Marie Antoinette

STEFAN ZWEIG

Marie Antoinette

The Portrait
of an Average Woman

Translated by Eden and Cedar Paul

GROVE PRESS
New York

First published in the United States in 1933 by The Viking Press Inc.

This edition is printed by special arrangement with Harmony Books, a division of Random House, Inc.

Printed in the United States of America

Library of Congress Cataloging-in-Publication Data

Zweig, Stefan, 1881–1942
  Marie Antoinette : the portrait of an average woman / Stefan Zweig ; translated by Eden and Cedar Paul.
    p. cm.
  Reprint. Originally published: New York : Viking Press, 1933.
  Includes index.
  ISBN-10: 0-8021-3909-4
  ISBN-13: 978-0-8021-3909-2
  1. Marie Antoinete, Queen, consort of Louis XVI, King of France, 1755-1793. 2. France—History—Louis XVI, 1774-1793. 3. Queens—France—Biography. I. Title

DC137.1 .Z82 2002
044'.035'092—dc21
[B]   2001058630

Grove Press
an imprint of Grove/Atlantic, Inc.
841 Broadway
New York, NY 10003

Distributed by Publishers Group West

www.groveatlantic.com

06 07 08 09 10   10 9 8 7 6 5 4 3

There is a history in all men's lives,
Figuring the nature of the times deceased;
The which observed, a man may prophesy,
With a near aim, of the main chance of things
As yet not come to life, which in their seeds
And weak beginnings lie intreasured.
Such things become the hatch and brood of time.

SECOND PART OF KING HENRY IV
Act III, Sc. 1

Table of Contents

Contents

Introduction

To tell the story of Marie Antoinette means to reopen a trial which took place more than a century ago, and one in which the accusers and the defenders volleyed invectives at one another. The accusers were responsible for the passionate tone of the discussion. To assail the monarchy effectively, the Revolution had to attack the Queen, and in the Queen the woman. Sincerity and politics are rarely to be found dwelling under one roof, and little justice is to be expected from the exponents and manufacturers of what is styled public opinion, when, to gain some demagogic end, they undertake the description of a character. In pursuance of the determination to send Marie Antoinette to the guillotine, no calumny was spared. Newspapers, pamphlets, and books denounced the "louve autrichienne" as guilty of every crime, every form of moral corruption, every perversion. In the very law-court, the public prosecutor did not hesitate to compare the "Widow Capet" with the most notoriously loose women of history, with Messalina, Agrippina, and Fredegond. Naturally, therefore, a decisive change of note was sounded when, in 1815, a Bourbon remounted the French throne. In order to flatter the dynasty, the picture of the bitch-wolf was painted out, and overlaid with the brightest and oiliest colours. In almost all the descriptions dating from this period, the Queen is decked with a halo, and we seem to sniff the incense as we read. Panegyric followed panegyric. Marie Antoinette's inviolable virtue was fiercely championed; her readiness for self-sacrifice, her kindness of heart, her spotless heroism, were celebrated in prose and verse; a veil of anecdotes, richly bedewed with tears, and woven for the most part by aristocratic hands, was prepared to half-conceal the transfigured countenance of the "martyred Queen."

In this matter, as in most, truth lies somewhere near the middle. Marie Antoinette was neither the great saint of royalism nor yet the great whore of the Revolution, but a mediocre, an average woman; not exceptionally able nor yet exceptionally foolish; neither fire nor ice;

xi

devoid of any vigorous wish to do good and of the remotest inclination to do evil; the average woman of yesterday, today, and tomorrow; lacking impulse towards the daimonic, uninspired by the will to heroism, and therefore (one might fancy) unsuited to become the heroine of a tragedy. But history, the demiurge, can construct a profoundly moving drama even though there is nothing heroic about its leading personalities. Tragical tension is not solely conditioned by the mighty lineaments of central figures, but also by a disproportion between man and his destiny. This disproportion is invariably tragical. It may manifest itself dramatically when a titan, a hero, a genius, finds himself in conflict with his environment, which proves too narrow and too hostile for the performance of his allotted task. Such is the tragedy of a Napoleon, prisoned on the remote island of St. Helena; of a Beethoven immured in deafness; of every great man denied scope for his powers. But tragedy arises no less when a momentous position, a crushing responsibility, is thrust upon a mediocrity or a weakling. Indeed, tragedy in this form makes a strong appeal to our human sympathies. A man out of the ordinary run is unconsciously impelled to seek a fate out of the ordinary run. His superdimensional temperament makes him organically inclined to live heroically, or (to use Nietzsche's word) "dangerously." He challenges the world because it is his nature to do so. Thus in the last analysis the genius is partly responsible for his own sufferings, since his inward vocation mystically craves for the fiery ordeal which can alone evoke his uttermost energies. His relentless fate drives him swiftly, and uplifts him as the storm a seagull.

The mediocrity, on the other hand, is temperamentally disposed towards an easy and peaceful existence. He does not want, does not need, tension, but would rather live quietly and inconspicuously, where the wind blows not fiercely and destiny does her work in milder fashion. That is why he adopts the defensive, that is why he grows anxious, that is why he flees, whenever an unseen hand tries to thrust him into the forefront of the fray. Far from craving for a position of historical responsibility, he shrinks from it. He does not seek suffering, but has to bear it when it is forced upon him. If he is ever compelled to transcend his own standards, the compulsion has come from without, not from within. Precisely because the average man, the mediocrity, lacks vision, lacks insight, his sorrow seems to me as great as—and perhaps more moving than—that of the true hero whose misfortunes stir the popular imagination; for poor Everyman has to bear his cross unaided, and has not, like the artist, the spiritual salvation of being able to transform his torment into work and thus give it lasting form.

The life of Marie Antoinette is perhaps the most signal example in history of the way in which destiny will at times pluck a mediocre human being from obscurity, and, with commanding hand, force the man or the woman in question to overstep the bounds of mediocrity. During the first thirty of her eight-and-thirty years, she pursued her inconspicuous course, though in an exalted sphere as far as social station was concerned; never transgressing the conventional standards whether for good or for evil; a tepid creature, an average woman; and, historically regarded, to begin with, nothing more than a lay-figure decked in a queen's robes. Had it not been for the outbreak of the Revolution, this insignificant Habsburg princess who had married a king of France would have continued, in her cheerful and untroubled play-world, to live her life after the fashion of hundreds of millions of women of all epochs. She would have danced, chattered, loved, laughed, made up her face, paid visits, bestowed alms; she would have borne children, and would at long last have died in her bed, without ever having lived in any true sense of the term. She would have been interred with pomp and ceremony, and the court would have worn mourning for the prescribed number of weeks; thereafter she would have vanished from human memory as completely as numberless other princesses, the Mary Adelaides and Adelaide Maries, the Anne Catherines and Catherine Annes, whose tombstones stand unread in the Almanach de Gotha. Never would any living creature have desired to study her vanished form or to reimagine the characteristics of her defunct spirit. But for her sufferings, no one would have known who she really was. More important still, had it not been for these same sufferings, she herself, Marie Antoinette, Queen of France, would not have known. For it is part of the fortune or misfortune of the average man that, unless fate calls upon him to do so, he is not moved to inquire about himself. No irresistible inner impulse stirs him to turn his curiosity in this direction. He allows his possibilities to slumber unutilized. Like muscles that are never exercised, his forces atrophy unless bitter need calls on him to tense them. A mediocrity must be spurred out of himself if he is to become all that he might be, and probably more than he has dreamed of becoming. For this, fate has no other whip than disaster. Just as an artist will often use some trivial motive for the display of great creative energies, so, now and again, destiny will avail herself of an insignificant hero, to demonstrate her capacity for weaving a tragedy out of weak and reluctant material. Marie Antoinette was a crowning instance of such an involuntary acceptance of the heroic role.

For with what transcendent art, with what a wealth of episodes, with how unparalleled a display of historical tensions, does the muse of history introduce this average woman into the stupendous drama of the opening phases of the French Revolution, as if deliberately emphasizing the clash of opposing forces around the primarily insignificant figure she had elevated to the rank of a star performer. With diabolical cunning, history began by making a spoiled darling of Marie Antoinette, who had the Kaiserhof as a home in childhood, wore a crown before she was out of her teens, had charm and grace and wealth in liberal measure when she was a young wife, and, in addition, was dowered with a light heart, so that she never troubled to ask the cost and value of these gifts. For years, she was so delicately nurtured that her senses were dulled and became carefree. But destiny, having raised her to the pinnacle of good fortune, dragged her down again with the utmost refinements of cruelty. With melodramatic roughness, this tragedy jumbled polar contradictions together. The Queen was inexorably torn from a hundred-roomed palace and thrust into a common prison, was hurried from the throne to the scaffold, from the gilded chariot to the tumbril, from luxury to privation, from being a centre of admiration to being an object of hatred, was plunged into deeper and ever deeper abysses of despair. Yet this mediocrity, buffeted by a heretofore indulgent fate, could never understand why the controlling powers had become hostile. All she knew was that she was unwarrantably belaboured, that red-hot pincers were tearing her poor flesh. Unaccustomed to suffering, she resisted and sought to escape. But with the ruthlessness of an artist who will not desist from his travail until he has wrung the last possibilities from the stubborn clay he is fashioning, the deliberate hand of misfortune continued to mould, to knead, to chisel, and to hammer Marie Antoinette until all the greatness derived from a long line of ancestors (though till now hidden) had been brought to light.

Amid torments and trials the afflicted woman, who had never been introspective, came at length to recognize the transformation. At the very time when she was stripped of the last insignia of power, she grew aware that in her there had dawned something novel and stupendous, and that but for her sufferings this dawn would never have begun. "Tribulation first makes one realize what one is." With mingled pride, agitation, and astonishment, she uttered these remarkable words, seized with a foreboding that through suffering her life, otherwise commonplace, would grow significant for posterity. The consciousness of a supreme duty lifted her character to a higher level than she had ever known. Just before the mortal, the transient frame perished, the immortal work of art was perfected. Marie Antoinette, the mediocrity, achieved a greatness commensurate with her destiny.

Marie Antoinette

CHAPTER I

A Child Marriage

UPON dozens of German, Italian, and Flemish battlefields, the Habsburgs and the Bourbons had engaged in deadly strife, each party hoping to make itself predominant in Europe. Now both sides were extenuated with fatigue. In the twelfth hour the longtime rivals perceived that their insatiable jealousies had served only to give free scope to the ambition of other ruling houses. The heretics of Britain were grasping at worldwide empire; the Protestant Mark of Brandenburg had become a mighty kingdom; Russia, a half-pagan land, aspired towards an immeasurably extended sphere of influence: recognizing these things (too late, as ever) the monarchs and their servants the diplomats began to ask themselves whether it would not be better to keep the peace instead of renewing the ancient struggle to their own detriment and to the advantage of upstarts. Choiseul at the court of Louis XV and Kaunitz as the adviser of Maria Theresa of Austria entered into an alliance; and, in the hope that this would be more durable than a breathing-space, more lasting than a truce, they decided that the friendship between the dynasties should be cemented by marriage. There had never been a scarcity of marriageable princesses in the House of Habsburg, and at this juncture, no less, there were many possible brides of various ages.

The French statesman began by trying to persuade Louis XV (grandfather though he was, and a man of more than questionable morals) to wed an Austrian princess, but His Most Christian Majesty made a quick remove from the bed of the Pompadour to that of a new favourite, the Dubarry. Nor did Emperor Joseph, recently widowed for the second time, show any disposition to couple with one of the three somewhat elderly daughters of Louis XV. The third possibility, and the most natural one, was to betroth the young Dauphin, the grandson of Louis XV, to a daughter of Maria Theresa. In 1766 matters came to a head with a serious proposal as concerned Marie Antoinette, then eleven years old. On May 24th, the Austrian ambassador in Paris wrote to the Empress: "The King has spoken in such a way that Your Majesty can regard the matter as settled."

But diplomatists would not be diplomatists if they did not plume themselves on making the simplest things difficult, and on the art of procrastinating whenever important negotiations are afoot. Intrigue was rife in this court and in that. A year, two years, three years passed without any definitive arrangements having been concluded. With good reason Maria Theresa became alarmed lest her troublesome neighbour Frederick of Prussia ("le monstre," as she bitterly named him) would not, by his Machiavellian arts, frustrate a scheme likely to promote Austrian influence; and she therefore brought all her amiability, ardour, and cunning to bear in an endeavour to make the French court fulfil what had been no more than a half-promise. With the indefatigability, of a professional go-between, and patiently turning her powers of state-craft to account, she saw to it that her daughter's virtues and beauties should become the talk of Paris. Showering gifts and courtesies upon the envoys, she hoped at length to get a "firm offer" from Versailles. Empress rather than mother, more concerned about the power of the Habsburgs than about her daughter's happiness, she turned a deaf ear to warnings that nature had not been kind to the Dauphin—that the young man was stupid and uncouth. If an archduchess is to become a queen, surely she need not expect happiness into the bargain? But the more urgently Maria Theresa demanded a sealed pledge, the more laggard seemed the crafty King of France. For three years Louis XV had been receiving portraits and reading eulogies of Marie Antoinette, and had declared himself on principle inclined to favour the proposed marriage. Yet he still hesitated to commit himself.

Meanwhile, in the rooms and the gardens of Schönbrunn, the inno-cent pawn with whom these important games of diplomatic chess were being played, the eleven-year, twelve-year, thirteen-year-old Toinette—short of stature, graceful, slender, unquestionably beautiful—was romp-ing with her sisters, her brothers, and her girl friends, but she troubled little about books and education. Of a lively temperament, and clever at getting her own way, she was able to twist round her fingers the governesses and the priests who had been told off to act as her instruc-tors, so that she managed to escape, for the most part, the tedium of lessons.

Maria Theresa, busied in affairs of State and giving scant thought to the needs and capacities of her offspring, discovered one day to her great distress that the future queen of France, though now thirteen, could write neither French nor German correctly, and was lacking in the most elementary knowledge of history or the other requisites of a sound education. In respect of music, the girl was little better off, though Gluck had been her teacher. There was no time to lose. With the utmost speed and at the last hour the self-willed and idle Toinette must be transformed into a cultured lady.

Above all, in view of the destiny that awaited her, it was essential that she should become a good dancer and that she should be able to speak French with a perfect accent. Maria Theresa hastened to engage the famous dancing-master Noverre, and two actors belonging to a French company then playing in the Austrian capital—the latter to give lessons in elocution. The French ambassador in Vienna having reported these developments to his chief, the prompt result was an angry protest: the princess who was to be the consort of the King must not hob-nob with strolling players! Fresh diplomatic negotiations followed upon the recognition that the education of the young woman provisionally chosen as the Dauphin's bride was a matter of prime concern to the French court; and in the end, upon the recommendation of the Bishop of Orléans, a certain Abbé Vermond was sent to Vienna as tutor.

It is to Vermond that we are indebted for the first authentic and detailed accounts of the young Archduchess. He was charmed. "She has a most graceful figure; holds herself well; and if (as may be hoped) she grows a little taller, she will have all the good qualities one could wish for in a great princess. Her character, her heart, are excellent." But the worthy abbé showed far more restraint in what he had to say about his pupil's accomplishments. Spoiled, inattentive, high-spirited, vivacious to a fault, Marie Antoinette, though quick of apprehension, had never shown the slightest inclination to busy herself with matters of serious import. "She is more intelligent than has been generally supposed. Unfortunately up to the age of twelve she has not been trained to concentrate in any way. Since she is rather lazy and extremely frivolous, she is hard to teach. During the first six weeks I inculcated the elements of literature, and found that she understood me very well when I gave her lucid explanations. Then she usually manifested a sound judgment—but I could not induce her to take the trouble to get to the bottom of a subject on her own initiative, though I felt that it was well within her power to do so. I came in the end to recognize that she would only learn so long as she was being amused."

Ten years later, twenty years later, almost all the statesmen who came in contact with Marie Antoinette complained of her reluctance to apply her thoughts though she was equipped with an excellent understanding, and of her proneness to become bored whenever a conversation grew serious; already when she was but thirteen there had become obvious the dangers implicit in her character—that of one who had abundant capacity and very little will. At the French court, however, during the epoch when the King's mistresses held sway, much more was thought of a woman's deportment than of her intrinsic worth. Marie Antoinette was pretty, of suitable standing, and of good character. These qualifications sufficed; so at length, in 1769, was sent the long-desired missive from Louis XV to Maria Theresa, in which the King formally demanded the young princess's hand for his grandson, the future Louis XVI, proposing Easter 1770 as the date for the marriage. The Empress was delighted. To this woman who had had to resign herself to so many sorrows there had come at last, it seemed, a ray of sunshine. The peace of her own realm, and therewith that of Europe was assured! Mounted couriers spurred forth to all the courts with the formal announcement that henceforward a blood-brotherhood had been established between the sometime enemies, Habsburg and Bourbon. "Bella gerant alii, tu felix Austria nube"; the old motto of the House of Habsburg held good once more.

The work of the diplomatists had been brought to a successful conclusion, but it now became plain that this had been no more than a fraction (and the easier fraction) of the task. To bring about an understanding between the Habsburgs and the Bourbons, to reconcile Louis XV with Maria Theresa, had been child's play in comparison with the unexpected difficulties that disclosed themselves when, in an affair so important, it was necessary to find a common platform for the ceremonial of the French and the Austrian courts. No doubt the respective chamberlains and their underlings had a whole year in which to elaborate an agenda for the marriage festivities—but what is a year, what are twelve months, when so many ticklish points of etiquette have to be thrashed out? The heir to the French throne was to wed an Austrian archduchess! What an infinity of tact was requisite to avoid disastrous blunders in numberless weighty details! What piles of ancient documents had to be studied with meticulous care! By day and by night the watch-dogs of convention at Versailles and at Schönbrunn had to cudgel their memories; by day and by night the envoys had to discuss the propriety of every possible invitation; mounted couriers must ride hell-for-leather bearing proposals and counter-proposals—for think what a catastrophe it would be (worse than half a dozen wars) if on this august occasion one of the ruling families were to be mortified by a breach of precedence!

Numberless learned dissertations were penned on either side of the Rhine, discussing such thorny problems as these: whose name should come first in the betrothal contract, that of the Empress of Austria or that of the King of France; which should first append his signature to the document; what presents should be given; the amount of the dowry; who should accompany the bride on her journey and who should receive her on arrival; how many knights, maids of honour, foot-soldiers, cavalrymen, ladies of the bedchamber, father-confessors, physicians, secretaries, and laundresses were to constitute the train of the Archduchess from Vienna to the frontier, and how many of these functionaries were to cross the frontier in attendance upon the future queen of France all the way to Versailles. But long before the periwigged pundits had come to an agreement concerning these matters, the courtiers of both sexes were wrangling with one another as to their respective rights to form part of the procession from Austria or to welcome it on French soil. Although the masters of the ceremonies worked like galley-slaves, when a year had passed they were still at odds over questions of precedence and the right to be present at court. During the eleventh hour, for instance, the attendance of the Alsatian nobles was erased from the agenda "in order to obviate the discussion of tedious problems of etiquette for whose settlement time is now lacking." Had not the date for bringing the discussions to a close been fixed by royal command, the guardians of Austrian and French ceremony would not, even to this day, have come to an agreement concerning the

"correct formalities" of the marriage—so that there would have been
no Queen Marie Antoinette, and perhaps no French Revolution!

Although the financial position alike in France and in Austria made
strict economy essential, both the monarchy and the empire were
resolved to celebrate the wedding with the utmost pomp and circumstance. Neither the House of Habsburg nor the House of Bourbon
would allow itself to be outshone by the other. The French embassy
in Vienna was too small to house the fifteen hundred guests. At top
speed annexes were run up, while simultaneously an opera house was
being built at Versailles for the wedding festivities. Both in the French
and in the Austrian capital these were happy days for the court pur-
veyors, the court tailors, jewellers, and carriage builders. Simply to
fetch the Archduchess, Louis XV ordered from Francien in Paris two
travelling carriages of unprecedented splendour constructed of rare
woods, coated with glass, lined with satin, lavishly adorned outside
with paintings, spotted all over with crowns; and, despite these glories,
beautifully light, magnificently sprung, and exceptionally easy to draw
along the roads. New court dresses, trimmed with costly jewels, were
provided for the Dauphin and the members of the royal train; the Pitt
diamond, the most famous brilliant of those days, glittered on Louis
XV's wedding hat; and Maria Theresa was determined that her daughter's trousseau should be no less sumptuous, with an abundance of
Mechlin lace, the finest linen, silk, and precious stones.

At length Durfort made his appearance in Vienna as special envoy
to fetch the bride, and his coming provided an attractive spectacle for
the Viennese, who were passionately devoted to such displays. Eight-
and-forty six-in-hands, among them the two wonderful carriages
already described, were driven slowly through the flower-bestrewn
streets to the Hofburg; the new uniforms and liveries of the hundred
and seventeen bodyguards and lackeys had cost a hundred and seventeen thousand ducats; and the cost of the whole train was estimated
at not less than three hundred and fifty thousand ducats.

Thereafter, festival followed upon festival: the official wooing; Marie
Antoinette's formal renunciation of her Austrian rights before the Holy
Bible, the crucifix, and lighted candles; congratulations from the court
and from the university; a full-dress military review; a gala performance at the theatre; a reception and ball in the Belvedere for three

thousand persons; a supper for fifteen hundred guests in the Liechten-stein Palace; and at length, on April 19th, marriage by proxy in the Augustinian Church, the Archduke Ferdinand representing the Dau-phin. The day was concluded by an affectionate family supper; and on April 21st came a formal farewell, with last embraces. At length, the reverential populace lining both sides of the road, Marie Antoinette, sometime Archduchess of Austria, drove away, in the chariot sent by the King of France, to fulfil her destiny.

To say farewell to her daughter had been hard for Maria Theresa. For years this weary and ageing woman (she was now well over fifty) had longed for the marriage as the crown of her desires, thinking that it would minister to the power of the House of Habsburg; and yet, at the last moment, she became filled with anxiety regarding the fate she had meted out to her daughter. When we read between the lines of her letters, when we study her life with an open mind, we cannot fail to recognize that this empress, the one great monarch of the Aus-trian line, had long felt the crown to be nothing but a burden. With endless labour, during interminable wars, she had defended her patch-work and artificial realm against Prussia and Turkey, against the East and the West, successfully maintaining its unity; but now, when objec-tively its position seemed secure, her courage flagged. She had a fore-boding that the empire to which she had devoted so much energy and passion, would suffer decay and disintegration in the hands of her successors. A far-sighted and almost clairvoyant stateswoman, she knew how loose were the ties that held together this chance assembly of multifarious nationalities, and that nothing but the utmost caution and reserve in conjunction with a shrewd passivity could prolong its life. But who was to continue the work which she had begun with such devoted care? Her children had been so great a disappointment to her that a Cassandra mood had developed. Not one of them displayed her own most outstanding qualities: patience, the power to plan and to persist, the capacity for renunciation, and a wise faculty for moderation. It would seem that from their father Francis of Lorraine restless ele-ments must have been introduced into their blood. One and all they were ready to throw away vast possibilities for the sake of a momentary pleasure. They were feeble folk, devoid of seriousness, lacking in faith.

and concerned only to achieve passing successes. Her son Joseph II, whom she had made co-regent five years earlier, filled with an heir's impatience, wooed the favour of Frederick the Great, who had persecuted and despised Maria Theresa for a lifetime. Joseph, too, was a great admirer of Voltaire, whom she, a pious Catholic, regarded as Antichrist. Archduchess Maria Amalia, whom Maria Theresa had likewise set upon a throne, by marrying her off to the Duke of Parma, hastened to scandalize Europe by her levity. In two months she had disordered the finances, disorganized the whole country, and amused herself with more than one lover. Another girl, in Naples, did the Empress little credit. Not one, indeed, of her daughters showed a serious disposition or seemed endowed with moral strength. Maria Theresa had a bitter feeling that the task to which, with incomparable self-sacrifice and application, she had devoted all her personal and private life, inexorably renouncing every possibility of enjoyment, had, after all, been futile. She would gladly have retired to a nunnery. Nothing but the justified dread that her incautious son would, with his rash experiments, quickly destroy what she had upbuilded, made her retain the sceptre of which her hand had long since wearied.

Nor was Maria Theresa, being a keen judge of character, under any illusion concerning the youngest of her brood, the spoiled darling Marie Antoinette. She knew the girl's spirit, good nature and cordiality, cheerful sagacity, uncorrupted humaneness; but she knew no less Toinette's defects, her immaturity, frivolousness, flightiness. Hoping even during the last hours to make a queen out of this temperamental hoyden, Maria Theresa had had Marie Antoinette to sleep in her own bedroom during the last two months before the departure. In lengthy conversations, the mother tried to prepare the daughter for the great position that awaited her. Hoping to win Heaven's favour, she took the girl on pilgrimage to Mariazell.

These endeavours bore no fruit. As the hour of departure approached, the Empress became more and more troubled in spirit. Her heart was full of gloomy forebodings, and she did her utmost to appease the powers of evil. Giving Marie Antoinette a written list of regulations for the conduct of life, she made the poor girl swear a solemn oath to reread this memorandum carefully month by month. Over and above her official dispatch, Maria Theresa wrote a private letter to Louis XV, imploring the old man (he was sixty, and therefore seven years older than herself) to show every possible consideration for the heedless girl of fourteen. Yet the mother remained uneasy. Before Marie Antoinette could have reached Versailles, Maria Theresa sent her daughter an additional exhortation to follow the guidance of the aforesaid document. "Let me recommend you, beloved daughter, to reread it on the twenty-first of every month. Be trusty in abiding by this wish of mine, this urgent request. The only thing I am afraid of is that you may sometimes be backward in saying your prayers, and in your reading; and may consequently grow negligent and slothful. Fight against these faults. . . . Do not forget your mother who, though far away, will continue to watch over you until her last breath."

While all the world was rejoicing over the daughter's triumph, the mother went to church and besought the Almighty to avert a disaster which she alone foresaw.

The huge cavalcade (there were three hundred and forty horses, which had to be changed at every posting-station) made its way slowly through Upper Austria and across Bavaria, approaching the imperial frontier by degrees, though delayed by innumerable festivals and receptions. Meanwhile, on the island which divides the waters of the Rhine between Kehl and Strasbourg carpenters and upholsterers were at work upon a singular edifice. Here the court chamberlains of Versailles and Schönbrunn were playing their trump cards. After endless deliberations as to whether the formal reception of the bride was to take place upon Austrian or upon French territory, a cunning man among them hit upon the Solomonic expedient of choosing for this purpose one of the small uninhabited sandbanks in the Rhine, between France and Germany, and therefore in no-man's-land. Here was to be erected a wooden pavilion for the ceremonial transference—a miracle of neutrality. There were to be two anterooms looking towards the right bank of the Rhine, through which Marie Antoinette would pass as Archduchess; and two anterooms looking towards the left bank of the Rhine, which she would traverse as Dauphiness of France after the ceremony. Between them would be the great hall in which the Archduchess would be definitively metamorphosed into the heiress to the throne of France. Costly tapestries from the archiepiscopal palace concealed the wooden planking;

the University of Strasbourg lent a baldachin; and the wealthy burghers of Strasbourg were glad to have their finest articles of furniture
hallowed by close contact with royalty. It need hardly be said that no
one of middle-class origin was really entitled to set eyes upon the
interior of this sanctum of princely splendour, but its guardians (as is
usual in such cases) were open to corruption by a liberal tip, and so, a
few days before Marie Antoinette's arrival, some German students,
spurred on by curiosity, made their way into the half-finished room.
One of these youths, not long past his teens, a tall fellow, with an eager
expression and with the stamp of genius upon his virile brow, could
not feast his eyes enough on the gobelin hangings, whose themes had
been taken from Raphael's cartoons. In Strasbourg cathedral he had
just had a revelation of the glories of Gothic architecture, and was
ready to show no less appreciation, no less love, for classical art. Filled
with enthusiasm, he was explaining to his less well-informed comrades
the significance of the beauties unexpectedly revealed to him by the
Italian master; but suddenly the flow of his eloquence ceased, he
showed disquiet, and knitted his dark eyebrows with something akin
to anger. He had just realized what the design on the tapestries represented—a myth that was certainly unsuitable as setting for a wedding
festival—the tale of Jason, Medea, and Creusa, the crowning example
of an unhappy marriage.

"What," exclaimed the talented youngster, ignoring the astonishment
of the bystanders, "is it permissible thus unreflectingly to display before
the eyes of a young queen entering upon married life this example of
the most horrible wedding that perhaps ever took place? Among the
French architects, decorators, and upholsterers, are there none who can
understand that pictures mean something, that pictures work upon the
senses and the feelings, that they effect impressions, that they arouse
ominous intimations? It seems to me as if a hideous spectre had been
sent to greet this lady at the frontier; this lady who is, we are told,
beautiful, and full of the joy of life!"

His friends found it difficult to assuage his anger, and had almost
to use force before they could make Goethe (for this was the student's
name) leave the wooden reception house. But when, not many hours
later, the members of the marriage train, glad at heart, and engaged in
cheerful conversation, entered the gaily decorated building, not one of

them was aware that the prophetic eyes of a great poet had already glimpsed the black thread of doom interwoven into the brightly coloured hangings.

The handing-over of Marie Antoinette was to signify her farewell to all the persons and all the things which linked her with the House of Habsburg. The masters of the ceremonies had devised a peculiar symbol of this change of mental and material habitat. Not only had it been decreed that none of the members of her Austrian train were to accompany her across the invisible frontier-line, but the sometime Archduchess was, on entering France, to have discarded every stitch of her native attire, was not to wear so much as shoes or stockings or shift that had been made by Viennese artificers. From the moment when she became Dauphiness of France, all her wrappings and trappings were to be of French origin. In the Austrian antechamber, therefore, in the presence of her Austrian followers, this girl of fourteen had to strip to the buff. Naked as on the day she was born, the still undeveloped girl disclosed her slender body in the curtained chamber. Then she was quickly re-dressed in a chemise of French silk, petticoats from Paris, stockings from Lyons, shoes made by the shoemaker to the French court, French lace. Nothing was she to keep that might be endeared to her by memory, not a ring, not a cross; for it would be a grave breach of etiquette were she to retain so much as a buckle, a clasp, or a favourite bracelet—and from this same moment she was to part company with all the familiar faces. Can we be surprised to learn that the poor child, overwhelmed by so much ceremonial and hurled (the word is not too strong) into a foreign environment, should have burst into tears?

Yet what could she do but pull herself together? She knew that exhibitions of sentiment were unseemly at a political wedding. Her French suite was awaiting her in the other room, and she would have been ashamed to present herself before them timidly, her eyes bedewed with moisture. Count Starhemberg, the best man, took her by the hand, and, followed for the last time by her Austrian companions, for two more minutes still herself an Austrian wearing French-made clothes, she entered the hall of transition where, in great state, the Bourbon delegation awaited her. The matchmaker who represented his master Louis XV delivered a solemn address, the marriage contract was read aloud, and thereupon ensued, while all held their breath, the great ceremony. It had been rehearsed as carefully as a minuet. The table in the centre of the hall symbolized the frontier. Before it stood the Austrians; behind it, the French. The best man relinquished Marie Antoinette's hand, which was taken by the French matchmaker, and he, with stately steps, led the trembling girl round the end of the table. As the measured minutes passed, keeping time with the advance of the members of the French suite to welcome their future queen, the Austrian nobles retired towards the door by which they had entered, so that they had quitted the hall at the very moment when Marie Antoinette had come to occupy a central position amid the members of her French court.

Soundlessly, with exemplary regard for the prescribed ritual, with ghostly magnificence, was this orgy of etiquette fulfilled; but at the last moment the terrified girl found the chill ceremonial unendurable. Instead of giving a cool and dignified response to the profound curtsy of the Comtesse de Noailles, sobbing, and with a gesture of appeal, she flung herself into the arms of her new lady-in-waiting. A touching scene, this, at the close of so much formality, though it was one which the high mandarins of the representation, whether they were French or whether they were Austrian, omitted to describe. In truth there was no place for sentiment, which is not tabulated among the logarithms of courtly procedure. The horses harnessed to the glass chariot were impatiently pawing the ground, the bells of Strasbourg cathedral were pealing, salvos of artillery were being fired; and, amid jubilations, Marie Antoinette quitted for ever and a day the carefree realm of childhood. Her destiny as a woman had begun.

The arrival of Marie Antoinette was a memorable occasion for the French people, which had not, of late years, been over-indulged with public spectacles. It was decades since Strasbourg had been favoured with the sight of a future queen of France, and probably none of those who aforetime had been seen in that city had been so charming as this Austrian maiden. With blue and sparkling eyes the girl—a fair-haired and delicately built creature—smiled from the glass chariot at the huge crowd of persons who had assembled from all the towns and villages of Alsace, adorned in their provincial dress. They, in their turn, welcomed the gorgeous procession with loud acclamations. Hundreds of children clad in white strewed flowers in its path; a triumphal arch had been erected; garlands decorated the gates; wine was flowing from the city fountains; oxen were roasted whole; in huge baskets, bread was provided for free distribution to the poor. When darkness fell, the houses were illuminated; strings of lanterns serpentined up the cathedral tower; the tracery of the magnificent building shone red in the fitful glare. Boats glided hither and thither on the surface of the Rhine, bearing lampions like great red oranges attached to their masts, or showing coloured torches waved by human hands. Coloured glass balls glittered from among the trees. On the island there was a grand fireworks display, and a set piece to exhibit, amid mythological figures, the interwoven monograms of the Dauphin and the Dauphiness. Till far on into the night the populace thronged the streets of the town and the banks of the river; bands played; lads and lasses danced merrily; there was a general feeling that the arrival of the blonde girl from Austria heralded a return of the Golden Age; and once again hope surged up in the embittered hearts of the French people.

But wonderful though this welcome was, there was already a rift in the lute, another boding of disaster in addition to the symbolic menace of the tapestry in the hall of reception. When next day, before proceeding on her journey westward, Marie Antoinette wished to hear Mass, she was greeted at the great doors of the cathedral, not by the venerable bishop, but by his nephew and coadjutor at the head of the diocesan clergy. Looking somewhat feminine in his flowing purple vestments, the young priest (who was man of the world more than priest) delivered a gallant and affecting speech which wound up with the courtly phrases: "You will be for us the living image of the beloved Empress whom Europe has so long admired and whom posterity will continue to venerate. The spirit of Maria Theresa, is about to unite with the spirit of the Bourbons." After listening attentively to this greeting, the train entered the comparative darkness of the lofty building. The priest led the girl princess to the altar, and there, with his finely shaped, bejewelled hand, lifted the monstrance for the benediction. He was Louis Prince de Rohan, in later days the tragi-comic hero of the affair of the diamond necklace. The hand which here in

Strasbourg invoked God's blessing on her head was the very hand which, long years afterwards, was to help in bespattering her crown with mire and in bringing her name into contempt.

Marie Antoinette could not linger in Alsace, although this semi-German French province had a home-like atmosphere. The King of France must not be kept waiting! Through many more triumphal arches and begarlanded gates, the bridal train wound its way towards the place of meeting, the forest of Compiègne, where, with a great park of carriages, the royal family was assembled to welcome this new member. Courtiers and court ladies, the officers of the King's guard, drummers, trumpeters, and buglers, spick-and-span in new clothes, stood in motley array. Under the May sunshine, the woods were bright with the play of colour. As soon as a fanfare from the respective trains had announced the near approach of the procession, Louis XV got out of his chariot to receive his grandson's bride. But Marie Antoinette was beforehand with him. Light of foot (this was one of her chief graces) she hastened up to him, and, schooled by Noverre, curtsied in due form to her new grandfather. The King, whose experiences in the Parc aux Cerfs had made him a connoisseur in the matter of girlish charms, and who was still susceptible, leaned forward with a tender content over this appetizing creature, helped her to rise, and kissed her on both cheeks. Not until after this did he introduce her future spouse, who, a lanky fellow five feet ten inches tall, was looking on with clumsy embarrassment. Now, contemplating the new arrival with his sleepy, short-sighted eyes, and without showing any particular zest, he kissed her on the cheeks formally, as etiquette demanded. A moment later, Marie Antoinette was seated in the chariot between grandfather and grandson, between Louis XV and the future Louis XVI. The old man seemed more inclined than the young one to play the role of bridegroom, chattering in sprightly fashion, and even paying court to the girl, while the husband-to-be leaned back in his corner, bored and tongue-tied. When the pair, who were not only betrothed but were already wedded per procurationem, retired for the night and went to sleep in separate rooms, this sorry lover had not yet spoken a single affectionate word to the fascinating flapper. In his diary, as summary of what had happened on so decisive a day, he penned the curt entry: "Entrevue avec Madame la Dauphine."

Six-and-thirty years later, in this same forest of Compiègne, another ruler of France, Napoleon, waited for another Austrian archduchess, Marie Louise, who had come to marry him. She was not so pretty, not so luscious a morsel as Marie Antoinette, the buxom and rather tedious though gentle Marie Louise. But Napoleon was no laggard in love, and hastened, at once tenderly and stormily, to take possession of his bride. On the evening of her arrival he asked the bishop whether the marriage by proxy in Vienna gave him full conjugal rights. Then, without waiting for an answer, he drew his own conclusions, so that next morning the pair had breakfast in bed together. But the husband who came to meet Marie Antoinette in the forest of Compiègne was neither a lover nor a man. He was only an official bridegroom.

The second wedding festival, the real one in succession to the proxy affair in Vienna, took place on May 16, 1770, at Versailles in the Chapel of Louis XIV. A court affair, a State affair, under the ægis of the Most Christian King, it was too private and too sublime and too sovereign for common folk to be allowed to catch a glimpse of it, even as a crowd waiting outside the doors. Only nobles of high descent, only those whose coats of arms bore many quarterings, could be granted access to the consecrated building, where, as the spring sunshine pierced the stained-glass windows, embroidered brocades, shimmering silks, all the glories of those set apart by privilege and wealth, flaunted themselves once more like the last beacon of an expiring world. The Archbishop of Rheims consecrated the marriage. He blessed the thirteen gold pieces and the wedding ring. Thereafter, the Dauphin put the ring on the fourth finger of Marie Antoinette's left hand, and gave her the gold pieces. Then the wedded pair knelt down to receive the prelate's blessing. The strains of the organ preluded the nuptial Mass. While the paternoster was being said, a silver canopy was held over the heads of the young couple. As soon as the religious ceremony was finished, the King and in due order of precedence his blood relations signed the marriage contract. It was an interminable document, a parchment on whose faded legend the curious can still decipher the badly penned signature "Marie Antoinette Josepha Jeanne," laboriously inscribed by the bride of fifteen. Beside the signature is a big blot of ink, the Dauphiness alone, among all the signatories, having botched her inscription in this ominous way. We may guess that there were whisperings among the bystanders!

Now, when the ceremony was over, the people was graciously allowed to participate in the rejoicings at the monarchical festival. Huge crowds (Paris was half depopulated for the nonce) thronged the gardens at Versailles—whose fountains and waterfalls, whose alleys and lawns and flower-beds are today freely opened to the profanum vulgus. The titbit of the show had been reserved for the evening, a display of fireworks which was to be the greatest ever seen at a royal court. But in such matters man proposes and the heavens dispose. In the course of the afternoon threatening clouds gathered, and at length the storm burst. Rain fell in torrents, and the populace, robbed of its spectacle, hastened back to Paris in wild disorder. Tens of thousands of the canaille, shivering with cold and drenched to the skin, hurried homeward through the streets; the trees in the park, likewise drenched, were bending before the blast—while behind the windows of the newly built "salle de spectacle," blazing with thousands of candles, began the great wedding feast, with which neither hurricanes nor earthquakes could be allowed to interfere. For the first and the last time, Louis XV was trying to outshine the magnificence of his immediate predecessor, the Grand Monarque.

Six thousand from among the blue-blooded of France had managed to secure cards of entry; not, indeed, to join in the banquet, but merely that they might look on reverently from the gallery while the two-and-twenty members of the royal house were busily plying knife, fork, and spoon. The spectators scarcely dared draw breath, lest they should disturb the sublimity of the moment, so that, apart from the noise that came from the supper-table, the only sounds were those made by an orchestra of eighty instrumentalists whose music—subdued to the solemnity of the occasion—re-echoed from among the marble pillars. Then, while the officers and men of the guard stood to attention, the royal family marched out between the bowing nobles, ranged in rows on either side. The festival was over, and it only remained for the husband who was destined to become King of France to fulfil what is the duty of Tom, Dick, and Harry on the wedding night. With the Dauphiness on the right and the Dauphin on the left, His Majesty conducted the wedded children, whose joint ages barely exceeded thirty years—to their sleeping apartment. Even in the bridal chamber etiquette must be maintained, for who but the King of France in person could hand the heir to the throne his nightgown, and who could perform a like service for the Dauphiness other than the most recently married lady of semi-royal rank; in this instance, the Duchess of Chartres? But even these distinguished assistants must not approach the nuptial couch. Apart from those who were to sleep in it, none could do that but the Archbishop of Rheims, who blessed it and sprinkled it with holy water.

At length the court left the youthful husband and wife to their privacy. Louis and Marie Antoinette were alone together for the first time since they had been married, and the rustling curtains of the great four-poster closed around an unseen tragedy.

CHAPTER II

Secret of the Alcove

WHAT first happened in the great four-poster was—nothing! It was with a disastrous double meaning that the young husband wrote next morning in his diary: "Rien." Neither the court ceremony nor yet the archiepiscopal consecration of the nuptial couch had sufficed to overcome the Dauphin's constitutional infirmity. Matrimonium non consummatum est; as far as its essential physical purpose was concerned, the marriage remained unfulfilled, today, tomorrow, for several years. Marie Antoinette had been coupled with a "nonchalant mari," with a negligent husband; and at first the general belief was that nothing but timidity, inexperience, or a "nature tardive" (today we should speak of "infantilism") had made the youth of sixteen impotent when put to bed with so fascinating a maiden.

"Toinette must not be in too great a hurry, for that, by increasing her husband's uneasiness, will only make matters worse," thought the mother, who was a woman of experience. Writing to her daughter in May 1771, she said that the latter must not take the disappointment too hardly, must not be peevish, "point d'humeur là-dessus"; recommended tenderness and caresses, "caresses, cajoleries"; yet even in this respect there must be moderation. "If you show yourself impatient, you may spoil the whole thing."

But when this distressing state of affairs had lasted a year, two years, the Empress began to grow anxious about the "conduite si étrange" of the young man. There could be no question as to his good will, for from month to month the Dauphin showed himself more and more affectionate towards his charming wife. His nocturnal visits were incessantly repeated, but always in vain, for some "maudit charme," some disastrous spell, always prevented a decisive finale to his embraces. Little Marie Antoinette, being ill informed about such matters, fancied that the only trouble was "maladresse et jeunesse," clumsiness and youth. Trying to make the best of a bad job, during the last days of 1771 she actually wrote to her mother denying "the false reports which are current here as to his impotence."

Maria Theresa, however, refused to be hoodwinked, and was determined to seek better information. Sending for van Swieten, her physician-in-ordinary, she begged his advice concerning the "froideur extraordinaire du Dauphin," and asked him whether anything could be done about it. The doctor shrugged his shoulders. If a girl with so many attractions could not liven up the Dauphin, he did not think that drugs would be of any avail!

Maria Theresa wrote letter after letter to Paris. Finally King Louis XV, whose experience in this domain had been multifarious to excess, took his grandson to task. Lassone, physician to the French court, was summoned; young Louis was subjected to physical examination; and at length it became plain that the Dauphin's sexual impotence was not what we should now term "psychogenic," but was due to a trifling organic defect—to phimosis. Details are given in a secret report sent from Paris to Madrid by the Spanish ambassador. It runs as follows: "Quien dice que el frenillo sujeta tanto el prepucio que no cede a la introducción y causa un dolor vivo en él, por el qual se retrahe S.M. del impulso que conviniera. Quien supone que el dicho prepucio está tan cerrado que no puede explayarse para la dilatación de la punta o cabeza de la parte, en virtud de lo que no llega la erección al punto de elasticidad necessaria."

Consultation followed upon consultation, as to whether the surgeons should intervene with the bistoury, "pour lui rendre la voix," as the cynical whisper ran in the anterooms. Marie Antoinette, who had meanwhile been fully informed about these things by experienced lady friends, did her utmost to persuade her husband to submit to surgical intervention. ("Je travaille à le déterminer à la petite opération, dont on a déjà parlé et que je crois nécessaire," she wrote to her mother in 1775.) But though five years had elapsed since his marriage, Louis XVI —as he had now become—was not yet an effective husband, and, being a young man of vacillating character, he found it impossible to make up his mind to so energetic a course. He hesitated, procrastinated, tried one futile measure after another, until the situation of the married pair, at once ludicrous and horrible, grew shameful to the Queen, was the scorn of the whole court, enraged Maria Theresa, and hopelessly humiliated the new King. Thus matters dragged on for another two years, making in all seven years of frustration. Then Emperor Joseph undertook the journey to Paris that he might inspire his rather pusillanimous brother-in-law with sufficient courage for the operation. The needful was done, and our pitiful Cæsar was enabled to cross his Rubicon. But as far as his wife's mental realm was concerned, that of which he now achieved the conquest had been hopelessly laid waste by these seven years of a preposterous struggle, by the two thousand nights during which Marie Antoinette, as woman and as wife, had suffered the most disastrous mortification that can befall one of her sex.

I doubt not that many of the more sensitive among my readers will be outraged at my having touched upon this thorny and most sacred mystery of the alcove. "Surely the matter could have been avoided!" they will exclaim. "Would it not have sufficed to refer to the monarch's ineffectiveness in the marriage bed in such veiled terms as to be practically incomprehensible, to evade discussion of the tragedy by leaving it wrapped in mystery, or at least to rest content with speaking in flowery and unintelligible metaphors of the 'lack of maternal joys'? Is it really essential to the study of a character that the author should emphasize such exceedingly private details?"— Certainly it is indispensable, for the multitudinous tensions, clashes and interlockings, subserviences and hostilities, which gradually developed between the King and the Queen, Louis's two brothers, and the court generally, with repercussions extending far and wide into the field of history, would remain incomprehensible if no frank explanation were given as to their true causes. More numerous and more momentous historical consequences than people are in general willing to admit have taken their rise in alcoves and behind the curtains of royal beds; but scarcely in any other instance is the logical sequence between an extremely private cause and a worldwide politico-historical effect so plain as in this tragi-comedy which concerned the conjugal relationships of Louis XVI and Marie Antoinette. Utterly insincere would be any description which should leave hidden away in the shadows what Marie Antoinette herself spoke of as the "article essentiel," the focus of her sorrows and expectations.

Besides, is it really a secret that I am disclosing when I speak frankly and straightforwardly about Louis XVI's impotence during the first seven years of his married life? By no means! Only the nineteenth century, with its morbid prudery, has made a noli-me-tangere of the unrestrained exposition of physiological facts. Throughout the eighteenth century, as in all previous ages, a king's competence or impotence, and a queen's fertility or barrenness, were regarded as public and not as private affairs, were looked upon as matters of State, because upon them depended the "succession," and therewith the fate of the whole country. The marriage bed was as obviously a part of human life as the font or the coffin. In the correspondence between Maria Theresa and Marie Antoinette, though all the letters passed through the hands of the official keeper of the archives and of the copyists, the Empress of Austria and the Queen of France wrote in the plainest terms about the details and the misadventures of this affair. Maria Theresa dwelt upon the advantages of husband and wife sleeping together as a rule, and gave her daughter plain hints as to the best way of turning to account any chance of intimate relations. The daughter, in her turn, never failed to report the arrival or non-arrival of the monthly periods, to describe her husband's repeated failures with a special mention any time when things went "un petit mieux," and finally—triumphantly—to announce a pregnancy. On one occasion the famous Gluck, the composer of *Iphigénie,* was entrusted with the carrying of such private news because he was leaving a day or two ahead of the courier. In the eighteenth century natural things were still regarded with naturalness.

Nor was it Toinette's mother alone who was well informed about the husband's impotence. All the ladies of the bedchamber, the other court ladies no less, knights and military officers, were continually talking about it. The body servants were no less well informed, "in the know," and so were the washerwomen at the court of Versailles. Even at his own table the King had to put up with many a rough witticism on the subject. Furthermore, since the impotence of a Bourbon monarch was a matter of such outstanding political importance, at foreign courts a keen interest was taken in the problem that pressed so urgently at the court of France. The reports of the Prussian, the Saxon, the Sardinian envoys are full of accounts of this ticklish problem. The most zealous among these diplomatists, Count Aranda, the Spanish ambassador, actually bribed some of the palace servants to bring him news as to the condition of the linen in the royal bed, wishing to perfect his physiological knowledge as to the actual state of affairs. All over Europe princes and kings, by letters and by word of mouth, were making fun of their maladroit colleague. Not only in Versailles, but in the streets of Paris and the whole land of France, the King's conjugal inefficiency was an open secret. People talked of it at the street corners. It found its way into print, lampoons on the topic being passed furtively from hand to hand. When Maurepas was made first minister, the general hilarity was stimulated by the circulation of the following cheerful versicles:

> Maurepas était impuissant,
> Le Roi l'a rendu plus puissant.
> Le Ministre reconnaissant
> Dit: Pour vous, Sire,
> Ce que je désire,
> D'en faire autant.

But what may sound amusing to us of a later generation had a momentous, nay perilous significance. During these seven years of impotence, the characters of the King and the Queen were warped, each in its own fashion—with political results which would be unintelligible had we no knowledge of the prime cause. The fate of this one marriage was intertwined with the fate of the world.

Incomprehensible, above all, would be Louis XVI's mentality if we knew nothing about this private trouble, for his character displays the typical clinical traits of an inferiority complex determined by a sense of defective virility. Because he had been impotent in the privacy of the conjugal bed, he became affected with inhibitions which robbed him in public life of the energy needed for creative activity. He was unable "to take the floor"; incapable of exercising his own will, and even more incapable of getting his own way on the rare occasions when his will stirred. Suffering from a sense of secret shame, awkward and shy, he did his utmost to avoid social functions, and was especially loath to associate with women. Though a good enough fellow, fundamentally eager to do the right thing, he was aware that everyone at court knew about his misadventures, so that he shrank into himself, wincing at the ironical smiles of the initiated. Occasionally, he tried to assume airs of authority, and to put on a semblance of manliness. Invariably, on these occasions, he overacted his part, becoming rough and brutal in his demeanour—such assumed roughness being unconvincing, a typical manifestation of the flight from reality. Never did he succeed in showing a natural self-confidence, least of all in his hereditary role of king. Because he had been unable to play the man in his sleeping apartment, he could not play the monarch in public.

Many of his personal tastes were ultra-virile; he was fond of outdoor sports and of hard physical toil; he learned the locksmith's craft, and the lathe he used in his workshop is still on show. But these circumstances, far from conflicting with the clinical picture just given, serve only to confirm it. He who is not really in all respects a man, has an unconscious longing to fulfil a "he-man's" part, seeking compensation for his hidden weakness in an exaggerated display of strength. By keeping the saddle for hours, hunting the boar and wearying one horse after another, by tiring out his muscles when wielding the hammer in his smithy, he found compensation in these proofs of his bodily strength, and could for a moment forget the fatal defect. It was agreeable to him to toil like Hephæstus, who, a titan at the forge, was a laggard in the service of Aphrodite. No sooner, however, did Louis throw aside his hunting costume or his workshop overall in order to put on full dress and strut among his courtiers, than he felt that something more than mere muscular strength was requisite to virility, and his embarrassment returned in full tide. Rarely was he seen to laugh, seldom did he look happy.

From the characterological outlook, the most disastrous consequences of this sense of weakness became apparent in his mental attitude towards his wife. There was a good deal in her behaviour which was repugnant to his taste. He disliked her unceasing round of social amusements, her perpetual noisy pleasure-seeking, her extravagance in money matters, her levity. A man able to play a man's part would speedily have asserted himself, and would have made his young wife conduct herself in accordance with his wishes. But how could he, who, night after night, was shamed and made ridiculous by his inefficiency as a spouse, assert himself as master in the daytime? Because of his sexual impotence, Louis XVI could make no headway against his wife. The longer this unhappy state of affairs lasted, the more did he fall into dependence, nay servitude. He gave her whatever she wanted, without demur, thus again and again by his complaisance ransoming himself from his sense of culpability. In the last analysis, will-power is but the mental expression of physical potency; and, lacking both, Louis had no aptitude for imposing the necessary restraint upon his wife's follies. It was the despair of the ministers of State, of Maria Theresa, of the whole court, to watch how the royal power was passing into the hands of a young and giddy-pated woman, and to note the inconsiderate way in which she was squandering her opportunities. Why, it may be asked, did not things improve after a trifling operation had made Louis a competent husband? The answer is simple. Too late! How familiar is the experience that the parallelogram of forces which becomes established during the early years of married life continues to function indefinitely, thanks to the mental relationships thus brought into being. Even when Louis XVI had been for some time seated on his throne, when he had become a husband in the full sense of the word and had procreated several children, he, who should have been the ruler of France, remained the thrall of Marie Antoinette, simply because to begin with he had been an ineffective husband.

The sexual impotence of Louis XVI had results that were no less sinister as regards the mental development of Marie Antoinette. Owing to the contrast between the sexes, one and the same disturbance has opposite results upon the masculine and the feminine nature. When a man is affected with sexual incapacity, he suffers from inhibitions and from irresolution. But when, in the female partner, her readiness to surrender herself to the male does not find its due fulfilment, the inevitable upshot will be irritability and lack of restraint with outbursts of excessive liveliness. By nature, Marie Antoinette was normal enough: a tender, womanly woman, foreordained to motherhood on the old, liberal scale, and only waiting, one may suppose, to submit herself to a real man. Temperamentally "foreordained," I mean. Her ill-starred destiny decreed that this creature of typically feminine sensibilities should enter into an abnormal union, and should be coupled with a man who was not fully a man.

Of course she was but fifteen at the time that the marriage should have been consummated, and it may reasonably be surmised that failure of consummation need not, at such a tender age, have seriously scarred her mind. According to our present lights and in view of our present social habits, we cannot regard it as physiologically unnatural for a girl to remain a virgin until she is two-and-twenty. But the case was peculiar in this way—in a way that makes uncanny nervous re-actions easily explicable. The husband to whose embraces she had, for reasons of State, been assigned, did not, during these seven years of pseudomarriage, leave her in a condition of untouched and untroubled chastity; again and again, for the space of two thousand nights, awk-wardly and fruitlessly he endeavoured to take possession of her youthful body. Year after year her sexual passions were fruitlessly stimulated in this unsatisfying, shameful, and degrading way, without a single act of complete intercourse. One need hardly be a neurologist or a sexologist to recognize that her superlative liveliness, her per-sistent and unavailing search for new satisfactions, her fickle pursuit of one pleasure after another, were typical outcomes of unceasing sexual stimulation by a husband who was unable to provide her with adequate gratification. Because she had never been stirred to the depths and then profoundly satisfied, this wife who was not really a wife after seven years of married existence craved for an atmosphere of perpetual movement and unrest.

By slow degrees, what to begin with had been no more than the high spirits of a spoiled child degenerated into a mania for pleasure, convulsive, morbid, regarded by the whole as scandalous—a ve-hement desire for pleasure against which Maria Theresa and all Marie Antoinette's friends fought in vain. Just as in the King unfulfilled virility gave rise to a passion for hard work in the smithy and for the excitement and fatigue of the chase, so in the Queen did these mis-directed and unsatisfied feelings find vent in passionate friendship for women, in flirting with handsome young men, in a fondness for make-up, and in similar inadequate emotional satisfactions. Night after night she would keep away from the marriage bed, the place of humiliation, and (while her husband who was no husband slept heavily after the hunt) would stay up till four or five in the morning at masked balls, at the gaming-table, at supper parties, often amid dubious company, warming herself at strange fires, an unworthy queen because wedded to an incompetent husband.

Many a moment of frantic melancholy showed, however, that this frivolity was unpalatable, and was the result of a futile search for amusement to escape from a gnawing sense of disappointment. Especially characteristic was her outburst when her relative, the Duchess of Chartres, gave birth to a still-born child. Thereupon she wrote to her mother: "However distressing, I only wish the same thing could happen to me!" Better a dead child than no child at all! Anything to escape from this degrading condition, anything that would enable her to feel that she was a normal wife, and not still a virgin after seven years of marriage. Only a sympathetic comprehension of the despair that underlay her craze for pleasure can explain to us the extraordinary change which took place when, finally, Marie Antoinette became wife and mother. Her nerves were tranquillized. Another, a second, Marie Antoinette appeared upon the scene, the self-controlled, strong-willed, intrepid woman she showed herself to be during the latter half of her life. But this transformation came too late. As in childhood, so in every marriage, the initial experiences are decisive. Decades cannot rid us of the troubles that have arisen from a primary though ostensibly trifling disturbance in the delicate and sensitive substance of the mind. There can be no perfect healing for these deep-seated and invisible wounds of the affective self.

In general, such a tragedy would be no more than a private affair; misadventures of the kind occur day after day behind closed doors. But in the case we are considering, the disastrous consequences of a conjugal failure extended far beyond the realm of private existence. Here husband and wife were king and queen, pitilessly exposed to the caricaturing concave mirror of public attention. What for others remained confidential, was, as far as they were concerned, a perpetual topic for gossip and criticism. The French attitude towards sexual matters has become proverbial. The wits of the French court naturally did not content themselves with compassionately noting what had gone wrong. It was inevitable that they should continually be asking themselves and one another how Marie Antoinette had sought relief, or would seek relief, for her husband's failure to perform his marital duties. They had before their eyes a handsome young woman, self-confident and coquettish, full of animal spirits, and in the heyday of her youth. They knew that she, who seemed made for love, was yoked to a man incapable of practising that sublime art. What, in these circumstances, could their idle brains busy themselves with but the problem: Who is cuckolding Louis?

Just because there were no solid grounds for suspicion, suspicion ran riot. If the Queen merely went out riding with some good-looking cavalier, with Lauzun or Coigny, for instance, the scandalmongers were sure that he must be her lover; if she took a morning stroll in the park with the ladies and gentlemen of the court, there was talk forthwith of the most incredible orgies. Wags were perpetually thinking and chattering about the love-life of the disappointed Queen, concerning which songs, lampoons, pamphlets, and pornographic poems were rife. At first the ladies-in-waiting kept such naughty verses in manuscript, hidden away in secret drawers, reciting them to one another furtively in the privacy of their boudoirs; but it was not long before the strains, growing louder, made themselves heard beyond the palace walls and outside the mansions of the nobility. They were printed, and were read by the common people. When revolutionary propaganda began, the Jacobin journalists had not far to look in order to discover arguments enabling them to represent Marie Antoinette as a prodigy of dissipation, as a brazen-faced adultress—and, in due course, the public prosecutor needed merely to extract an unsavoury item or two from this Pandora's box filled with gallant calumnies in order to bring the Queen's slender neck under the guillotine.

We see, then, how in this case the consequences of a disorder in married life extended over the confines of personal fortunes and misfortunes deep into the realm of universal history. The destruction of the royal authority did not begin with the storming of the Bastille, but in Versailles. It was no chance matter that the news of the King's impotence and the malicious falsehoods about the Queen's nymphomania spread so rapidly from the halls of the palace to become the property of the whole nation. There were secret family and political reasons for this leakage. The fact was that in this palace there lived four or five persons, Louis's closest blood relations, who had a strong personal interest in the frustration of Marie Antoinette's hopes. First and foremost there were the King's two brothers, to whom the failure to consummate the royal marriage was most welcome, seeing that his anatomical defect and his dread of the surgeon's knife interfered, not only with the normal course of his marriage, but also with the normal course of the succession—giving these younger brothers unexpectedly good chances of mounting the throne. The elder of the two, Count of Provence and subsequently Louis XVIII (for he reached his goal at last, God alone knows by what crooked ways), had always found it hard to put up with the prospect of playing second fiddle throughout life, instead of wielding the sceptre himself. But Stanislas Xavier, as he then was, was likewise an inefficient husband and was childless; so the third of the brothers Charles Philip, Count of Artois, and in due time Charles X, had most to gain by Louis XVI's impotence, for he had sons who might succeed to the throne.

To the Count of Provence and the Count of Artois, therefore, Marie Antoinette's plight was a matter for rejoicing, and the longer the deplorable state of affairs lasted, the more confirmed were they in their happy expectations. Their fury, then, can well be imagined when, in the seventh year of the marriage, the King's virility was at length fully established, and the sexual relations between himself and his wife became normal. Stanislas Xavier never forgave his sister-in-law for this downfall of his hopes, and he tried to secure by intrigue what had become impossible of attainment along the straight path. From the day when Louis XVI became a father, his brother the Count of Provence and several other relatives were among the most dangerous of his adversaries. The Revolution found zealous assistants at court; princely hands helped to open the doors to it and supplied it with some of its best weapons. The secret of the alcove did more than anything else to undermine monarchical authority.

Almost always, indeed, there are hidden influences at work in the shaping of destiny, and the great majority of events of worldwide importance are but the expression of some inward personal conflict. One of the most cunning wiles of history is the way in which consequences of incalculable moment are developed out of seemingly trifling occasions; this was not the first, and certainly it was not the last time when a sexual disturbance transiently affecting one man threw the whole world into disorder. The impotence of Alexander of Serbia, his erotic enslavement to Draga Mashin (the woman who freed him from this trouble), the assassination of the pair, the summoning of Peter Karageorgevitch to the throne, the increasing enmity between Austria and Serbia, and finally the Great War, developed with the relentlessness of an avalanche. History, casting her mystic shuttle to and fro, weaves the rune of fate out of the frailest gossamer threads. In the life-story of Marie Antoinette, the grotesque and, except for herself, seemingly unimportant experiences of the first nights and years of her marriage, were decisive, not only in shaping her character, but also in moulding the destinies of the world.

For the time being, however, the storm was still invisible. How distant were all these consequences and complications from the merry child of fifteen, who joked with her awkward bed-fellow, and who, with cheerfully beating heart and brightly smiling eyes, looked forward to ascending the steps of a throne—from which she would be torn, and forced to mount the scaffold. The gods give no sign to one for whom they have predestined the drawing of the black marble from the bag. They allow their intended victim to pursue an untroubled course while the fountains of destiny are being unsealed from within.

CHAPTER III

Début at Versailles

Down to our own day, Versailles seems the most magnificent, the most challenging gesture of autocracy. Without obvious reason, in a flat piece of country a few miles west of the capital, there stands on an artificial mound a huge palace looking down through hundreds of windows upon artificial water-ways and artificially designed gardens, forth into vacancy. There is no river to promote traffic and intercourse; the place is not a junction of important roads or railways. A chance product, the petrified caprice of a great ruler, this palace flaunts its unmeaning splendour before our astonished eyes.

That was what Louis XIV, inflamed with Cæsarean ambition, wanted! Versailles was to be a shining altar set up that it might minister to his overweening vanity, might foster his trend towards self-idolization. A convinced autocrat, dictatorial by temperament, he had victoriously imposed his will to unity upon a disintegrated land: prescribing order for his realm; a code of morals for society; etiquette for his court; unity for the faith; and purity for the French tongue. This will to unity had radiated from his person, and therefore all resplendence was to be consecrated in his person. "L'état c'est moi." I am the centre of France; I am the navel of the world. It was to symbolize his outstanding position that the Roi Soleil removed his palace from the capital. By establishing it amid vacancy he emphasized the fact that a king of France had no need of the great city, of its citizens, of the masses, as supports of or justifications for his power. Enough for him to stretch out a commanding arm, and forthwith from swamp and sand there arose pleasure-gardens and woods, cascades and grottoes, the most sumptuous palace in the world. From this astronomical point, arbitrarily chosen by the monarch, the sun was henceforward to shine upon his kingdom. Versailles was built to give France a tangible demonstration that the people was nothing and the king everything.

Creative power, however, is always vested in particular individuals. The crown passes from head to head, but the power and majesty that have been associated with it are not necessarily transmitted by inheritance. Those who succeeded to the huge palace, to the firmly stablished realm, Louis XV and Louis XVI, were narrow of outlook, infirm of purpose, with much aptitude for enjoyment but no vivifying urge. As far as externals went, there was no change under their rule. Boundaries, language, morals, religion, the army—all were as they had been under the Grand Monarque. His resolute hand had set too deep an imprint for a hundred years to erase it; but soon the forms became void of content, for they lacked the ardency of the generative impulse. Under Louis XV there were changes in the significance of Versailles, though the old imagery persisted. Three or four thousand servants in gorgeous livery still thronged the alleys and the courtyards; there were still two thousand horses in the stables; dances, receptions, masquerades, went on in accordance with the prescribed routine; fine gentlemen and ladies clad in brocades, silks, and other gorgeous robes, flashing with jewels, pranked it in the mirrored and gold-pilastered halls; Versailles was, as of old, the most distinguished, the most refined, the most cultured court in Europe.

What had been aforetime the expression of a mighty flux of power, was now like a mill grinding without grist, and had become spiritless and unmeaning. When the Grand Monarque was gathered to his fathers, another Louis, great-grandson of the former, mounted the throne. The new king, however, succeeding like the fourteenth Louis at the age of five, proved, when he grew to man's estate, to be no ruler worthy the name, but the slave of a succession of light women. True, he assembled archbishops, ministers of State, military commanders, architects, men of letters, and musicians around his throne; but just as he himself was no Louis XIV, so were these satellites no longer worthy to rank with Mazarin, Turenne, Mansart, Colbert, Molière, Racine, and Corneille. They were place-hunters, flatterers, cantankerous beings, eager to enjoy rather than to beget great enterprises, parasitic on the works of their predecessors, incapable of transfusing their own with a firm will and a vigorous spirit. In this marble forcing-house no bold designs were any longer conceived, no resolute innovations, no writings of note, for only the marish growth of in-

trigue and galanterie could flourish in the hothouse air. It was not
achievement which now counted, but the power to form a cabal; not
merit, but the favour of the mighty. He who would abase himself
most humbly at the levee of the Pompadour or the Dubarry, would
rise to the highest position. Words counted more than deeds, semblance more than fundamental reality. Each working for his own ends
—or combining, if they combined, only as log-rollers—these men
played their part as kings, as statesmen, as priests, as soldiers, with
much grace, doubtless, but without any far-reaching purpose. One and
all they had forgotten France, the reality of things, and were concerned
only about their careers and their pleasures. Versailles, installed by
Louis XIV as the Forum Maximum of Europe, declined under Louis
XV to become no more than a stage for private theatricals, where the
leading roles were played by titled amateurs—the most artificial and
the most expensive theatre the world had ever known.

On these splendidly decorated boards there now appeared, with
mincing gait, a débutante of fifteen summers. She was a probationer,
a dauphiness. But the spectators knew that this fair-haired little Archduchess of Austria would, within a few years, become one of the two
star performers at Versailles; and it was natural that the future queen
should be the cynosure of all eyes. The first impressions were extremely
favourable. With her bewitchingly slender form she recalled a Sèvres
figurine; her tint was that of coloured porcelain; she had cheery blue
eyes, a mobile, well-formed arrogant mouth, and an ingratiating smile.
Even when she pouted, she was fascinating. Her deportment was
beyond criticism. She walked as if on wings, danced divinely, and yet,
born in the purple, she held herself confidently as she made her dignified progress along the Gallery of Mirrors, and dispensed greetings
to right and to left without a trace of embarrassment. Various ladies
at court who, in the absence of a prima donna, had fancied themselves
able to play the leading role, recognized in the immature girl a victorious rival.

There was only one complaint as to her behaviour, but this was
unanimously voiced by the more strait-laced members of court society.
The child showed a puzzling inclination to throw off all restraint even
in these sacred halls. She was, in fact, a romp and, at times, a regular

tomboy, when, with flying skirts, she larked with her young brothers-in-law. She could not readily adapt herself to the dreary tameness, to the chill reserve, which here at the French court were expected of the spouse of a crowned head. On great occasions her conduct was immaculate, for she had been reared in the trammels of Spanish-Habsburg etiquette, which was no less pompous than that of France. But in the Hofburg and at Schönbrunn, formal behaviour was kept for appropriate seasons. When there were important receptions, ceremony was put on like a gala dress, to be laid aside with all convenient speed as soon as the servants had shut the doors behind the departing guests. Thereafter relaxation ensued; manners became homely once more; the children of the reigning house could amuse themselves as lustily as if they had been ordinary mortals. Doubtless etiquette held sway at Schönbrunn, but it was not slavishly worshipped. In France, on the contrary, at a court full of affectation and grown old before its time, people no longer lived for life's sake but merely in order to show off. The higher their rank, the more close-meshed the network of taboos. There was never a spontaneous gesture, and naturalness of any kind was an unpardonable offence against good taste. From morning till night and from night till morning, "deportment" reigned supreme; and any transgressor of the rules of this tedious game aroused the animosity of the cringing courtiers who were at once actors and audience and whose whole purpose in life was to live in and for the royal theatre in the palace of Versailles.

Neither as child and Dauphiness, nor yet in later years as Queen, had Marie Antoinette any inclination to take the preposterous game seriously; she was always inclined to make light of the ceremonial sanctity in Versailles; she could not grasp, never would she be able to grasp, the tremendous importance of correct obeisances, of precedence, and all the rest of it. Self-willed, mutinous, uncontrolled, she was everlastingly in revolt against rules and regulations. Typically Austrian in her lack of punctilio, not to say lack of discipline, she wanted to live and let live, and could not endure without respite the intolerable insistence upon matters of no importance whatever. Just as at home she had shirked her lessons, so here did she seize every opportunity of evading the admonitions of her strict lady-in-waiting, Madame de Noailles, whom she mockingly nicknamed "Madame Etiquette." The unconscious longing of this poor child who had too early been made a pawn in the political game was to get what was sedulously withheld from her amid all the luxuries of her station, namely a few years of unalloyed childhood.

A crown princess has no longer any business to be a child! Her attendants were leagued together in order to keep her in mind of her duty and to see that she maintained an inviolable dignity. Those mainly responsible for her education, for her "breaking in," over and above the chief lady-in-waiting who was a religious devotee, were her husband's three aunts, the daughters of Louis XV, bigoted and ill-natured old maids whose virtue was unchallenged by any breath of scandal. Madame Adelaide, Madame Victoire, Madame Sophie, these three Parcæ, took charge of Marie Antoinette in what seemed the friendliest fashion. In their retired nook she was initiated into the strategy of the petty warfare at court, was taught the art of "médisance," of backbiting, of underground intrigue, and was shown the technique of pin-pricking. At first the new lessons were amusing to the inexperienced young woman, and, in all innocence, she re-echoed the malicious utterances; but, being fundamentally straightforward, it was not long before she found herself out of tune with such exhibitions of ill-nature. To her misfortune, perhaps, she never learned to assume a false front, never learned to conceal either her likings or dislikings; and her sound instincts soon led her to throw off the tutelage of her aunts. Nor had the Comtesse de Noailles better luck with her pupil. At fifteen, at sixteen, the girl's impetuous temperament made her perpetually rebel against "la mesure," against moderation, and against the regular allotment of the daily round. But in this last matter there was no respite. Here is her own description of one of her days:

"I get up at half past nine or ten o'clock, dress, and say my morning prayers. Then I have breakfast, and go to see my aunts, where I generally find the King. This takes until half past ten. Thereafter, at eleven, I go to have my hair dressed. Next comes the levee, which all may attend, except persons without rank or name. I rouge my cheeks and wash my hands before the assembled company; then the gentlemen withdraw, the ladies remain, and I dress myself in their presence. Now it is time for church. If the King is at Versailles, I go with him, with my husband, and my aunts to Mass. If the King is away, I go alone with the Dauphin, but always at the same time. After Mass we have our dinner in public, but this is over by half past one, for we both eat very quickly. Then I am with the Dauphin for a time, and when he has business to do I retire to my own room, where I read, write, or work. Needlework, for I am embroidering the King a coat, which gets forward very slowly, though I hope that, with God's grace, it will be finished in a few years from now. At three o'clock I go again to my aunts, with whom the King is at this hour. At four, the Abbé comes to me, and at five my clavecin teacher or singing-master, till six. At half past six I almost always go to my aunts, unless I go out. I should tell you that my husband almost always goes with me to my aunts. From seven till nine we play cards; but when it is fine, I go out, and then the cards are not in my room but at my aunts'. At nine o'clock we have supper, and when the King is not there the aunts have supper with us. But when the King is there, we go to the aunts after supper. We wait there for the King, who usually comes at about a quarter to eleven. While waiting, I lie down on a big sofa, and go to sleep until the King comes. When he is away, we go to bed at eleven. That is how I spend my day."

In this daily routine, there was little place left for amusements, though it was for these, above all, that her impatient heart yearned. The hot young blood racing through her veins made her want to run, to laugh, to play the fool; but at the first sign of anything of the kind "Madame Etiquette" would raise an admonitory finger, and would declare that this, that, and the other—in fact, everything Marie Antoinette really wanted to do—was incompatible with the position of a Dauphiness.

Abbé Vermond, who had been her tutor in Vienna, and was now her confessor and reader rolled into one, had an even harder time of it with her. It was true that Marie Antoinette was still very backward as regards book-learning, for her education had been far below the average in quality. At fifteen, while she had forgotten a good deal of her German, she had not yet gained an adequate mastery of French; her handwriting was extremely bad; her literary style was marred by numberless inelegances and faults in spelling, and she had to have her letters drafted for her by the worthy Abbé. Besides this, he read aloud to her for an hour every day, and also made her read to herself—for Maria Theresa was continually asking about her daughter's reading. The Empress had her doubts about the accuracy of the statement that her Toinette read or wrote every afternoon.

"Do try to get your head well stocked with good reading," writes the mother. "You need it more than almost anyone. I have been waiting two months for the Abbé's list, and I am very much afraid that you have neglected this matter, and that the donkeys and the horses have used up the time which ought to have been set aside for reading. Be careful not to neglect this matter during the winter, since reading is about all that you are capable of, for you know little of music or drawing or dancing or painting or other accomplishments."

Unfortunately Maria Theresa had good ground for her suspicions. Little Toinette, with mingled simplicity and shrewdness, was well able to twist Abbé Vermond round her finger—and a Dauphiness cannot be coerced or punished. What should have been the reading hour, almost always degenerated into an hour of idle chatter. She learned nothing or next to nothing, and her mother's most earnest persuasions could never make her diligent. The possibilities of a normal and healthy education, of a sound development, had been marred by forcing her into premature marriage. Here was Marie Antoinette, a child in years, burdened with the title and dignity of a wife, and in a royal station which gave her immense prestige; yet she was expected to sit at a desk and master the elements of education like any other schoolgirl. One moment she would be treated as a great lady, and the next she would be berated like a child. Her chief lady-in-waiting wanted her to show a fine deportment; her aunts wished her to take part in court intrigues; her mother wanted her to educate herself; but in her own heart she desired to enjoy life and youth. It was owing to this perpetual conflict between her age and her position, between her will and that of others, that there arose in a temperament which might otherwise have developed straightforwardly an uncontrollable unrest, and an impatient craving for liberty. In due time, these failings were to have a disastrous influence upon Marie Antoinette's fate.

Maria Theresa was fully informed concerning her daughter's dangerous position at the foreign court; and she knew, likewise, that the unsteady young creature lacked the instinctive capacity requisite for the avoidance of the traps and snares of palace intrigue. That was why she sent to Paris, not only as ambassador, but also as the Queen's trusty counsellor, the ablest among her diplomats, Count Mercy. Writing to him with singular frankness, she said: "I dread my daughter's youth, the effect which undue flattery may have upon her, her idleness, and her lack of any inclination for serious activity. Let me urge you to keep a watchful eye upon these matters, and to see to it that she does not fall into bad hands—for I have every confidence in you."

The Empress could not have made a better choice. Born in the Low Countries, but wholly devoted to his imperial mistress; a man who knew the life of court, and yet was no courtier; a cautious thinker without being cold; clear-headed, if not a man of genius—this wealthy and unambitious bachelor fulfilled his position of trust with the utmost tact. Thanks to his detailed reports, the anxious mother in far-off Schönbrunn was able to keep watch on her daughter as if through a telescope. She knew every word that Toinette spoke, every book that the young woman read—or failed to read. She knew what dresses were worn, how the days were spent, with whom the girl had conversation, what mistakes were being made. All these things Maria Theresa learned because Mercy had taken his measures with so much care, and had cast a fine-meshed net around his protégée.

"I have made sure of three persons in the service of the Archduchess, one of her women and two of her menservants, who give me full reports of what goes on. Then, from day to day, I am told of the conversations she has with Abbé Vermond, from whom she hides nothing. Besides this, the Marquise de Durfort passes on to me everything she says to her aunts. I have also sources of information as to what goes on whenever the Dauphiness sees the King. Superadded are my personal observations, so that there really is not an hour of the day as to which I am not instructed concerning what the Archduchess may have said or done or heard. . . . I have made my inquiries thus extensive because I know how essential it is to Your Majesty's tranquillity that you should be fully informed."

This faithful retainer reported with pitiless sincerity all that he heard and all that he could find out. Since reciprocal thefts from the ordinary post were at that time one of the chief arts of diplomacy, Mercy's private dispatches were sent to the Empress by special messengers. The letters were kept even from the chancellor and from Emperor Joseph by being enclosed in covers bearing the inscription "tibi soli."

Marie Antoinette, who was not of a suspicious nature, seems often to have wondered how it was that Schönbrunn could be kept so well posted up concerning every detail of her life; but she never imagined that the grey-haired and fatherly ambassador was her mother's private spy, or that Maria Theresa's letters of exhortation, inspired by such comprehensive information, had many of them been sent at Mercy's instance. For it was only through an appeal to the maternal authority that the ambassador could exert any control over the unruly young woman! Being the representative of a foreign though friendly court, it did not become him to read the Dauphiness moral lectures; he dared not presume to instruct, or ostensibly to influence, the future queen of France. That was why, whenever he wished to gain some useful end, he arranged for the sending of one of those affectionate but admonitory letters from Vienna which Marie Antoinette received and opened with a palpitating heart. Although subservient to no one else in the world, the giddy girl was timid where her mother was concerned, and reverently bowed her head before even the harshest criticism from that quarter.

Thanks to this unceasing supervision, Marie Antoinette was saved, during the first years of her residence in Versailles, from the greatest of all the dangers to which she was exposed, that of her own unruliness. A guardian spirit, her mother's powerful and far-sighted intelligence, was thinking on her behalf; her levity was kept under restraint by her mother's resoluteness. Maria Theresa was doing her utmost to atone for the wrong she had committed in sacrificing her youthful daughter to reasons of State.

Good-natured, cordial, and unreflective, Marie Antoinette had no dislike for the people who formed her immediate environment. She was really fond of her grandfather by marriage, Louis XV, who seemed to her an extremely friendly old gentleman; she got on tolerably well with her maiden aunts and with "Madame Etiquette"; she had confidence in her good confessor, Vermond; and she felt a child's respect, tinged with liking, for her mother's friend Mercy the ambassador. But they were all elderly folks, serious-minded, solemn, grave in their demeanour and self-controlled in their actions. Our lassie wanted friends and comrades of her own age, playmates and not merely teachers, supervisors, and counsellors; she wanted persons with whom she could associate on frank, cheerful, and confidential terms; the youth in her thirsted for youth in others. But whom could she find as playmates in the hopelessly formal edifice of cold marble? She might well look for comradeship to her husband, who was only a year older than herself, but this clumsy associate—occasionally in the sulks, often embarrassed, and in his embarrassment not infrequently rough—avoided any real intimacy with his wife. No more than she, had he had the smallest desire to be married so early, and a good while elapsed before he could make up his mind to be even reasonably civil towards the girl from foreign parts.

Who, then, was left for her to play with but Louis's younger brothers, the Count of Provence and the Count of Artois? With these lads of fourteen and thirteen respectively, Marie Antoinette often had a gay time enough. Getting hold of various costumes, they dressed up and played at private theatricals; but all the properties and the clothes had to be hustled out of sight as soon as "Madame Etiquette" drew near, for a Dauphiness must not be caught play-acting. Her craving for amusement, and for the signs of a little tender affection, had curious results at times. On one occasion she applied to Mercy begging him to arrange for a dog to be sent to her from Vienna, "un chien Mops" [a pug]. Another time, Madame de Noailles discovered to her horror that the future queen of France had called the two little children of one of her waiting-maids into her room and was romping with them on the floor regardless of her fine clothing. From the first hour to the last, the free, the natural girl and woman in Marie Antoinette was fighting against the unnaturalness of the environment into which she had been introduced by marriage, against the stifling atmosphere of hooped petticoats and tight-lacing. To the end of her days the frivolous Viennese felt herself a stranger amid the formalities of the thousand-windowed palace of Versailles.

CHAPTER IV

Fight for a Word

"Don't meddle in politics, don't interfere in other people's business," was Maria Theresa's reiterated advice to her daughter—superfluous advice, in truth, for Marie Antoinette thought nothing in the world of the smallest importance except her own pleasure. Being in love with herself, a typical young Narcissus, she was inexpressibly bored by everything that required careful consideration or systematic thought; and it was not through any will of her own that within the first year after her advent she became involved in the petty palace intrigues which, at the court of Louis XV, had replaced the broadly conceived statesmanship of his predecessor. At the time of her arrival, there were two main parties at Versailles. The Queen had died two years before, so, as far as women were concerned, precedence and authority should have accrued to the King's three daughters. But they, being stupid and narrow-minded, being no more than bigots with a taste for meddling, could make no better use of their position than to insist upon sitting in the front seats when Mass was being said, and upon having precedence at receptions. Tedious and spiteful old maids, they could exert no influence over their royal father, who was absorbed in his pleasures (which were all grossly sensual). But because they were without influence, because they had no positions to give away, even the least among the courtiers cared nothing for their good will, and all the honour and glory of court life ("honour" in a very dubious sense) had accrued to Madame Dubarry, the King's latest mistress.

Sprung from the dregs of the populace, with a past which certainly would not bear investigation, and having (if rumour be true) spent some time in a brothel before she was promoted to be the King's bed-fellow, she got her complaisant protector to buy her a titled husband, Count Dubarry, a most accommodating person, who disappeared for ever from the scene immediately after the paper marriage. All the same, the sometime street-walker made the name of Dubarry acceptable at court. For the second time, before the eyes of Europe, was played a ludicrous and degrading farce in which the Most Christian King had the lady who was well known to be his mistress received by all his court as a distinguished noblewoman. Her position thus legitimized, the King's inamorata lived in the great palace at Versailles, her apartments separated by only three rooms from those of the scandalized daughters, and connected with the King's quarters by a specially built staircase. With her own well-tried body, and with those of willing but hitherto sexually inexperienced pretty girls whom she brought to the old voluptuary in order to stimulate his declining passions, she kept Louis XV in her toils, so that the only way to the King's favour lay through her salon. Naturally the hangers-on at court crowded round her, since she held the reins of power; foreign envoys danced attendance in her anteroom; kings and princes showered gifts upon her; she could have ministers dismissed, could allot lucrative posts, could get palaces built, and could squander the royal treasure in various other ways. The wanton charms of her bosom were set off by costly jewels; huge gems sparkled on her hands, which were ardently kissed by eminences and princes and aspirants; while her abundant brown locks were adorned by an invisible queenly crown.

Thus the King's illegitimate partner became the chief dispenser of the royal favour; and a daring courtesan, flattered by all and sundry, was able to assume the airs and to wield the influence of a queen. Meanwhile, in their retirement, the King's daughters, their noses much out of joint, were lamenting their hard fate, were railing under their breath at the impudent strumpet who was bringing the court into disgrace, was making their father an object of scorn, was usurping the powers of government, and was rendering a decent, Christian family life impossible. With the venom inspired by their own involuntary virtue (their sole possession, for they had neither charm nor wit nor dignity), these three daughters loathed the whore of Babylon who had virtually replaced their deceased mother on the throne. From morning till night, their only thought was to sneer at her, to despise her, and to do her an ill turn whenever opportunity offered.

Now, by the favour of fortune, there appeared at Versailles this foreign child, Marie Antoinette, an Austrian archduchess by birth—only fifteen, but, through her position as wife to the heir to the throne, by right the first lady in the land. It was a welcome task to the three spiteful old maids to play her off against the Dubarry; and from the first moment of her arrival, it was their chief aim to make the unsuspecting girl a pawn in their game. They would thrust her forward, and, while they themselves were unnoticed in the background, she should help to lay the unclean beast low. Thus with every semblance of affection they drew the little princess into their circle. Without an inkling of what was afoot, within a few weeks the girl became involved in a fierce struggle.

At the time of her arrival, Marie Antoinette had known nothing of such women as the Dubarry, nor of the peculiar position acquired by this particular specimen at Versailles. The court of Maria Theresa was a "strictly moral" one, and no word about a king's mistresses had ever been uttered in the hearing of the little innocent. At the very first supper she had noticed among the other court ladies a buxom and beraddled woman gorgeously dressed, who looked at her inquisitively. A countess, she was told; Countess Dubarry. But her worthy aunts were not slow to enlighten her as to the realities of the situation, for a few weeks later we find Marie Antoinette writing to her mother concerning the "sotte et impertinente créature." Frankly, unreservedly, she passed on to Maria Theresa all her dear aunts' backbiting about the Dubarry, and was open-mouthed in talk with her daily associates— to the great amusement of the court, which in general was profoundly bored, and relished such sensations. The fact was that Marie Antoinette had taken it into her little head (or, rather, her aunts had put it into her little head) to rid Versailles of this audacious intruder who was flaunting her plumes like any peacock that strutted about the grounds of the royal palace. According to the rigid etiquette that prevailed at Versailles, no lady of lesser rank could address a lady of higher rank uninvited, but must reverentially wait until the superior began the conversation. Now that there was no queen, the Dauphiness was, of course, the chief lady of the court, and she made abundant use of her privilege in this respect. Coolly, smilingly, and challengingly, she let Countess Dubarry wait and wait and wait for a word. Week after week, month after month, the impatient courtesan went hungry. The scandalmongers and toadies were not slow to note the fact; they took a fiendish delight in this duel; the whole court basked in the warmth of the fire kindled by His Majesty's daughters. Everyone kept eager watch on the Dubarry, sitting in ill-concealed wrath among the ladies while the froward little minx chattered like a magpie to everyone else, but to her said never a word. Towards Madame Dubarry Marie Antoinette persistently showed a frozen countenance—looking through the bejewelled Countess as if she had been a window-pane.

Now the Dubarry was by no means ill-natured. A woman of the people, she had the characteristic merits of the lower classes; she was friendly and forthcoming, prepared to be jovial and comradely to all who would respond in kind. Her vanity made her ready to be agreeable to anyone who would flatter her. She was prodigal in her gifts to those who asked a boon, and was anything in the world rather than spiteful or envious. But for the very reason that she had risen with such bewildering speed from the ranks, the Dubarry loved to make the most of her newly acquired power; she wanted to enjoy the fruits of luxury in all men's sight, and in all women's; she rejoiced in making a fulsome display of her unseemly position; and, in especial, she longed to have it regarded as a seemly one. Her prime wish was to sit in the first rank among the court ladies, to wear the most sparkling jewels, to have her wardrobe stocked with the most resplendent gowns, to drive in the finest chariots drawn by the speediest horses. Her royal lover, a devoted slave, refused her none of these things. But this was not enough. Playing in the tragi-comedy of illegitimate power, and reminding us in this respect of the first Napoleon, her supreme ambition was to be recognized by the legitimate powers of this world. The upshot was that Countess Dubarry, though princes fawned upon her and though she was the spoiled darling of the courtiers, still had an overwhelming and unfulfilled desire; to be "recognized" by the young woman who was indubitably the chief lady of the realm, to be cordially welcomed by this archduchess of the House of Habsburg. But not only did the "petite rousse" (thus, beside herself with anger, did Madame Dubarry nickname Marie Antoinette), this little gaby of sixteen who could not speak French correctly, and who could not even, because of her husband's impotence, surrender an undesired virginity; not only did the sometime archduchess turn up her nose at the Dubarry and give her father-in-law's mistress the cut direct in the face of the whole court—the Dauphiness openly and shamelessly made fun of the

Countess who, as far as real power went, undoubtedly took precedence
of every other woman in France. Such contumelious treatment was
unendurable!

In this Homeric contest, there can be no question that Marie Antoinette had the right of it. She was of higher rank, and had no need to
vouchsafe a word to the "lady" in question, who, as a mere countess,
was far beneath the Dauphiness, even though seven million diamonds
might glitter upon her person. Yet the Dubarry was backed up by the
actualities of power, for she controlled the King. Nearing the last
stages of moral decay, indifferent to the State, his family, his subjects,
and the world, an arrogant cynic ("après moi le déluge")—all that
Louis XV now cared for was his tranquillity and his pleasures. He let
events run their course, caring not a jot for the morality of his court,
well knowing that if he wanted to play the disciplinarian he would
have to begin with himself. He had reigned long enough, and for the
few years that remained he wanted to live for himself alone, though
everything should crumble around him and fall into utter ruin as soon
as he left the stage. It was inevitable, therefore, that this war of the
women which had suddenly broken out should be a great annoyance
to him. In accordance with his epicurean principles, he would have preferred to have nothing to do with the affair. But the Dubarry was
incessantly dinning in his ears that she could not allow herself to be
humiliated by a young minx from Austria, that she could not bear
being made ridiculous before the whole court; King Louis must protect her, must safeguard her dignity, and therewith his own. At length
the King grew weary of such frequent scenes and of such floods of
tears. Sending for Marie Antoinette's first lady-in-waiting, Madame
de Noailles, he let her know which way the wind was blowing. He
began by uttering a few amiable commonplaces about his grandson's
wife. By degrees, however, he interwove a little criticism into his
observations. The Dauphiness, he said, was talking somewhat too freely
about what came under her eyes, and it would be well to let her know
that such behaviour could not fail to have a bad effect in the intimacies
of family life. Madame de Noailles hastened to transmit this warning
to Marie Antoinette, who retailed it to her aunts and to Vermond. The
latter, needless to say, passed it on in due course to Mercy, who, as

Austrian ambassador, thinking above all of the alliance between Austria and France, was greatly concerned, and sent an express messenger to Vienna that the whole affair might be laid before the Empress.

Here was a painful situation for Maria Theresa, the pietist, the bigot, to deal with! In Vienna, through the instrumentality of her famous Committee of Public Morals, she was accustomed to give short shrift to ladies of easy virtue by having them confined in reformatories. Was she now to tell her own daughter to be civil to a creature of that sort? How could she venture to disregard the wishes of the King of France? The mother, a rigid Catholic, and the stateswoman were in sharp conflict. Ultimately, being an experienced diplomatist, she managed to evade the need for coming to a personal decision, and referred the whole business to the Imperial Chancellery. She did not write in person to her daughter, but instructed Kaunitz, her first minister, to send Mercy a rescript urging Marie Antoinette to remember her political duties. In this way the requisite moral formalities were observed, but at the same time the young woman was given a strong hint to better her ways. Kaunitz wrote: "To refrain from showing civility towards persons whom the King has adopted as members of his own circle is derogatory to that circle; and all persons must be regarded as members thereof whom the ruling monarch himself looks upon as his confidants, no one being entitled to ask whether he be right or wrong in doing so. The choice of a reigning sovereign must be unreservedly respected."

The language, though plain to a fault, left Marie Antoinette cold, for she was being perpetually spurred on by her aunts. When the letter was read aloud to her, in her easy-going way she said to Mercy: "Yes, yes; all right"; but in her inmost heart her thought was that, whatever the old buffer Kaunitz might say, no chancellor had any right to interfere in her private affairs. Having noted how angry the "sotte créature" was at being publicly ignored, the arrogant Dauphiness found that this wrath added succulence to the jest. As if no reproof had reached her by a circuitous route, she persisted, with cheerful malice, in her policy of silence. Day after day she encountered the favourite at dances, festivals, round the gaming-table, and even at the King's board, watching with glee how the Dubarry trembled with expectancy and looked askance whenever she (the Dauphiness) drew near. Well, the King's mistress might wait till the day of judgment! All she could get out of Toinette was a disdainful and icy stare. The civil words which Dubarry, the King, Kaunitz, Mercy, and (in secret) even Maria Theresa wanted remained unspoken.

War to the knife had been declared. As at a cockfight, the courtiers gathered round the two contending women, who maintained a resolute silence; one of them with the tears of impotent wrath in her eyes, and the other with a smile of contemptuous superiority wreathing her lips. Wagers were freely laid as to whether the legitimate or the illegitimate she-ruler of France would win the battle. It was years upon years since Versailles had witnessed so amusing a spectacle.

When matters had reached this pass, the King grew seriously annoyed. Accustomed, within the palace at any rate, to exercise a Byzantine discipline (so that when he merely batted an eyelash everyone hastened to do his will before he had troubled to give plain expression to his desire), he, the Most Christian King of France, had now for the first time since his majority to encounter resistance. A half-grown girl was daring to scout his openly expressed wishes.

The simplest plan would, no doubt, have been to bid the refractory young woman to his presence and give her a good talking-to, but even this demoralized old cynic had some remnants of scruple, and hesitated to command his grandson's wife to hold friendly converse with his mistress. In his perplexity, therefore, Louis XV did precisely what Maria Theresa had done in hers, metamorphosing a private matter into an affair of State. To Mercy's great surprise he was summoned by the French Ministry for Foreign Affairs to an audience with the King, not in the official audience chamber, but in the apartment of Countess Dubarry. The singular choice of locality led him to expect what was coming, and his expectations were promptly fulfilled. The only person there to receive him was the first minister; but hardly had he exchanged a few words with the latter when Countess Dubarry entered, greeted him warmly, and went on to explain in considerable detail how unjust it was to suppose that she harboured any unfriendly sentiments towards the Dauphiness. The accusation was a gross calumny! The Austrian ambassador found it extremely embarrassing to be so suddenly transformed from the representative of the Empress into the confidant of the Dubarry, and he had recourse to vague diplomatic utterances. Then a concealed and curtained door was noiselessly opened; Louis XV came in, and His Majesty took charge of the ticklish conversation.

"Hitherto," said the King to Mercy, "you have been spokesman of the Empress. For a little while I should like you to be good enough to act as mine." He went on to speak frankly about Marie Antoinette. She was very charming; but young, and perhaps a thought too high-spirited. Wedded, as she was to a man who did not know how to keep her under control, she was made a pawn of by all sorts of cabals, and allowed herself to be guided by evil counsellors. (Of course, Louis was referring to his own daughters, Marie Antoinette's aunts by marriage!) He therefore begged Mercy to do all that was possible to induce the Dauphiness to modify her behaviour.

Mercy was not slow to grasp that the affair had become one of high politics; he had been given a direct commission which must be instantly discharged; the King was insisting upon unqualified surrender. Sending an express to Vienna, the ambassador did his best to temper the asperities of the situation, touching up the Dubarry's portrait in the friendliest possible colours. The Countess was not such a bad sort after all, and she demanded nothing more than a trifle, namely that the Dauphiness should, just once, say a word to her in public. While awaiting the answer to his dispatch, he visited Marie Antoinette and made the strongest possible representations. In fact he threatened her a little, breathing the ominous word "poison," for it was notorious that at the French court inconvenient persons of the highest rank had been got rid of by this means.

Then, with all the eloquence he could command, he went on to describe the way in which a palace dispute, if it pursued its course unchecked, might lead to a breach between the Habsburgs and the Bourbons. This was his highest trump. He made Marie Antoinette understand that if the alliance, her mother's life-work, were now to be broken, the blame would lie at her door.

The heavy artillery had its due effect. Marie Antoinette was intimidated. With tears of anger in her eyes, she promised the ambassador that, on a day that was fixed between them, when there was to be a card-party, she would say the required word to the Dubarry. Mercy drew a breath of relief. God be praised, the alliance had been saved.

Frequenters of the court now looked forward to a dramatic spectacle. From one to another the word had been passed that in the evening, after so long a delay, the Dauphiness would for the first time address Madame Dubarry. The stage was carefully set. The ambassador and Marie Antoinette had come to an agreement about the matter. At the end of the card-party, Mercy was to go up to the Dubarry and enter into conversation with her. Then, as if by chance, the Dauphiness was to come that way, catch sight of the ambassador, say good-evening to him, and seize the opportunity of uttering a word or two to the King's favourite as well. All the plans had been admirably drafted, but unfortunately the performance did not run smoothly as per program, for the aunts grudged their hated rival the triumph of a public success. They had made up their minds that the fire-proof curtain should be lowered before the signal could be given for the duet of reconciliation. Marie Antoinette had the best intentions in the world when she went to the card-party, and Mercy carried out his role to perfection. Haphazard (to all seeming), he went up to Madame Dubarry and began to talk to her. Meanwhile, likewise as previously arranged, Marie Antoinette began her circuit of the hall. Conversing now with this lady, now with that, now with a third, she prolonged somewhat unduly this last exchange of trivialities—being perhaps a little anxious and excited, and maybe out of temper. Still, there now remained only one lady between her and the Dubarry. In two minutes, in a minute, she would reach Mercy and the favourite.

But at this decisive moment Madame Adelaide, the most venomous of the three old maids, played her great coup. Stepping up briskly to Marie Antoinette, she said in a commanding tone: "It is time for us to leave. We will go and await the King in my sister Victoire's room." Marie Antoinette, taken by surprise, alarmed, utterly lost courage. She could not find the energy to refuse, nor yet the presence of mind, before leaving, to utter a swift and indifferent, yet decisive word to the waiting Dubarry. Flushed, confused, she turned upon her heel and fled, running rather than walking; and the word—the long-desired,

commanded, diplomatically wrestled for, and faithfully promised word
—remained unspoken. The position was even worse than it had been;
a fresh slight had been inflicted, and the planned reconciliation had
come to naught. The mischief-makers at the court rubbed their hands
with delight; and even in the servants' hall the menials giggled as they
told one another how Madame Dubarry had fruitlessly been kept waiting. But the Countess was in a fine rage; and, a more important matter, so was Louis XV. "Well, Monsieur de Mercy," said he acidly to the
ambassador, "you don't seem to have achieved much. Apparently I
must come to your aid!"

The King of France had uttered threats in his anger; Madame
Dubarry was in a tantrum; the Austro-French alliance was tottering;
the peace of Europe was endangered. The ambassador promptly reported to Vienna. There was nothing for it but that Maria Theresa
should intervene, for no one else in the world had any influence over
this stiffnecked and inconsiderate child. The Empress, indeed, was
greatly distressed, nay alarmed, at the turn affairs had taken. When
she sent her daughter to France, she had been animated by the sincere
desire that the child should not become involved in the troubled current of political life. She had written to her ambassador as follows:
"I may tell you frankly that I have no wish for my daughter to
acquire a decisive influence upon public affairs. My own experience has
taught me only too well how crushing a burden is the government of
a huge monarchy. Besides, I know my daughter's youth and levity,
together with her lack of application (to say nothing of her ignorance)
—considerations which intensify my fears that she could do little to
promote the success of the work of government in a monarchy which
is in so chaotic a condition as that of France at the present time. If my
daughter can give no help in the matter, or if the condition of the
monarchy should go from bad to worse, I would rather that some
minister of State were blamed for it than my daughter. . . . I therefore cannot make up my mind to talk to her about politics or affairs
of State."
But this time, alas, the unhappy woman had to be false to her own
counsel, since she now had grave reasons for political anxiety at home.
Obscure and unsavoury intrigues were going on in Vienna. Months

before, Frederick the Great, whom she regarded as Lucifer's emissary on earth, and Catherine of Russia, whom she mistrusted no less, had approached Austria with a proposal for the partition of Poland, and the Empress's conscience had been uneasy ever since because the idea had secured enthusiastic approval and support from Kaunitz and her co-regent Joseph II. "The partition is essentially unjust, and to us can only be harmful. I earnestly deplore the proposal, and must avow that I am ashamed to show my face." She had been quick to recognize this political scheme for what it was—a crime, an act of rapine perpetrated against a defenceless and blameless people. "By what right can we plunder an innocent whom we have always plumed ourselves on protecting?" In genuine indignation, she rejected the plan, regardless of the fact that her moral disapproval might be regarded as mere weakness. "I would rather be thought weak than dishonourable," she said with combined nobility and shrewdness. It was long since Maria Theresa had ceased to be an autocrat. Joseph II, her son and fellow-ruler, dreamed of nothing but war, expansion of the Empire, and reforms; whilst his mother, who was well aware how unstable and artificial a realm was Austria, could think only of maintaining and safeguarding the extant. It was in order to counteract Maria Theresa's influence, that Joseph had been wooing the favour of the great soldier, Frederick II, who had so long been his mother's bitterest enemy; and, to make matters worse, the Empress saw with consternation that Kaunitz, who had been her most faithful servant and whom she had raised from obscurity to power, had turned towards the rising star of her son.

Worn out by the cares of State superadded to these private contrarieties, disappointed in her hopes both as mother and as empress, Maria Theresa would gladly have laid down the sceptre. Her strong sense of responsibility alone kept her on the throne. In many respects her situation was strangely akin to that of her descendant, Francis Joseph who, no less tired, continued to hold the reins of power till 1916. She foresaw that her son Joseph, a man of fickle and restless disposition, a reformer in a hurry, would, when left to himself, promptly spread disquiet throughout a realm already difficult to control. To the last, therefore, this pious and upright woman battled on behalf of what, to her, was the highest thing in the world—honour.

"I must admit," she wrote, "that never before in my life have I been so profoundly troubled. When an unrighteous claim was made on my territories, I stiffened my back and put my trust in God. But on the present occasion, when I have to recognize, not merely that right is not on my side, but that obligation, justice, and equity are fighting against me, I can get no rest. My uneasy heart continually reproaches me with the likelihood that I shall try to benumb myself or others, or that I shall endeavour to make duplicity pass for straightforwardness. Loyalty and faith seem to have forsaken me for ever—the greatest treasures, and the true sources of strength when one monarch is in opposition to others."

Frederick the Great, however, had a tough conscience, and said mockingly in Berlin: "The Empress Catherine and I are a pair of brigands; but this devout Queen-Empress—I wonder how she has been able to arrange matters with her confessor!" He pressed for a settlement, while Joseph II insisted that war would become inevitable if Austria did not comply. At length, with many tears, with a sore conscience and a sad heart, Maria Theresa gave way. "I am not strong enough to manage affairs alone, and I have consented to follow the lead of others, though to my grievous distress." When signing, she excused herself on the ground that "all wise and experienced men" had advised her to do so. Yet she knew that she was to blame, and in trembling awaited the day when the secret treaty and its consequences would become known to the world. What would France say? Would that country, in view of the Austro-French alliance, look on indifferently at the robbery of Poland by Austria, Prussia, and Russia, or would it protest against a partition which Maria Theresa herself knew to be unjust? (Had not the Empress with her own hand erased the word "rightfully" from the Decree of Occupation?) Everything turned, now, upon the mood of Louis XV. Would he be friendly or hostile?

It was while these cares were so urgent, while these pangs of conscience were so acute, that Maria Theresa received from Mercy the alarming news that King Louis was extremely angry with Marie Antoinette, and had plainly manifested his displeasure to the writer of the dispatch. The distressing information reached Vienna at a time when the French ambassador, Prince de Rohan, had been so effectively befooled that, giving his whole time and energy to pleasure parties **and** the chase, he was quite unaware of any scheme for the partition of Poland being afoot. Now, because Marie Antoinette would not speak the necessary word to Countess Dubarry, the partition of Poland might very well lead to war! Maria Theresa was greatly alarmed. If she, at fifty-five, had had to sacrifice her conscience to reasons of State, was her daughter, a chit of sixteen, to show herself more royalist than the King, more moral than her own mother? A letter was therefore written in more strenuous terms than ever, designed to make the mutinous girl eat humble-pie. Of course not a word was said about Poland or concerning reasons of State, the assumption being that the matter was, after all, a trifle. These false pretences must have come hard to the Empress. She wrote as follows:

"The dread and embarrassment you show about speaking to the King, the best of fathers, about speaking to persons you are advised to speak to! What a pother about saying 'Good day' to someone, a kindly word concerning a dress or some such trumpery. Mere whimsies, or something worse. You have allowed yourself to become enslaved to such an extent that reason and duty can no longer persuade you. I cannot keep silent about the matter any longer. After your conversation with Mercy and after all that he told you about the King's wishes and your duty, you actually dared to fail him. What reason can you give for such conduct? None whatever. It does not become you to regard the Dubarry in any other light than that of a lady who has a right of entry to the court and is admitted to the society of the King. You are His Majesty's first subject, and you owe him obedience and submission. It behoves you to set a good example, to show the courtiers and the ladies at Versailles that you are ready to do your master's will. If any baseness, any intimacy, were asked of you, neither I nor another would advise you to it; but all that is expected is that you should say an indifferent word, should look at her beseemingly—not for the lady's own sake, but for the sake of your grandfather, your master, your benefactor!"

This cannonade (in which the projectiles were not thoroughly honest arguments) broke down Marie Antoinette's defences. Unruly, self-willed, defiant, obstinate, all the same she had never ventured to defy her mother's authority. The Habsburg domestic discipline triumphed as usual. To save her face, Marie Antoinette penned a few words of protest. "I do not say that I refuse to address her, but I cannot agree to speak to her at a fixed hour on a particular day, known to her in advance, so that she can triumph about it." This was nothing but a rearguard skirmish. In truth, the young woman had decided to capitulate.

New Year's Day 1772 witnessed the final decision of this heroic-comic war of the women; a decision which proved a signal victory for Madame Dubarry and a defeat for Marie Antoinette. Once more the stage was set in due form; once again all the frequenters of the court gathered together as witnesses. New Year greetings were being given. In order of precedence, one after another the ladies of the court filed past the Dauphiness, among them the Duchesse d'Aiguillon, wife of the minister of State, with Madame Dubarry. Marie Antoinette, having said a few words to the duchess, turned her head more or less in the direction of Madame Dubarry and (while the onlookers held their breath lest a syllable should be lost) uttered the momentous words for which so strenuous a combat had been waged. "Il y a bien du monde aujourd'hui à Versailles"—there are quite a lot of people here today. That was all that Marie Antoinette could bring herself to say, but in the then state of affairs at court as in Europe at large, it was of enormous importance, more momentous than the winning of a province, more exciting than would have been any of the much-needed reforms. At length, the Dauphiness had spoken to the King's favourite. Marie Antoinette had capitulated, and Madame Dubarry was victor on the field. General harmony had been restored, and fine weather followed the storm. The King received the Dauphiness with open arms, embracing her tenderly as if she were a long-lost child; Mercy thanked her in moving tones; the Dubarry strutted through the hall like a peacock; the aunts were more embittered than ever; the whole court was in a buzz from attics to cellars—and all because Marie Antoinette had said to Madame Dubarry: "Il y a bien du monde aujourd'hui à Versailles."

In truth it was a memorable utterance, for this commonplace remark was the seal of a great political crime, was the price paid for King Louis XV's tacit acceptance of the partition of Poland. The nine words expressed compliance with the will, not of Madame Dubarry alone, but also of Frederick of Prussia and Catherine of Russia. Not only was Marie Antoinette humbled, but a whole country had thereby been brought low.

Marie Antoinette's youthful pride had suffered defeat. For the first time she had bowed her neck, but she was not to do so again until it bowed beneath the guillotine. Her prolonged refractoriness had made it plain enough that this soft-hearted and frivolous creature, "la bonne et tendre Antoinette," had a tough spirit when she felt her honour at stake. She said acrimoniously to Mercy: "I have spoken to her once, but that is as far as I shall go. Never again shall the woman hear the sound of my voice." She made it plain to her mother, too, that, though she had given way this once, no further sacrifices were to be expected of her. "Of course I shall always be ready to forgo my prejudices and repugnances, provided that I am not asked to do anything ostentatious or which conflicts with my sense of honour." Her mother, outraged at this first sign of flat insubordination on the part of her chick, wrote a tart reply: "You have made me laugh by your notion that either I or my ambassador could ever advise you to do anything contrary to your sense of honour, or even anything in the least unbecoming. It really makes me anxious that you should show so much agitation about these few words; and when you declare that you will never speak to Madame Dubarry again, I tremble for you." Once more: "You must speak to her as to any other lady received at court. You owe it to the King and to myself." These admonitions were fruitless. Vainly did Mercy and others try to persuade her to adopt a friendly attitude towards Madame Dubarry, and thus make sure of being always in the King's good graces. Such adjurations were shattered against the Dauphiness's newly acquired self-confidence. In this matter she had made up her mind once for all, and neither threats nor cajoleries could induce her to open her lips to the Dubarry. She had spoken nine words to the King's favourite, and no power on earth would make her utter a tenth.

On New Year's Day 1772, Madame Dubarry triumphed over an archduchess of Austria, over the Dauphiness of France; and it might have been expected that the famous cocotte, now that she had such powerful allies as King Louis and Empress Maria Theresa, would continue her campaign against the future Queen. But there are battles after which the victor, recognizing the might of his adversary, becomes alarmed at his own success, and begins to wonder whether it will not be wiser for him to vacate the battlefield on his own initiative and offer terms of peace. Madame Dubarry was by no means easy in mind after her triumph. She had cherished no animosity against Marie Antoinette, and had merely demanded this trifling satisfaction as a salve to her wounded pride. Having got her own way, the good-natured woman actually felt ashamed of her public victory. Nay more, she was anxious; and shrewd enough to know that her power rested upon insecure foundations, upon the gouty legs of a man well up in years. Louis was already sixty-two. Any day an attack of apoplexy might lay him low, and next morning the "petite rousse" would be Queen of France. A "lettre de cachet," ordering imprisonment in the Bastille, was easily signed!

Turning these considerations over in her mind, Madame Dubarry hastened to make the sincerest efforts to conciliate Marie Antoinette. Again and again she appeared at the latter's evening parties, and although the hostess never deigned to notice her, she was careful to avoid any sign of pique. Again and again she sent messages to the Dauphiness declaring her heartfelt devotion. She tried to win Marie Antoinette's favour by speaking well of her to the King. Since these methods proved unavailing, she had recourse to a desperate measure. If her sometime adversary could not be won over by affectionate zeal, perhaps good will could be purchased. It was well known at court (the affair of the diamond necklace ten or twelve years later was but a crowning instance of a prevailing trend) that Marie Antoinette had a craze for costly trinkets. Following the train of thought which was subsequently to be followed by Cardinal de Rohan, Dubarry fancied that expensive gifts might prove a lure. A famous jeweller, the Boehmer who was subsequently concerned in the necklace affair, had a pair of diamond ear-rings whose value was estimated at seven hundred thousand livres. It seems likely that Marie Antoinette had expressed admiration, and that the Dubarry knew she had taken a fancy for them. However this may be, one day, through the instrumentality of a lady-in-waiting, Madame Dubarry let the Dauphiness know of her willingness to persuade Louis XV to make a present of the diamond ear-rings to his granddaughter-in-law. Marie Antoinette, however, did not vouchsafe a word in reply to the shameless proposal. The next time she encountered the King's favourite, it was once more to give her the cut direct. Not for all the crown jewels in the world should this Dubarry woman, who had once publicly humiliated her, hear another syllable from her lips. At seventeen she had acquired a new pride, a new self-assurance. Besides, what need had she of gems provided by others' favour? She knew that it could not be long before she would be wearing a queen's diadem.

CHAPTER V

Conquest of Paris

O N DARK evenings, from the little hills adjoining Versailles, one who looked eastward saw the skies glowing with the lights of Paris. So near was the capital that it could easily be reached on foot in less than four hours, while a carriage took only a third of the time. What could be more natural than that, on the second, third, or fourth day after the wedding, the Dauphiness should propose a visit to the metropolis of her future realm? But the essence, or rather the futility, of ceremonial resides in the determination to suppress or to caricature the natural in all its manifestations. As far as Marie Antoinette was concerned, there was an invisible barrier between Versailles and Paris —the barrier of etiquette. The heir to the throne of France, accompanied by his spouse, could not visit the capital until His Majesty's consent had been asked and accorded. Everything must be done in due form. But this "joyeuse entrée" of Marie Antoinette was a thing which her affectionate relatives wished to postpone as long as possible. No matter how deep the grudge the great ones at court might bear one another—the bigoted maiden aunts, Madame Dubarry, and the ambitious younger brothers the Counts of Provence and Artois, they all joined hands in blocking Marie Antoinette's road to Paris. They did their utmost to prevent her enjoying a triumph which would make too obvious her coming rank. Week after week, month after month, the camarilla discovered some new hindrance, found some new pretext, so that six months, a year, two years, three years passed, and still the Dauphiness was prisoned in the golden cage of Versailles. At length, in May 1773, Marie Antoinette lost patience, and took the offensive. Since the masters of the ceremonies continued to shake their powdered heads forbiddingly whenever she expressed her wish, she applied direct to Louis XV. To the old man the request seemed perfectly reasonable, and, being always disinclined to say no to a pretty woman, he acceded forthwith—much to the annoyance of the obstructionist clique. He told his grandson's charming wife that she could choose whatever day she best liked for the formal entry.

Marie Antoinette fixed upon the 8th of June. But now that the King had given her permission, the mischievous young woman thought it would be amusing—in secret—to make flinders of the detested palace rules and regulations which had so long kept her from visiting Paris. Just as many affianced lovers, knowing that stolen waters are sweet and that bread eaten in secret is pleasant, enjoy their first night of love without waiting for the priestly blessing and without taking the trouble to inform their parents and elders about the matter —so did Marie Antoinette persuade her husband and her brother-in-law to make a private visit anticipatory of the official appearance in Paris. A few weeks before the "joyeuse entrée" they had their horses put to late in the evening; then, masked and in fancy dress, they drove to the opera ball in the Mecca of their desires, in the forbidden city. Since, next morning, they all appeared punctually at early Mass, the escapade remained undiscovered. It brought no trouble upon the offenders, and nevertheless Marie Antoinette had for the first time revenged herself on the detested etiquette.

Since she had already tasted the paradisaical fruit of Paris, her public and formal entry into the city was all the more fascinating. The King of Heaven smiled on the occasion no less than did the King of France. This eighth of June was a brilliant and cloudless summer day, which had lured forth vast crowds as spectators. The progress from Versailles to Paris took place through double lines of onlookers, shouting acclamations and waving their hats frantically, while flags fluttered and garlands of flowers added colour to the scene. The Maréchal de Brissac, Governor of Paris, was waiting at the gates of the city, and respectfully handed these peaceful conquerors the keys of the fortress, lying on a silver platter. Within the fortifications, the women of the Great Market, clad in their best attire, were massed to welcome Marie Antoinette (how different a welcome from that of a later day!); and to offer her the fruits and flowers of the season. Salutes were fired from the Invalides, the Hôtel de Ville, and the Bastille. Slowly the State carriage wound its way across the city, along the Quai des Tuileries as far as Notre Dame. Everywhere, at the cathedral, at the monasteries, at the university, the couple were received with set speeches; they drove through triumphal arches built for the occasion; but their heartiest welcome came from the common people. By tens of thousands, by hundreds of thousands, the folk had gathered together from every street and alley of the huge town; and the sight of the Dauphiness, so unexpectedly charming, and herself charmed, aroused indescribable enthusiasm. When, at length, from the balcony of the Tuileries, Marie Antoinette looked forth over the vast assembly, she cried out, almost in alarm: "Mon Dieu, how many of them there are!" Maréchal de Brissac, who was standing beside her, instantly rose to the occasion. He bowed to her, and answered with typical French gallantry: "Madame, I hope His Highness the Dauphin will not take it amiss, but you have before you two hundred thousand persons who have all fallen in love with you."

Her first encounter with the French people made a profound impression upon Marie Antoinette. Though but little inclined to reflection, she was quick of perception, her tendency being to judge all that happened in accordance with her immediate personal impressions—for she saw only the surface of things. Today, when for the first time in her life she had seen so huge an assembly of the nameless masses (a hot tide of affectionate frenzy sending its waves in a swelling flood to her very feet), she became enabled to grasp the formidable splendour of the position to which destiny had uplifted her. Hitherto at Versailles she had merely been addressed as "Madame la Dauphine," one title among a thousand others, the topmost rung no doubt of the long ladder of nobility, but an empty term, a chill concept. At length there had become plain to her, here in Paris, the ardent promises conveyed by the phrase "heiress to the throne of France." Awestruck by the experience, she wrote to her mother:

"Last Tuesday there was a festival which I shall never forget. We made our entry into Paris. We were received with all imaginable honour. Though this was pleasant enough, what touched me much more was the affection and the zeal of the poor people, which, though crushed by taxation, was overflowing with joy at the sight of us. When we were driving to the Tuileries, the press was so great that we were blocked for three quarters of an hour without being able to move forward or backward. . . . On our way home from the palace, we waited for half an hour upon an open terrace. Darling Mother, I do not know how to describe to you the transports of delight and affection which were then manifested to us. Before we finally drove away, we kissed our hands to the people, at which they were greatly pleased. How fortunate to be in a position in which one can gain widespread affection at so little cost. Though the cost be small, such love is infinitely precious. The fact was borne home to me, and I shall never forget it."

These are the first genuinely individual words to be found in Marie Antoinette's letters to her mother. Her mobile nature was easily impressed, and it was natural that she should be greatly moved and gratified by the unearned and passionate manifestation of love. But impressions quickly made can also be quickly effaced, and she who would "never forget" was in truth forgetful. After two or three further visits to the capital, she took such acclamations as a matter of course, obviously due to her rank and station, accepting them gladly enough, but with the childlike heedlessness wherewith she accepted all the gifts of life. Though it had seemed so wonderful to her that she should rouse the warm enthusiasm of the crowd, so wonderful that she should be loved by this unknown people, henceforward she regarded it as her unchallengeable right to be adored by twenty millions, and had not the glimmer of a notion that rights imply duties, or that even the most devoted love will languish when nothing is done to requite it.

At her first official journey, Marie Antoinette had effected the conquest of Paris, but simultaneously Paris had conquered Marie Antoinette. From this day on, she had a passion for the great city. Often, too often, did she drive to this alluring metropolis, so bountiful in its offers of pleasure. Sometimes she went in state, by day, and attended by the court ladies; sometimes after nightfall, accompanied only by a few intimates, to visit a theatre or a ballroom and to amuse herself to the top of her bent, "incognito," and in ways that were not always unexceptionable. Now that she had broken loose from the monotony of daily life at Versailles as prescribed by the court calendar, this half-child, this wild girl, had come to realize how infinitely boring was the thousand-windowed marble-and-stone box where she had been immured, the court with its bows and curtsies and cabals, with its full-dress parades. She knew now how insufferably tedious had been her aunts, spiteful and sour old maids, with whom she had had to go to Mass in the mornings and to sit knitting through the long evening hours. Ridiculously, spectrally artificial seemed to her the cheerless and constrained life of the court, with its rigidly prescribed attitudes. She had sickened of the eternal minuet, of its endless repetitions of the same figures, the same circling movements, and of the horror that ensued when the most trifling false step was made. How delightful, in comparison, was the unrestraint of Paris with its vigorous current of life. She felt, there, like one who emerges from a hothouse into the fresh air. In the gigantic metropolis, in its tumultuous confusion, one could lose oneself, one could dive into deep waters, one could escape from the inexorable daily curriculum and play with happy chance. One could be oneself, one could enjoy oneself, instead of posturing without cessation before a mirror. The natural upshot was that twice or thrice a week a chariot filled with gaily clad ladies drove from Versailles to Paris, to return only in the grey of morning.

What did Marie Antoinette see of Paris? During her early visits, curiosity led her to seek out whatever was worth seeing—the museums, great houses of business and manufacture, a popular festival or two, and once even an exhibition of pictures. Therewith, however, as far as Paris was concerned, her cultural needs were satisfied for the next twenty years. Henceforward she devoted herself indefatigably to amusements, going regularly to the Opera, the Comédie Française, the Italian Theatre, to routs, masked balls, and gaming-houses—in a word, enjoying "the night side of Paris," the "pleasure-city" beloved of rich American women today. Especially was she fascinated by masked balls at the Opera House, for, a prisoner of her position, nothing but a mask could set her free. A masked lady can allow herself to jest and romp in a way which would be unpermissible to Madame la Dauphine. Under such conditions Marie Antoinette, while her tiresome and incompetent husband was snoring in bed at home, could exchange lively sallies with unknown gentlemen; she could chatter as frankly as she pleased with a charming young man named Fersen, a Swedish count. She could dance until her lithe body was healthily tired; she could laugh to her heart's content. How gloriously could she live her own life in Paris!

But not once during these years did she enter a middle-class domicile; not once did she attend a sitting of the Parliament of Paris or of the Academy; not once did she visit a hospital or a market; not once did she try to learn something of the daily life of the French people. Always, on these Parisian escapades, Marie Antoinette kept within the narrow but glittering circle of upper-class pleasures, thinking she had done enough for the "bon peuple" by responding with an indifferent smile to its enthusiastic greetings—though again and again the populace was ranged in double lines to acclaim her, and again and again the nobles and the well-to-do bourgeois jubilated when, in the theatre, she made her appearance in the royal box. Her joyful leisure, her unceasing round of amusements, her noisy pleasure-parties, seemed to her sanctioned by popular approval when, as she drove into Paris she saw the "people" flocking homeward weary after the day's work, and when she saw them once again returning to toil at six in the morning, as she drove home to bed. What reason had she to suppose that there was anything wrong with her policy of live and let live? With the foolish impetuosity of youth, Marie Antoinette fancied that the whole world was pleasure-full and carefree because she herself was heedless and happy. But, while thus renouncing the formalities of court life and enjoying herself to her heart's content in Paris, she imagined she was maintaining her popularity. In actual fact, secluded for nearly two decades on these drives to and fro in her luxurious chariot, she caught never a glimpse of the real people and the real Paris.

The powerful impression of her first official reception by Paris had worked a transformation in Marie Antoinette. Self-confidence is always promoted by others' admiration. A young woman whom thousands have assured she is beautiful, is made more beautiful by her knowledge of her beauty. At Versailles the Dauphiness had been no more than a shy girl, who felt herself alien and superfluous in unfamiliar surroundings. Now an uprush of pride which was not wholly free from surprise at its own existence swept away uncertainty and timidity. Vanished was the fifteen-year-old girl who, under tutelage of ambassador and confessor, of aunts and other relatives, had glided through the halls of Versailles curtsying to every court lady. Of a sudden Marie Antoinette acquired the "dignity proper to an exalted station." Bracing herself from within, winged by the presence of admiring inferiors, she sailed past them almost as if they had ceased to exist. Everything in her had undergone a change. The woman, the individuality, began to break through. Even her writing underwent a remarkable modification. Hitherto it had been a clumsy, childish hand; the letters were large and round. Now it became the strong and elegant penmanship of a grown woman. To the end of her days, indeed, her script betrayed the impatience and the heedlessness of her character; but henceforward it was that of an independent personality.

The girl, pulsing with the ardency of youth, was ripening to live the life of a woman, was becoming ready to love. Political considerations, however, had fettered her to a dullard, who was not yet fully a man; and since Marie Antoinette, her heart still untouched, knew no other man than Louis to love, at eighteen she fell in love with herself. The sweet poison of flattery was circulating in her veins. The more she was admired, the more did she crave for admiration; and before she could legally flaunt it as queen, she wanted to rule the court, the capital, the whole realm, thanks to her womanly charms. Directly she became aware of the wakening of any power, she was eager to exert it.

As luck decreed (and such luck is rare) the young woman had a fine opportunity of making a first test whether she could impose her will upon the court and the town of Paris. Gluck had finished his *Iphigénie*, and wanted to have it produced in the French capital. Success in this matter was regarded as of the utmost importance by the court of Vienna, which was musically inclined, so Maria Theresa, Kaunitz, and Joseph II expected the Dauphiness to smooth the composer's path. Now, in artistic matters, Marie Antoinette's aptitudes were mediocre; she had little knowledge of music, painting, or literature. Perhaps she had a certain amount of natural taste; but she was devoid of independent preferences, being inclined merely to accept the prevailing fashion in such matters, and showing a transient interest in anyone who had already secured recognition. Devoid of insight, she never read a book to the end; invariably sought to avoid serious conversation; lacked the earnestness, veneration, diligence, and reflectiveness that are indispensable preliminaries to any decision worthy of the name. For her, art was never anything more than one of the ornaments of life, one pleasure as an interlude among others more delightful; she could only enjoy art that did not fatigue—and she therefore never enjoyed true art. She had trifled with music, as with all else. The lessons Gluck had given her in Vienna had taught her very little; at the clavecin she was a dilettante, just as she was when she thought fit to take part in amateur theatricals or to sing to an intimate circle. It need hardly be said that she, who never even noticed the presence of her fellow-countryman Mozart in Paris, was utterly incapable of understanding what was new and splendid in *Iphigénie*. But Maria Theresa had warmly commended her to do her best for Gluck; and, in an amused way, Marie Antoinette had a liking for this seemingly fierce man, broad in the beam and jovial.

What, more than all, enlisted her in his service was that she wished to try her strength in Paris against those who were supporting Italian and French opera against what they termed "the barbarian invasion." She insisted, therefore, that Gluck's new opera, which the court musicians had declared "unpresentable," should at once be given a fair trial. The unruly and choleric Bavarian, animated with the characteristic obstinacy of the great artist, did not make it easy for her to advance his cause. At the rehearsals, he berated the ladies of the cast so savagely that these spoiled darlings complained bitterly to their titled lovers. He dragooned the instrumentalists, who were not used to the demand for such exactitude; and, in general, played the tyrant in the opera-house. His mighty voice could be heard resounding from behind the closed doors as, time after time, he threatened to make an end of the whole business and return to Vienna. Nothing, in fact, but dread of the Dauphiness prevented an open scandal.

April 13, 1774, was fixed for the first night; the members of the court had reserved their seats and ordered their carriages. Then one of the singers fell ill, and the understudy was called upon to take his place. "No," said Gluck commandingly, "the opening performance must be postponed." The management was in despair, and asked him what he could be thinking of. The court had already made its arrangements. Surely a composer—and one who was only a bourgeois and a foreigner—would not dare, because he thought one tenor might not be as good as another, to interfere with the plans of serene highnesses? "I don't care what you say," shouted the stubborn musician, in a fine rage. "Rather than give way, rather than have my opera unsatisfactorily produced, I would throw my score into the fire!" He rushed off to his patroness Marie Antoinette, who was diverted by the wild man's antics. Unhesitatingly she espoused the cause of her "bon Gluck." The court chariots were counter-ordered, and, greatly to the annoyance of the princes, the first night was postponed until the nineteenth. Sending for the lieutenant of police, the Dauphiness took measures to ensure that Their Highnesses should not vent their anger upon the uncourtly musician by hissing him. With all possible emphasis and publicity, she made her fellow-countryman's cause her own.

In actual fact the first night of *Iphigénie* was a triumph, but rather for Marie Antoinette than for Gluck. The newspapers and the public were cold. They declared: "While it must be agreed that there are fine and even sublime passages here and there in *Iphigénie*, they are inter- spersed among many that are commonplace, and among others which are extremely dull." As always in artistic matters, a bold innovator has to make his own audience, and rarely succeeds with uninstructed readers, spectators, or auditors. Still, Marie Antoinette had brought the whole court to the opening performance. Even her husband, who in general would have been unwilling to sacrifice his chances of bringing down a stag for the sake of the music of the spheres, and to whom the chase was more important than all the arts put together, had been forced to put in an appearance. Since the mood of the house was un- satisfactory, Marie Antoinette loudly applauded every aria. From polite- ness her brothers-in-law, her sisters-in-law, and the courtiers and court ladies generally, had to chime in—with the result that, despite currents of adverse feeling, the production of *Iphigénie* was a famous event in the history of music. Gluck had conquered Paris. Marie Antoinette, too, had publicly imposed her will upon the capital and upon the court. This was the first victory of her personality, the first great demonstration made by the young wife in the face of all France. Only a few weeks were to elapse before the title of queen was to confirm her in a position of power which she had already autocratically won for herself by her own unaided energy.

CHAPTER VI

The King Is Dead, Long Live the King!

O
N April 27, 1774, King Louis XV, when out hunting, suddenly declared himself extremely tired, and, suffering from severe headache, he returned to his favourite palace of the Trianon. During the night his doctors found that he had fever, and they summoned Madame Dubarry to his bedside. Next morning, seriously alarmed about his condition, they ordered his removal to the adjoining great palace of Versailles. Inexorable death itself must comply with the still more inexorable laws of etiquette; a king of France could not be allowed to be seriously ill or to die elsewhere than in the royal bed of state. "C'est à Versailles, Sire, qu'il faut être malade."

There were promptly assembled six physicians, five surgeons, three apothecaries, fourteen skilled attendants in all. Each of them felt the royal pulse every ten minutes. But, after all, the diagnosis was only made by chance. In the evening, when one of the servants was holding a candle near the King's bed, a bystander noticed the well-known and ominous red spots on the face, and news ran like wildfire through the building that His Majesty had smallpox. A gust of terror traversed the huge palace; dread of infection (there actually were some more cases a few days later); and, above all, anxiety on the part of the courtiers as to what their position would be if King Louis died.

His daughters showed the courage of true piety, keeping watch over the sick man throughout the day, while at night-time Madame Dubarry sat by his bedside. The heirs to the throne, on the other hand, the Dauphin and the Dauphiness, were forbidden by court regulations to visit the sick man. They must not run any risk of infection, for during the last three days their lives had become much more valuable. Meanwhile there was a singular cleavage among the frequenters of the court. Those of the older generation, the powers of yesterday, the aunts and the Dubarry, trembled as they watched the dying man, knowing full well that their sun would set when he drew his last breath. In the other rooms were assembled the coming generation, the future King Louis XVI, the future Queen Marie Antoinette, and the Count of Provence who, so long as his elder brother remained childless, naturally looked upon himself as heir to the throne. In the Œil de Bœuf, the great anteroom which separated the sick-chamber from the hall where the rising generation sat, waited the mass of the courtiers, vacillating, uneasy, not knowing whether to turn their faces towards the sunset or the sunrise.

The King had never a chance, for his exhausted body was in no condition to make headway against so serious an illness. Bloated, covered with pocks, it seemed decomposing while he yet lived, although his consciousness was fully maintained. His daughters and Madame Dubarry displayed great hardihood in keeping their stations, for, though the windows were wide open, the stench in the room was almost intolerable. The doctors speedily recognized that the case was hopeless; so now began another struggle, that for the dying man's sinful soul. To begin with, however, the priests refused to draw near the sick-bed, to hear Louis's confession, or to administer Holy Communion. Before they would consent to do this, the King, who had been a slave to his lusts, must give plain signs of repentance. First of all the main cause of offence must be swept away, the harlot still watching beside her paramour. It was cruel for King Louis, in this dread hour, to be coerced into dismissing the one human being he was really fond of. Yet he had no choice, being now obsessed by the spectre of hell fire. In stifled tones, he bade farewell to Madame Dubarry, who drove forthwith to the neighbouring château of Rueil to wait there in the faint hope that, after all, her protector might recover.

Now, at length, confession and communion were possible. His Majesty's confessor, the man who for eight-and-thirty years had held a sinecure at the royal court, entered the sick-room. The door was closed behind him, for the courtiers in the anteroom were not, of course, privileged to hear the King's confession. What a pity! The register of his doings in the Parc aux Cerfs would have been so interesting! Watch in hand, they ticked off the minutes, that they might at least know how long it took a Louis XV to recount all his sins and excesses. To their surprise, the confessor reappeared after sixteen minutes, and soon it was disclosed that Louis could not yet be granted absolution; that the Church demanded from a monarch who had not opened his heart to it for nigh on forty years, and who had lived in open sin before the very eyes of his children, a deeper humiliation than that of auricular confession. For the very reason that he had occupied so outstanding a position, for the very reason that he had fancied himself lifted above the need of complying with the spiritual law, the ecclesiastics insisted that he must abase himself more profoundly than any other before the Almighty. The transgressor who had been a king must make public avowal of his faults. Then only would he be readmitted to the rites of the Church.

There was a wonderful spectacle next morning, when the mightiest autocrat of Christendom had to do penance before his assembled subjects. Troops were ranged on the steps of the palace, and the Swiss Guards formed a double line from the chapel to the sick-room. The drums were sounded while the high dignitaries of the Church marched in solemn procession, and the Host was borne along beneath a canopy. The Dauphin and his two brothers, with their wives, each holding a lighted candle, followed the archbishop and his train as far as the bedroom door. At the threshold, they halted and knelt down. Only the King's daughters and those princes who were not in the line of succession were allowed to enter the room with the clergy.

In the breathless silence, the auditors could hear the cardinal carrying on a low-toned conversation with the King, and through the open doors he could be seen administering Holy Communion. Then, turning to the doorway and uplifting his voice, he spoke to the assembled court, as follows: "Gentlemen, the King instructs me to tell you that he asks God's pardon for his offences and for the scandalous example he has set his people; that if God vouchsafes the restoration of his health, he will devote himself to repentance, to the support of religion, and to relieving the lot of his people." Thereupon a murmur came from the dying man. Only those close beside him could hear the words: "I wish I had been strong enough to say that myself."

What ensued is a tale of horror. It was not so much that a man was dying as that a swollen and blackened corpse was falling to pieces. None the less, as if the energy of all his Bourbon ancestors had been concentrated in his carcass, Louis XV continued to wrestle for many days against impending annihilation. They were terrible days for everyone concerned. The servants almost fainted from the abominable stink; the three daughters were exhausted by their prolonged watching; the physicians knew that death was inevitable; more and more impatiently did the court await the fall of the curtain. In the stables the horses stood harnessed, for, to minimize the risk of infection, the new Louis with all his followers was to remove to Choisy the instant the old King had drawn his last breath. The outriders would leap into their saddles, the trunks were already packed, everyone was waiting for the sign. At one of the bedroom windows a candle was burning, and its extinction was to show that the monarch's vital spark had expired. At length, on Tuesday, May 10, 1774, the struggle was over, and the prearranged signal was given. The murmur of the onlookers rose, and swelled; shouts passed from room to room: "The King is dead, long live the King!"

Marie Antoinette was sitting apart with her husband in a small room. Suddenly they heard a strange clamour, growing ever louder, drawing ever nearer, though the words were unintelligible. Then the door burst open. As if blown by a storm, Madame de Noailles entered, knelt, and was the first to kiss the new Queen's hand. Behind her came the others, more and more and more, the whole court, for everyone was eager to pay homage, to show zeal by being among the first to offer congratulations. There was a rattle of drums, the officers drew their swords, and from hundreds of lips again came the cry: "The King is dead, long live the King!"

Marie Antoinette went forth as Queen from the room she had entered as Dauphiness. With a sigh of relief, those who remained to perform the last rites lifted the black and unrecognizable corpse of Louis XV swiftly into the coffin which had long since been held in readiness, having instructions to bury it with scant ceremony. Meanwhile, the royal chariot bore a new king and a new queen through the gilded park-gates of Versailles. The people in the streets shouted joyously as they drove by, inspired with the old delusive hope that with the passing of the late king their miseries would come to an end, and that a new world would begin under the new ruler.

Madame Campan, the elderly collector of gossip, relates in her memoirs (which are on one page mellifluous, and on the next bedewed with tears) that, when the news of Louis XV's death was brought to Louis XVI and Marie Antoinette, they fell upon their knees, and sobbed a prayer: "Lord God, guide us and protect us, for we are too young to rule." A touching anecdote doubtless, and one that would be appropriate in a fairy-tale; but unfortunately, like so many of the anecdotes about Marie Antoinette, it has the trifling drawback of being a clumsy invention. It obviously fails to square with what we know of the psychology of the couple. Louis XVI was cold-blooded as a fish, and the last thing likely is that he could have been profoundly affected by an occurrence which, in common with the whole court, he had been expecting for a week or more. Still less is the tale suited to the character of Marie Antoinette, who with untroubled spirit accepted this gift of the moment like all others which fortune threw into her lap.

Not that she had shown herself eager for the succession, impatient to grasp the reins! She never dreamed of playing such a part as her mother played, of becoming a second Elizabeth of England, a second Catherine of Russia. She lacked energy for so lofty a role, was too slothful, too narrow of outlook. As always in the case of mediocrities, her wishes were wellnigh exclusively personal. She had no political ideas that she would have liked to stamp upon the world; no inclination to subjugate or to humiliate others. From earliest youth, her main characteristic had been a longing for independence. She did not want to dominate; but, on the other hand, she would not allow herself to be dominated or even influenced by others. To be queen meant for her nothing more than increased scope for personal freedom. After more than three years' tutelage and supervision, for the first time she felt herself able to throw off restraint, now that no one was there who could call her to order—for her mother dwelt across the frontier, hundreds upon hundreds of miles away; and her husband was submissive to her stronger will, so that she could laugh contemptuously at his timid protests when he ventured to make any. Raised at length from the position of Dauphiness to that of Queen, the only rule to which she was subject was that of her own caprices. She need pay no further heed to the nagging of her aunts, need no longer ask the King's permission before going to an opera ball. Over and done with were the pretensions of her detested adversary the Dubarry, who on the morrow would be hounded into retirement at Luciennes. Never again would the diamonds of the sometime favourite sparkle at court suppers; no longer would princes and kings throng her boudoir to kiss her hand.

Proudly, and taking no shame in her pride, Marie Antoinette assumed the crown. Her true mentality is shown, not in Madame Campan's fable, but in the words she wrote to her mother on the occasion: "Although God decreed that I should be born in the rank I now occupy, I cannot but marvel at the dispensation of Providence thanks to which I, the youngest of your children, have been chosen to be queen over the finest realm in Europe." One who fails to hear in these words the overtone of delight has a deaf ear. Precisely because she was aware only of the greatness of her position and failed to realize the responsibilities it would entail, was Marie Antoinette so cheerful and carefree on ascending the throne.

She mounted it amid shouts of acclamation. Neither she nor Louis had done anything or promised anything, and yet both the young rulers were greeted with enthusiasm. "Surely a new Golden Age will begin," thought the credulous people, "now that the courtesan who was so spendthrift has fallen from power, now that the old epicurean and voluptuary Louis XV has been safely entombed; now that we have a king who is simple in his tastes, thrifty, modest, and pious; now that we have a queen who is so charming, so young, and so kindly." Portraits of the pair were displayed in every shop-window; all they did was heartily approved of; and even the court, weary of the old regime, began to take heart. "Now," thought the courtiers and court ladies, "we shall have a round of dances and parades, cheerfulness and joy of life, the rule of youth and freedom." It was a relief to everyone that Louis XV was dead and done with, and the very tolling of the bells in the church towers of France seemed to convey a joyful message, as if summoning the populace to a festival.

Only one person in Europe was deeply moved, and even seriously alarmed, at the death of Louis XV. Empress Maria Theresa was filled with gloomy forebodings. Thirty laborious years had taught her how burdensome is a crown, while during the same period as a mother she had learned the weaknesses and defects of her daughters. As regards the youngest of these, she would have been glad if the ascent to the throne could have been postponed until the frivolous and unruly creature had ripened a little, and had learned to guard against the temptations of unthriftiness. Writing to Mercy on receipt of the tidings that Louis XV had breathed his last, she said: "I am greatly distressed by your news, and am still more concerned with thoughts of my daughter's fate, which cannot fail to be either wholly splendid or extremely unfortunate. There is nothing to calm my apprehensions in the situation of the King, the ministers, or the State. She herself is so young, has never had any power of application, nor ever will have—unless with great difficulty."

To her daughter's proud letter announcing the promotion, Maria Theresa replied in a melancholy strain: "I do not compliment you on your new dignity, which is dearly bought, but which will become even more costly unless you can go on leading the quiet and innocent life you have led during these three years thanks to the kindness and complaisance of one who has been as a father to you, and a life which has secured for you the approbation and the love of your people. This is all the better for your present position, but you must know how to preserve it and to use it for the good of the King and of the State. You are both of you still extremely young; the burden is a heavy one; I am distressed, much distressed about it. . . . All that I can say, all that I can wish for, is that neither of you should be in a hurry. Look at things for yourselves; change nothing; let matters go on as they are. Otherwise chaos and intrigue will become insurmountable, and, my dear children, you will find yourselves in such a tangle that you will be unable to extricate yourselves."

From afar, from the altitude of decades of experience, the experienced ruler sees the posture of affairs in France much better than those who are actually living in the country, and is fully aware of the general instability. She urgently implores the new King and Queen to keep on the friendliest terms with Austria and thus to safeguard the peace of the world. "Our two monarchies only need repose so that we can set our affairs in order. If we work with closely joined hands, no one will interfere with us, and Europe will enjoy the happiness of tranquillity. Then all the other nations will be happy as well as our own."

Most urgently does the mother warn the daughter about the risks of frivolousness, about the dangers that wait upon one who thinks of nothing but pleasure. "That is what I am most afraid of in your case. You must learn to interest yourself in serious matters, for this may be most useful if the King should ask your counsel. . . . Be careful to avoid misleading him into any great or unusual expenditure. . . . Everything depends upon being able to continue in the line of this happy beginning, which has been fortunate beyond expectation, and which will make you both happy by making your people happy."

Marie Antoinette, much moved by her mother's earnestness and anxiety, made promise after promise. She acknowledged that she had a weakness as far as serious undertakings were concerned, and vowed amendment. But the mother's prophetic sense was too strong for this to bring appeasement. She could no longer believe that good fortune awaited the French realm, or her daughter who was its queen. Consequently, at the very time when the whole world was making much of Marie Antoinette and envying her good luck, Maria Theresa wrote to Mercy with a sigh: "I fancy her good days are past."

CHAPTER VII

Portrait of a Royal Couple

A LWAYS and everywhere during the first weeks of a new reign, engravers, painters, sculptors, and medal-makers have their hands full of work. In France, likewise, on this occasion, people hastened to put away pictures and busts of Louis XV—no longer "Louis le Bien-Aimé"—and to replace them by garlanded images of the new pair of rulers. "Le Roi est mort, vive le Roi."

The medallion designers did not need much flattery in order to produce a somewhat Cæsarean impression by their reproductions of the worthy countenance of Louis XVI. Were it not that his neck was rather short and thick, the new King's face was not devoid of a certain nobility. He had a smooth and somewhat receding forehead; a vigorous-looking nose; full and rather sensual lips; a fleshy but well modelled chin of a rounded shape; in fine, unquestionably a congenial profile. Where touching-up was most needed was in respect of his eyes and the way he used them, for he was so short-sighted that without a lorgnette the man failed to recognize even his closest acquaintance three paces away. It was not easy, without departing from the original, for the engraver to give his heavy-lidded, pallid, and watery eyes some semblance of authority. Being of cumbrous build, he held himself badly, and it was therefore difficult for the court painters to make him look imposing in full royal rig. Grown prematurely obese, awkward in his movements, with an awkwardness that was intensified to the pitch of ludicrousness by his bad sight, Louis XVI, though he was nearly six feet high and had no stoop, made a poor showing on official occasions (la plus mauvaise tournure qu'on pût voir). He tramped across the shining parquet floors of Versailles heavily and with swinging shoulders "like a peasant at the plough-tail"; he could neither dance nor play tennis; if he tried to walk fast he was apt to stumble over his sword. Well aware of his bodily maladroitness, the poor fellow was embarrassed by the knowledge, and his embarrassment served only to make matters worse; with the result

76

that the first impression produced upon anyone who set eyes on the King of France was that he was looking at a country bumpkin.

Yet Louis XVI was neither stupid nor narrow-minded. The trouble was that, just as his short sight made him gawky in his movements, so did his timidity or shyness (in the last analysis probably due to his lack of sexual virility during the early years of his marriage) gravely hinder him in the manifestation of his intelligence. It was a serious effort for him to carry on a conversation, knowing as he did that his thought-processes were slow and lumbering. The King, therefore, was consumed with anxiety when faced by shrewd, witty, and clever persons, whose thoughts were lively and whose words flowed from their lips quickly and easily. In such circumstances, his doltishness made him ashamed. Grant him time to arrange his ideas, however, avoid hurrying him to a decision or an answer, and he could do well enough; could surprise even such a sceptic as Joseph II or Pétion by his excellent commonsense. Though never brilliant, he had a sound intelligence which worked satisfactorily as soon as he could overcome his shyness. In general, however, he preferred writing down his thoughts instead of uttering them by word of mouth; and he was fond of reading, for books are quiet and unobtrusive, and do not try to hustle the reader. Having read widely, he was well informed upon historical and biographical matters; and he was continually working to improve his English and his Latin, being helped in this endeavour by a remarkably good memory. His documents and his housekeeping books were in perfect order. Evening after evening, in a clear round hand which was almost copperplate in its perfection, he recorded the trifling incidents of his life ("Stag-hunting . . . got one. . . . Have had a fit of indigestion") in a diary which fills us with amazement because it utterly ignores matters of historical importance. This journal presents us with the image of a man of mediocre intelligence, with no power of independent thought, designed by nature to become a trustworthy collector of taxes or other civil servant of lower grade; fitted for any sort of mechanical and subaltern activity carried on out of the limelight; anything, anything in the world, except the position of a monarch.

What was really amiss in Louis XVI's make-up was that he had lead in his veins. Nothing came easily to him. Well intentioned though he was, he had continually to overcome a constitutional inertia, a sort of

perpetual sleepiness, before he could do anything, before he could
think or even feel. His nerves were like rubber bands that have lost
their elasticity. He lacked tension. This inborn obtuseness of sensibility
rendered him inapt for notable achievement in the effective realm.
Love (whether in the mental or in the physiological sense), pleasure,
desire, anxiety, pain, fear—none of these passions could pierce his
tough hide; and even immediate peril to his life could not stir him
out of his lethargy. When the revolutionists were storming the Tuileries, his pulse was not quickened by a single beat per minute; and
during the night before he was guillotined the two pillars of his
wellbeing, sleep and appetite, remained unperturbed. He never grew
pale, though a pistol were held to his breast; anger never flashed from
his myopic eyes; nothing could alarm him—and nothing could arouse
his enthusiasm. He did not care to use his body except in hard physical
exercise, such as his locksmith's work or the chase. What required
delicate movements for its attainment (in himself or others)—art,
music, the dance—made not the slightest appeal to his emotions. No
muse and no god could make his torpid senses vibrate; not even Eros.
Never during the twenty years and more of his married life did Louis
XVI covet any other woman than the one his grandfather had chosen
for him as wife. He was content with her, happy after his fashion, just
as he was always well content because he made so few demands.
It was a sorry trick that fate played on him to demand from
one of so inert and slothfully animal a nature the most important
decisions known to the history of the eighteenth century; it was unfair
to expect a man who was only interested in the surface of things to
play a leading part in face of a political catastrophe of worldwide
importance. He was a man of contemplation, not a man of action.
Physically robust though he was—at the point where action begins,
where the muscles should tense themselves voluntarily for attack or
for defence, he became pitifully weak. Every demand for prompt and
effective resolution threw Louis XVI into the most terrible perplexity.
He could only give way, could only do what others wanted, for all he
himself wanted was repose, repose, repose. To anyone who was urgent,
to anyone who took him by surprise, he would promise whatever was
asked; and with the same slack readiness would promise the opposite
to the next comer. Merely to approach him, merely to address him, was

to take him by storm. Owing to this incredible weakness, Louis XVI was again and again guiltlessly guilty, dishonourable while his intentions were honourable, the tool of his wife and of his ministers of State, a King's figure in a puppet-show, happy enough when people left him to his own devices, but despairing and a man to drive others to despair when called upon to rule. If the revolutionists, when they wanted to rid themselves of this simple fellow, had, instead of slicing through his thick neck with the "national razor," found for him some hut in the countryside with an acre of garden attached and a post where he had some insignificant duties to perform, they would have made him far happier than did the Archbishop of Rheims with the crown of France, which for twenty years he wore without pride, without pleasure, and without dignity.

Not even the most courtly of court bards ever ventured to extol this good-natured but ungainly man as a great imperator. On the other hand, the leading artists of France vied with one another to glorify the Queen in every possible way and in all types of phraseology; in marble, terra-cotta, unglazed porcelain, pastel, ivory miniatures, and eloquent verses—for her countenance, her whole demeanour, were in perfect conformity with the late-eighteenth-century ideal. Delicately built, slender, elegant, graceful, playful, and coquettish, from the first hour when, at the age of nineteen, she ascended the throne, she became the goddess of the Rococo, the type of fashion, and a model for all persons of taste. If a woman wished to be regarded as beautiful and attractive, she tried to resemble the Queen.

Yet Marie Antoinette cannot be said to have had either a remarkable or a peculiarly impressive face. Of a sharply cut oval form, with small and piquant irregularities such as the thick lip characteristic of the Habsburgs and a forehead that was rather too flat, it did not charm either by the promise of much intelligence or by any physiognomical trait. Something chilly and vacant seemed to emanate from this immature face, which not until the later years of her womanhood was to lose its inexpressiveness as of polished enamel and to acquire a certain measure of majestic force and resoluteness. The only features that seemed to indicate a liveliness of feeling were the soft and extremely beautiful eyes, which at one moment would be brimming with tears and the next sparkling with amusement. They were of a half-tone blue, and short-sighted like her husband's, though in her case short sight seemed to give them a touching expression. But there was nothing to indicate firmness of will or strength of character in this pale oval. All that the acute observer could trace was evidence of a soft and yielding disposition, that of a woman who would be guided by her moods, and, feminine through and through, would swim always with the stream of sensibility. It was this delicate charm which everyone admired in Marie Antoinette. The only real beauties she possessed were her luxuriant hair, shading from pale blond into pale red; the purity of her complexion, which was as delicate as alabaster; her full-bosomed figure; the perfect line of her ivory-smooth and delightfully rounded arms; the carefully manicured hands—all the bloom and the aroma of developing maidenhood—but too fleeting and too sublimated a charm to be conveyed by any of her portraits.

Even the most skilful of these portraits withholds from us the essential elements of her nature, the explanation of the personal influence she wielded. What can a portrait do but fix for after generations some rigid posture of the original, and (as all agree) the real witchery of Marie Antoinette was to be found in the inimitable grace of her movements. Not until she became vivacious, did she disclose the native harmony of her body. When she was walking through the lines of courtiers in the Gallery of Mirrors at Versailles; when, with coquettish relaxation, she leaned back on a sofa to converse; when she impetuously ran as if on wings up the stairs; when, with a natural grace, she stretched forward her dazzlingly white hand to be kissed, or affectionately threw her arms around the waist of one of her friends—every movement seemed the spontaneous result of feminine bodily intuition. Horace Walpole, a man who was not easily carried off his feet by admiration, said that when she was standing still she was the statue of beauty, and when she was in motion she was grace personified. In very truth she rode like an amazon. Whenever her lithe and shapely body came into play, she excelled the loveliest women of her court, not only in adroitness, but also in physical attractiveness. Walpole, who was so delighted with her, strenuously denied the contention that she sometimes danced out of time, saying, in courtly fashion, that if there were any disharmony, then the music must have been wrong. Her own instinct, her own conscious or half-conscious knowledge of how she looked best, made Marie Antoinette love to display herself in movement. That was her true element. Sitting still, on the other hand, listening, reading, reposeful thinking, and even (in some measure) sleep, were an intolerable tax upon her patience. She liked to buzz hither and thither, to be always beginning some new task which she would never finish, to be continually occupied without any serious exertion; she loved to feel that time was not standing still with her, or that she was out-running time. To be quick at her meals, content perhaps with eating a sweetmeat or two; to sleep only for a short time, never to think long, to be perpetually on the go, frittering away her days—such were her desires. The twenty years, or rather less, during which Marie Antoinette was Queen were characterized by an unceasing movement in an orbit around her own ego. Since, outside this orbit, she had no goal, nor any inward conviction of an aim, from the human and political standpoint she was circling in the void.

It was her instability, her lack of firm anchorage, her squandering of energies that were great but incessantly misapplied, which her mother took so much amiss in Marie Antoinette. Maria Theresa, equipped with a profound knowledge of human nature, knew that the gifted and inspired girl might have made a hundredfold better use of her powers than she did. Marie Antoinette merely needed to exert her will in order to be what she was fundamentally, and she had royal powers; but it was her doom that an irresistible desire to have an easy and comfortable time led her perpetually to live below her proper spiritual level. Typically an Austrian woman in this respect that, though unquestionably talented even to excess, she was utterly lacking in such resolution as might have made her turn her gifts to good account—she heedlessly scattered her talents while gadding in search of amusements. "Her first movement," wrote her brother Joseph II, "is invariably a right one; and if she would only persist in it, if she would only reflect a little more, would only disregard cross-currents, she would get on splendidly." But this "little more reflection" was irksome to her impetuous temperament. Any other thought than was extemporized was a labour, and intellectual labour was repugnant to her capricious and nonchalant disposition. She wanted always and everywhere to be at play, to keep on the surface of things. Above all no toil, no genuine work. When Marie Antoinette talked, it was only with her mouth, and never with her head. If anyone spoke to her, she listened in a scatter-brained way. As a conversationalist, although she was alluring by her amiability and her glittering levity, she let every thought drop as soon as it had come into her mind. She could never talk nor think nor speak to an end; she could never get her hackles into anything in order to suck meaning and facts out of genuine experience. That was why she did not want any books, any State documents, anything of serious moment that would require patient attention to understand; and it was unwillingly that she impatiently scribbled the most necessary of letters. Even in her epistles to her mother the careful reader can often note a desire to get an irksome duty over and done with. "Above all let me avoid anything that will make life a burden, let me avoid anything which will foster gloom or dullness or melancholy!" Such was her attitude, and a man who played up to her slothfulness seemed to her a man of supreme intelligence; whereas he who demanded that she should exert her brains was a tedious pedant, and with a flirt and a flutter she would escape from reasonable counsellors to the light atmosphere with which the courtiers and court ladies of her own kidney provided her. "Let me enjoy myself! Why should I bother to think things over, to calculate, and to economize?" Such were her dominant feelings, and such were the dominant feelings of her circle. Live the life of the senses and not the life of reflection! It was the motto of a whole generation, the motto of persons of station in the latter part of the eighteenth century—of the generation to which, symbolically, Marie Antoinette had been assigned as Queen, that, in full sight of all men, she should live and should die with it.

No novelist could have invented a more glaring characterological contrast than that which existed between this pair. Down to the finest nerve-fibrils in their bodies, the rhythm of their circulation, the subtlest manifestations of their respective temperaments, Marie Antoinette and Louis XVI showed an extraordinarily instructive antithesis in their qualities and peculiarities. He was heavy, she was light; he was inert, she was mobile; he was dull, she was sparkling; his nerves were obtuse, hers were sensitive. The difference spread far into their mental life. He was irresolute, she was quick to make up her mind; he pondered long before answering, she was always ready with her yes or her no; he was strictly religious, she was in love with the things of this world; he was modest and unassuming, she was coquettishly self-assertive; he was pedantic, she was frivolous; he was thrifty, she was extravagant; he was over-serious, she was immoderately light-hearted. He felt most at his ease when alone, whereas she delighted in the noise and the bustle of social life. He ate slowly and abundantly like an animal, and had a taste for the heavier wines; she never touched wine, ate little, and that speedily. His element was sleep, hers the dance; his world was the day, hers the night; so that the clocks that ticked off their hours of activity might have been respectively regulated in accordance with the movements of the sun and of the full moon. Towards eleven at night, when Louis XVI went to bed, Marie Antoinette began to wake up thoroughly; one day at the card-table or in the gaming-house, another day at a ball. She did not turn over in her bed until he had already been away for many hours at the chase. Their habits, their tastes, their daily and nightly rounds, were utterly disharmonious. For most of their married life, Marie Antoinette and Louis XVI could not be said to live together, any more than for the most part (to the great distress of Maria Theresa) they occupied the same bed.

Am I describing a marriage troubled by quarrels, one in which the partners were perpetually at odds, one in which separation seemed almost imminent? By no means! The marriage was one with which both husband and wife were well content; and, had it not been for Louis's initial impotence, with all the distressing consequences described in a previous chapter, it could have been accounted an extremely happy union. After all, if there is to be friction in wedded life, both partners must be endowed with a fair amount of energy; will must clash with will; there must be a collision between rival hardnesses. Both Marie Antoinette and Louis XVI did their utmost to avoid friction and tension; he from bodily and she from mental indolence. "My tastes do not accord with the King's," writes Marie Antoinette lightly in a letter to a friend. "He is only interested in hunting and in mechanical work. . . . I know you will agree that I should not look particularly well standing beside a forge, that the part of Vulcan would not suit me; and I fancy the role of Venus would be more uncongenial to him than my tastes—of which, indeed, he does not disapprove."

The fact was that Louis XVI regarded her noisy, bustling life of pleasure-seeking with considerable disfavour; but, being a slacker, he never tried to put a stop to it. He smiled good-humouredly at her unrestraint; and, at bottom, was proud to have a wife so charming and so much admired. Insofar as he was capable of taking a clear line, this worthy fellow, in his loutish but honest way, had completely surrendered his will to the woman who so greatly excelled him in good looks and intelligence. Aware of his inferiority, he sedulously drew aside lest he should stand in her light. She, in turn, though she smiled at him a little for being so complaisant a husband, had no malice in her smile; for, in a careless way she was rather fond of him, looking upon him much as if he had been a huge, rough-coated St. Bernard, whom it was amusing to pat from time to time, because he never gave her any trouble, and was obedient to her slightest nod. In the long run, were it only from gratitude, she would never be unkind to this pachydermatous spouse. He always let her follow her own whims, withdrew unobtrusively when he felt he was not wanted, never entered her room unannounced, proved an ideal husband in that (thrifty though he was) he paid her debts again and again without complaint, according her every freedom, and remaining devoted to her, in his frigid way, to the end of the chapter. The longer Marie Antoinette lived with Louis XVI, the more did she come to esteem the character of one who deserved respect notwithstanding his weaknesses. Although they had been coupled for diplomatic purposes, by degrees they became good comrades, so that in this respect the marriage compared very favourably with most royal marriages of the time.

As for love, which is a great word and a sacred one, the less said about love in this connexion the better. Louis was not virile enough to love; his heart was too cold. On the other hand, Marie Antoinette's liking for her husband was tinged too much with compassion, kindly consideration, and at times even condescension, was too lukewarm a mixture of these multifarious ingredients, to be worthy of the name of love. As far as the crudities of bodily intercourse were concerned, from a sense of duty and for reasons of State this highly strung and sensitive woman had to give herself to her husband; but it would be absurd to suppose that so easygoing and sluggish a fellow could have aroused and then gratified erotic tension in a woman of brisk and lively disposition. Joseph II, returning to Vienna after his visit to Paris, said bluntly: "She has absolutely no love for him." Marie Antoinette herself, writing to her mother, says that, of the three brothers, Louis, "whom God has bestowed on me as husband," is "still" the one she is fondest of. The "still" which thus slipped itself into the lines betrays more than the writer wots of. The implication is: "Since I could not get a better husband, this good fellow is 'still' an acceptable substitute." The word suffices to disclose how tepid, so far as love was concerned, were the relationships between husband and wife.

Maria Theresa, who had much worse things to put up with as regards news concerning her daughter in Parma, might have been satisfied with this elastic conception of marriage if only Marie Antoinette had shown a little more power of dissimulation, a little more tact in her behaviour; if she had understood better how to conceal from others that she regarded her royal spouse qua man, as null, as "une quantité négligeable"! But what her mother found it hard to forgive in Marie Antoinette was that the latter forgot to maintain the formalities, and thus forgot to maintain her husband's honour. As luck would have it, one of the Queen's careless words came to Maria Theresa's ears. Count Rosenberg, a gallant old gentleman who had been one of the Empress's political associates, went on a visit to Versailles. Marie Antoinette took a fancy to him, and had so much confidence in him that after his return to Vienna she wrote a rambling letter in which she described how she had fooled her husband when the Duc de Choiseul had requested an audience of her. "As you may imagine, I did not see him without speaking about the matter to the King, but you will never guess how cleverly I arranged things so as not to seem to be asking permission. I told him that I had a fancy to see Monsieur de Choiseul, and that my only difficulty was to settle upon a day. Everything went off so well that the poor man ('le pauvre homme') himself arranged the most convenient hour when I could see the duke. It seems to me that I made a pretty extensive use of a woman's rights on this occasion."

Carelessly Marie Antoinette penned the phrase "le pauvre homme" just as it came into her head, sealing and dispatching her letter without

anxiety, thinking only that she was telling Rosenberg an amusing anecdote, since for her it was merely an expression of kindliness when she
referred to her husband in this way. In Vienna, however, a different
interpretation was put upon words which implied that sympathy or
tender feeling had been diluted with contempt. Maria Theresa was
quick to recognize that it was a dangerous breach of tact for the Queen
of France, in a private letter, to speak of the Most Christian King as a
"pauvre homme." It implied that in her husband the Queen did not
even honour the monarch. If she could actually write such a phrase, in
what sort of words was the scatter-brained young woman likely to
make mock of the ruler of France at garden-parties and routs when
lightly conversing with the Lamballes and the Polignacs, and with the
young men who danced attendance on her? The feeling at Vienna was
that order must promptly be taken about the matter, and so strongly
worded a letter was written to Marie Antoinette that many decades
elapsed before the Imperial Archives would allow its publication. The
Empress, in fact, gave her daughter the Queen a good dressing-down!

"I cannot hide from you that a letter you have written to Rosenberg
has caused me the most profound consternation. What a style! What
levity! What has happened to the good, the generous heart of her who
was Archduchess Antoinette? I can see in your letter nothing but
intrigue, base hatred, a spirit of persecution, banter: intrigue worthy of
a Pompadour, or of a Barry, but utterly unworthy of a queen, a great
princess, and a princess of the House of Lorraine and Austria, who
should be full of kindness and decency. Your too speedy success and
the danger that you will have your head turned by flattery have made
me tremble for you throughout the winter, during which you have
hurled yourself into a life of pleasure and preposterous display. This
frantic pursuit of pleasure without the King as your companion, or
when you know that if he does accompany you it is by complaisance
merely and that he will not enjoy himself, and that it is by complaisance likewise that he lets you have your own way—upon all these
matters I have touched with disquietude in my previous letters. But my
uneasiness has been only too fully confirmed by this last letter. What
language to use! 'Le pauvre homme'! What sign is there of the respect
and gratitude you owe him for his kindness? I leave you to think the
matter over, and will say nothing more on that topic, although I might

say a great deal. . . . But, foreseeing the difficulties in which you may become involved, I cannot hold my peace, loving you as I do; and I foresee the difficulties more clearly than ever, since you are so light-minded, so impulsive, so heedless. Your good luck will not last for ever, and by your own fault you will be plunged into the depths of misfortune. The trouble arises because you lead so terribly dissipated a life and never apply your mind to anything. What books do you read? Yet you venture to thrust your finger into every pie, to meddle with affairs of State, with the choice of ministers! What is the Abbé doing? What is Mercy doing? I suppose they are in your bad graces, since they do not flatter you grossly, but show their love for you in a way which they hope will make you happy and not so as to amuse you or so as to profit by your weaknesses. You will recognize the truth some day, but then it will be too late. I hope I shall not live until misfortune overtakes you, and I pray God to cut short my days before this happens, since I can no longer be of any use to you, and I could not bear to lose my child or to see her unhappy—you whom I shall love tenderly until the last moment of my life."

Is she not exaggerating when she writes this long tirade and forebodes disaster, merely because her high-spirited daughter, writing in jest, had spoken of the King as "the poor man"? Hardly so; for in this instance Maria Theresa was not so much concerned about the phrase that had slipped from her daughter's pen as about the things of which that phrase was symptomatic. The words concerning which the Empress seemed to be making such a pother had thrown a flood of light on the scant respect shown for Louis XVI, not only by the wife of his bosom, but by the court circle in general. It was natural that she should become uneasy. Her thoughts may well have run as follows. "If, in any realm, contempt for the monarch has already undermined the essential props of monarchy within his own family, how can it be expected that the other pillars and buttresses shall stand firm in times of trouble?" How could a threatened monarchy persist without a monarch? How could a throne be supported by mere supers, for whom the monarchical idea was no longer any part of their essential being? An irresolute king and a worldly-minded queen, the former thinking too slowly and the latter never stopping to think at all—how could such a pair maintain the dynasty when storms gathered to assail it? The Empress, though not really in a rage with her daughter, felt alarmed about her prospects.

Contemplating the pair from our modern angle, what grounds can we find for righteous wrath against this king and this queen of France? What reasons have we for condemning them? Even the Convention found it extremely hard to produce evidence in favour of the charge that this "poor man" had been a tyrant and a malefactor. At bottom there was not a grain of malice either in him or in his wife. Like most mediocrities, they were neither harsh nor cruel; not even ambitious or grossly vain. The pity of it was that even in their merits they could not transcend the qualities of average middle-class specimens of our race: a reasonable measure of good nature, a fair amount of considerateness, temperate benevolence. Had they been born into a time as commonplace as themselves, they would have been esteemed, and would have made a tolerably good showing. But neither Marie Antoinette nor Louis was competent to undergo the internal transformation that would have enabled them to manifest a sublimity of spirit fit to cope with an epoch that became dramatically intense; and they were much better able to die with distinction than to live strongly and heroically.

CHAPTER VIII

Queen of the Rococo

WHEN Marie Antoinette, the daughter of his old adversary Maria Theresa, mounted the French throne, Frederick the Great, the hereditary enemy of Austria, became uneasy. He sent letter after letter instructing the Prussian ambassador in Paris to keep close watch on her political plans. He had good reason to scent danger. Marie Antoinette had merely to exert her will, to take a little trouble, and all the threads of French diplomacy would have been in her hands. Europe was governed by three women, Maria Theresa, Marie Antoinette, and Catherine of Russia. But, fortunately for Prussia and disastrously for herself, Marie Antoinette was not in the least attracted by the great historical possibilities that loomed before her. She had no thought of trying to understand the time in which she lived; her utmost ambition was to kill time. The crown was but a new toy. She wanted to enjoy power instead of using it.

From the outset, the Queen's mistake was that she wished to conquer as woman instead of as queen. Her petty feminine triumphs were of more moment to her than any she might have achieved in the stupendous domain of history. Because, for her trivial mind, the royal position was only a matter of outward form devoid of spiritual content, in her hands what should have been a mighty task shrivelled to become a temporary amusement, and an exalted function was for her mere play-acting. To be queen meant no more to Marie Antoinette, for fifteen years or so, than to be admired as the smartest, the most coquettish, the best dressed, the most spoiled, and above all the best amused woman at court; to be the arbiter elegantiarum, the person who set the tone for a society rich in artificial distinction and one which regarded itself as the world. Throughout this period she acted with unrivalled grace and charm, playing her role as perfect queen of the Rococo in her private theatre at Versailles, which was built over an abyss.

Yet how poverty-stricken was the repertory of this social comedy:

a passing flirtation and a few insignificant intrigues, very little genius
and a great deal of dancing. In all this play-acting she had no adequate
partner to take the role of king, no man to act the hero as counterpart to her heroine. The audience, meanwhile, was always the same,
bored and ostentatious; though outside the gilded bars of the cage,
twenty millions of French people were looking to her to be an effective
ruler. Blinded by self-approbation, she would not desist from this silly
comedy, being never weary of befooling herself with unmeaning nov-
elties. Even when the growling of the thunder in Paris had already
become audible in the gardens of Versailles, she would not desist.
The Revolution had forcibly to drag her from this petty Rococo stage
into the huge and tragical theatre of real history before she could
be brought to grasp how profound had been the error which, throughout all these years, had made her choose so insignificant a part, really
that of a soubrette, though apparently that of a fine lady in a drawing-
room, when fate had given her the chance of devoting her whole soul
to the work of a true heroine. Recognition came too late, and yet not
altogether too late. For when events had moved so far that to live as
a queen was no longer possible and only to die as a queen remained
open to her, she became equal to the occasion in the tragic epilogue
to the pastoral comedy. When sport became earnest and she was bereft
of her crown, in her heart of hearts she became a true queen.

Almost inconceivable to us seems the heedlessness displayed by
Marie Antoinette, a heedlessness which made her for nearly two
decades sacrifice the essential to the unimportant, duty to pleasure, the
grave to the gay, France to Versailles, the real world to the world of
her fantasies. The best way of understanding the absurdity of her
behaviour is to take a map of France and mark on it the narrow space
in which she spent almost all the years of her reign. One who does so
will be amazed. The area is so confined that upon a small-scale map
it shrinks to little more than a point. From Versailles to Trianon, to
Marly, to Fontainebleau, to Saint-Cloud, and to Rambouillet, six places
in all—separated one from another by no more than a few leagues—
she moved back and forth perpetually in her busy tedium. Not once
did she feel any desire to overstep the boundaries of this pentagram

in which the stupidest of all devils, the devil of pleasure, held her prisoner. Not once during a space of almost a fifth of a century did the Queen of France wish, or at any rate give way to the desire, to make acquaintance with her own realm, to see the provinces she had to rule, the seas that washed the French coast, the mountains, fortresses, cities, and cathedrals of a far-flung and multiform land. Not once did she steal an hour in order to visit one of her subjects or even to think about her subjects at all; not once did she cross the threshold of a middle-class domicile. The world that lay beyond the narrow circle within which the nobility moved was for her practically non-existent. Not a notion had she that round about the opera-house of Paris there stretched a gigantic town, filled with poverty and discontent; that beyond the ponds of Trianon, well stocked with mandarin ducks and overfed swans, beyond the lawns on which the peacocks flaunted their plumes, behind the show village, the Hameau—clean of front and titivated up by the court architect—the peasants' houses were falling into ruins and the barns were empty. She never knew that millions upon millions of the French people toiled and hungered, alternating between hope and despair. Maybe nothing but such ignorance, nothing but the lack of any will to know about the hardships of the world, could have given the Rococo its bewitching grace, its facile, careless charm. None but those who are unacquainted with the realities of life can play so light-heartedly. But a queen who forgets her people is taking great risks. Marie Antoinette might have questioned, but would not question, the world. A glance would have told her what was going on, but she would not look, she did not want to understand. She wanted to go on living in her sanctuary, youthful and unmolested. Following a will-o'-the-wisp, she moved ever in a circle, missing her opportunities, and, a marionette among the other marionettes of the court, she wasted the years of her prime—years that could never be recalled.

Such was her undeniable fault. With unprecedented levity she ignored one of the mightiest tasks ever imposed by history, carelessly evading the gravest issues of the century. An undeniable fault, and yet a venial one, explicable as it is by the strength of a temptation which even one more staunch of fibre would hardly have been able to resist. Suddenly removed from the nursery to the marriage-bed, summoned before she had fully awakened to womanhood to wield supreme power, not yet ready for any such calling, still little more than a child, this young woman, simple, not particularly intelligent, not endowed with any exceptional strength of disposition, found herself gyrating in a circle of planetary admiration; and her eighteenth-century court was peculiarly, was knavishly well adapted to lead a girl astray. It was trained in the use of the subtle poison of flattery, ever ready to fascinate with unmeaning trifles, past master in the university of galanterie and in the Phæacian art of extracting the utmost pleasure out of life. Experienced, all too experienced, in allurements, intimately acquainted with every foible of the mind, the courtiers knew from the start how best to bewitch the heart of an immature maid, still curious about herself. From the first days of her reign, Marie Antoinette was surrounded by the incense-fumes of extravagant idolization. Whatever she said was acclaimed as wonderfully clever; whatever she did was a law to others; whatever she wanted was done. If she displayed some capricious fancy, next day it became the fashion. Did she commit a folly, the whole court enthusiastically imitated her. To be near her was to be in the sunshine for this vainglorious and ambitious crowd; for her to glance at them was the bestowal of a gift; her laugh entranced them; her coming was a festival. When she gave a reception, all the ladies, the oldest as well as the youngest, those of highest rank no less than those who had only just been admitted to the court, made the most convulsive, the most strenuous, the most ridiculous endeavours to enlist her attention, to secure a gracious word; or, if this last was not to be achieved, at least to be noticed and not to be overlooked.

Whenever she appeared in the streets, the populace, thronging to see her, shouted acclamations. When she entered the theatre, the audience rose in mass to salute her. If she passed a mirror, contemplating her own image she saw a very pretty young woman, gorgeously apparelled, beaming with delight at her own triumph, carefree and happy, as good-looking as the handsomest women at court, and therefore (since for her this court was the world) the handsomest woman in the world.

How could one with the heart of a child, how could one with no more than a moderate amount of energy, defend herself against the intoxication of such happiness, mingled as it was with all the piquant and the sweet essences of feeling, with the covetous admiration of men, the envious admiration of women, the devotion of the crowd, her own pride? How could she fail to be a victim of levity when everything came so lightly, so easily; when as much money as she wanted was obtainable by merely scribbling her name upon a piece of paper; when precious stones, gardens, and palaces could be secured at will by writing the word "payez" on an invoice; when the soft breezes of joy soothed all her nerves? How could she be other than careless and light-hearted when life seemed to rise as if on wings?

This levity of outlook was not a fault peculiar to Marie Antoinette, for it was characteristic of her generation. It was her unhesitating acceptance of the spirit of her time which made her the typical representative of the eighteenth century. The Rococo, the too highly cultivated and most delicate blossom of an ancient civilization, a century of delicate and idle hands, of spoiled and coddled minds, wanted, before it perished, to express itself in a particular figure. No kings, no males, could have incorporated this century of the lady in the picture-book of history. A woman's figure, a queen's figure, was essential for its symbolization, and Marie Antoinette thus became the emblematic queen of the Rococo. Among the heedless, the most heedless of all; among the spendthrift, the most spendthrift; among the gallant and coquettish women, the most gracefully gallant and the most deliberately coquettish—she gave the plainest and the most memorable expression to the manners and to the artificialities of the eighteenth century. Madame de Staël wrote of her: "I think it is difficult to put more grace and more kindliness into civility than she does. She shows a peculiar affability which does not allow us to forget that she is queen, and yet always produces in us the impression that she herself has forgotten it." Marie Antoinette played with life as if she were playing upon a delicate and fragile instrument. Instead of becoming a great figure for all time, she became the embodiment of her own epoch. Even though she squandered her energies upon trifles, her existence had its peculiar significance, in that it was a fitting expression of and an appropriate close to the eighteenth century.

What is the first thought of the Queen of the Rococo when she wakes of a morning in her palace at Versailles? To read the reports from the capital or from the provinces? To scan the letters from her ambassadors, to learn whether her armies have been victorious; to inquire whether war has been declared against England? Nothing of the sort! Marie Antoinette did not get to bed until four or five. She has slept only a few hours, for her restless temperament is almost independent of repose. The day begins with an imposing ceremony. The mistress of the robes appears with the chemises and other articles of apparel essential to the morning toilette. By her side stands the first lady's maid. The latter, making obeisance, holds out to the Queen a folio volume into which patterns of all the dresses in the wardrobe have been pinned. Marie Antoinette has to decide which gown she would like to don. How difficult, how responsible is the choice, seeing that for each season of the year twelve dresses prescribed for State occasions, twelve others for evenings of private entertainment, and twelve robes of ceremony are available, to say nothing of the hundreds which have to be renewed year by year. Think of what a disgrace it would be for the queen of fashion to wear the same toilette often! Then there are the négligés, the slip-bodices, the lace fichus, the caps, the cloaks, the waistbands, the gloves, the stockings, the underclothing of all kinds stored away in an arsenal which keeps an army of tailoresses, sempstresses, and maids busy. The selection usually takes a considerable time; but at length, by special pins in the patterns, an indication has been given of the clothes Marie Antoinette wishes to wear today: the State robe for the reception; the dishabille for the afternoon; the full dress for the evening. That part of the business of the day is over; the pattern book is taken away, and the chosen dresses are brought in.

Need we be surprised that when raiment has become of such supreme importance, the chief dressmaker, the divine Mademoiselle Bertin, should exert more influence over Marie Antoinette than the ministers of State—for these latter can be replaced by the dozen, whereas Bertin is unique and incomparable.

By origin she had been nothing more than an ordinary dressmaker belonging to the lower classes of the population; she was gruff, aggressive, opinionated, and anything but good-mannered; but, being a supreme mistress in her trade, she had unbounded influence over the Queen. For her sake there was a palace revolution at Versailles nearly eighteen years before the real revolution began. Mademoiselle Bertin had made short work of the rule of etiquette which forbade any bourgeois or bourgeoise the entry into the petits cabinets of the Queen; this artist of scissors and needle had achieved what proved beyond the power of Voltaire or of any of the great writers or painters of the day— she was received by the Queen in private interviews. When she appeared twice a week with her schemes for new creations, Marie Antoinette left the court ladies to their own devices and held a private council with the venerated modiste, to discuss some new fashion that should be still more grotesque than that of yesterday. It need hardly be said that Bertin, being a shrewd woman of business, turned these privileges to pecuniary account. After she had induced Marie Antoinette to accept some costly "creation," she proceeded to fleece the court and the rest of the nobility.

Over her establishment in the Rue Saint-Honoré it was announced in gigantic letters that she was dressmaker by special appointment to the Queen; and she never hesitated to keep her other clients waiting, telling them arrogantly, when she at length arrived: "I have just been working with Her Majesty." Soon she had a regiment of tailoresses and sempstresses in her service, for the more elegant Marie Antoinette's dresses, the more impetuously did the ladies of the court vie with one another not to be outshone. Many of them would bribe the faithless Bertin to cut them a dress after a model which the Queen herself had not yet worn. Luxury in these matters spread like a contagious fever. The unrest throughout the country, the dispute with the Parliament of Paris, the war with England, did not agitate this futile court society half so much as the new puce which Mademoiselle Bertin had brought into fashion, or some exceptionally audacious cut of the hooped skirt, or an unprecedented shade of silk just turned out at Lyons. Every lady who valued herself felt bound to monkey the exaggerations of the mode, and a husband remarked with a sigh: "Never before have Frenchwomen spent so much money simply in order to make themselves ridiculous."

To be queen in this domain, above all, seemed to Marie Antoinette her unequivocal duty. After she had been three months on the throne,

she had become the model for the world of fashion in respect alike
of gowns and of hairdressing, so that her triumph was the talk of all
the drawing-rooms and of all the courts of Europe. The Hofburg was
no exception in this respect, and a disagreeable echo came from that
quarter. Maria Theresa, who could have wished Toinette to be better
occupied, sent back to Mercy in Paris a picture showing her daughter
decked out in the most preposterous way, with an angry request to be
informed whether this was the counterfeit presentment of an actress
or that of the Queen of France. Also she gave the young woman a
scolding, which had no more effect than earlier ones: "You know I
have always held that it is well to be in the fashion to a reasonable
extent, but that one should never be outré in one's dress. A good-
looking queen, endowed with charm, has no need of such follies. On
the contrary, simplicity of attire enhances these advantages, and is
more suitable to her exalted rank. Since, as Queen, you set the tone,
all the world will hasten to follow you even when you stray into wrong
paths. But I, who love my little Queen and watch her every footstep,
cannot hesitate to warn her of her frivolousness in this matter."

The second great task of the morning was the dressing of the
Queen's hair. Happily in this matter likewise she had the assistance
of a great artist, Monsieur Léonard, the indefatigable and unrivalled
Figaro of the Rococo. In superb style, aping the gentleman, he drove
a six-in-hand every morning from Paris to Versailles to practise his
craft on the Queen with comb, washes, and towels, inventing new
devices from day to day. Just as Mansart, the famous architect, surmounted the houses built by him with the artificial roof which goes
by his name, so did Monsieur Léonard construct above the forehead
of every lady of rank a towering edifice of hair decked with symbolical
ornamentations. To begin with, by means of huge hairpins and a
lavish expenditure of stiff pomade, the hair was strained upwards from
the temples like a huge flaming candle, about twice the height of the
pointed head-dress of a Prussian grenadier; then, in free space, eighteen
inches above the eyebrows, began the artist's plastic realm. Not only
were landscapes and panoramas, with fruit, gardens, houses, ships, the
sea in a storm, the whole motley world, modelled with the comb on the
summit of this "pouf" or "quésacos" (the latter name was taken from

a pamphlet by Beaumarchais)—but, to provide for sufficiently frequent changes in fashion, the event of the day had to be symbolized in this superstructure. Everything which these humming-bird brains were interested in, all that was inside these heads which were mostly full of emptiness, had to be flaunted on the top of the coiffure. When Gluck's opera was the centre of attention, Léonard promptly designed a coiffure à la Iphigénie, with black mourning ribbon and Diana's half-moon. If the King was inoculated with smallpox, due notice of this remarkable occurrence was taken by the appearance of "poufs de l'inoculation." When the American rebellion was the centre of fashionable interest, the "coiffure de la liberté" made its appearance upon the heads of the ladies. When the populace was on the verge of famine, and the bakers' shops in Paris were being plundered, the frivolous society of the court could find nothing better to do than to record the remarkable incident in ladies' head-dresses as "bonnets de la révolte." These artificial structures surmounting empty heads grew continually loftier and more absurd. By degrees the towers of hair, built up with the aid of solider foundations and more numerous artificial plaits, attained such an altitude that ladies could no longer sit in their carriages, but had to pull up their skirts and kneel down. The very doorways in the palace had to be made higher, to save marchionesses and countesses from having to stoop as they went from room to room, and the ceilings of the boxes in the theatres were reconstructed as arches. A good many caricatures have come down to us showing what a nuisance such colossal structures were to the lovers of the dames in question. But, as everyone knows, women are always ready to sacrifice themselves on the altar of fashion, and it was manifest that the Queen would not have regarded herself as worthy of her great position had she not taken the lead in such follies.

Once more there came a critical echo from Vienna: "I cannot refrain from touching upon a matter which many of the newspapers have brought to my notice. I refer to the way in which you are dressing your hair. They tell me that from the roots on the forehead it rises as much as three feet, and is made higher by the superaddition of plumes and ribbons." Trying to turn the matter off, the daughter assured her dear mother in reply that in Versailles people were so much used, now, to the sight of such lofty head-dresses that no one in the world (by the "world" Marie Antoinette meant the hundred noble ladies at court) saw anything out of the ordinary in them. Master Léonard, with a cheerful heart, therefore continued to build higher and ever higher—until it pleased Almighty God to decree a change of fashion, so that next year the towers were razed—only to be replaced by a yet more costly style of head-gear, that of ostrich feathers.

As for the third great concern of Marie Antoinette's toilette, it related to the question whether a woman could be dressed from day to day in some new creation without having an appropriate change of ornaments. Of course not! Obviously, moreover, a queen needed larger diamonds and thicker strings of pearls than any other woman. She must have more rings and circlets and bracelets and brilliants and hair-chains and gems, finer shoe-buckles and more bejewelled borders to the fans painted by Fragonard, than the wives of His Majesty's younger brothers or any other ladies of the court. No doubt she had brought a considerable stock of gew-gaws with her from Vienna, and Louis XV had given her as a wedding present a casket of family trinkets. But what was the use of being a queen if one could not be continually buying new, lovelier, and more costly gems? Marie Antoinette, as everyone at Versailles knew (and it will soon become plain that danger arises when such matters are proclaimed from the housetops) had gone mad about ornaments. She simply could not resist when her shrewd and subtle jewellers, Boehmer and Bassenge—Jewish immigrants from Germany—showed her in satin-lined boxes their latest works of art, wonderful ear-pendants, rings, and diamond-headed pins. Besides, these good fellows made it easy for Her Majesty to buy. They paid due honour to the Queen of France by charging her double prices, but gave her long credit, and would always repurchase the old trinkets at half their value. Unaware that there was anything discreditable in such usurious transactions, Marie Antoinette incurred debts all over the place, confident that in case of need her thrifty spouse would come to her rescue.

Another growl from Vienna: "I have news from Paris to the effect that you have been buying bracelets at a cost of two hundred and fifty thousand livres, with the result that you have thrown your finances into disorder and have heaped up a burden of debt; and that, to find a way out of the difficulties thus incurred, you have sold your diamonds very cheap. These reports wring my heart, especially when I think of the future." Again: "A queen only degrades herself by decking herself out in this preposterous way; and she degrades herself still more by unthrifty expenditure, especially in such difficult times. I know too well how extravagant are your tastes, and I cannot keep silent about the matter, for I love you too heartily to flatter you. Do not forfeit, through frivolities of the kind, the good name you acquired to begin with. Everyone knows that the King is extremely modest in his expenditure, so the whole blame will rest on your shoulders. I hope I shall not live to see the disaster that is likely to ensue."

Diamonds are expensive, fine gowns are expensive, and although on coming to the throne the kind Louis had doubled his wife's allowance, there must have been a hole in her purse, for it was almost always empty.

How was she to keep herself in funds? Luckily the devil had provided her with a paradise easy of access—the gaming-table. Louis XIV had done his utmost to stop high play at court, and gambling was not one of Louis XV's vices, so when Marie Antoinette came to the throne playing for money at Versailles was as innocent a way of passing the evening as billiards or dancing. The usual game was lansquenet for moderate stakes. But the new Queen rediscovered for herself and for others the notorious faro which, as we learn from Casanova, was the favourite hunting-ground of eighteenth-century card-sharpers. Courtiers and court ladies alike recked little that Louis XVI had forbidden gambling under high penalties. The police had no access to the Queen's salons. Nor did Marie Antoinette's frivolous associates care a jot that the King would have frowned at sight of their gaming-tables heavily laden with gold pieces. They gambled to their hearts' content, for the doorkeepers had been instructed to give the alarm when Louis was coming. Thereupon cards, counters, and money disappeared as if by magic beneath the table. When the monarch arrived upon the scene, all were chattering merrily—to laugh heartily as soon as "the poor man" departed to his early rest, and to resume their game without a qualm.

In order to liven up the play and increase the turnover of coin, the

Queen admitted to her gaming-table anyone who had money in his purse. Touts and night-hawks were quick to avail themselves of their opportunities; and it was not long before rumour was rife in Paris that cheating at cards was the order of the day in the Queen's drawing-room. Besides King Louis, there was only one person who failed to be aware of the fact, Marie Antoinette, who did not want to know, because she was blinded by her craving for amusement. When she was in the vein, when the passion for high play took possession of her, nothing could restrain her. She gambled night after night far on into the small hours; and once, to the scandal even of the court, until All Saints' Day was well advanced.

This new development brought another rumble of discontent from the Hofburg: "Gambling is unquestionably one of the worst of pleasures, attracting evil company and giving rise to malicious talk. It allures those who are given to it by the passion for gain, and they are always duped by their desires, for irrefutable calculation shows that one who plays honestly cannot win in the long run. Let me beg you, then, my dear daughter, not to give way to this passion. Let me beg you to wean yourself of it without transition. Who is better fitted to advise you than I, who have had a similar experience in my own person? If I do not get a satisfactory answer from you on this point, I shall apply direct to the King, in order to save you from greater misfortune. I know too well what consequences will ensue, and that you will lose caste before the public, above all abroad—which will be a great distress to me, since I love you so tenderly."

Dress, make-up, and gambling, however, occupied only half the day and half the night. The short hand of the clock circled inexorably twice in the twenty-four hours, and there was still vacant time to be killed. How was Marie Antoinette to amuse herself? Riding, hunting, were old-time royal amusements; but of course one must have company on these occasions, or one would be bored to death. Seldom would it be one's own husband, for a livelier companion was preferable, one's brother-in-law the Count of Artois, or some other high-spirited gentleman. Often, just for a joke, one could ride a donkey instead of a horse; not so distinguished-looking, doubtless; but when one's grey-coated mount pranced a little, it was not so far to fall, and then the court could have the most enchanting glimpses of "frilly thingumbobs" and the well-shaped legs of a queen. In winter one went out driving, warmly wrapped up; or one skated. In summer one could amuse oneself of an evening with firework displays and with open-air dances or with concerts by night in the park. A few paces down from the terrace and, with a chosen companion or two, one was fully protected by the darkness, and one could amuse oneself to one's heart's content—quite honourably, of course, but playing with danger as with all the other things of life.

What matter if a spiteful courtier should write and publish a broadsheet penned in verse describing the nocturnal adventures of the Queen and entitled "Le lever de l'aurore"? The King, thick-skinned as well as indulgent, did not feel such pin-pricks, and Marie Antoinette had had a gay time of it. The great thing was that she should never be alone; that she should never have to spend a long evening at home over a book, seated by the fireside with Louis; that she should be ever on the go, and lively from one week's end to another.

When a new fashion came in, Marie Antoinette was the first to adopt it. As soon as the Count of Artois introduced horse-racing from England (his only contribution to his native land!) the Queen was to be seen upon the grandstand, surrounded by dozens of anglomaniac young coxcombs, laying wagers, vastly entertained by this new titillation of the nerves. In most cases such a blaze-up of enthusiasm did not last long. She would be bored on the morrow by what had fascinated her yesterday. Nothing but perpetual change in the round of pleasures appeased her nervous unrest, which (unquestionably) was dependent upon the secret of the royal alcove.

Among a hundred successive forms of enterprise, the only one whose charms persisted—and the one which wrought most mischief to her reputation—was that for masked balls. It was an enduring passion because it provided a twofold enjoyment: that of remaining a queen; and that, since the mask of black silk made her queenship no longer recognizable, of being able to disport herself on the brink of amorous adventures—not, as at the gaming-table, staking mere money, but subjecting herself as woman to the hazard of the die. Decked out as

Artemis or wearing some coquettish domino, she could shake off the chill and exalted trappings of etiquette to descend into the warm turmoil of ordinary human life; could enjoy the aroma of love-making, the proximity of temptation, the half-surrender to passion; could, for a while, let her hand rest with a fervent pressure on the arm of an elegantly dressed young Englishman or a bewitching Swedish cavalier —showing Axel Count von Fersen, in a few venturesome words, how greatly he pleased the woman who, alas, being a queen, must safeguard her virtue.

Marie Antoinette did not know, or chose to ignore, that these vagaries of hers, magnified into libertinage by the gossips at Versailles, were the talk of the drawing-rooms; she did not know, or chose to ignore, that when on one occasion a wheel of the royal carriage broke, and for twenty paces or so she had to take a fiacre in order to reach the Opera House, reports of this and similar trifling follies and misadventures found their way into underground news-sheets as accounts of amorous excesses. Futile as usual were her mother's exhortations: "If what you did were always done in the King's company, I should hold my peace, but what distresses me is that almost invariably you gad about apart from him, and in the company of all that is worst and youngest in Paris, so that the Queen, this charming Queen, is generally the eldest of the company! The newspapers, the leaflets, which used to delight me because they had so much to say about my daughter's magnanimity and kindness of heart, have suddenly changed their tone. I read in them nothing except accounts of horse-races, gambling, the turning of night into day, so that I can no longer bear to look at them; but I cannot prevent people talking to me about them, for everyone knows how devoted I am to my children, so that naturally they tell me what gossip is current. I often shut myself away from society lest I should hear of these matters."

No representations of this kind had any influence now upon the unreasonable young woman with whom matters had gone so far that she could not understand why people did not understand her. What objection could there be to enjoying life to the full, since life had no other significance than enjoyment? With alarming frankness she unbosomed herself to Mercy concerning such maternal reproofs: "What does she want? I am terrified of being bored."

"I am terrified of being bored"—in these words Marie Antoinette summed up the whole attitude of her generation and of the society in which she moved. The eighteenth century was drawing to a close; it had fulfilled its aim; the realm had been firmly established; Versailles had been built; the rules of etiquette had been perfected. What more was there to do? Since there was no war (this was before France had come to the support of the rebel British colonies across the Atlantic), the marshals had become mere lay-figures in uniform; the bishops, in a generation which no longer believed in God, were but gallant gentle-men in purple cassocks; the Queen, who had not at her side a King worthy of the name and had no heir to the throne to educate, was but a lively woman of the world. All of them faced an era in which mighty currents were beginning to flow, and faced it in a mood of mingled tedium and incomprehension. From time to time, with greedy hands, they snatched a few glittering drops out of the turmoil. Because the tumultuous element sparkled so interestingly round their fingers, they played with it like children dipping their hands over the thwarts of a boat. Not one of them perceived that the flood was rising quickly and ever more quickly, so that, when at last the danger became ap-parent, flight would have been too late, the game was already lost, their lives were forfeit.

CHAPTER IX

Trianon

LIGHTLY, caressingly, Marie Antoinette picked up the crown as a gift. She was still too young to know that life never gives anything for nothing, and that a price is always exacted for what fate bestows. She did not think she would have to pay a price. She simply accepted the rights of her royal position and performed no duties in exchange. She wanted to combine two things which are, in actual human experience, incompatible; she wanted to reign and at the same time to enjoy. Her desire was that all should fulfil her wishes as Queen while she gave free rein to every caprice; she wanted the power of the ruler and the freedom of the woman, wanted, in fact, to have it both ways, wanted her new position to redouble without drawback the intensity of her young and passionate life.

But no freedom was possible at Versailles. In the brightly lit galleries, every step one took was open to the public gaze. Every movement was controlled, every word was bruited abroad by a treacherous wind. Here she could neither be alone nor enjoy "solitude à deux." At Versailles she could find neither repose nor yet relief from tension. The King was, so to say, the mainspring of a huge striking clock, which inexorably recorded the hours. Every action from birth to death, from getting up in the morning to going to bed at night, the very moments of amatory dalliance, became actions of State. The ruler, to whom everything belonged, was here a part of the show, and did not belong to himself. But Marie Antoinette detested control of any kind, and for this reason, almost immediately after she became Queen, she asked her obliging husband to provide her with some corner of retirement where she need not be Queen. Thereupon Louis XVI, half through weakness and half in a lover's mood, bestowed on her the summer palace of the Little Trianon, a tiny realm, but her very own, superadded to the vast realm of France.

In itself this was no splendid gift which Marie Antoinette received from her husband; nothing more than a toy which was to amuse and engross her idleness for more than ten years to come. Its builder had not designed the palace as permanent residence for a royal family, but only as a "maison de plaisir," as a "buen retiro," as a house of accommodation—and Louis XV had made a plentiful use of it as an unwatched love-nest for his amusements with the Dubarry and other light-of-loves. (I speak of the Little Trianon, and not of the Great Trianon, which was built by Louis XIV for Madame de Maintenon.) King Louis's suppers with the ladies upon whom he bestowed his affections were served upon a cleverly constructed table made after the manner of a modern lift, so that the spread board could rise discreetly into the banqueting-room from the basement, and the lord of the earth and his lady could remain unobserved by any menial. For this intensification of erotic comfort, the worthy Leporello was granted a bonus of twelve thousand livres, over and above the seven hundred and thirty-six thousand livres of which the whole pleasure-house had drained the State treasury.

Marie Antoinette took over this retired nook in Versailles park when it was still warm after the late King's sudden death and Madame Dubarry's eviction. The Little Trianon was one of the most graceful creations of French taste, delicate in design, perfect in execution, a dainty casket for the elegant maiden queen. A villa in the neo-classical style, its windows giving upon beautiful lawns and gardens, well out of sight of Versailles and yet conveniently near, this palace was no greater and scarcely more luxuriously furnished than a private country mansion of today. There were seven or eight rooms in all; an entrance hall, a dining-room, a boudoir, a large drawing-room, a bedroom, a bathroom, a miniature library (lucus a non lucendo, for, according to universal witness, Marie Antoinette never opened a book until the last weeks of her imprisonment, except for a few light novels whose pages she fluttered).

Within this Lilliputian palace, during the years of her tenancy, the Queen made few changes. Having excellent taste in such matters, she was careful to introduce nothing that should be ostentatious, pompous, or too obviously expensive into rooms that were deliberately intended to produce an impression of privacy and comfort. On the contrary, all was done with a light, delicate, and reserved touch, in that new style which is as wrongfully termed "Louis Seize" as America has been christened after Amerigo Vespucci. We ought, rather, to speak of the "Marie Antoinette style," for it is she whom these subtle and charming characteristics recall. They have nothing in common with the stout and massive Louis XVI or with his crudities of person and character. Everything at the Little Trianon reminds us of the frivolous and bewitching feminine figure whose portrait still hangs on the walls. From the bed to the snuff-box, from the clavecin to the ivory fan, from the sofa to the miniature, all is of a uniform type, the choicest materials embodied in the most inconspicuous forms, seemingly fragile and yet durable, a combination of classical lines and French grace. The style is one still congenial to us, reminding us, as does no earlier style, of the dominion of a cultivated and tasteful lady, contrasting by its intimacy and its harmony with the dramatic pomposity of Louis Quinze and Louis Quatorze.

The boudoir, for light conversation and equally light amusements, was, therefore, the centre of the house, rather than the great, echoing reception-rooms. Here, a carven and gilded wooden panelling replaced the stiff marble of the more formal apartments; there were soft silken hangings instead of stiff satin and heavy brocades. As to colour, a mat cream, a delicate cherry, a pale blue prevailed. The whole interior was designed to form an appropriate setting for women in the springtime of life, for pleasant and intimate gatherings, for cheerful unconcern. Thus the costly and coquettish furnishing of the Little Trianon gave appropriate harbourage to the statuettes of Clodion, to the paintings of Watteau and Pater, to the silver-toned chamber music of Boccherini, and to the other most select products of eighteenth-century art. Nowhere else did the playfulness of spirit which prevailed among the French high nobility just before the troublous days of the Revolution find so unalloyed an expression. For all time the Little Trianon will remain the most refined, the most fragile, and yet the most indestructible shrine of this essentially artificial blossoming. Here ultra-sophisticated enjoyment secured perfect expression in a domicile and in the figure of its owner. The zenith and the nadir of the Rococo, maturing to a climax in the last hour before its death, is, even in our own day, best symbolized by the little clock placed in the centre of the chimney-piece in Marie Antoinette's boudoir.

It was a doll's house, this Little Trianon, and, characteristically enough, its windows commanded no glimpse of the world of living men; of Paris, of the town of Versailles, of the farms in the working countryside. Ten minutes suffice for a survey of the whole place, and yet, small though it was, as far as Marie Antoinette was concerned it was more important than the whole of France where dwelt her twenty million subjects. Here she felt emancipated from obligations, whether to ceremonial, to etiquette, or even to morality. In order to make plain that in this petty realm she and no one else was supreme, she issued her decrees in her own name instead of that of her husband, subscribing them "de par la reine"—much to the annoyance of sticklers for tradition at court, who continued to lay great stress upon the Salic Law. The servants did not wear the royal livery of red, white, and blue, but her own red and silver. Even her husband, the Most Christian King of France, appeared at the Little Trianon as a guest. Tactful and complaisant as ever, he was careful not to turn up uninvited or at inconvenient times, strictly respecting the domestic privacies of his wife. All the same, the good fellow was glad enough to come when asked, finding life in this quiet "country house" far more agreeable than in the great palace, for, "par ordre de la reine," strict ceremonial was discarded at the Little Trianon. Here the Queen, and the King when present, did not "hold court." They could loll on the grass in an easy undress. There was no need to worry about precedence, for all were good companions. Stiffness, and sometimes even the most elementary dignity, were laid aside.

At the Little Trianon Marie Antoinette felt really at home; and soon she had become so much fascinated by the ease of an informal life that she found it hard when she had to go back to Versailles in the evening. Having once tasted the freedom of her "country house," her court duties became more and more irksome to her, so that she was increasingly prone to shake off the responsibilities of her representative position (and, perhaps, to evade her conjugal obligations) by withdrawing ever more frequently, day after day, to her beloved dove-cot. Could she have followed her preferences unhesitatingly, she would never have left Trianon. In general, as was her wont, she did follow her preferences, and, for practical purposes, the summer palace became her residence. Her bedchamber had only a single bed in which there

would hardly have been room for her bulky husband. The last intimacies of married life took place only when Marie Antoinette desired.
As Balkis Queen of Sheba visited Solomon, so did Marie Antoinette
visit King Louis, at her own sweet will—or when her mother wrote
too acrimoniously about the "lit à part." Not once, so far as we know,
was the worthy Louis her guest in the single bed at the Little Trianon,
for this summer palace was Marie Antoinette's inviolable kingdom,
her island of Cythera, wholly consecrated to her own pleasures—among
which her connubial duties were certainly never reckoned. Here she
wanted to live her own life without hindrance; to be nothing but the
spoiled, honoured, and uncontrolled young woman who, busied among
a thousand trifles, forgot everything else; forgot her realm, her spouse,
the court, time, and the world—and, often (perhaps these were her
happiest hours) forgot even herself.

At Trianon her idle spirit had at length found occupation, upon a
toy which was continually being refurbished. Just as her dressmaker
had to design an unending succession of new dresses, and just as her
jeweller had to be perpetually finding her new trinkets, so was Marie
Antoinette unceasingly engaged upon the re-adornment and the renovation of her tiny realm set apart among the great pleasure-grounds of
Versailles. Superadded to dressmaker, jeweller, dancing-master, and
music teacher, were now the architect, the landscape gardener, the
painter, the decorator; new ministers of her petty kingdom, helping her
to while away the weary hours and to empty even faster than before
the treasury of the State. The garden, above all, interested Marie Antoinette, for it seemed to her essential that it should differ in every
respect from the old-fashioned precincts of the great palace of Versailles.
It must be the most up-to-date, the most stylish, the most peculiar, the
most coquettish of the day; a genuine Rococo apanage to her Rococo
country mansion. In this matter once again, consciously or unconsciously, Marie Antoinette was following the taste of the new times.
Cultivated persons had grown weary of Le Nôtre's ideas of horticul-
ture; of his lawns shaped with a ruler, of his hedges shaved with a
razor; of the formalities designed at the draughtsman's table, the
ornamentations which were to show in boastful spirit that Louis the
Roi Soleil had impressed the forms he desiderated, not only upon the

kingdom, the nobility, the estates, and the nation, but also on God's own countryside. People were sick unto death of this green geometry, of this "massacre of nature." As in many other respects, so likewise in respect of the futility of much that was styled landscape gardening, Jean Jacques Rousseau found the apt phrase for his generation when, in *La nouvelle Héloïse,* he demanded a "natural park."

Beyond question Marie Antoinette had never read *La nouvelle Héloïse.* If she had heard of Jean Jacques Rousseau, it could only have been as librettist and composer of the charming pastoral *Le devin du village.* Nevertheless, Rousseau's views were part of the contemporary atmosphere. Dukes and marquises were profoundly moved, and their eyes were even bedimmed with tears, when the conversation turned upon this distinguished advocate of primitive innocence (in private life, homo perversissimus!). They were profoundly grateful to him because, after the customary stimuli had lost effect, he had found a last spur for their jaded senses: sporting with naivety, playing of innocence, the masquerade of naturalness. It need hardly be said, therefore, that at this juncture Marie Antoinette, likewise, wanted a "natural" garden, a blamelessly innocent landscape, which must be the most natural of new-fangled natural gardens. With this end in view, she summoned to her aid the most noted, the most highly refined horticultural artists of the day, that, in the most artificial way possible, they might design and create for her an ultra-natural garden.

As fashion decreed, this "Anglo-Chinese garden" was to represent, not merely nature, but the whole of nature. In the microcosm of a few square kilometres, there was to be a quasi-microscopic reproduction of the entire cosmos. However circumscribed the area, it was to contain French and Indian and African trees, Dutch tulips, magnolias from southern climes, a lake and a river, a mountain and a grotto, a romantic ruin, rural dwellings, Greek temples and oriental glimpses, Dutch windmills, North and South, East and West, all that was most natural and all that was most eccentric, all that was most artificial and all that had the stamp of the utmost genuineness. At the outset the architect had planned to introduce into his garden-plot a volcano spouting fire and also a Chinese pagoda, but, fortunately, these proposals were, for once in a way, found too costly.

Spurred on by the Queen's impatience, hundreds of workmen,

guided by the plans of architects and painters, began to conjure up
a designedly purposeless and artificially natural landscape. First of all,
as an indispensable requisite of a pastoral scene, there must be a brook
that murmured gently on its course through the meadows. Since there
was no local spring to tap, the water had to be brought in pipes all
the way from Marly, and much gold as well as water ran through the
conduit! Still, the essential aim was achieved, for at Trianon the
streamlet meandered just as if it had cut its own way. Flowing gently
down into an artificial pond adorned with an artificial island, the
waters burbled on agreeably beneath graceful bridges, and were deep
enough to become the haunt of dignified swans. A rock which might
have formed the theme of anacreontic verses reared its noble head,
surmounted by a romantic belvedere, hollowed by an artificial cave
and its flanks coated with artificially implanted moss. There was nothing to show that this touchingly simple scene had been designed upon
countless water-colour drawings; or that the whole lay-out had been
foreshadowed by twenty plaster models, wherein the pond and the
streamlet were represented by fragments of looking-glass, the fields and
the trees as in a jig-saw puzzle by painted and adhesive imagery.

But this first installation was by no means the last. Every year the
Queen had some new fancy for beautifying her miniature kingdom
with more highly artificial and more "natural" additions and altera-
tions. She would not wait until the old bills had been paid before
incurring fresh obligations; she had found a congenial amusement and
wished to make the most of it. Ostensibly casual in their appearance,
but in truth carefully designed by her artificers, further expensive trifles
were continually being added to the garden, in order to enhance its
charm. A tiny temple, consecrated to the god of those days, a temple
of love, crowned a hillock; in its open classical rotunda was one of
Bouchardon's finest sculptures, a Cupid carving his deadly bow out
of the club of Hercules. The aforesaid love-grotto in the rock was
skilfully provided with loopholes, so that a pair that had sought this
retirement for amorous dalliance could glimpse any approaching intruders and escape being taken by surprise. Winding paths led through
the little wood; the lawns were planted with rare exotic flowers; and
ere long one could notice amid the greenery a small music pavilion,
a beautiful octagon of white marble. These various enchantments were

so gracefully, so tastefully intertwined into a whole, that, in very truth, their extreme artificiality became inconspicuous. But the fashion demanded yet more genuineness than this. In order to make nature more natural than ever, in order to provide the most refined side-shows which should have the absolute veracity of life, various supers were engaged to intensify the genuineness of this expensive pastoral comedy: real peasants of both sexes; real milkmaids with real cows, real calves and pigs and rabbits and sheep, real scythemen and reapers and shepherds and hunters and launderers and cheese-makers—to mow lawns and wash clothes and manure the soil and milk the cows, so that the puppet-show should proceed in lively fashion.

Dipping deeper than before into the public purse, Marie Antoinette had a life-size stage built hard by Trianon for these spoiled children out of a bandbox—the famous "Hameau," fully provided with byres and hayricks and barns, with dove-cots and fowl-houses. Mique, the distinguished architect, and Hubert Robert, the famous painter, designed, and superintended the building of, eight little peasant farms, true to type, with thatched roofs, farmyards and dung-heaps, all complete. Lest these fire-new make-believes should appear spurious amid the costly pretence of their "natural" surroundings, it was thought advisable to imitate (as far as externals were concerned) the poverty and decay of the actual dwellings of the countryfolk. Rifts were made in the walls; the plaster was romantically chipped away in patches; shingles were ripped off here and there. Hubert Robert painted cracks' in the woodwork, so that it might seem touched by the hand of time; and the chimneys were carefully smoked. So much for externals. Within, however, these apparently ruinous cottages were equipped with every possible convenience; with mirrors and stoves, with billiard-tables and comfortable couches. All must be clean and in perfect order.

When Marie Antoinette, bored beyond measure or suffering from a fit of the blues, felt impelled to play Jean Jacques Rousseau, and, with some of her court ladies, to undertake the "work" of butter-making, there must be nothing that could soil her fingers. If she visited Brunette and Blanchette in the cow-house, it need hardly be said that before her coming the floor had been sedulously cleaned by an unseen hand, that the beasts' hides had been curried and combed with the utmost care so that one looked like alabaster and the other like mahogany, and that the foaming milk was received, not in the wooden buckets used by ordinary peasants, but in porcelain vases made at Sèvres and adorned with the Queen's monogram.

This Hameau, today a lovely ruin, was for Marie Antoinette an out-of-doors theatre, the site of a stimulating comédie champêtre. At a time when, throughout France, the unhappy peasants were beginning to grow riotous, when the real countryfolk, crushed by the burden of taxation, were uproariously demanding relief from their intolerable miseries—in this Potemkin side-show there prevailed a preposterous and mendacious comfort. Sheep were led to pasture by ribbons of blue silk tied round their necks. The Queen, with a parasol held over her head by one of her ladies, came to look on sometimes while the washer-women did their work in the rippling brook. This simplicity was so splendid, so moral, so agreeable; everything was so clean and charming in this little paradise; life here was as bright and resplendent as the milk which spurted from the cows' udders. Marie Antoinette wore dresses of thin muslin, rural in their simplicity, and had herself painted in them for a few thousand livres a picture. She enjoyed the most innocent pleasures, cultivating the "goût de la nature" with all the frivolousness of satiety. She fished; she culled flowers; she went walking (rarely alone) along the winding paths; she ran across the lawns; she watched her "good peasants" at their work; she played catch-ball. She and her intimates danced minuets and gavottes upon the flower-bespangled turf instead of upon parquet flooring; they hung swings between the trees; they played hide-and-seek among the cottages and in the shady paths; they rode, amused themselves in countless ways, and had little dramas staged in this natural theatre, being audience and actors by turns.

The passion for private theatricals was the most recent of Queen Marie Antoinette's discoveries. She had begun by the building of a tiny private theatre (which still stands, and is beautiful in its lovely surroundings) for performances by Italian and French companies. This caprice cost her 141,000 livres. Then she was suddenly bitten by the idea of appearing herself on the boards. Her light-hearted companions were ready enough to share her enthusiasm for the new venture. Her brother-in-law the Count of Artois, Madame de Polignac, and other members of the court circle were delighted to join in the frolic. The King put in an appearance several times in order to admire his wife's performances as leading lady. After this innovation, it was carnival-time at Trianon all through the year. Festivals were held in honour of her royal spouse, of his brothers, and then in honour of foreign guests of royal rank to whom Marie Antoinette wished to show off her magic realm. On these occasions coloured glass lanterns —amethyst, ruby, and topaz—twinkled out of the darkness among the trees; there were splendid firework displays; and the strains of sweet music sounded from the middle distance. Banquets were served to hundreds of guests; booths were built in which could be enjoyed "all the fun of the fair"; the guileless landscape served as a refined background to riotous luxury. There was no need for a "natural life" to be tedious. Marie Antoinette had not come to the Trianon in order to go into retreat or in order to live a life of reflection, but simply that she might amuse herself better and with more freedom from restraint.

The final account for the Trianon was not cast up until August 31, 1791. The total was 1,649,529 livres; but in reality, if various ignored items are added in, the total amount was more than two millions. This no doubt was merely a drop in the Danaid sieve of the royal unthrift and general mismanagement of expenditure; still, it was a preposterous sum in view of the disorder of French finances and of the poverty that prevailed throughout the land. When on trial before the Revolutionary Tribunal, the "Widow Capet" had to admit: "It is likely enough that the Little Trianon cost huge sums of money, and perhaps more than I intended, for I gradually became involved in unexpected disbursements."

In the political field, as well, the Queen had to pay dearly for her caprices. By leaving the camarilla to its own devices at Versailles, she robbed court life of vital significance. The lady whose function it was to hand her her gloves, and the one who reverently placed the nightstool for the Queen's use; the maids of honour and the knights of honour; the thousand guardsmen, servants, and other underlings— what was left for them to do when the Queen spent all her time at Trianon? Day after day they sat unoccupied in the Œil de Bœuf, the guardroom, and the servants' hall; and, just as a machine unused is eaten up by rust, so did this neglected court become ever more

dangerously envenomed with gall. Ere long matters had reached such
a pass that, by a tacit understanding, good society began to keep away
from court festivals. The arrogant "Austrian woman" might amuse
herself as best she pleased in her "little Schönbrunn," in her "little
Vienna," but she must do it alone. The French nobility, as ancient as
the Habsburgs, had too good an opinion of itself to be satisfied with
occasional bowing and scraping at a formal reception. More and more
conspicuous, more and more plain-spoken, became the new Fronde,
the "cave" that was formed by the blue-bloods of France against the
Queen after she had forsaken Versailles. The Duc de Lévis has given
us a lively account of the position.

"In an age of pleasure and frivolity, intoxicated by supreme power,
the Queen had no fancy for submitting herself to constraint, and she
found court ceremony tedious. It seemed clear to her that in so enlightened a century, when prejudices had been whistled down the
wind, the occupants of a throne could free themselves from the shackles
which custom had imposed upon them. She thought it absurd to
suppose that the loyalty of the common people could depend upon
the number of hours which the royal family spent in a circle of bored
and boring courtiers. . . . Except for a few favourites, chosen for some
whim or because of a successful intrigue, everyone was excluded from
the royal presence. Rank, service, repute, birth, were no longer warrants for admission into the intimacies of the reigning family. Only on
Sundays could persons furnished with proper introductions see Their
Majesties for a few minutes. But most of those to whom this privilege
was granted soon found it nothing better than a corvée, since they
were given no thanks for putting themselves about to attend at court.
Coming to realize that it was foolish to make a long journey merely
in order to secure an ungracious reception, they preferred to stay at
home. . . . Versailles, a scene of such magnificence in the days of
Louis XIV, when all Europe was eager to come thither for lessons in
good taste and good manners, now became nothing more than a minor
provincial town, which one visited with reluctance and whence one
departed as speedily as possible."

From afar, Maria Theresa had been quick to recognize the danger:
"I know well enough how tedious and futile is a representative position; but, believe me, you will have to put up with both tediousness

and futility, for otherwise you will suffer from much more serious inconveniences than these petty burdens—you more than most rulers, since you have to queen it over so techy a nation."

But when Marie Antoinette did not want to understand, those who tried to reason with her were wasting breath. What a fuss her mother and the rest of them were making because she preferred to live a mile away from Versailles! Yet the truth of it was that this mile severed her for life from her court and from her people. Had Marie Antoinette continued to hold her court at Versailles, surrounded by the French nobility and amid the customary pomps and ceremonies, in the hour of peril she would have had the support of her royal relatives and of all the distinguished and powerful persons in France. If, on the other hand, she had followed the example of her brother Joseph, and had democratically endeavoured to get into touch with the common people, she would have been idolized by hundreds of thousands of Parisians and by the millions of the inhabitants of France. But Marie Antoinette, individualist to the core, cared nothing about making herself agreeable either to the aristocracy or to the plebs; she thought only of herself, and, thanks to this caprice which made her withdraw to the Trianon, she became unpopular with all ranks. Because she was too eager to be alone in her happiness, she was alone in her unhappiness; and she had to pay with her crown and her head for her devotion to a childish toy.

CHAPTER X

The New Society

SCARCELY had Marie Antoinette settled into her bright and cheerful abode, when she began to ply a new broom. The first thing was to get rid of the elders, for old people were wearisome and ugly. They could not dance; they could not take life easily; they were continually preaching foresight and thoughtfulness, whereas the Queen had had more than enough of leading-strings and lectures in her days as Dauphiness. Away, then, with her strict governess, Madame Etiquette, the Comtesse de Noailles; a queen no longer needs a governess, for she can do whatever she likes! Abbé Vermond, the confessor and counsellor provided by her mother, the instructor who was to see to it that she conned her lessons diligently, must keep his due distance now. She wanted young people around her, merry folk, who would not spoil sport by the foolishness of taking life too seriously. It really mattered very little whether these amusing companions were persons of high rank, of good family, of blameless character; nor did the Queen care whether they were able and cultured, for cultured people were generally pedantic and tiresome. Enough that her associates should be witty, should be able to tell spicy stories, and should cut a good figure at parties. Entertainment, entertainment, entertainment—that was Marie Antoinette's first and last demand from her intimates. She surrounded herself, therefore, "with all that is worst and youngest in Paris," as Maria Theresa exclaimed with a sigh; or, to quote her brother, Joseph II, she became the centre of a "soi-disante société" which seemed to him to consist of most undesirable persons. Ostensibly disinterested, they really formed a coterie of place-hunters who, while ministering to the Queen's pleasure, were able to obtain for themselves fat sinecures, or, amid a profusion of gallantries, sought opportunities for pouching lucrative pensions.

There was, indeed, one prize bore who from time to time marred the serenity of the gay circle. He could hardly be kept out of it, for (though the fact was almost ignored) he was the husband of this lively woman, and, furthermore, the monarch of France. Honestly in love with his charming spouse, Louis the complaisant, having been careful to ask permission, would visit Trianon; would watch how the young folks were amusing themselves; would, now and then, put in a word of timid protest when the conventions were too flagrantly disregarded or when the disbursements were piled up beyond reasonable measure. On such occasions, however, the Queen merely laughed, and her laugh put an end to the discussion. Besides, the cheerful company of idlers had a sort of contemptuous liking for the King, who was ready to sign "Louis" at the foot of the decrees with which Queen Marie Antoinette assigned them well-paid posts. The good fellow did not give any trouble. He remained for an hour, or perhaps as long as two hours, and then he toddled back to Versailles, to his books or to his smithy. Once, when he overstayed his welcome, and the Queen was fretting to start for Paris with her gay companions, she secretly put on the clock an hour, and the King, not noticing the fraud, went home obediently to bed at ten o'clock instead of eleven, while the elegant rabble laughed uproariously as soon as his back was turned.

It need hardly be said that such jests did not tend to promote the conception of royal dignity. But what could Trianon make of so ungainly, so clownish a man? When anecdotes were in question, he could not cap "a good one" by a better; and there was no laughter in his composition. Timid and shy, looking as if he had a belly-ache, he sat yawning and tired out among those who did not become really lively before midnight. He never went to masked balls; he did not play hazard; he did not pay court to any of the ladies. No one had any use for this excellent but tedious creature, who was utterly out of his element in the society at Trianon, in the realm of the Rococo, in the Arcady of giddiness and high spirits.

The King, then, did not count as participator in the new society. His brother, the Count of Provence, who hid ambition behind a mask of indifference, likewise thought it more prudent to avoid compromising his dignity by associating with these young madcaps. Since it was necessary that some male representative of the royal family should accompany the Queen in her pleasurings, the Count of Artois, Louis XVI's youngest brother, took over the office of guardian angel. Shallowpated, frivolous, impudent, but subtle and not without cleverness of a kind, he suffered from the same dread as Marie Antoinette and was affected with the same disinclination—the dread of being bored, and the disinclination for occupying his mind with serious topics. A libertine, a spendthrift, amusing and elegantly dressed, vainglorious, superficial rather than deeply stirred by passion, he was the leader of the company whenever there was question of some new sport, some new fashion, some new pleasure; with the result that he soon had more debts than the King, the Queen, and the whole court put together. These qualities, however, made him a fit companion for Marie Antoinette. In truth she neither liked him nor loved him, although there was much gossip at court about their relations. The real fact was that he was able to act for her as a sort of rearguard in her extravagances. Brother and sister-in-law being drawn together by their mania for pleasure, they speedily became inseparable.

The Count of Artois, therefore, was the chosen commander of the bodyguard upon Marie Antoinette's daily and nightly excursions in the realm of amusement. The circle of madcaps was a small one, and, except for the brother-in-law, there were perpetual changes in the leading posts. The Queen was indulgent to nearly all offences on the part of her satellites; to their debts and to their arrogant pretensions; to their challenging and unduly familiar conduct; to their love-affairs and to the scandals in which they often became involved. But there was one thing she could not forgive, and that was when they began to bore her. For a time Baron Besenval was first in her good graces, a Swiss nobleman of fifty with the domineering ways of an old soldier; thereafter she gave the preference to the Duc de Coigny, "un des plus constamment favorisés et le plus consultés." These worthies, in conjunction with the ambitious Duc de Guines and the Hungarian Count Esterhazy, were entrusted with the remarkable duty of consoling the Queen when she was suffering from an attack of German measles—whereon tongues wagged with the malicious inquiry which four from among the court ladies King Louis would select to nurse him if he were in a like situation.

A fixed star in this firmament was the Comte de Vaudreuil, lover of Marie Antoinette's favourite companion, Madame de Polignac. Somewhat in the background remained the shrewdest and the most refined of the whole band, the Prince de Ligne, the only one who did not feather his nest while at the Trianon, and also the only one to preserve respectful memories of the Queen, as shown by what he wrote about her in the memoirs published in his old age. Variable stars in the constellation at Trianon were "handsome" Dillon and the young hothead the Duc de Lauzun, both of whom were for a time risky companions of a queen who was still a virgin against her will. Mercy, the Austrian ambassador, was hard put to it to get the Duc de Lauzun out of Marie Antoinette's entourage before he had won something more than her sympathy. Comte Adhémar could sing prettily to his own accompaniment on the harp, and he was a good actor; qualifications which sufficed to make him envoy to Brussels and then ambassador in London. Few of these courtiers, however, went far afield, most of them preferring to remain in close proximity to their royal patroness and to secure remunerative positions at court. Not one of them, with the solitary exception of the Prince de Ligne, was a man of intelligence; not one of them tried to make a worthy political use of the power which Marie Antoinette's friendship gave him; not one of these masquerade heroes of the Trianon became a real heroic figure upon the stage of world history. Nor had Marie Antoinette a true respect for any of them (with the before-mentioned exception), It cannot be doubted that this young and coquettish woman allowed them more freedoms than were becoming in view of her position as queen, but the decisive fact remains that neither in mind nor in body did she wholly surrender herself. He who was to hold a unique position in her affections, the only man who was ever to stir her heart profoundly, was still hidden in the shadow of a coming time. We may well suppose that the bustle of the supernumeraries who surrounded her must have assisted to hide his proximity and his presence.

More dangerous to the Queen than these untrustworthy and transitory cavaliers were Marie Antoinette's women friends, for here strangely mingled affective energies played a sinister part. By temperament Toinette was a thoroughly natural, an essentially feminine woman, gentle, tender, ready to surrender herself to the embraces of the male; but during these first years of her married life her inefficient husband was unable to gratify her physiological requirements. Forthright by disposition, she had need of someone who would relieve her spiritual and bodily tensions, and since, for propriety's sake, she would not (or would not yet) seek it from a man, Marie Antoinette at this juncture involuntarily turned towards a woman friend.

It was natural enough that a tone of tender affection should be manifest in the Queen's friendships with women. At sixteen, at seventeen, at eighteen, Marie Antoinette, though ostensibly a married woman, was of an age when girls at boarding-schools are typically predisposed towards passionate friendship one for another—and, though married, she had not yet been deprived of her maidenhood. Taken early from her mother and separated from a governess to whom she was sincerely attached, wedded to a man who was neither competent from the physical point of view nor affectionate from the spiritual, she had, as a matter of course, the inclination to find relief in a passion for somebody, for anybody, a longing which is as appropriate to the nature of a girl as its perfume is to a flower; and hitherto this passion had not found vent. The girlish trivialities of walking hand-in-hand, or with arms round one another's waists, giggling together in a corner, romping up and down a room with one of her own sex and age, the formation of a mutual admiration society of two maidens—such simple manifestations of springtime had not as yet blossomed in her youthful body. At sixteen, at seventeen, at eighteen, at nineteen, at twenty, Marie Antoinette had not experienced one of these youthful enthusiasms in which what is most manifest is, not the sexual element (though this may be stormy enough), but a timid enthusiasm which is the premonition of a true sexual awakening.

It was only to be expected, I repeat, that Marie Antoinette's first relationships with women friends should be strongly tinged by the tender emotion—and it was also natural that at the French court, where the French attitude towards matters sexual was dominant, such unconventional behaviour on the part of a queen should be grossly misinterpreted. Cultivated to excess, nay perverted, the French courtiers and court ladies were incapable of understanding these natural manifestations, so that it was not long before whispers began to circulate concerning the Queen's Sapphic inclinations. "There have very generally been ascribed to me two tastes, that for women and that for lovers," writes Marie Antoinette, self-assured, frankly, and serenely to her mother; straightforwardly and even arrogantly despising the court, public opinion, and the world. She had not yet become acquainted with the thousand-tongued power of calumny; she was still able to give herself unreservedly to the delight of being at length able to love someone, to confide in someone; and she threw caution to the winds in the determination to show her women friends with what absolute devotion she could let her heart go out to them.

The Queen's first favourite, Madame de Lamballe, was a comparatively fortunate choice. Belonging to one of the best families of France, and therefore with no greed either for money or for power; endowed with a tender and sentimental disposition, not overburdened with brains, but for that reason having no taste for intrigue; a person of little account, and quite free from ambition—she responded to Marie Antoinette's affection with sincere friendship. Her morals were above reproach; her influence was restricted to the Queen's private life; she did not demand places for her friends or for her relatives; she made no attempt to meddle with affairs of State. She did not run a gaming-table, did not involve Marie Antoinette more deeply in the hunt for pleasure, but was tranquilly and unobtrusively loyal, until (amid the general break-up of the old regime) her death during the September massacres put the seal on her friendship.

One evening, however, her fire was suddenly extinguished as a candle is blown out. At a court ball during the year 1775 the Queen noticed a young woman with whom she had not previously been acquainted, rendered touching by a modest grace, with a face pure as an angel's and a delicately girlish figure. Inquiring who the stranger was, Marie Antoinette was informed that it was the wife of Jules de Polignac. The passion she conceived for the Comtesse de Polignac was not, like her fondness for the Princesse de Lamballe, the outcome of a human sympathy gradually increasing to become a friendship, but a sudden and overwhelming interest, a clap of thunder, a sort of superheated falling in love. Going up to the young lady, the Queen asked her why she so seldom appeared at court. "I am not well enough off to figure on State occasions," replied the Comtesse de Polignac artlessly. The Queen was charmed by such sincerity, for how pure of soul must be the bewitching woman who could unhesitatingly avow a lack of means which was regarded in those days as the supreme disgrace! Was not this the ideal, the long-desired friend? Instantly Marie Antoinette invited the Comtesse de Polignac to become a regular attendant at court, showing so marked a preference for her as to arouse general envy. The Queen walked about arm-in-arm with her, had her to stay at Versailles, insisted on her constant companionship, and once actually removed the whole court to Marly simply in order to be close at hand during her friend's confinement. Within a few months, the impoverished noblewoman had become supreme, not only over Marie Antoinette, but likewise over the whole circle in which the Queen moved.

Unfortunately, however, this tender and innocent angel had not come down from heaven but sprang from a family up to the eyes in debt and one which was eager to turn such unexpected favour to pecuniary account, so that it was not long before the minister of finance could have told a pretty tale about the matter. To begin with, debts were paid to the tune of 400,000 livres; the daughter received 800,000 livres as dowry; the son-in-law was given a commission as captain, and a year later a landed estate as well, bringing in an income of seventy thousand ducats; the father was granted a pension; while the complaisant husband, who had really long since been replaced by a lover, received the title of duke, and one of the most lucrative positions in France, that of postmaster-general. The sister-in-law, Diane de Polignac, though a woman of bad reputation, became one of the Queen's ladies-in-waiting; Comtesse Jules, in due time, was allotted the position of governess to the royal children; her father, as if the pension were not enough, was appointed ambassador; the whole family wallowed in money and in honours, and was able, over and above this, to empty a cornucopia filled with privileges into the greedy hands of their friends. In the end, through this one whimsy of the Queen's, the Polignac family came to cost the State half a million livres a year. "Almost unexampled," wrote Mercy to Vienna, much out of humour, "is it that in so short a time the royal favour should have brought such overwhelming advantages to a family." Not even Madame de Maintenon, not even the Pompadour, cost as much as this favourite, this angel with downcast eyes, this modest and gentle Polignac.

Those who were not themselves swept into the whirlpool, stood at the marge contemplating it with astonishment, unable to understand the abandonment with which the Queen allowed her name, her position, her reputation to be misused for the benefit of this gang of plunderers. Everyone knew that Marie Antoinette, in respect of mental endowments, energy, and uprightness, was worth a hundred of the worthless creatures who constituted her daily entourage. However, when character vies with character, what becomes decisive is skill rather than force, strength of will rather than intelligence. Marie Antoinette was slack whilst the Polignacs had a keen eye to the main chance; she was easy-going and they were tenacious; she stood alone, whereas they had consolidated themselves into a clique which deliberately kept the Queen away from the rest of the court; they held her in their toils by ministering to her craze for amusement. Of what avail was it that her poor old confessor Vermond should reprove his sometime pupil by saying: "You are not strict enough regarding the morality and the reputation of your friends male and female"; or that, with remarkable boldness, he should add: "Misconduct of all kinds, immorality, a tarnished or a lost reputation, seem to be titles for admission to your society!" Such words of admonition counted for nothing as against affectionate prattle when Marie Antoinette strolled arm-in-arm with her favourite; prudent counsel was effectively counteracted by persistent and calculated cunning. Madame de Polignac and her clan had discovered the open sesame when they discovered how to entertain the Queen, how to relieve her sense of tedium; and after a few years Marie Antoinette had become utterly enslaved by this cold and designing band. In Madame de Polignac's salon, one would support another's application for a well-paid post. They reciprocally endorsed each other's requests for pensions and sinecures, regardless, to all seeming, of their own private welfare. The upshot was, that, while the Queen took no heed, the last golden trickles among the drying well-springs of the State treasury continued to pour their riches into the hands of a few. The ministers of State were helpless in face of these intrigues. "Faites parler la reine"—"Do your best to ensure that Her Majesty shall show you favour"—they answered, shrugging their shoulders, whenever anyone asked them a favour. Rank and title, positions and pensions, were now granted in France by Marie Antoinette alone, and the Queen's hand, in these matters, was invisibly guided by the violet-eyed, the lovely, the gentle Polignac.

Fostering her pleasure, the clan surrounded Marie Antoinette by an insurmountable barrier. Others at court were not slow to perceive it, realizing that behind this wall lay the Earthly Paradise. There posts were granted; there pensions were to be had for the asking; there, with a merry jest, with a well-turned compliment, could be secured a favour for which others had fought for decades and done yeoman's service. In that blessed precinct there prevailed perpetual cheerfulness, joy, freedom from care; and all the treasures and graces of the world awaited one who could find his way into the Elysian fields of the royal favour. Need we be surprised that there was increasing bitterness among those who were kept outside the enclosure; the members of the old, the accredited, the meritorious nobility, who had not the entry to the Trianon, and whose palms (likewise itching) were never soothed by the golden rain? "Are we then of less account than these impoverished Polignacs?" murmured the Orléans, the Rohans, the Noailles, the Marsans. "Now that we at length have a young, a modest, well-behaved King, one who is not the plaything of his mistresses, now that it is no longer necessary to woo the favour of the Pompadour or the Dubarry, are we still expected to seek the good graces of a she-favourite in order to get what belongs to us by right and tradition? Shall we continue to put up with being thus cold-shouldered or ignored by the young woman from Austria whose chosen companions are youths from foreign parts and women of dubious reputation, when, if she knew the dignity of her station, she would consort with noblemen and noblewomen of native birth and ancient lineage?" The excluded closed their ranks, and day by day they became more numerous. It was not long before, from the desolate windows of Versailles, hatred with a hundred eyes glowered at the lightsome and unsuspecting play-world of the Queen.

CHAPTER XI

A Fraternal Visit

Towards the close of the year 1776 and at the carnival of 1777 Marie Antoinette's pleasure-hunt attained its climax. The Queen was never missing at a horse-race, a dance at the Opera House, a masked ball. She never got home until day had dawned, and she persistently avoided the marriage-bed. Till four in the morning she would sit at the gaming-table, her losses and her debts the topic of general condemnation. In despair, Mercy sent dispatch after dispatch to Vienna: "Her Majesty has utterly forgotten her dignity. . . . It seems impossible to show her the error of her ways . . . the different varieties of pleasure follow one another with such rapidity that it is hard to find a moment in which to speak to her of serious matters." It was long, he said, since Versailles had been so deserted as during this winter. During the last month, the occupations of the Queen, or rather her pleasures, had neither changed nor diminished. It was as if an evil demon had taken possession of the young woman; never had her restlessness been more crazy than in this decisive year.

Now a new danger threatened. In 1777 Marie Antoinette was no longer the simple girl of fifteen who had arrived in France to play the part of Dauphiness. She was two-and-twenty, voluptuously beautiful, an extremely attractive woman, and it would have been unnatural if she had remained cold and unmoved amid the erotic, the sensually overstimulating atmosphere of the Versailles court.

Her female relatives who were more or less of the same age as herself, her women friends, had long since borne children; every one of them had a really effective husband, or at least lovers. She alone, more beautiful than them all, more desirable and perhaps more desirous than any member of her circle, excluded from amatory relationships by the unfortunate condition of her husband, had never yet allowed her feelings to go out to a man in self-surrender. She had tried to gratify her longing for the tender passion by diverting it towards members of her own sex, to enter into intimate personal relationships which should relieve her from the vacancy and tedium of court society. But this did not suffice her; and since she was a thoroughly natural and normal woman, nature began to claim its rights.

More and more, in her association with the young gentlemen of her circle, Marie Antoinette began to lose the untroubled confidence of her early poise. True, she still shrank from going to extremes; but she was continually playing with fire, and in this sport she could not control her treacherous blood. She grew pale and red by turns; she trembled in the proximity of these youths whom she unconsciously desired; she was confused at times; her eyes brimming over with tears, and she had an ever-renewed craving for gallant compliments. We read in Lauzun's memoirs of a remarkable scene in which, after she had just lost her temper with him, Marie Antoinette suddenly flung her arms round him, and then, frightened and ashamed, fled from the spot. This account has the stamp of truth, and there is also a report from the Swedish ambassador relating to her manifest passion for young Count Fersen which discloses the same condition of amorous irritability. It was plain that this sexually ungratified woman was nearing the limits of self-control. Although she tried to fight down her passions, and perhaps because she tried to fight them down, her nerves could no longer endure the hidden tension.

As if to fill in the details of the clinical picture, Mercy at this juncture was reporting to Vienna that the Queen suffered from sudden attacks of "affectations nerveuses," or what in those days were termed "the vapours." For the time being, the consideration of her squires saved Marie Antoinette from going to the extreme of an actual breach of the marriage bond, for Lauzun and Fersen fled the court as soon as they perceived that the Queen's interest in them was passing the bounds of decorum. There can be no doubt, however, that if either of these young men with whom she had flirted so liberally had chosen to push his suit in a favourable moment, he would have found little difficulty in effecting the conquest of a virtue which was no longer vigorously defended from within. Up till now Marie Antoinette had been lucky enough to be saved from the last decisive step. But the danger was ever more imminent; the moth was fluttering nearer and nearer to the candle-flame; another flap or two of the wings, and rescue from the destructive element would have become impossible.

Did the watch-dog set on guard over her by her mother know of this danger? Presumably he did, for his warnings against Lauzun, Dillon, and Esterhazy, make it clear that the experienced old bachelor had a better understanding of the real causes of Marie Antoinette's trouble than she had herself. He realized, too, what a catastrophe it would be if the Queen of France were to give herself to the embraces of an illicit lover before she had presented her husband with a lawful heir. This disaster must be averted at all costs. Mercy, therefore, sent a dispatch to Vienna begging Emperor Joseph to come to Versailles and see if he could set matters right. The Queen must, if possible, be rescued from herself.

Joseph II's journey to Paris had a threefold aim. It was his purpose to have a heart-to-heart talk with the King, his brother-in-law, concerning the ticklish subject of Louis's non-fulfilment of his essential duties as a husband. Secondly, with the authority of an elder brother, Joseph designed to give his pleasure-loving sister a scolding which should make her fully aware of the risk both political and personal in which she was becoming involved. Thirdly, by renewing the ties with the little sister he had not seen for seven years, he would cement the alliance between the ruling houses of France and Austria.

These three tasks were imposed on him by reasons of State. Joseph II, however, had a fourth object, a private one; he wanted to turn his visit to account in order to make of himself a more striking figure in the world, and to arouse the utmost possible admiration for his own personality. Essentially honourable and straightforward, fairly able though not highly talented, above all excessively vain, he had for years suffered from a malady of the spirit which is characteristic of crown princes. He was annoyed because, though a grown-up man, he was still unable to rule as he thought fit; because on the political stage he was eclipsed by his famous and greatly admired mother; because, as he bitterly expressed it, he was only "a fifth wheel on the coach." Precisely because he knew that it would always remain impossible for him to excel Maria Theresa in ability and in moral authority, precisely because he was aware that so long as his mother lived his part would be a subordinate one, he wanted to make this subordinate role as conspicuous as possible. Since, in the eyes of Europe, she embodied the heroic conception of

sovereign power, he would be the "people's emperor," the modern, philanthropic, unprejudiced, enlightened father of his country. Donning
a smock, he walked behind the plough-tail; wearing the dress of an
ordinary citizen, he would mingle with the crowd; just to see what it
was like, he had himself locked up for a time in the Spielberg—being
careful that the whole world should know of these exhibitions of modesty and simplicity. Until now, however, Joseph II had only been able
to play the affable caliph before an audience of his own subjects. The
journey to Paris at length gave him a chance to strut the boards in
view of a wider world. For weeks in advance the Emperor had been
studying how best to play Modesty with the utmost refinement of
detail.

In some measure Emperor Joseph was able to fulfil this private purpose. He did not, of course, succeed in cheating history. His record on
the debit side shows mistake after mistake: the hasty introduction of
half-baked reforms, disastrous crudities; and perhaps the only thing
that delivered Austria from a ruin that was already threatening was
his premature death. But legend is kindlier and more credulous than
history, and in the domain of legend he prevailed. For a long time
tales were current about the "people's emperor." Shilling-shockers
galore describe how a distinguished-looking unknown, wrapped in a
plain mantle, performed gracious deeds and loved a simple country
maiden. The end of these novelettes is always the same: the unknown
throws back the flap of his cloak, and the onlookers see beneath it,
with astonishment, a gay uniform. The stranger goes on his way with
the profound remark: "You will never know my name; I am the
Emperor Joseph!"

Absurd as the phrase sounds, it is based upon a trustworthy instinct,
for, with a touch almost of genius, it caricatures Joseph's peculiarities.
On the one hand he wished to play Modesty; and, on the other hand,
he had an itch that he should be duly admired for this same modesty.
His journey to Paris was characteristic in this respect. On no account
would he travel as Emperor Joseph II. He did not wish to attract attention to himself. He went "incognito" as Count Falkenstein; and much
stress was laid upon the importance of respecting his privacy. It was
carefully, tediously prescribed that no one, not even the King of France

was to address him in any other way than as "Monsieur." He did not wish to stay in palaces, and would only make use of ordinary post-chaises for his conveyance. It need hardly be said that every court in Europe was kept fully informed as to his movements! At Stuttgart, the Duke of Württemberg played him a scurvy trick, issuing orders that the signboards should be taken down from the inns, so that the "people's emperor" had no option but to sleep in the ducal palace.

All the same, the new Haroun al Rashid maintained his incognito which was no incognito with the utmost strictness to the very end. Driving into Paris in an ordinary fiacre, he put up at the Hôtel de Tréville, today the Hôtel Foyot, registering under the name of Count Falkenstein. When he reached Versailles, he hired a room in a second-rate sort of house, sleeping there, as if at the fighting-front, in a camp-bed, covered only by his cloak. Nor was he mistaken in his calculations. To the common folk of Paris, whose King lived always in the lap of luxury, a ruler of this sort seemed very remarkable indeed. A sensation was created by an emperor who went to the infirmaries and tasted the soup served to the inmates; who attended the sittings of the Academies; became an auditor at the Parliament of Paris; associated with boatmen and shopkeepers; inspected the Deaf-and-Dumb Institute, went to the Botanical Gardens, was shown over a soap factory, hob-nobbed with handicraftsmen. Joseph saw a great deal in Paris—and was delighted to be the cynosure of all eyes. He charmed everyone by his affable behaviour, and was himself even more charmed by the enthusiastic approval his friendliness encountered. One of the strangest elements of his strange character was that he was fully aware of the mingling of the false and true in his play-acting, for he wrote from Paris to his brother Leopold: "You are worth more than I am, but I am more of a charlatan, and in this country one must be that. I am simple by set purpose and from modesty, deliberately over-playing my part, with the result that I have aroused an enthusiasm which I find positively embarrassing. I have had a pleasant time here, but I am well content to leave, having had enough of my role."

Over and above achieving a personal triumph, Joseph was able to fulfil his political aims. Above all he had much less difficulty than he had expected in the discussion of the ticklish subject with his brother-in-law. Louis XVI, straightforward and cheerful, was perfectly frank with Joseph. Frederick the Great had tried to queer the pitch by instructing his ambassador Baron Goltz to make it widely known in Paris that Emperor Joseph had written to him (Frederick): "I have three brothers-in-law who are all contemptible creatures: the one at Versailles is feeble-minded; the one in Naples is a fool; and the one in Parma is an idiot." In this instance the "bad neighbour" was unsuccessful in his attempts to sow discord, for Louis XVI had not a trace of vanity, and the poisoned shaft could not penetrate the armour of his good nature. The brothers-in-law had some straight talk, and, on closer acquaintance with Louis XVI, Joseph II could not but find something to respect in him. "The man is a weakling, but no fool. He has some ideas of his own, and a fair measure of sound judgment, but is apathetic both in mind and in body. His conversation is sensible enough, but he has no taste for culture and is devoid of curiosity. For him the 'fiat lux' has never yet been spoken, and the matter of which he is made is still without form and void." Within a few days of his arrival, Joseph II had the King well in hand. The two came to a good understanding about political matters; and it is obvious that the Emperor must have found little difficulty in persuading his brother by marriage to submit to the operation needed for the cure of the phimosis.

More difficult, because more responsible, was Joseph's attitude towards Marie Antoinette. The sister had awaited her brother's visit with mixed feelings, happy that at length she was to have a chance of frank discussion with a blood relation, and the one she was fondest of; but also full of anxiety because of the blunt and didactic way in which the Emperor was prone to berate his little sister.

Writing to her not long before, he had scolded her as if she had been a schoolgirl: "What can you be thinking of to interfere in public affairs as you do; to dismiss ministers and appoint others in their place; to send one of them to rusticate in his country-seat; to create new and costly posts at court? Have you ever troubled to ask yourself what right you have to intervene in the affairs of the French government and the French monarchy? What studies have you made that entitle you to imagine your advice or opinion counts for anything, especially in public matters, which need wide knowledge? You are nothing more than an amiable young woman who never thinks of anything but her amusements, her dresses, her daily pastimes. You never read, never hear any-one talk sense for a quarter of an hour during a whole month, never think anything out, and, I am certain, never give a moment's reflection to the possible consequences of what you say or do." The spoiled dar-ling of the Trianon was not used to such scoldings, and we may well imagine that she must have had an attack of palpitation when the court chamberlain informed her that Count Falkenstein had reached Paris and next day would put in an appearance at Versailles.

But things passed off better than she had expected. Joseph II was diplomatic enough to refrain from playing Jupiter Tonans—at any rate to begin with. He paid her a few well-turned compliments concerning her charming appearance, saying that when the time came for him to marry he would like to have a wife as pretty as his sister. In fact he was the gallant rather than the elder brother. Maria Theresa had been as sound in her judgment as usual when, writing to Mercy shortly before this visit, she had said: "I am not afraid that he will take too harsh a view of the Queen's actions. What I dread rather is that, since she is so pretty and so charming, and since she can converse with so lively a wit, and so becomingly, she will meet with his approval (and that he himself will have his head turned a little by her flattery)."

That was what happened! The cordiality of his good-looking sister, her sincere delight at seeing him once again, the respect with which she listened to whatever he had to say, in conjunction with his brother-in-law's good nature and with the triumph he had secured through play-ing Modesty in Paris, sufficed to tie the dreaded pedant's tongue; the bear was tamed by being given plenty of honey. His first impression was a kindly one: "She is an amiable and refined woman, not quite grown up yet, little inclined to take careful thought; but fundamentally well behaved and virtuous, with a ready wit and an insight which has often surprised me. Her first impulse is always a sound one; and if she would only follow it, while giving a little more thought to the matter, and paying less heed to the legion of prompters by whom she is surrounded, she would be really perfect. She has, however, a strong leaning towards pleasure, and since her foible is well known, people play upon it, and she is always most ready to listen to those who can serve her turn in this respect."

While Joseph II seemed to be giving himself up unreservedly to the

enjoyment of the various festivals his sister had arranged for his welcome, he was, unnoticed, making his own shrewd observations. Above
all it became plain to him that Marie Antoinette had "no affection for
her husband." She was utterly indifferent to Louis, and treated him
with a most unbecoming disdain. Nor had the Emperor much difficulty
in discovering that she kept bad company, that she was a "giddy-pate"
for whom the Polignacs were most undesirable associates. In one
respect, however, he was relieved of his apprehensions. We may suppose, in view of King Louis's condition, that he had anticipated the
worst; but he now felt certain that, though she had flirted rather out-
rageously, his sister was still a virtuous woman, "enfin, jusqu'au
présent"—so far, at any rate. Notwithstanding the dissoluteness of those
with whom she kept company, her morality was in truth better than
her reputation. Still, after all that he had seen at the French court, he
could not but be uneasy about the future, and it seemed expedient to
say a few vigorous words of warning. Several times there were clashes
between the brother and the sister in public. For instance, on one occasion he told her roughly that she was of no use to her husband. Again,
he spoke of the Duchesse de Guémenée's card-room as "un vrai tripot,"
nothing better than a gambling-hell—and the duchess was one of the
Queen's intimates. But public reproof made Marie Antoinette extremely
angry, so that at times the sparring between brother and sister became
acrimonious. The young woman's defiant spirit resented such tutelage;
yet at the same time she could not but be aware of the justice of his
criticisms and reproaches, and she knew full well that her own weaknesses made trusty guardians of the sort eminently desirable.

It seems uncertain whether the two ever really talked matters out.
In a subsequent letter, doubtless, Joseph II reminded Marie Antoinette
of a certain conversation they had had when seated upon a stone bench;
but obviously he could not have come to the bottom of things on such
casual occasions. During his two months' stay in the country, Joseph II
achieved a general survey of France, learning far more of the country
than its King knew, and far more of his sister's perils than she herself
was aware of. But he also realized that, since her levity was incurable,
no admonitions would have any permanent effect; that in an hour
whatever he might say would have been forgotten, especially if she
wanted to forget. To influence her by word of mouth was impossible.

He therefore decided to draft an "instruction" which should embody his observations and reflections, and, in the hour of parting, he handed her this lengthy document (it ran to thirty pages) with the request that she should read it after his departure. "Litera scripta manet." His written warnings would remain to guide her after he had gone.

This "instruction" throws more light on Marie Antoinette's character than any other document which has come down to us, for Joseph II wrote in good faith and was animated by the best intentions. Though somewhat turgid in style and rather too preachy-preachy for modern taste, it manifests the writer's diplomatic adroitness, for the Emperor of Germany was careful to avoid giving a queen of France direct orders concerning her behaviour. He did no more than moot one question after another, writing a sort of catechism intended to make his sister (disinclined for serious thought) give her mind to matters of primary importance. He wanted to incite her towards self-knowledge and to awaken her sense of responsibility. Insensibly, however, the questions became an indictment, their apparently fortuitous succession concreting itself into a register of Marie Antoinette's sins of omission and commission. Above all, Joseph II reminded her how shockingly she had wasted her time.

"You are grown up now, and no longer have the excuse of being a child. What will happen, what will become of you, if you still hesitate?" With terrifying insight he answered his own question as follows: "An unhappy woman and a still more unhappy queen." Still in this question-and-answer form he recapitulated instance after instance of her remissness, throwing a cold and clear light upon her conduct towards the King. "Do you really seek opportunities? Do you honestly respond to the affection he manifests for you? Are you not cold, distrait, when he caresses you or when he speaks to you? Do you not show yourself bored, and even disgusted? This being so, how can you expect that a man of cold temperament should make advances to you and should love you warmly?" Inexorably he showed his sister, accusing her, though always in the interrogatory style, how, instead of subjecting herself to the King, she turned his clumsiness and weakness to account in order to make herself the centre of attention and to win success for herself instead of for her husband. "Do you try to make yourself necessary to him; do you endeavour to convince him that no one loves him more sincerely than you, and that no one has his glory and his happiness more at heart? . . . Do you ever suppress any of your own wishes for his sake? . . . Do you occupy yourself with matters which he has neglected in order to produce the impression that you are meritorious where he has failed? . . . Do you sacrifice yourself to him in any way? . . . Do you maintain an inviolable silence as concerns his errors and infirmities? Do you make appropriate excuses for them, imposing silence upon those who dare to allude to them?"

For page after page, Emperor Joseph dilates upon his sister's craze for pleasure: "Have you ever troubled to think of the effect which your friendships, your intimacies, may have upon the public if you fail (as you do) to give your esteem to persons who are in every respect irreproachable and trustworthy, seeing that in this way you produce the impression of participating in and authorizing vice? . . . Did you ever reflect upon the disastrous consequences of playing hazard as you do, on the bad company which assembles on these occasions, and of the tone which prevails? . . . Recall what has happened under your own eyes, and then bear in mind that the King never plays games of chance, and that it is therefore scandalous for you alone in the family to give such evil customs your support. . . . In like manner think for a moment of the contretemps you have had at the Opera balls, and of the misadventures there of which I have learned from your own lips. I will not hide from you my opinion that of all your amusements these are indubitably the most unseemly, especially in view of the fact that your squire on such occasions is your brother-in-law, who counts for nothing. What use, then, is there in going incognito, pretending to be someone other than you are? Do you honestly believe that you are not recognized? Really, everyone knows who you are; and, when you are masked, people say many things in your presence which it is not suitable for you to hear, but they are said to tickle your ears and to make you fancy that they have been said in all innocence. . . . The place has, in fact, a very evil reputation. Why, then, do you go? Do you want frank conversation? You cannot, in such circumstances, have a frank conversation with your friends, for the mask makes it impossible. Nor do you go there simply to dance. Why these escapades, this unseemliness? Why do you rub shoulders with a crowd of libertines, of loose women, of strangers, listening to improprieties, and perhaps uttering them? ... Really this sort of thing does not become you. ... I cannot but insist that it has been the chief cause of offence and scandal for those who are sincerely attached to you and whose thoughts run in respectable channels. The King is left alone all night at Versailles, while you defile yourself by mixing with the canaille of Paris!"

Joseph urgently reminded his sister of their mother's advice that she should improve her mind. It was surely time for Toinette to undertake some serious reading. Two hours a day would not be too much, and would make her shrewder and more reasonable for the remaining twenty-two hours out of the twenty-four. Then, in the course of these admonitions, of this lengthy sermon, comes a prophetic word which retains its full impressiveness today. If his sister does not follow his counsel, says Joseph II, he foresees disaster. Here are his actual words: "In very truth I tremble for your happiness, seeing that in the long run things cannot go on like this. ... The revolution will be a cruel one, and perhaps of your own making." The sinister word is here breathed for the first time. Maybe, like most seers, Joseph did not fully understand his own foreboding; but a decade later Marie Antoinette was to grasp the significance of her brother's warning.

CHAPTER XII

Motherhood

THIS visit from her brother, Emperor Joseph II, may seem a trifling episode in the life of Marie Antoinette, but the fact was that it effected a most decisive transformation. Within a few weeks there became manifest the fruits of Joseph's talk with Louis XVI concerning the secret of the royal alcove. The necessary operation having been successfully performed, the husband was able to address himself to his marital duties with appropriate vigour. As early as August 19, 1777, Marie Antoinette reported to Vienna: "As regards my virgin state, it is unfortunately still the same. However, I do not despair, for things are certainly going a little better. The King is more forthcoming, and in his case this means a great deal." On August 30th there is at length sounded a victorious fanfare. After countless defeats in this Seven Years' War of Eros, the "nonchalant mari" had stormed the undefended fortress. "I have attained the happiness which is of the utmost importance to my whole life. More than a week ago my marriage was thoroughly consummated. Yesterday the attempt was repeated, with results even more successful than the first time. I was in the mind, to begin with, to send a special messenger to my beloved mother, but I was afraid this might attract too much attention and arouse gossip. Besides, I wished to be quite sure that matters were all right. I don't think that I am with child yet, but at any rate I have hopes of becoming so from moment to moment."

This happy turn in events did not long remain a secret. The Spanish ambassador, best informed of the whole diplomatic corps, was actually in a position to acquaint his royal master with the precise date (August 25th), adding: "Since the event is so interesting and a matter of such grave public moment, I took the opportunity of talking about it to Messieurs Maurepas and Vergennes, the ministers of State, not together but separately, and both of them have confirmed my private information. Moreover, it transpires that the King mentioned the matter to one of his maiden aunts, declaring with the utmost frankness: 'I find the pleasure very great, and I regret that so long a time has passed without my being able to enjoy it.' His Majesty has become more cheerful than he used to be, and no one can fail to note that the Queen has blue circles round her eyes far more often than of yore."

All the same, the young wife's jubilation concerning her husband's vigour was premature, seeing that Louis XVI did not devote himself to the "new pleasure" with nearly as much zeal as to the chase. Only ten days later we find Marie Antoinette writing to her mother: "The King is not fond of sleeping in the same bed with me. I do my best to ensure that there shall not be a total separation between us in this matter. Sometimes he comes to pass the night with me, and I think it would be a mistake for me to urge him to do so more often." Maria Theresa was sorry to hear the news, for she regarded the matter as one "of the first importance"; but she agreed with her daughter that it would be unwise to be importunate, while giving Toinette a hint to adapt her sleep-time as far as might be to that of her husband.

Vienna had to wait a good while for the much-desired information that a pregnancy had at length been the outcome of this lukewarm marriage, for it was not until the following April that the impatient wife had good reason to believe herself with child. At the very first indication, Marie Antoinette wanted to dispatch a special messenger to the Hofburg, but the physician of the bedchamber, although privately willing to bet a thousand louis d'or that the Queen was right, advised her to wait a little longer. On May 5, 1778, Mercy, who was a cautious man, reported it to be practically certain that the Queen was expecting. At length, on July 31st, at half past eleven in the evening, Marie Antoinette first became unmistakably aware of the fœtal movements, and the pregnancy was officially announced to the court on August 4th. "Since then," wrote the Queen to the Empress, "the movements have been frequent, which is a great joy to me." It amused her to announce his fatherhood to the husband who had been such a laggard in a way which was extremely original. Entering his presence, she pulled a long face, as if she had been ill-used, saying: "I have come, Sire, to complain of one of your subjects who has been so audacious as to kick me in the belly." The worthy Louis was puzzled for a moment, then laughed with a comfortable pride, and, almost taken aback by his unanticipated efficiency, clasped his wife in his arms.

The public announcement was followed by multifarious ceremonies. Te Deums were sung in the churches; the Parliament of Paris sent congratulations; the archbishop ordered that prayers should be offered up for a happy course of the pregnancy; extreme care was taken in the choice of a woman who, when the time arrived, would be in a position to act as wet-nurse to the royal baby; and a hundred thousand livres were held in readiness for distribution among the poor. All the world was agog waiting for the great event, and not least the accoucheur, for whom the Queen's delivery was a gamble, seeing that the birth of an heir to the throne would bring him a pension of forty thousand livres whereas he would get only ten thousand if he brought a princess into the world. The members of the court circle, however, were scarcely less excited than he as they waited for the Queen to be brought to bed, seeing that, in accordance with a custom hallowed by centuries, the delivery of a queen of France was anything but a private family affair. Her travail and delivery must be witnessed by all the princes and princesses and by the court grandees in general. It was a privilege of their high rank, and not one of them would dream of renouncing it, barbarous though it was and likely enough to be prejudicial to the health of the woman in childbirth. From all the provinces, from the most distant castles and palaces, the would-be spectators assembled in crowds. Even the smallest garret in the little town of Versailles was occupied, and the presence of newcomers sent up prices with a run until they reached thrice the usual level.

At length, on December 18th, the ringing of bells announced that the labour pains had begun. Madame de Lamballe hastened to the Queen's bedroom, followed by the ladies-in-waiting. At three in the morning King Louis, the princes, and the princesses were awakened; pages and guardsmen galloped off to Paris and Saint-Cloud to summon everyone of royal blood or princely rank that they might be present on the great occasion. A few minutes after the physician of the bedchamber had loudly announced that the Queen was in labour, a mob of noblemen and noblewomen forced its way into the room. They seated themselves in order of precedence in the armchairs round the bed. Those for whom there was no place left in the chairs, climbed on benches ranged beside the walls, lest they should miss sight and hearing of any movement, any groan, of the woman in torment. The air in the confined space grew intolerably stuffy, laden with the breath of the fifty or more spectators, and with the sharp odour of vinegar and essences. No one thought of opening a window, no one made any move, and the scene of public torture lasted for seven hours, until at length, at half past eleven in the morning, Marie Antoinette gave birth to the child—alas, a daughter.

The royal infant was reverently carried into the dressing-room, to be washed, and then handed over to the care of the governess. The King proudly followed in order to inspect this belated fruit of his loins with due admiration, and behind him trailed, inquisitive as ever, the whole court, when suddenly there came a shout from the accoucheur: "Air and hot water! Her Majesty must be bled." The Queen had had an attack of congestion of the head and had lost consciousness, half suffocated by the pestilential atmosphere and perhaps by the effort she had made to repress her cries of agony in the presence of the fifty spectators. She lay motionless, breathing heavily among the pillows. The alarm was general; the King opened a window with his own hand, and the room was cleared. No hot water was forthcoming. The court flunkeys had been thinking only of medieval ceremony, and had ignored the most obvious need on such occasions—to have plenty of hot water in readiness. The surgeon, therefore, ventured to open a vein in the foot without further preparation. Blood flowed freely; the Queen opened her eyes; she was saved. Now there was an outburst of general rejoicing; people threw their arms round one another, congratulated one another, wept with joy; and the bells of the churches announced the glad tidings far and wide.

The woman's torment was over, and the mother's happiness had begun. Even though the happiness was not unalloyed, even though a salute of only one-and-twenty guns could be fired in honour of the birth of a princess instead of a salute of a hundred and one guns in honour of the birth of an heir to the throne, Versailles and Paris were bubbling over with delight. Mounted couriers were sent to all the countries of Europe; alms were distributed throughout the country; an amnesty was declared, numerous debtors and criminals being released; at the King's court, a hundred young engaged couples were provided with new clothing, wedded, and given a dowry. When the

Queen went to Notre Dame to be churched, this hundred of couples (the minister of police had been careful to choose good-looking ones) were awaiting her arrival and vociferously acclaimed their benefactress. There were fireworks and illuminations for the populace in Paris, with wine flowing from the public drinking-fountains, free distribution of bread and sausages, and free entry into the Comédie Française, the charcoal-burners being seated in the King's box and the fishwives in that of the Queen. The poor folk, too, were to have a jolly time! Rejoicings, in fact, were universal. Louis XVI could become cheerful and self-assured now that he was a father; Marie Antoinette as a mother would be a happy, serious-minded, and conscientious woman. The great hindrance had been swept out of the way, the royal marriage had been safeguarded. The parents, the court, the wide land of France could be well pleased, and did actually show themselves well pleased by participation in public festivals.

Yet there was one person, not in France, who was but partially satisfied—Maria Theresa. No doubt her favourite daughter's position had been improved by the birth of this female grandchild, but it was not yet consolidated. As empress, as stateswoman, the Austrian ruler had dynastic considerations more at heart than private family happiness. "We absolutely need a dauphin, an heir to the throne." With the wearisome iteration of a litany came admonitions to her daughter to be careful now, above all, to avoid the "lit à part," to shun any manifestation of levity. As month after month passed without tidings of a new pregnancy, Maria Theresa grew acrimonious in her complaints of how bad a use Marie Antoinette was making of her conjugal opportunities. "With the King it is early to bed and early to rise. Since the Queen keeps such different hours, how can one have happy expectations? . . . When they see one another only in passing, no real success can be hoped for." Her urgency grew continually greater. "Up till now I have been discreet, but in the end I shall grow importunate; it would be a crime if no more children were born of this royal race." There was only one thing left to live for. "I am becoming impatient, and at my age I have not long to wait."

But this last joy of knowing that a king of France with Habsburg blood in his veins had been born was not to be granted her. Marie Antoinette's next pregnancy came to an untimely end. A too vigorous movement when closing one of the carriage windows brought on a miscarriage, and before the impatiently expected grandson was born, or was even on the way, Maria Theresa died on November 29, 1780, of inflammation of the lungs. She had cherished two wishes amid numberless disillusionments and disappointments. The first, as aforesaid, to live until her grandson had been born as heir to the French throne remained unfulfilled. The fulfilment of the other, that she might die before her best-loved child was laid low by misfortune through folly and lack of understanding was vouchsafed to the pious mother.

Not until a year after Maria Theresa's death did Marie Antoinette give birth to a son. In view of the menace of disaster during the first childbed, the "full-dress parade" was abandoned on this occasion, and only the Queen's closest relatives had access. Things went easily on the whole, but when the new-born child was taken away the Queen was still too weak to ask whether it was a boy or a girl. However, as soon as she was a little better the King came to her bedside, tears flowing down his cheeks, as he said in his sonorous voice: "Monsieur le Dauphin demande entrée."

Amid general rejoicings the folding doors were thrown wide and the Duke of Normandy, washed and wrapped in his swaddling clothes, was brought back to the happy mother. All the ceremonies proper to the birth of a crown prince could at length be carried out. Once again Cardinal de Rohan crossed Marie Antoinette's path at a decisive moment, for it was he who baptized the infant. An excellent wet-nurse was ready to suckle the young prince, a woman who had been encouragingly nick-named "Madame Poitrine." A royal salute of a hundred and one guns was fired, so that Paris was speedily acquainted with the good news. Then came a succession of festivals, more numerous and more splendid than those which had followed the birth of the princess. The guilds, one and all, sent delegations to Versailles, each attended by musicians, and the ceremony of their reception occupied nine days. The members of the chimney-sweeps' guild triumphantly carried a chimney on the top of which were seated little chimney-sweeps singing merrily; the butchers' guild drove a fat ox; the sedan-chairmen had a gilded chair in which fancy-dress figures of a wet-nurse and a little dauphin were seated; the shoemakers bore babies' shoes, the tailors a miniature uniform of the regiment the Dauphin was one day to command, the blacksmiths an anvil which they hammered in a musical rhythm. As for the locksmiths, since they knew the King had a special taste for their craft, they had conceived a wonderful device, bringing a huge and artfully contrived lock out of which, when Louis XVI, with the zeal of a craftsman, unlocked it, there sprang a tiny dauphin marvellously fashioned in steel. The market-women, in their turn, many of them the same women who a few years later were to hail the Queen with the vilest invectives and obscenities, had decked themselves out in black silk dresses and recited an address penned by Laharpe. Special services were held in the churches; there was a great banquet in the Hôtel de Ville; the war with England, poverty, and other disagreeables were forgotten. For the moment there were no discontents, since even those who would soon be revolutionists and republicans overflowed with displays of ardent royalism. Collot d'Herbois, in due time to become chairman of the Jacobin Club, but now no more than a play-actor in Lyons, composed a piece in honour of "the august princess whose goodness and virtues have conquered all hearts." He who would eventually sign Louis Capet's death warrant now invoked heaven's blessings on the royal pair:

Pour le bonheur des Français,
Notre bon Louis seize
S'est allié pour jamais
Au sang de Thérèse.
De cette heureuse union
Il sort un beau rejeton.
Pour répandre en notre cœur
Félicité parfaite,
Conserve, ô ciel protecteur,
Les jours d'Antoinette.

The populace was still at one with its rulers; the Dauphin had been born, not only to his royal parents, but also to the country at large, and his arrival was an occasion for universal delight. Fiddlers and trumpeters appeared at every street corner; in towns and villages drums were beaten and people sang and danced merrily. Everyone loved, everyone praised the King and the Queen who had at length so valiantly performed their duty.

The disastrous spell was broken. Twice more did Marie Antoinette become a mother. In 1785 she gave birth to a second son, the future Louis XVII, a vigorous and healthy boy, "a typical peasant youngster." In 1786, as the fruit of her fourth and last pregnancy, was born Sophie Béatrix, who died just before reaching the age of one year. With motherhood began the first transformation in Marie Antoinette, not so far a decisive metamorphosis, but the beginning of a decisive one. Her pregnancies necessitated several months' abstinence from the life of unmeaning amusement; she soon began to find it more agreeable to play with her children than to stake money at the gaming-table; the tender emotion which, for want of a better object, had been squandered upon carousals, had at length found a normal outlet. The way to a life of reflective self-knowledge seemed to be opening. Could she have a few tranquil and happy years, she would herself grow tranquil, this lovely woman with the gentle eyes. Turning away from futilities, she would be content to watch her children growing up, to see them gradually taking hold of life. But this respite was never to be accorded her by fate. At the very time when Marie Antoinette's internal unrest was waning, a period of unrest was beginning for the world.

CHAPTER XIII

The Queen Becomes Unpopular

THE birth of the Dauphin marked the zenith of Marie Antoinette's power. By producing an heir to the throne she had become, as it were, queen for a second time. Once again the acclamations of the crowd had shown that the French people, many disappointments notwithstanding, still had inexhaustible love for, inexhaustible trust in, the ruling house; had made it plain with how little trouble the sovereigns of this nation could have continued to hold its affection. What was now needed was that Marie Antoinette should take a decisive step —from Trianon back to Versailles, to Paris, out of the Rococo world into the real one, out of her giddy entourage back to the old nobility and to the people. Then all would be well. But when she had recovered from giving birth to the Dauphin, she heedlessly returned to her life of pleasure, resuming, as soon as the popular festivals were over, the costly and disastrous amusements at the Little Trianon. Now destiny lost patience with her, and she crossed the water-parting of good fortune. Thenceforward her course led downward towards the abyss.

Not that, to begin with, there were any striking developments. All that could be noticed was that court life at Versailles grew increasingly dull. Fewer and ever fewer gentlemen and ladies appeared at the receptions, and those who did come were cool and aloof in their attitude. They maintained the proprieties, but only for form's sake and not for that of the Queen. They bowed, they curtsied, they kissed the royal hand; but they did not woo the favour of a private conversation, and their countenances were gloomy and uncongenial. It was the same with the middle and lower classes. When Marie Antoinette visited the theatre, she was no longer received with jubilation by the auditorium, and in the streets the familiar cries of "Vive la Reine!" were stilled. There was not as yet any manifest hostility, but there was no further sign of that cordiality which had given an agreeable warmth to respect. The sovereign lady was still revered, but there was no affection for the woman. The King's wife was served with due attention, but not with affectionate interest. People did not openly disregard her wishes, but they preserved a chilly silence—the harsh, malicious, repressive, and ominous silence of a conspiracy.

The headquarters of this conspiracy was at the four or five royal palaces; the Luxembourg, the Palais Royal, the Château of Bellevue, and Versailles itself. They were in league against Trianon, the Queen's residence.

The ill-natured chorus was led by the three maiden aunts. They had never forgotten how, as Dauphiness, the young woman had given them the go-by, and how as Queen she had thrust them into the background. In an evil temper because they no longer played an influential part at court, they had retired to Bellevue. There, neglected and bored, they spent the first triumphal years of Marie Antoinette's reign, not a soul paying heed to them, now that devotion centred round the young and bewitching Queen, whose little white hands held the reins of power. But at length, when Marie Antoinette was becoming unpopular, the gates of the Château of Bellevue were frequently opened. The numerous ladies who were not invited to Trianon, the disregarded "Madame Etiquette," the dismissed ministers of State, various ill-favoured women whose morals were irreproachable because no one cared to make love to them, gentlemen who had been snubbed, unsuccessful place-hunters, all who detested the "new trend" and sighed for the "good old days" of piety and decency (which were of course in great measure illusory) gathered together in this cave of Adullam.

The aunts' rooms at Bellevue were transformed into a poison distillery, where the evil-tongued gossip of the court was bottled for public consumption, accounts of the "Austrian woman's" latest follies, the "on dits" about her supposed love-affairs. Here was the arsenal of scandal, the notorious "atelier des calomnies." Here were composed spiteful couplets, winged words which flew from Bellevue to Versailles, and thence farther afield. Bellevue became the forcing-house for scandal, or a vat for the preservation of all that time would fain have left behind, of the living corpse of the disillusioned, the discrowned, that which was over and done with, the mummies of a dead world, the vestiges of a history whose tale was told, but which lingered on to take vengeance for being regarded as out-of-date. The envenomed shafts, however, were not aimed at "the good King," for whom a sanctimonious commiseration was always expressed, but at Marie Antoinette, the young, the radiant, the fortunate Queen.

More dangerous than this toothless yesterday, which could no longer bite but could only vent its spleen, was the new generation of those who had never tasted the sweets of power and had become weary of being kept in the background. In its exclusiveness and indifference, Versailles had cut itself off so completely from the real France that it was wholly unaware of the new currents of thought which were agitating the land. An intelligent, a cultured middle class had come into being. The new bourgeois had been taught by Jean Jacques Rousseau that they possessed rights, and, looking across the Channel, they saw in England a government which was democratic at any rate in form. Those of their order who returned to France after taking part in the American War of Independence brought tidings of a remarkable country where differences of caste had been abolished by the notions of equality and liberty. In France, however, they found nothing but rigidity and decay, for which the incapacity of the court was largely responsible. When Louis XV died, there had been a universal hope that an end had at length come to the dominion of the King's mistresses, to the regime of a tainted patronage; but instead of a change for the better, the rule of the Pompadours and the Dubarrys had been replaced by that of other women who still had no thought for France, by that of Marie Antoinette swayed by Madame de Polignac from behind the scenes. With growing bitterness, the enlightened bourgeoisie saw how France's position of power in the world was being forfeited, how the State debts were increasing, how the army and the navy were in evil case, how the colonies were being lost at the very time when neighbouring lands were in process of energetic development. More and more vigorously and more and more widely, therefore, stirred the will to make an end of misgovernment and neglect.

There were good reasons why the concentrated discontent, which was inspired by genuinely patriotic and national feelings, should make Marie Antoinette its chief target. The whole country knew that the King was incapable of effective decision, that he did not count as a ruler, and that therefore the Queen's influence was all-powerful. Two possibilities were open to Marie Antoinette. She might, following her mother's example, have seriously, actively, energetically undertaken the work of government; or she might have left politics severely alone. The Austrian group was continually though vainly endeavouring to guide her into the courses of statecraft. One who aspires to rule, or to play even a modest part in the work of government, must spend a few hours every day in the perusal of relevant documents; but the Queen had no taste for reading. One who would make sovereignty effective must listen to ministerial reports and must think them over carefully; but Marie Antoinette found it tiresome to think. For one with her levity of temperament, merely to give careful hearing was a great exertion.

"She scarcely listens to what I say," wrote Mercy to Vienna, "and it is almost impossible to discuss serious matters with her or to rivet her attention upon an important affair. The pursuit of pleasure holds her in thrall." The best that could be hoped for was that she would sometimes consent to answer him when, commissioned by her mother or her brother, he became pressing. "Tell me what I ought to do, and I will do it," she would say, and thereupon she would actually go from Mercy to the King. By the next day, however, she had forgotten the whole thing. Her intervention in matters of State never got beyond the stage of "a few impatient impulses." At length, at the court of Vienna, Kaunitz had to resign himself to circumstances. "It is absolutely useless to count upon her. We must content ourselves, as in the case of a defaulting debtor, to get what little we can out of her." Writing to Mercy, he said that, after all, it must be remembered that at other courts, likewise, women played no part in politics.

If she would only have refrained altogether from interfering with matters of State! Then, at least, she would have had no responsibility, and no one could have blamed her when things went awry. But, prompted by the Polignac clique, she was continually interfering when there was question of changing a minister of State, or of the occupancy of some other post of importance. She did what is the most dangerous thing anyone can do in politics; she talked at large without having the remotest acquaintance with the subject; she amateurishly thrust her fingers into every pie, interfering in matters of the utmost moment; she used her overwhelming influence with the King exclusively on behalf of her favourites.

"When anything serious is at stake," complained Mercy, "she is timid

and undependable; but when she is egged on by the perfidious in-
triguers who surround her she does everything she can to fulfil their
behests, even though she recognizes that their demands are inexpedient." The Comte de Saint-Priest, one of the ministers of State, declared that nothing had done more to bring the Queen into odium
than her impulsive meddling, her unwarranted nominations to posts.
Since, in the view of the bourgeoisie, she was really responsible for the
guidance of State affairs, and since the various generals and ambassadors and ministers she had appointed were for the most part incompetent, since France was drifting ever more swiftly towards bankruptcy,
the blame for these disasters was placed upon the Queen's shoulders,
although, from her own outlook, she had done nothing more than
provide a few delightful persons with good positions. Whoever in
France was a devotee of progress, the restoration of public order, justice,
creative activity, was up in arms against the spendthrift, heedless, but
perpetually cheerful mistress of the Little Trianon, who was sacrificing
the love and the welfare of twenty million persons to the twenty ladies
and gentlemen who formed the arrogant clique of her favourites.

The widespread dissatisfaction of those who wanted a new system, a
better ordering of public affairs, a more sensible distribution of responsibility, had long been in need of a rallying-point. At length it was
discovered in a single house, in one man. This embittered adversary
likewise had royal blood in his veins; as at the Château of Bellevue,
the palace of the King's aunts, the reaction foregathered, so did the
Revolution become centred round the Duke of Orléans in the Palais
Royal. Thus from two fronts, mutually opposed, a campaign against
Marie Antoinette was simultaneously opened. Louis Philippe Joseph
was temperamentally inclined towards enjoyment rather than towards
ambition; he was a rake, a spendthrift, a gambler, and a dandy, distinguished neither by ability nor by malice. An aristocrat and a mediocrity, he had the weakness characteristic of uncreative natures, a vanity
directed only towards externals. Marie Antoinette had mortified this
vanity, for, with a quip about her cousin's achievements as a warrior,
she had prevented the bestowal on him of the office of lord high
admiral of France. The Duke of Orléans had not been slow to take up
the gauntlet. Sprung from a branch of the royal house as old as that

to which Louis belonged, wealthy and independent, he did not hesitate to run counter to the King's will in the Parliament of Paris and to treat the Queen as a declared enemy. It was natural, therefore, that he should become the leader of the malcontents. Anyone who wished to make head against the Habsburgs and against the ruling line of the Bourbons, anyone who regarded an unlimited monarchy as antiquated and oppressive, anyone who favoured the establishment of a rational and up-to-date democratic system in France, now sought the protection of the Duke of Orléans. At the Palais Royal (the first of the revolutionary clubs, conducted in this case under the ægis of one in whose veins monarchical blood ran), there assembled innovators, liberals, constitutionalists, Voltairians, philanthropists, and freemasons. Mingled with these were various other discontented elements: those who were heavily in debt, disgruntled aristocrats, cultured bourgeois to whom no positions in the public service were open, unemployed lawyers, demagogues, journalists—fermenting energies which, a few years later, were to animate the shock troops of the Revolution. The mighty spiritual army with which France was to fight its way to liberty was assembled here under the leadership of the weak and self-satisfied Duke. The war-cry had not yet been uttered, but everyone knew what it would be, everyone knew the trend of the movement: "Against the King, and above all against the Queen!"

Between these two groups of adversaries, the revolutionists and the reactionaries, there stood in solitary grandeur the man who was perhaps the most dangerous of all the Queen's enemies, her brother-in-law "Monsieur," Stanislas Xavier, Count of Provence, in later days to mount the throne as King Louis XVIII. A cautious intriguer, treading delicately, moving like a shadow, he had no intention of compromising himself by premature adhesion to either of the rival groups, but swung like a pendulum to right and to left, waiting till destiny should reveal the moment for taking a definitive inclination. While he was by no means sorry to note the increasing difficulties in which his brother's government was becoming involved, he carefully refrained from public criticism. Dark and silent as a mole, he burrowed and mined while biding his time. When Louis XVI and Louis XVII had run their course, and when the Napoleonic interlude was over, the Count of Provence at length became Louis XVIII, fulfilling what had since early childhood been his supreme ambition by mounting the steps of the throne. For a while his expectations had risen high. The seven tragical years during which Louis XVI's marriage remained unfruitful had been for him the seven plentiful years of the Bible. Then his hopes of the succession were dashed because at length his sister-in-law was with child. When Marie Antoinette was delivered of a daughter, he wrote the following avowal to King Gustavus of Sweden: "I do not hide from myself that this matter has been a home thrust. . . . As far as outward appearances are concerned, I was soon able to master myself, and I have behaved with the same decorum as before, though without any demonstration of joy, which would have been regarded as (and would really have been) mendacious. . . . It has not been easy for me to master the inner man, who still rises in revolt from time to time; but I can keep him in good order even if I cannot entirely subdue him."

The birth of the Dauphin was, to all seeming, a final blow to his hopes. The way was absolutely blocked, and he was forced into those devious and hypocritical paths which were ultimately, though not for another thirty years, to lead him to the long-desired goal. The enmity of the Count of Provence was not like that of the Duke of Orléans an open flame of hatred, but a fire of envy that smouldered beneath the ashes of misrepresentation. As long as the power of Marie Antoinette and Louis XVI was unchallenged, this secret pretender to the crown kept his own counsel, giving no sign of his schemes. It was not until the Revolution opened that he began his suspicious machinations, the holding of strange conferences in the Luxembourg. Subsequently, when he had fled to England, he issued challenging proclamations wherein he valiantly dug into the graves of his brother, his sister-in-law, and his nephew, in the hope (ultimately fulfilled) that in their coffins he would find the crown he hoped to wear.

Did the Count of Provence do anything yet more sinister? Is it true that, as many authorities have declared, he played a still more Mephistophelean part? Did his ambitions as pretender go so far as to lead him to print and circulate pamphlets throwing discredit on Marie Antoinette's honour? Can it be possible that he arranged for the theft of certain documents so that the unhappy little boy, Louis XVII, who had secretly been rescued from the Temple, was dragged to a fate whose details remain obscure even to this day? There was a good deal in the behaviour of Stanislas Xavier to give rise to such suspicions. This much is certain, that immediately after mounting the throne King Louis XVIII, partly by money and partly by force, got hold of and destroyed various letters which he had written long before as Count of Provence. Again, does not the fact that he did not venture to have the body of the poor boy who died in the Temple interred as Louis XVII seem to imply that Louis XVIII did not really believe in the death of Louis XVII, but supposed that a changeling had died in prison in the young King's stead? However these things may be, Stanislas Xavier was well able to keep his own counsel and to cover up his trail; and today the underground galleries he drove in the attempt to mine his brother's throne have long since fallen in. This much alone is certain, that, among her bitterest adversaries, Marie Antoinette had no more dangerous foe than this ambushed and inscrutable man.

After ten wasted years on the throne, Marie Antoinette was already encompassed on all sides, so that by 1785 the animosities directed against her had become virulent. The groups hostile to the Queen— comprising most of the nobility and half of the bourgeoisie—had consolidated their position, and were awaiting a sign for the attack. But the authority of the hereditary monarchy was still firmly established, and no resolute plan of campaign had hitherto been formed. There was nothing more than chatterings and whisperings, the whizz of feathered shafts traversing Versailles. Every one of these arrows was tipped with poison, and they were aimed, not at Louis, but at the Queen. Printed or written leaflets were passed from hand to hand beneath the table and were quickly hidden in the clothing when a stranger drew near. Distinguished noblemen wearing famous orders would visit the bookshops of the Palais Royal and, having been led by the bookseller into a back room would, when the door had been carefully shut, purchase the latest lampoon directed against the Queen. Ostensibly printed in London or Amsterdam, it would really be damp from the press, probably machined in the Duke of Orléans's own palace or in the Luxembourg. Unhesitatingly these blue-blooded pur· chasers would pay more gold pieces than such pamphlets had pages. They seldom ran to over ten or twenty of these, but were richly illustrated with lascivious copperplate engravings, and peppered with malicious jokes. Such a spicy pasquinade was one of the most acceptable presents a man could give to his beloved—if the lady had not been honoured by an invitation to the Trianon. The gift would bring more pleasure than a costly ring or fan. Penned by unknown authors, printed by hidden hands, secretly distributed, these derogatory writings fluttered like bats through the park-gates of Versailles into the boudoirs of the court ladies, and they also made their way into the châteaux of the provinces; but when the lieutenant of police tried to run the offenders to earth he found himself checked by invisible powers. They insinuated themselves everywhere. The Queen would find one at table when she unfolded her napkin; the King would come across one on his writing-desk among his official documents. When Marie Antoinette went to the theatre, one of them would be pinned to the balustrade in front of her seat, a malicious versicle; and when at night she leaned out of window for a breath of air she would hear the strains of the street ditty which everyone was singing, and which opened with the inquiry:

> Chacun se demande tout bas:
> Le Roi peut-il? Ne peut-il pas?
> La triste Reine en désespère . . .

and which, after giving various erotic details, ended with the threat:

> Petite Reine de vingt ans
> Qui traitez aussi mal les gens,
> Vous repasserez en Bavière.

These pamphlets and "polissonneries" of the early days were much milder than those which were circulated a few years later; ill-natured, certainly, but not positively outrageous. They were intended to annoy rather than to inflict a deadly wound. It was not until the Queen was with child, and this unexpected event had disappointed the hopes of various aspirants to the throne, that the tone became venomous. Now, when the statements were manifestly false, the lampooners began deliberately to speak of the King as impotent and of the Queen as an adulteress, with the obvious design (of course in Stanislas Xavier's interest) of stigmatizing any issue Marie Antoinette might have as bastards. It was especially after the birth of the Dauphin, incontestably the rightful heir to the throne, that this polemic tended to assume its worst form. The Queen's intimate friends, Madame de Lamballe and Madame de Polignac, were pilloried as mistresses of the arts of Lesbian love; Marie Antoinette was described as a nymphomaniac with perverse inclinations; Louis was a poor weakling on whom his wife had put the horns; the Dauphin was a bastard. Let me give another example of a spicy epigram then current:

> Louis, si tu veux voir
> Bâtard, cocu, putain,
> Regarde ton miroir,
> La Reine et le Dauphin.

By 1785 the concert of calumny was in full swing. No more was needed than that the Revolution should shout in the streets what for years had been whispered and rhymed in the drawing-rooms, and Marie Antoinette was prejudged before ever she was indicted at the Revolutionary Tribunal. It was the court which really drafted the indictment. The axe of hatred which severed the Queen's neck had been put into the executioner's hands by the delicate and bejewelled fingers of members of the aristocracy.

Who composed these lampoons? That is really a minor question, since the poetasters were for the most part writing to order, for pay, and not to fulfil any purposes of their own. When, in the days of the Renaissance, distinguished noblemen wanted to sweep some adversary out of their path, they hired a bravo or bought a dose of deadly poison. The eighteenth century, having grown philanthropic, used more refined methods. People stabbed a political opponent, not with a dagger now, but with a pen, using moral and not physical weapons to overthrow an adversary—slaying by ridicule. As luck would have it, towards 1780 some extremely able pens became available at a price: Beaumarchais, the author of immortal comedies; Brissot, who was to be one of the tribunes of the Revolution; Mirabeau, the genius of liberty; Choderlos de Laclos, a novelist as well as a distinguished general. These, though men of exceptional talent, were, being in low water, purchasable on easy terms. Behind such gifted lampoonists stood hundreds of others, courtiers, commoners, men with dirty finger-nails and empty stomachs, ready to write anything they were asked; honey or poison, epithalamia or invectives, hymns or pamphlets, long or short, acerb or tender, political or unpolitical, to suit the employer's taste.

Besides, a writer of this sort equipped with both boldness and skill could earn his fee twice or thrice over. First he was paid the stipulated sum (through an intermediary, of course, while the prince or nobleman who gave the commission remained discreetly in the background) for a lampoon of the Pompadour, the Dubarry, or at this juncture Marie Antoinette. Then, turning informer for the nonce, he could privately acquaint the court with the fact that such and such a libel was being printed in Amsterdam or London, and could thus earn a round sum from the treasury or the police, who would be able to take steps for the suppression of the noxious pamphlet. Thirdly, one who, like Beaumarchais, was cunning and bold enough to keep in safe hiding one or two copies of the defamatory print to whose utter destruction he had pledged himself, could threaten to have a new edition printed, altered or unaltered. This last was a merry jest indeed, which in Vienna, under Maria Theresa, brought for its able discoverer the punishment of fourteen days' imprisonment, and then, as compensation in timid Versailles, a sum of a thousand gold gulden and a further indemnity of seventy thousand livres.

Speedily it became known to the hawkers of this kind of wares that pamphlets directed against Marie Antoinette were, at the moment, the best-paying proposition, and even that there was no serious risk attached to their sale—so naturally the trade was brisk. Thus did hatred and avarice join forces in the composition and diffusion of these scurrilous documents. Nor was it long before their purpose was achieved. From end to end of France, Marie Antoinette became an object of popular detestation both as woman and as queen.

"The Austrian woman" was not ignorant of these machinations; she knew all about the lampoons, and guessed in what quarter they originated. She disdained, however, to pay serious heed to them. With inborn and unteachable Habsburg pride, she thought it better to despise dangers than to go out to meet them with prudence and caution. Contemptuously she wiped off the mud with which her dress had been splashed. In the course of a letter to her mother she casually remarked: "We are suffering from an epidemic of satirical verses, directed against the notables of the court, both men and women, and French wit has not refrained from aiming its shafts even against the King. Nor, indeed, have I been spared."

That was all she had to say about the lampoons. She did not even trouble to be angry. What could it matter to her if a few blow-flies settled upon her gown? Thrice armoured by her royal dignity, she regarded herself as invulnerable to these paper darts. She forgot, or she did not understand, that a single drop of this poison of calumny which has entered the circulation of public opinion can multiply like the virus of a contagious fever with which not even the ablest of physicians can cope. Smilingly she made light of the danger. To her way of thinking, words were but chaff in the breeze. A violent storm was needed to awaken her to a sense of danger.

CHAPTER XIV

A Thunderclap in the Rococo Theatre

IN THE beginning of August 1785 the Queen was busier than usual, though not because the political situation was peculiarly ominous and because the rising in the Netherlands was putting the Franco-Austrian alliance to a very severe test. To Marie Antoinette her Rococo theatre at the Little Trianon was of much greater importance than the wider stage on which the affairs of the world were being played. What she was so eager about just now was a new first night. Beaumarchais's *Le Barbier de Séville* was to be produced in the palace theatre, with a distinguished cast. The Count of Artois in his own exalted person was to appear as Figaro, Vaudreuil was to play the Count, and the Queen was to represent the merry girl Rosine.

The famous comedy penned by Monsieur de Beaumarchais? Surely not the work of the man known to the police as Monsieur Caron, who ten years earlier had written that infamous pamphlet entitled *Avis important à la branche espagnole sur les droits à la couronne de France* in which the impotence of Louis XVI had been proclaimed to the world; the man who had at that time been vainly hunted by the authorities, and who had had the impudence to send his pamphlet to the enraged Maria Theresa? Surely not the man who had called the Empress Mother a "friponne"; Louis XVI, a fool and a "mauvais sujet"? Surely not the man who, when in Vienna, had been arrested by imperial command as a blackmailer, and who, when prisoned in Saint-Lazare had been punished, as was customary in those days, by a caning on admission? Yes, it was the very same! When her pleasures were in question, Marie Antoinette had a short memory; and Kaunitz did not exaggerate in saying that her follies were "continually increasing and being embellished."

What made her indiscretion all the more flagrant was that, besides having grossly offended her mother, this industrious and talented adventurer and writer of comedies had monstrously defied the royal authority. A hundred and fifty years after the event, none can fail to remember the ignominious defeat of a King by an imaginative writer, and yet the Queen would seem to have completely forgotten it within four years. In 1781, the censorship, having keen nostrils, had become aware that Beaumarchais's latest comedy *Le Mariage de Figaro* smelt of gun powder. There was enough explosive in it to blow the old regime to smithereens, and the ministerial council unanimously forbade its production. Beaumarchais, however, extremely sensitive to anything which might touch his fame or restrict his income, found a hundred ways of bringing up the question of his play over and over again. At length he managed to arrange that it should be read aloud to Louis himself, who would give a final decision. Dullard though he might be, the worthy King was not stupid enough to overlook the spirit of revolt that breathes through this magnificent comedy. "The man makes fun of everything in the State which ought to be respected," he angrily exclaimed. "Do you mean to say that it must not be staged?" asked the Queen, greatly disappointed, for to her an interesting first night was of much greater importance than the welfare of the State. "Certainly," rejoined Louis XVI. "You can be sure of that."

One might have supposed that this would be an end of the matter. The Most Christian King, the absolute ruler of France, had forbidden the production of *Le Mariage de Figaro,* and there was nothing more to say. An end as far as Louis was concerned, but not by any means an end for Beaumarchais. He had no thought of striking his flag, being well aware that it was only upon coins that the royal head counted for anything, only as the subscription to official documents that the royal signature had weight, whereas the real ruler of the country was the Queen, and the Queen, in turn, was ruled by the Polignacs. He would, therefore, appeal to this supreme authority!

The prohibition of the stage performance had made the comedy fashionable, and the author gave readings of it in one drawing-room after another. With the mysterious impulse towards self-destruction which was characteristic of the degenerate society of those days, the nobility became enthusiastic about the drama, first of all because it made fun of their own order, and secondly because Louis XVI had considered it unbecoming. Vaudreuil, Madame de Polignac's lover, was impudent enough to have the play performed in his private theatre. But this was not enough. The King must be publicly put in the wrong and Beaumarchais must publicly be put in the right. It was necessary to stage *Le Mariage de Figaro* in the royal theatre, in the theatre of the King who had prohibited it, and because the King had prohibited it. Secretly (one may presume with the knowledge of the Queen, to whom Madame de Polignac's smile was more important than her husband's prestige) the actors and actresses were charged to study their parts; tickets had been issued; the carriages were already driving to the theatre—when, at the last moment, Louis decided to assert his authority. He had forbidden the performance, and now his dignity as a monarch was being publicly challenged. An hour before the curtain ought to have been rung up, he stopped the whole affair by a "lettre de cachet." The lights were extinguished, and the members of the distinguished audience had no resource but to drive home again.

Once more, surely, the matter must be settled. No, for it seemed amusing to the Queen's clique to give plain demonstration of a power which excelled that of a crowned weakling. The Count of Artois and Marie Antoinette brought pressure to bear, and the King, weak of will as ever, gave way to his wife's demand. All he insisted on was that, to save his face, modifications should be made in the most challenging passages—which everyone already knew by heart! *Le Mariage de Figaro* was announced for production on April 27, 1784. Beaumarchais had triumphed over Louis XVI. To the malcontents among the nobility the evening was made sensational by the fact that the King had wanted to forbid the production and had expressed a hope that the piece would be a failure. The crush was so great that the doors were broken down and the iron railings bent. The French aristocrats applauded vigorously and listened with rapture to the comedy which, in the moral sphere, rang their own death-knell—not having the ghost of a notion that this was the first public manifestation of revolt, was the herald of the storms of the Revolution.

Any stir of decent feeling, of tact, of understanding, would assuredly, in such circumstances, have induced Marie Antoinette to refrain from participation in the staging of a play by Monsieur de Beaumarchais. Assuredly it was unfitting that a pamphleteer who had besmirched her honour and had made the King ludicrous in the eyes of all Paris should be able to boast of having had one of his characters impersonated by the daughter of Maria Theresa, by the wife of Louis XVI, two monarchs who had placed him under lock and key as a rogue? But since his victory over the King, Beaumarchais had become the rage in Paris; and, for the Queen, fashion was the supreme law. What did honour and respectability matter? After all, this was only play-acting! Besides, what a bewitching part was that of the roguish maiden! How did the text run?: "Imagine the prettiest little woman in the world, gentle, tender, lively, fresh, appetizing, nimble of foot, slender-waisted, with rounded arms, dewy mouth; and such hands, such feet, such teeth, such eyes!" What woman at court had such white hands, such soft and well-rounded arms, as the Queen of France and Navarre? Who else was so fitted to play this delightful role? Away, then, with hesitation. Summon Dazincourt from the Comédie Française to train these distinguished amateurs in the niceties of plastique. The Queen would order a lovely dress from Mademoiselle Bertin. They would all have a really amusing time once more, and be able to rid their minds of the perpetual quarrels at the court, to cease thinking about the ill-nature of affectionate relatives and the tiresome futilities and inconveniences of political life. Day after day, therefore, Marie Antoinette was busied over the forthcoming production of *Le Barbier de Séville* in her graceful little white-and-gold theatre, all unaware that the curtain was about to rise upon another comedy in which, unwittingly, she had been chosen to play the chief part.

The rehearsals of *Le Barbier de Séville* were drawing to a close. Marie Antoinette still had her misgivings. Would she really look young enough and pretty enough as Rosine? Would not her friends in the stalls, spoiled darlings, exacting, declare that she was not sufficiently light in her movements, not enough at her ease? Would they not regard her performance as amateurish? What a lot of trouble a Queen had to bear! Why was Madame Campan, with whom she was to go through her part once more, so late? Ah, here she was at last, at last; but what was the matter with her? She seemed in a great state of excitement.

At length Madame Campan recovered her composure, to some extent, and was able to explain stammeringly that, the day before, Boehmer, the court jeweller, had come to her much perturbed, asking her to procure for him without delay an audience of the Queen. The

Saxon Jew's story had been rambling and foolish. A few months ago, he said, the Queen had secretly purchased from him the famous and costly diamond necklace, and had arranged to pay for it by instalments. But the first instalment was long overdue, and not a ducat had yet been paid. His creditors were pressing him, and he needed money forthwith.

What was Madame Campan talking about? What diamonds? What necklace? What money? What instalments? At first it was all incomprehensible to Marie Antoinette. Of course she knew about the diamond necklace which the two jewellers, Boehmer and Bassenge, had made. Once, twice, three times they had offered it to her, for 1,600,000 livres. Of course she would have liked to buy it, but she could not get any money out of the ministers of State. They were always talking about the deficit. The jewellers must be a pair of swindlers. What impudence to declare that they had sold it to her secretly, and that she had agreed to pay for it by instalments—that she was in their debt! There must be some preposterous misunderstanding. Yes, she did remember, thinking things over, that quite recently, perhaps a week ago, she had had a strange letter from Boehmer and Bassenge in which they had thanked her for something, and had referred to a costly trinket. Where was the letter? Oh, yes, she had burned it. Always a scatter-brain, she seldom read a letter to the end, and this one, subservient and incomprehensible, had been promptly destroyed. What did the men really want of her? She made her secretary write a note to Boehmer. After all, there could be no such flaming hurry, and to-morrow would be inconvenient. August 9th would do well enough, for meanwhile she wanted her wits about her for the rehearsals of *Le Barbier de Séville*.

When Boehmer kept his appointment on August 9th, he was pale with emotion. The story he had to tell was so utterly perplexing, so past all understanding, that to begin with the Queen thought the man must have gone mad. He spoke of a Countess of Valois, "an intimate friend of Your Majesty."—"What on earth do you mean?" asked Marie Antoinette. "A friend of mine? I have never had such a lady among my intimates!"—Anyhow, Boehmer went on, this Countess Valois had inspected the necklace and had declared that the Queen wished to buy it secretly.—"Then His Eminence the Cardinal de Rohan . . ."—"That fellow?" interjected Marie Antoinette. "A man I detest and to whom I have never spoken a word!"—". . . took possession of the necklace, stating that he had been commissioned to do so by Your Majesty."

Crazy as the tale seemed, there must have been some truth at the bottom of it, for poor Boehmer's face was beaded with sweat as he spoke, and he was trembling all over. The Queen was furious that an unauthorized use should have been made of her name, and she commanded the jeweller to write a full account of the whole affair. By the twelfth of August this strange document, which is still to be seen in the archives, was in her hands. When she read it, she thought she must be dreaming. Her wrath became intensified as she passed from one line to the next, for so gross a fraud seemed unprecedented. An example must be made of the rogues. For the moment, however, she said nothing of the affair to the ministers of State, and even kept it from her most intimate friends; but on August 14th, she told the King about the mysterious business, and made him pledge himself to defend her honour.

In due time Marie Antoinette was to realize that she would have done better to have this obscure intrigue thoroughly investigated forthwith. But careful thought, caution, and foresight, were foreign to her headstrong and impetuous nature; furthermore, her good sense was least to be trusted when her pride was touched.

Outraged as she was, in the document Boehmer had brought her the Queen's attention was throughout concentrated upon one name, that of Louis Cardinal de Rohan whom for years she had loathed with all the uncontrol of her impulsive character, and whom she believed capable of any atrocity. Not that this worldly-minded nobleman in holy orders had ever, so far as she knew, done anything to harm her. As already described, on her coming to France he had welcomed her at the great doors of Strasbourg cathedral in a most flattering address. He had baptized her children, and had done his utmost to win her friendship. Fundamentally there was no opposition between their respective temperaments. On the contrary, Cardinal de Rohan was the masculine counterpart of Marie Antoinette, as light-minded as she, as superficial and as lavish in expenditure, and as indifferent towards his spiritual duties as she was towards her royal obligations. He was a mundane priest, just as she was a mundane sovereign; he was bishop, as she was queen, of the Rococo. He would have been a most suitable member of the little circle at Trianon, this man with his polished manners, his pose of witty boredom, his fondness for doing things on the grand scale. One might have expected that they would be on excellent terms: the elegant, handsome, frivolous, mellow-tongued cardinal; and the pleasure-seeking, gay, pretty queen with her light-heartedness and her taste for high play. Nothing but chance that had sown enmity between them. Yet how often do we find that those who are most alike become the most irreconcilable of foes.

It was, in truth, Maria Theresa who had driven a wedge between Rohan and Marie Antoinette; the Queen's detestation of the Cardinal was inherited from the mother, or was at any rate taken over from the mother, was a suggested dislike. Louis de Rohan had been ambassador in Vienna before he became cardinal in Strasbourg, and in the former position he had aroused the fierce anger of Maria Theresa. Expecting to welcome a diplomatist, she had found a presumptuous chatterbox. The Empress could easily have forgiven him for being of second-rate intelligence, and could perhaps have turned this weakness to good account, seeing that an able ruler may derive many advantages from having a foreign power represented by a simpleton. She might even have pardoned him for his love of display, although it revolted her when this self-conceited servant of Jesus made his appearance in Vienna with two sumptuous chariots each of which had cost forty thousand ducats; with a princely stud of horses; with gentlemen of the bed-chamber; with runners and lectors; with stewards and major-domos; with a multitude of lackeys dressed in green silk liveries and wearing plumes; with a suite which put that of the imperial court into the shade.

These things she might have forgiven, but there was one point upon which Maria Theresa was inexorable. Where religion and morality were concerned, her strictness knew no bounds. She was a bigot in these respects, and it was intolerable to her that "a man of God" should lay aside his sacred habiliments in order to wear a brown shooting-jacket, and, surrounded by fawning ladies, to bring down 130 head of game in a single day. What made matters worse, to her way of thinking, was that this priestly diplomat's loose, spendthrift, and frivolous behaviour, instead of arousing general indignation, secured widespread approval in Vienna, in her Vienna of the Jesuits and the Committees of Morality. The Austrian nobility, which was weary of the thrift and strictness of the court at Schönbrunn, drew a breath of relief when invited to participate in such refreshing and distinguished luxury and display; they were delighted to associate with this gentlemanly windbag. Above all, the ladies of the Austrian capital, who had been bored to death by the severities of the strait-laced puritanical widow, flocked to Rohan's lively supper-parties. Supremely annoyed, Maria Theresa wrote to Mercy: "Our women, young and old, pretty or ugly, have all alike been charmed by him. They idolize him, and for his part he seems to be well pleased here, for he declares that he would like to stay even after the death of his uncle the Bishop of Strasbourg."

Worse than all, the mortified Empress had to put up with it when her confidant Kaunitz spoke of Rohan as his dear friend; and when her son Joseph, who was always amused when he could say "yes" to his mother's "no," struck up an intimacy with Rohan. She could only look on with a wry face while this popinjay was making his notions of the way to enjoy life current in her family, in the court, in the whole city of Vienna. But Maria Theresa could not bear that her strictly religious capital should become a frivolous Versailles, a light-minded Trianon; she could not endure that the nobles at the Habsburg court should give themselves up to adultery and fornication; this plague should not be allowed to become endemic in Vienna, and so Rohan must be recalled. Letter after letter went to Marie Antoinette, designed to ensure that this "contemptible creature," this "vilain évêque," this "man with a hopelessly corrupt mind," this "volume farci de bien de mauvais propos," this "mauvais sujet," this "vrai panier percé," should be recalled. The wrath of the Empress found vent in terms of abuse worthy of an infuriated fishwife. She raged and stormed, wrote at last almost beseechingly in her despair, demanding to be "freed" from the emissary of Antichrist. In fact, very soon after Marie Antoinette became Queen, she obediently saw to it that Louis Rohan was dismissed from his ambassadorship at Vienna.

But when a Rohan falls, he falls upwards. To compensate him for the loss of his diplomatic mission, he was made a bishop, and shortly afterwards grand almoner, thus becoming the highest ecclesiastical dignitary at the court, the man through whose hands passed the King's benefactions. His own revenues were enormous, for not only was he bishop of Strasbourg, but also landgrave of Alsace, abbot of the rich abbey of Saint-Vaast, chief superintendent of the royal hospitals, vicar-general of the Sorbonne—and, God alone knows why, member of the Academy! But considerable though his income certainly was, his expenditure was greater still, for Rohan squandered money with both hands. At a cost of millions he rebuilt the episcopal palace in Strasbourg; he gave the most expensive banquets; he lavished money upon his light-of-loves; but the most wasteful of his passions was that for Cagliostro, who cost him more than seven mistresses. Soon it was an open secret that the bishop's finances were embarrassed, and Christ's servant was seen more often in the offices of Jewish money-lenders than at church, more often in the company of pretty ladies than in that of learned theologians. The Parliament of Paris had just been conducting an inquiry into the extravagant management of the hospital whereof Rohan was chief superintendent. Need we be surprised, then, that from the first the Queen should have been convinced that this Brother Lightfoot had organized the swindle of the necklace in order to raise funds for himself?

"The Cardinal has made use of my name like a vile and clumsy coiner. The probability is that, when he acted as he did under pressure of an immediate need for money, he believed he would be able to pay the jeweller at the appointed time without anything having been discovered," wrote Marie Antoinette to Joseph II. We can understand the bitterness which made her regard Rohan as unpardonable. During the last fifteen years, since first meeting him in front of Strasbourg cathedral, Marie Antoinette, strictly obeying her mother's commands, had not addressed him a single word, but had flouted him in the face of the whole court. It seemed to her, therefore, a base act of revenge that he should have dragged her name into a conspiracy of cheats; and of all the attacks on her honour which had been made by the French nobility, she regarded this as the craftiest and the most audacious. Passionately, with tears in her eyes, she implored the King to make a public example and mete out the severest punishment to this deceiver, who was really, though she did not know it, not deceiver but deceived.

The King, being completely subservient to his wife, did not trouble to take thought when she asked him to do something for her, she who herself never weighed the consequences of her actions or her wishes. Without scrutinizing the details of the charge, without asking for documents, without questioning either Boehmer or the Cardinal, he unreflectingly made himself the tool of a giddy-pated woman's wrath. On August 15th he astonished the ministerial council by announcing his intention to have the Cardinal arrested immediately. The Cardinal? The Cardinal de Rohan? The statesmen looked at one another in amazement and alarm. At length one of them ventured to ask whether it was not rather too strenuous a measure, whether it might not produce an unfortunate effect, to lay by the heels so exalted a personage, a high dignitary of the Church—to lock him up as if he were a common malefactor. But public disgrace was what Marie Antoinette demanded as chastisement. It was at length to be made plain to all that the Queen's good name was not to be trifled with. Most unwillingly, much disquieted, with anxious forebodings, the ministers at length gave way. A few hours later came an unexpected climax. Since the Feast of the Assumption was also the Queen's name-day, a court was held at Versailles to offer her congratulations. The Œil de Bœuf and the galleries were thronged with courtiers and other persons of importance. Among them, as chief performer, was the unsuspecting Rohan, for it was his business to fulfil his pontifical function on this august occasion. There he waited, ready to discharge his office, in the anteroom to the King's chamber, the place for those who had the privilege of the "grande entrée"—wearing a white surplice over his scarlet cassock.

But Louis XVI did not appear in state as was expected, accompanied by his wife, that they might go together to Mass. Instead there came a lackey to summon Rohan into the private apartments. There stood, biting her lips and with averted gaze, the Queen, who vouchsafed no acknowledgment to the Cardinal's greeting. No less cold and uncivil was Baron Breteuil, the minister of State, a personal enemy. Before Rohan had had time to consider what could be wanted of him, the King said bluntly: "My dear cousin, I want to know all about the diamond necklace which you bought in the Queen's name."

Rohan turned pale. He was not prepared for this.

"Sire," he said stammeringly, "I was myself deceived, but I have deceived no one."

"If so, my dear cousin, you have no occasion for anxiety. But I am awaiting your explanation."

Rohan did not know what to answer. He saw Marie Antoinette's threatening look, and words failed him. His confusion aroused the King's compassion, and the kindly Louis tried to make things easier for him.

"Write what you have to say to me about the matter," said the King, and thereupon he, Marie Antoinette, and Breteuil left the room.

When Louis returned, His Eminence had written about fifteen lines, by way of explanation, and these he handed to the King. A woman named Valois had commissioned him to get the necklace for the Queen. He realized now that she had cheated him.

"Where is this woman?" asked Louis.

"Sire, I do not know."

"Have you the necklace?"

"It is in this woman's hands."

Now Louis summoned the Queen, Breteuil, and the keeper of the seals, and had the report of the jewellers read over to him. He next asked about the written authorization, ostensibly signed by the Queen, on which Rohan had acted. The latter, utterly crushed, said:

"Sire, I have the document. Obviously it must have been a forgery."

"Obviously," replied the King. Still, although the Cardinal offered to pay for the necklace, he said severely: "Sir, in the circumstances I have no choice but to have the seals placed on your house and to put you under arrest. The Queen's name is precious to me. Aspersions have been cast upon it, and I must neglect nothing which can put matters right."

Rohan besought the monarch to spare him this disgrace, especially at such an hour, when he was about to enter the house of God and to say the pontifical Mass before the assembled court. The King, pliable and good-natured as usual, was shaken by the manifest despair of the man who was himself a victim. But Marie Antoinette could no longer contain herself. With tears of anger in her eyes she asked Rohan how he could possibly have believed that she, who for eight years had addressed him never a word, would have employed him as a go-between in order to buy the necklace behind her husband's back. To this reproach the Cardinal could find no answer. He was now unable to understand how he could ever have been fool enough to become involved in the imbroglio. Louis was sorry for him, but said: "I hope you will be able to justify yourself! Meanwhile, however, I shall do my duty as King and husband."

The interview was over. The nobles were waiting impatiently in the crowded reception-room. Mass ought to have begun long since. What in the name of wonder could be the cause of such a delay? There was a feeling of storm in the atmosphere!

Suddenly the folding-doors leading into the King's private apartments were thrown open. The first to appear was the Cardinal de Rohan in his scarlet cassock, pale of countenance and with pinched lips; behind him, Breteuil, the old soldier, red in the face like a weather-beaten peasant, his eyes sparkling with excitement. Having reached the middle of the room, Breteuil shouted an order to the captain of the bodyguard: "Arrest Monsieur le Cardinal!"

Amazement was general. A cardinal to be arrested! A Rohan! And in the King's anteroom! Was the old swashbuckler Breteuil tipsy? No! Rohan made no move, showed no indignation, but with hanging head surrendered to the guards. Almost shuddering with alarm, the courtiers formed into a double line, and running the gauntlet of inquisitive, shame-provoking, embittered glances, there now strode from room to room and down the stairs the Prince de Rohan, grand almoner of the King, cardinal of the Holy Catholic Church, landgrave of Alsace and prince of the Empire, member of the Academy, and the holder of countless other dignities, while behind him, as if the prince had been no more than a galley-slave, stalked the weather-beaten soldier as guardian.

Rohan was kept waiting for a time in one of the little guardrooms on the ground floor; awakening from his stupor, the prisoner took advantage of the prevailing consternation to pencil a few lines on a sheet of paper instructing his private chaplain to burn with all possible speed the documents that would be found in a red portfolio. These, as subsequently transpired at the trial, were the forged letters purporting to have been written by the Queen. One of the Cardinal's mounted couriers galloped off with this message to the Hôtel de Strasbourg and reached his master's house before the police (who were taking their time) arrived to place the papers under seal; and before the grand almoner of France, who should have said Mass before the king and the court, had been conveyed to the Bastille. Meanwhile orders had been issued for the arrest of all who had been confederates in this obscure affair. As for the Mass, no Mass was said at Versailles that Assumption day. What would have been the use? Who would have been in a sufficiently devotional mood to listen to the holy words? The court, Paris, and soon the country at large, were stunned by the news as by a bolt from the blue.

Behind the closed door remained the Queen, her nerves still twitching with anger. The scene had excited her terribly, but at length she had been able to deal with one of her calumniators, with one of those who were making crafty attacks upon her honour. Would not all well-disposed persons now hasten to congratulate her upon the arrest of this rascal? Would not the court extol the energy of the King who had for so long been reputed a weakling, of the King who had sent this unworthiest of priests to the Bastille? But, strange as it must have seemed to her, no one came. With embarrassed countenances, even her closest friends, the women who had been her chief associates for so long, kept out of her way. It was very still at Trianon and at Versailles. The nobles did not trouble to conceal their indignation that one of their privileged class should have been treated with so much dishonour; and the Cardinal de Rohan, who would be let off lightly if he would bow to Louis's personal judgment, having recovered from his first alarm, coolly rejected the royal grace and claimed the right to be judged by the Parliament of Paris. Marie Antoinette, though at the outset in so desperate a hurry, began to become uneasy. She was not pleased with her success. That evening her ladies-in-waiting found her in tears.

Soon, however, her habitual high spirits returned. Foolishly self-deceived, she wrote to her brother Joseph: "For my part, I am delighted that we shall no longer hear anything about this horrid affair." This was August. The trial before the Parliament of Paris could not possibly take place earlier than December, and perhaps it would not begin until after the New Year. Why should she trouble her pretty head about the matter? If people wanted to gossip or to murmur, let them do so. What matter? Make-up and the new dresses! No need to stop the performance of a delightful comedy because of such a trifle. The rehearsals continued, and the Queen, instead of studying the police reports relating to the great trial (about which there was no immediate urgency, and which might perhaps be yet further postponed), went on studying the part of the lively Rosine in *Le Barbier de Séville*. It would seem, however, that even in this matter her constitutional indolence must have made her careless, for otherwise she would surely have laid to heart Basile's remark anent calumny—words which seem prophetic of her own fate.

"Calumny! You don't really know what you are disdaining when you disdain it. I have seen persons of the utmost probity laid low by it, or nearly so. Believe me, there is no false report however crude, no abomination, no absurd falsehood, which the idlers in a great city cannot, if they take the trouble, make universally believed—and here we have tittle-tattlers who are past masters in their art. . . . First of all they circulate a faint rumour which skims the surface of the ground like a swallow just before a storm, pianissimo and murmurous, so that it seems to pass without leaving a trace; but really, in its passage, it has implanted its poisonous germs. Some ear has heard it, some mouth repeats it, and, piano, piano, it reaches other ears. The mischief has been done. It sprouts like a mushroom, spreads like a swelling wave, rinforzando as it moves from one to another, until it becomes the very devil; so that, all of a sudden, who can tell how, the calumny has taken shape, is enlarging, is growing steadily, under all men's eyes. It extends the range of its flight, its great wings making the roar of a whirlwind, of a whirlwind which, amid rolling thunder, sweeps everything into its resistless eddy, until, through Heaven's will, it becomes a general clamour, a public crescendo, a universal chorus of hatred and contempt. Who can stand up against such a typhoon?"

But Marie Antoinette was, as usual, hard of hearing, or slow of understanding. Had it been otherwise, she would surely have realized the bearing of this famous declamation upon her own fortunes. The production of *Le Barbier de Séville* on August 19, 1785, signalized the last act of the Rococo comedy. Incipit tragœdia.

CHAPTER XV

The Diamond Necklace

WHAT had really happened? To give a credible account of the matter is far from easy, for the true story of the affair of the diamond necklace would be rejected as wildly improbable if, instead of having actually happened, it were merely the theme of a sensational novel. The old adage is a sound one. Truth is stranger than fiction. The imaginative writer cannot but feel sometimes that he would do well to make his bow to the public and retire gracefully, since life so easily outbids his fantasies. Even Goethe, who in *Grosskophta* tried to make a stage play out of the necklace affair, only consolidated into a heavy jest what was, in verity, one of the boldest, most stimulating, most scintillating farces in history. There is not a comedy of Molière's in which we find so motley and so amusing a crowd of humbugs and humbugged, of deceivers and deceived, of clever fools, as in this lively hotch-potch in which a thievish magpie, a fox equipped with all the wiles of charlatanry, and a clumsy and credulous bear are the leading characters in the craziest tragi-comedy known to history. At the centre of every genuine comedy, there must be a woman. The figure round whom this affair of the diamond necklace circled had been a neglected child, daughter of an impoverished nobleman and a dissolute serving-maid. A barefooted wench, this child had picked up a livelihood by stealing potatoes out of the fields or by minding cows for a pittance. When her father died and her mother became a street-walker, the girl took to begging as her only resource, and at seven, by a stroke of luck, she approached the Marquise de Boulainvilliers with what seemed the incredible patter: "Give alms to a poor orphan sprung from the blood of the Valois!" What! Was this lousy and affamished little creature in truth of royal blood? Could she, indeed, be a descendant of that famous line? Though incredulous, the Marchioness told her coachman to pull up, and she questioned the little beggar-girl exhaustively.

In the affair of the diamond necklace, we must throughout be prepared to accept preposterous improbabilities. The girl Jeanne was in very fact the legitimate daughter of Jacques-Rémy, who, though a poacher, a drunkard, and a terror to the whole countryside, was unquestionably an offspring of the House of Valois, which was just as old and just as distinguished as the House of Bourbon. The Marquise de Boulainvilliers, profoundly touched by the sad fate of such royal spawn, took Jeanne and a smaller sister under her care and had them brought up at a seminary for young gentlewomen. When she was fourteen, Jeanne was taught various trades, such as those of tailoress and sempstress; she learned to wash and iron clothes; and was finally admitted to a convent for daughters of the nobility. Soon, however, it became apparent that little Jeanne was unfitted for a cloistered existence. Her father's vagrant blood was circulating in her veins, and at two-and-twenty she and her sister ran away from the nunnery. Penniless, but high-spirited and adventurous, they turned up in Bar-sur-Aube. There a sprig of the lesser nobility, Nicolas de Lamotte, an officer in the gendarmerie, fell in love with her, and married her, though rather late in the day, for the priestly blessing only forestalled by a month the birth of twins. The husband was neither exacting nor jealous, and under his ægis Madame Lamotte, or "Madame Lamotte-Valois," was able to give free rein to her tastes while ostensibly leading a respectable petty-bourgeois life. However, "the blood of the Valois" demanded its rights, and from the first Jeanne had had but one thought—to climb, no matter how. She importuned her benefactress the Marquise de Boulainvilliers until the latter secured for her the entry to Cardinal de Rohan's palace at Zabern. Being clever as well as pretty, she was able to play upon the weaknesses of the Cardinal. Through her intermediation (presumably at the cost of wearing an invisible pair of horns) her husband was appointed captain in a regiment of dragoons and had his debts paid.

Might not Jeanne have now been satisfied? By no means! This was but one step in an ascending career. Her spouse Lamotte had received his commission as captain from the King, but thereafter, on his own responsibility, he dubbed himself count. Now that she had so fine a name as "Comtesse de Lamotte-Valois," was she to rest content with vegetating in the provinces upon a modest pension paid to herself, supplemented by her husband's pay as cavalry officer? It would have been absurd! To a pretty and unscrupulous woman, determined to plunder the vain and the foolish, such a name was worth a hundred thousand livres a year. In order to open their campaign, this precious pair rented a mansion in the Rue Neuve-Saint-Gilles, prattled to money-lenders about the huge estate to which the countess was rightfully entitled as a descendant of the Valois, and kept open house with the funds thus obtained—although the plate was only hired for each occasion from neighbouring silversmiths. When their creditors began to press for payment, the Comtesse de Lamotte-Valois fobbed them off by telling them she was going to Versailles to push her claim at court.

It need hardly be said that she did not know a soul in these exalted circles, and that she might well have wearied her pretty legs week after week standing to demand admission without ever finding her way into the Queen's anteroom. But, being a skilled adventuress, she had already planned her great coup. While among other petitioners in Madame Elisabeth's waiting-room, she suddenly fell into a faint. Everyone crowded around her, her husband disclosed her exalted name, and, with tears in his eyes, explained that weakness resulting from years of semi-starvation could alone account for the fainting fit. Amid general sympathy this thoroughly healthy invalid was carried home upon a stretcher; two hundred livres were sent to her forthwith; and her pension was increased from eight hundred livres to fifteen hundred.

But this was no more than a beggarly allowance for a Valois! Since the first trick had been successful, she would repeat it a second and a third time, so she fainted in the Countess of Artois's anteroom, then again in the Gallery of Mirrors through which the Queen was about to pass. Unfortunately Marie Antoinette, upon whose generosity this prize beggar had especially counted, heard nothing of the lady's syncope; and since a fourth attack of the kind at Versailles would have raised suspicions, the precious pair returned to Paris without having made much by their trouble. They were, in fact, far from having achieved the object of their desires. Of course they were extremely careful to avoid giving themselves away, and made a great to-do about the gracious fashion in which the Queen had welcomed them as her dear relatives. Since there was no lack of nincompoops eager to scrape acquaintance with the Comtesse de Lamotte-Valois who had been so highly honoured by the Queen, plenty of fat sheep soon presented themselves for the shearing, and their credit was temporarily re-established.

The two deeply indebted mendicants were speedily surrounded by a regular court, presided over by a certain Rétaux de Villette who had the title of first secretary, and who not only shared in the rogueries of the distinguished countess, but also had a place in her bed. The "second secretary," Loth, was a priest. Coachmen, lackeys, and maidservants were hired, so that ere long all went merry as a marriage bell in the Rue Neuve-Saint-Gilles. There were many amusing card-parties, which were not indeed lucrative for the pigeons who came to be plucked, but the presence of ladies of easy virtue made up for that. Still, the earnings at faro and similar games did not suffice to make income balance expenditure; creditors were ever more urgent in their demands for payment, and after a few months came threats to put the bailiffs in. Once again our worthy couple had reached the end of the tether, and, if they were to save themselves from prison, they must widen the scope of their operations.

For a swindle in the grand style at least two things are needed, a great swindler and a great fool. The fool was not far to seek, being no other than that illustrious member of the Académie Française, His Eminence the Bishop of Strasbourg, the Grand Almoner of France, Cardinal de Rohan. Wholly a man of his own epoch, neither shrewder nor stupider than others, this charming prince of the Church suffered like so many of his contemporaries from the malady of his century: credulity. Few people seem able to live for any considerable time without faith, and since Voltaire had put religious belief out of fashion, superstition had taken its place in the salons of eighteenth-century society. A golden age thus dawned for alchemists, cabalists, rosicrucians, charlatans, necromancers, and miraculous healers. No gentleman or lady of rank or fashion could refrain from consulting Cagliostro, from dining with the Comte de Saint-Germain, and from sitting among the convulsives beside Mesmer's magnetic tub. Precisely because they were so clear-sighted, so wittily frivolous; for the very reason that the generals no longer took their duties, the queens their dignity, the priests their God, seriously—"enlightened" men and women of the world found their only way of escape from an intolerable sense of vacancy in sporting with the metaphysical, the mystical, the supra-sensual, and the incomprehensible; and, however wide-awake they might seem, they fell a ready prey to every variety of humbug and adventurer.

Among these spiritually impoverished persons, the most credulous of all was His Eminence the Cardinal de Rohan, who was in the toils of the most skilful of humbugs, a pope among the swindlers of his day, the "divine" Cagliostro. Giuseppe Balsamo had made a nest for himself in the Zabern episcopal palace, and displayed marvellous skill in conjuring his patron's money into his own purse. Since augurs and cheats recognize one another at the first glance, Cagliostro and the Comtesse de Lamotte-Valois were soon as thick as thieves. Informed by Cagliostro (who was thoroughly acquainted with the Cardinal's secret desires), the Valois knew that Rohan's supreme ambition was to become first minister of France; and she knew likewise what he dreaded as the only serious obstacle in his path, Marie Antoinette's inexplicable dislike. For an artful woman, to know a man's weaknesses means to have him in tow; and our dainty swindler promptly twisted a rope at the end of which she would be able to make the episcopal bear dance for so long as he could still sweat money.

In April 1784 the Comtesse de Lamotte-Valois began to drop casual remarks to the effect of how much confidence her "dear friend," the Queen, reposed in her; and more and more the unsuspicious Cardinal came to believe that this pretty little woman would be an ideal advo-cate with Marie Antoinette. He frankly admitted how profoundly he had been mortified because, for years past, Her Majesty had not vouch-safed him so much as a glance, and that he knew of no greater happi-ness than the possibility of serving her reverently. If only someone could at length convince the Queen of his devotion and loyalty!

Appearing to be much moved, this "intimate friend" promised to plead his cause with Marie Antoinette; and already in May, to Rohan's astonishment, she told him something which convinced him that her influence was powerfully at work. The Queen, she said, was no longer adversely inclined, and, to show her change of mood (though it would be inexpedient to do anything too pronounced for the moment), Marie Antoinette would, at the next formal reception, privately nod to the

Cardinal in a particular way. We are all apt to believe what we want to believe, and to see what we want to see. Rohan actually imagined that at the next reception he had noticed a certain "nuance" in the Queen's response to his salutation, and paid hard cash to the go-between as a reward.

But the Valois wanted to use the golden touch far more effectively than this. In order to get the Cardinal more firmly in her snare, she felt it necessary to show him a more tangible sign of the royal favour. What about some letters? Was not forgery one of the arts to be expected from an unscrupulous secretary who shared her house and her bed? Unhesitatingly Rétaux drafted, ostensibly in Marie Antoinette's handwriting, letters from the Queen to her friend Valois. Since their pigeon gulped these down as genuine, the obvious cue was to follow up the lucrative path. Why not rig out an interchange of letters between Rohan and the Queen, so that the plunderers could dip their fingers more deeply into the Cardinal's pouch? Acting on the Valois's advice, the besotted Cardinal composed a detailed justification of his previous behaviour, spent days correcting the manuscript, and finally handed over a fair copy of the document to this woman who was priceless in more senses of the term than one. Surely she must be a sorceress as well as the Queen's intimate? Within a few days the Comtesse de Lamotte-Valois brought a little note penned upon gilt-edged rep note-paper, adorned in one of the corners with the fleur-de-lis. The proud Queen sprung from the House of Habsburg, the woman who had hitherto cold-shouldered him, now wrote to the Cardinal as follows: "I am delighted that I need no longer regard you as blameworthy. It is not yet possible to grant you the audience you desire. I will let you know as soon as circumstances permit of this. Meanwhile be discreet." The bamboozled victim could not contain himself for joy. Acting on the Valois's advice, he wrote letter after letter to thank Her Majesty; and the more he was filled with pride at the thought of standing high in Marie Antoinette's good graces, the more successful was the Comtesse de Lamotte-Valois in emptying his pocket. The bold scheme was making good headway.

The only trouble was that the other person in the comedy, Queen Marie Antoinette, did not really form part of the cast. How could the dangerous game be continued on its present lines? Rohan might be the most credulous idiot in the world, but he would not for ever go on believing that the Queen was greeting him when in reality she was giving him the cut direct and would never address a word to him. Before long the Cardinal would certainly smell a rat. It was necessary for the conspirators to play a bolder move in their game of chess. Since it was certain that the Queen would never speak to him, could not someone be found to impersonate Marie Antoinette, someone with sufficient histrionic ability to make the fool believe that he had had an interview with the Queen? Darkness has always been a great aid in the rogue's armamentarium. Would it not be feasible to arrange for a tryst after nightfall, to utilize some well-shaded alley in Versailles park? Then Rohan could meet somebody drilled to act as the Queen's double who would say a few words conned beforehand. In the night, all cats are black; and, being in the mood to be humbugged, the worthy Cardinal would be led by the nose just as easily as he had been by Cagliostro's hocus-pocus and by the forged letters on gilt-edged notepaper. But where, at short notice, could a young woman be found to "double" the part, as the modern film producers say? Where but in the region frequented by "ladies" of all sorts and sizes, tall and short, fat and thin, brunette and blond, walking to and fro for professional purposes; in the gardens of the Palais Royal, the paradise of Parisian harlots? "Count" de Lamotte set out in search of what was wanted, and he soon put his hand upon the needed impersonator, a young lady named Nicole, known afterwards as the Demoiselle d'Oliva, or the Baronne d'Oliva. Ostensibly a modiste, her main concern in life was to serve gentlemen rather than ladies. Lamotte easily persuaded her to the undertaking, for, as the gentleman's wife explained to the judges, the girl was "exceedingly stupid." On August 11th this servant of the pandemian Venus was conveyed to lodgings at Versailles, and with her own hands the Comtesse de Lamotte-Valois dressed the young woman in a white muslin gown, a skilful imitation of the one which the Queen is seen wearing in the portrait painted by Madame Vigée le Brun. On with a wide-brimmed hat to shade her face as much as possible and to cover her carefully powdered hair, and then out and away with the rather alarmed little woman who was for a few minutes to represent the Queen of France in conversation with the grand almoner of the monarchy. The most audacious piece of knavery in all history was under way.

Swiftly, silently, the pair of rogues with their pseudo-queen sped across the terrace at Versailles. Heaven was kind to them on this moonless night. They mounted to the grove of Venus, where, since it is so thickly shaded by pines, cedars, and fig trees, barely more than the outline of a face and figure could be discerned. The place formed an admirable setting for the trick that was to be played. But the poor little cocotte began to tremble. Into what sort of an adventure had she allowed these strangers to inveigle her? She would have liked to run away. Her teeth chattered with anxiety as she held the rose and the letter which, as arranged, she was to hand to a distinguished gentle-man who was coming to speak to her at the appointed spot. Hark, there was the sound of footsteps on the gravel. A man loomed in the darkness, Rétaux the secretary, who, in the livery of one of the royal servants, was conducting Rohan to the meeting-place. Nicole felt her-self vigorously thrust forward, and her two companions vanished as if they had been swallowed up by the night. She stood alone. No, not alone, for, tall and slender, a stranger approached: the Cardinal.

How foolishly this stranger behaved. Making a profound obeisance, almost to the ground, he kissed the hem of the little prostitute's gar-ment. Now it was Nicole's business to hand him the rose and the letter. But in her confusion she dropped the rose and forgot the letter. The utmost she could do was, in stifled tones, to stammer out the few words she had learned by heart: "You may hope that the past will be forgotten." This brief utterance seemed to delight the unknown gentle-man beyond measure. Again and again he bowed, and, in broken words, murmured his subservient thanks—although the poor little modiste could not understand why. All that she knew was that a deadly fear overcame her lest she should say something that was not in the programme, and thus give the game away. Thanks be, at this juncture, there sounded another footstep on the gravel, a hasty one this time, and an excited whisper: "Come away quickly, quickly, Madame and the Countess of Artois are close at hand." The warning (it was part of the plot) sufficed. The Cardinal took alarm, and departed swiftly with Lamotte, whose wife led away little Nicole. With pal-pitating heart the pseudo-queen of this comedy slunk past the palace where, behind the closed shutters, the real Queen was sound asleep, heedless of the drama that had been played outside.

The trick proved gloriously successful. The Cardinal was bereft of his senses. Hitherto his suspicions had from time to time been aroused, so that again and again he had had to be reassured. The alleged significant nod was but a half-proof, and even the letters were dubious. But now, when, as he believed, he had spoken to the Queen in person, and had learned from her own lips that she had forgiven him, he regarded the Valois's every word as gospel truth. He was ready to follow her lead through thick and thin. That evening there was no happier man in the fair realm of France. He looked forward confidently to becoming first minister and the Queen's favourite.

A few days later the Valois announced to the Cardinal another signal proof of Marie Antoinette's favour. Her Majesty—of course Rohan knew the kindliness of her heart—wanted to bestow fifty thousand livres upon a noble family that had fallen upon evil days—but at the moment she was short of cash. Would the Cardinal be good enough to undertake this gracious service on her behalf? Rohan, in his exuberance, never stopped to wonder that the Queen, whose revenues were enormous, should be stinted in funds. Indeed, all Paris knew that she was heavily burdened with debt. Sending for an Alsatian Jew named Cerf-Beer, a money-lender, he borrowed the requisite sum, and handed it over to the Valois. She and her husband had found the string which could make their puppet work. Three months later they tugged it still more vigorously, telling him that the Queen was again in want of money, and the Cardinal subserviently pawned his furniture and his plate that he might satisfy his patroness without delay.

These were heavenly days for Count and Countess de Lamotte. The Cardinal was away in Alsace, but his money jingled in their pockets. They need no longer trouble about the future since they had found so fine a pigeon to pluck. It would be enough, from time to time, to write a letter to Rohan in the Queen's name, and he would hand over as many ducats as they wanted. They would have a gay time of it, and take no thought for the morrow. In those days it was not only noblemen, sovereign princes, and cardinals who were credulous and light-minded, for the infection had spread to the very cheats who practised on the credulity of their wealthy patrons. A country house at Bar-sur-

Aube with beautiful gardens and a well-stocked farm was purchased; the owners of the easily acquired property took their meals off golden platters, and drank from crystal goblets; the best society was eager to enjoy the honour of associating with the Comtesse de Lamotte-Valois. A jolly world, in which fools and dupes abounded!

One who, at the gaming-table, has thrice drawn the highest card, will be ready to stake his all on the fourth chance. Hazard thrust the ace of trumps into the Valois's hand. At one of her parties a guest told her that the court jewellers Boehmer and Bassenge were in trouble. The poor fellows had sunk their capital and a good deal of their credit in the most wonderful diamond necklace human eyes had ever seen. It had been intended for Madame Dubarry, who would certainly have bought it had not the smallpox so suddenly made an end of Louis XV. Then it was offered to the Spanish court, but without success. Queen Marie Antoinette, who was crazy about such trinkets, and was not wont to boggle at a high price, besought her husband to purchase the gems; but the skinflint would not disburse sixteen hundred thousand livres. The jewellers were up to the neck; interest charges were gnawing away at the lovely diamonds; probably they would have to break up the splendid necklace, and sell the stones—at a great loss—one by one. Would it not be possible for the Comtesse de Lamotte-Valois, who was on such intimate terms with Marie Antoinette, to persuade her royal friend to buy this beautiful piece of workmanship after all? By instalments, of course, and on the most favourable terms. No doubt a liberal commission would be paid to the intermediary! The Valois, wishing to foster the legend of her influence with the Queen, was graciously pleased to say she would do her best in the matter, and on December 29, 1784, the two jewellers brought the precious necklace for inspection to the Rue Neuve-Saint-Gilles.

What a wonderful sight! The Valois's heart almost stopped beating. Just as these diamonds sparkled in the sunlight, so did glittering thoughts course through her shrewd and impudent brain. Would she not be able to persuade that jackass of a cardinal to buy the diamond necklace secretly for the Queen? Very soon he was back in Paris from Alsace, and the Comtesse de Lamotte-Valois had her tale ready for him. There was to be a new sign of royal favour. The Queen

wanted (of course without her husband's knowledge) to buy a costly
trinket. A go-between whose discretion could be relied upon would be
needed, and Her Majesty, to show her confidence in Rohan, had
chosen him to fill this honourable position. A few days later, the
Comtesse was able to tell the delighted Boehmer that a purchaser had
been found—the Cardinal de Rohan. On January 29th, in the Hôtel de
Strasbourg, terms of purchase were arranged. The price was to be
sixteen hundred thousand livres, payable within two years in four six-
monthly instalments. The necklace was to be handed over on February
1st, the first instalment becoming payable on August 1, 1785. The
Cardinal wrote the conditions with his own hand, and gave the agreement to the Valois, who was to submit it to "her friend," the Queen.
Next day, January 30th, she came back with Her Majesty's answer.
The Queen was perfectly satisfied with the conditions.

However, the donkey who had hitherto been so tractable jibbed just
outside the stable. Sixteen hundred thousand livres was a large sum of
money, was no trifle even to this spendthrift prince of the Church. If
he were to disburse so vast an amount, he must be safeguarded in some
way, must at least have a document signed by the Queen authorizing
him to make the purchase. Something written and signed? Of course!
(What did one keep a secretary for?) Next day the Comtesse de
Lamotte-Valois brought back the contract which Rohan had so carefully penned, and, lo and behold! in the margin beside each clause was
inscribed the word, manu propria, "Approved!" while at the end of
the document was the "holograph" signature, "Marie Antoinette de
France."

Now, had he had any gumption, this grand almoner of the court,
member of the Academy, ex-diplomat, and in his dreams future first
minister, would assuredly have been aware that the Queen of France
never signed any documents except by her Christian name without any
addition. The signature "Marie Antoinette de France" was enough at
the first glance to betray the handiwork of an extremely incompetent
forger. But how could Rohan doubt, since the Queen had secretly
accorded him a personal interview in the grove of Venus? He pledged
his honour that he would never let this momentous document out of
his hands and would never show it to anyone. The following morning,
on February 1st, the jeweller brought the necklace to the Cardinal,

who himself took it to the Valois the same evening, wishing to convince himself that it would be conveyed to the Queen by trusty hands. He was not kept waiting long in the Rue Neuve-Saint-Gilles. Soon a manly footstep was heard on the staircase. The Comtesse begged the Cardinal to withdraw into an adjoining room, from which, through a glass door, he would be able to watch the transfer of the valuable purchase. He was in fact able to observe the entry of a young man, dressed in black (of course it was once more Rétaux, the redoubtable secretary), who presented himself with the words: "By order of the Queen." Thoroughly reassured by this magic phrase, Rohan handed over the casket to the Valois, who, in turn, gave it to the mysterious emissary. The latter disappeared as swiftly as he had come, and with him the necklace vanished until the last trump. Much moved, Rohan bade farewell and departed. He could not be kept waiting long for a due return for his friendly offices. The Queen's secret helper would soon become the King's chief servant, the first minister of France!

A few days later a Hebraic jeweller called at the headquarters of the Paris police to complain, as representative of his outraged colleagues, that a certain Rétaux de Villette was offering remarkably fine diamonds for sale at such low prices as to arouse strong suspicion that they must have been stolen. The minister of police sent for Rétaux. The latter explained that the diamonds had been entrusted to him for sale by one of the King's relatives, the Comtesse de Lamotte-Valois. "Countess" —"Valois"—these fine-sounding appellations worked like a charm upon the official, and made him dismiss Rétaux, who had suffered nothing worse than a fright. Still, the incident was enough to impose caution. The Countess, who had promptly broken up the necklace into its component parts, realized that the risk of hawking the separate brilliants in Paris would be too great, so she packed her husband off to London, his pockets stuffed with diamonds—greatly to the advantage of the jewellers of Bond Street and Piccadilly, who were able to purchase precious stones at figures far below their market value. Hurrah! now there was plenty of money, far more money than even this accomplished female swindler had ever dreamed of making. Intoxicated by her success, she did not hesitate to flaunt her newly acquired wealth. She had a carriage drawn by four English mares; lackeys with magnificent liveries; a Negro servant whose clothes were trimmed with silver lace; carpets, tapestries, bronzes, plumed hats; a bed with appointments of scarlet velvet. When the worthy couple removed to their distinguished residence at Bar-sur-Aube, no less than four-and-twenty carts were needed to convey the articles of luxury which had hastily been got together. To the inhabitants of this little provincial town, the arrival must have seemed like a tale from the *Arabian Nights' Entertainment.* Richly caparisoned horsemen led the train of the new Grand Mogul. Then came the English berline, pearl-grey, upholstered in white. On the satin wrap which the occupants of this splendid vehicle used to keep warm the legs which would have been better employed in escaping across the frontier, were embroidered the arms of the House of Valois, with the motto: "Rege ab avo sanguinem, nomen, et lilia"—From the King, my ancestor, I derive my blood, my name, and the lilies. The sometime officer in the gendarmerie was gloriously decked out. He had rings on all his fingers, a huge diamond buckle on his shoes; three or four watch-chains glittered on his heroic breast; and his wardrobe, as we learn from the inventory made public during the trial, contained no less than eighteen new silk or brocade suits, trimmed with Mechlin lace, and having buttons of chased gold. His wife was equally resplendent, for she glittered with jewels like a Hindu idol. Never before had the burgesses of Bar-sur-Aube seen such a display of wealth, which exercised its customary magnetic attraction. The titled folk of the neighbourhood flocked to the Valois mansion, to guzzle and swill at the banquets that were given. Troops of lackeys served the most delicate food upon costly plate; musicians discoursed sweet music; a modern Crœsus, the Count strode through his princely mansion, scattering money with both hands.

Here, once more, the story of the diamond necklace is so fantastically absurd as to become incredible. Surely the fraud should have been discovered within a few weeks? How was it possible for the two rogues to make so lavish a display of their plunder? Were there no police in France? But the Valois had not reckoned without her host. If matters should take an ill turn, at any rate she had a fine front-rank man. Should the bubble burst, the Cardinal de Rohan would see to it that no harm came. It would not suit the grand almoner of France to become involved in a scandal, and still less in an affair that would make him intolerably ridiculous. Rather than that should happen, he would, without a grimace, pay for the necklace out of his own pocket. Why worry, then? With such a partner in the business, they could sleep soundly in their damask bed. In actual fact they seem to have been quite free from anxiety, the Valois herself, her excellent husband, and the secretary who was so skilful with his pen. They gave themselves up to the unalloyed enjoyment of the revenues they were so adroitly extracting from the inexhaustible coffers of human stupidity.

There was, however, a trifle which disturbed the good Cardinal. He had fully expected, at the next official reception at court, to see the Queen wearing the precious diamond necklace; and he had perhaps hoped for a word from her or a confidential nod, for some kind of recognition which would be intelligible to him though its meaning would be hidden from others. But there was nothing of the sort! Marie Antoinette coolly ignored him, and there were no diamonds flashing upon her white neck. At length, in his bewilderment he asked the Valois: "Why does not the Queen wear the necklace?" The gay deceiver was never at a loss for an answer, and replied: "Her Majesty is reluctant to wear her necklace until it has been fully paid for. Then she will give King Louis a surprise."

Again the patient jackass buried his nose in the hay and was well contented. April passed into May, and May into June. Nearer and nearer drew the first of August, the day fixed for the payment of the opening instalment of four hundred thousand livres. To secure a respite, the tricksters hit upon a new expedient. The Queen, said the Comtesse de Lamotte-Valois, had been thinking matters over, and had come to the conclusion that the price was excessive. Unless the jewellers would agree to a rebate of two hundred thousand livres, Her Majesty had decided to send the trinket back to them. The artful dodger counted upon a lengthy period of chaffering. She was mistaken. The jewellers, who had asked a fancy price and who were in a tight corner, declared, without parley, that they would agree to the proposed reduction in price. Bassenge wrote a letter announcing the firm's consent, and, with Rohan's approval, Boehmer delivered it to Marie Antoinette on July 12th, when he was taking the Queen some other jewels which she had really ordered. The letter ran as follows:

"Your Majesty, it is with the utmost gratification we venture to think that the last arrangement proposed to us, to which we have agreed with zeal and respect, affords a new proof of our submission and devotion to Your Majesty's orders, and it gives us great satisfaction that the most beautiful diamond necklace in the world is at the disposal of the greatest and best of Queens."

To one not "in the know," this involved epistle is, at the first sight, incomprehensible. Still, if the Queen had read it attentively and had given careful thought to its twisted phraseology, surely she would have asked herself in surprise: "What arrangement? What diamond necklace?" But on this occasion as upon a hundred others, Marie Antoinette failed to read the document attentively to the end; she found such a labour too tedious; and she was never a woman given to serious reflection. She opened the letter and glanced at it as Boehmer 'had asked her to do. Then, since she had no inside knowledge of what had been going on, the purport of the involved verbiage eluded her, so she sent her maid to call Boehmer back that he might furnish an explanation. Unfortunately the jeweller had already left the palace. Oh, well, she would find out in due time what the fool meant! She would see him again by and by. Meanwhile, she cast the letter into the fire.

This destruction of the letter, this renouncement of further inquiry into a matter she did not understand, seems—like nearly all the incidents in the affair of the diamond necklace—almost incredible. Even so careful and competent and trustworthy a historian as Louis Blanc considered the Queen's prompt refusal to face the issues thus opened before her a sign that she must have known something about the shady affair. In reality, however, her hasty destruction of the document was characteristic. Afraid of her own heedlessness and dreading the espionage to which she was subjected at court, she had made it a practice never to keep any letters (those from her relatives excepted). When the palace of the Tuileries was stormed by the mob in 1792, not a scrap of writing addressed to her was found in her writing-desk. The pity of it was that what in most respects was a useful precaution proved in this particular instance to have been a rash action.

Thus, by a concatenation of circumstances, the disclosure of the fraud was delayed until the last moment. But no sleight-of-hand could postpone the coming of the first of August, and Boehmer wanted his money. The Valois made one last frantic wriggle in the attempt to defend herself—a bold one, for she threw her cards face upwards on the table and bluntly informed the jewellers: "You have been cheated. The signature to the guarantee in the hand of the Cardinal is forged, but he is rich enough to pay you, and will pay you." Her hope was that this would avert the blow. Her reasoning was logical enough. She believed that Boehmer and Bassenge would go to Rohan in a fine rage, would thrash the whole story out with him, and that he, afraid of making himself an object of scorn in the eyes of the court and of the country at large, would keep a still tongue in his head and would quietly pay over the fourteen hundred thousand livres. The jewellers, however, were guided, not by logic but by fear; they were afraid of losing their money! Knowing that the Cardinal was up to the eyes in debt, they refused to have any further dealings with him. Boehmer and Bassenge were both assured, in spite of what the Valois had told them, that Marie Antoinette was privy to the affair. If otherwise, would she not have replied to the above-quoted letter? She was much more able to pay their bill than the windbag of a Cardinal. Besides, in the worst event (so they falsely believed), she still had the necklace, and that was pledge enough.

The rope that was being used to lead a fool by the nose was now stretched to breaking-point. The huge edifice of falsehood and reciprocal misunderstanding fell with a crash when Boehmer came to Versailles and begged audience of the Queen. Within a minute of their encounter both he and Marie Antoinette knew that a gross fraud had been perpetrated, but not until the trial took place would it transpire who had been the arch-cheat.

From a study of the multifarious official documents and other utterances concerning this most complicated of all trials, the irrefutable fact emerges that Marie Antoinette had absolutely no inkling of the scandalous way in which her name and her honour were being misused. As far as legal responsibility was concerned, she was guiltless, a victim of and not a confederate in the most audacious piece of roguery known to history. She had never received the Cardinal at a private interview, had never become acquainted with the fraudulent Comtesse de Lamotte-Valois, had never handled a single one of the brilliants belonging to the necklace. Nothing but deliberate malice, nothing but intentional calumny, can involve Marie Antoinette in any way with the doings of this prize adventuress and this feeble-minded Cardinal. It cannot be too often reiterated that the Queen was unwittingly and innocently entangled in the dishonourable affair by a gang of swindlers, forgers, thieves, and fools.

All the same, Marie Antoinette cannot be "discharged from court without a stain upon her character." The fraud was so successfully staged because the tarnish upon her reputation gave courage to the cheats, and because those that were gulled were predisposed towards unhesitating belief in any act of heedlessness upon the Queen's part. Had it not been for the levities and follies of Trianon, continued year after year, this comedy of lies would have been inconceivable. No one in his senses would ever have ventured to suspect Maria Theresa, for instance, of carrying on such a clandestine correspondence as that relating to the diamond necklace, or that she would have given such a man as the Cardinal an assignation after nightfall in Versailles park. Rohan and the jewellers would never have swallowed the tale that the Queen was short of money and wanted, on the quiet, through a go-between, to buy an expensive diamond necklace and pay for it by instalments—unless Versailles had for years been buzzing with evil-tongued whispers about nocturnal adventures in the park, about jiggery-pokery with the royal jewels, and about unpaid debts. Neither would the Valois have been able to upbuild such an imposing edifice of lies, had not the foundation-stone been laid by the Queen's frivolous and unseemly behaviour, and had not Her Majesty's dubious reputation constituted the scaffolding. Though in all the preposterous intricacies of the necklace affair Marie Antoinette was, in a sense, blameless, she remains blameworthy that so gross a swindle could have been attempted and victoriously achieved under cover of her name.

CHAPTER XVI

Trial and Sentence

WITH his usual keenness of insight, Napoleon recognized Marie Antoinette's crowning error in the diamond necklace trial. "The Queen was innocent, and, to make sure that her innocence should be publicly recognized, she chose the Parliament of Paris for her judge. The upshot was that she was universally regarded as guilty." There lies the truth. This was the first occasion on which Marie Antoinette lost her self-confidence. Whereas she had always contemptuously disregarded evil tongues, ignored chatter and calumny, she now referred her cause to a tribunal which heretofore she had despised—the tribunal of public opinion. For years she had behaved as if she neither heard nor saw the shower of poisoned arrows. But when, in a sudden and almost hysterical fit of temper, she demanded an open trial, she disclosed how bitterly her pride had been wounded by the envenomed shafts. She was determined that Cardinal de Rohan, whom she regarded as the most audacious of the gang, should, being more conspicuous than the rest, atone for all. Unfortunately, however, no one but the Queen believed that the poor fool had acted in bad faith or with hostile intent. Her brother shared the general opinion in this matter. Writing to Mercy under date September 2, 1785, Joseph II said: "I have always known the Grand Almoner to be inconceivably light-minded and hopelessly extravagant; but I must avow that I hesitate to believe him capable of such a piece of rascality, of so black a crime, as that of which he is now accused." Still less did Versailles believe in Rohan's guilt; and murmurs soon became rife to the effect that the Queen had had the Cardinal thus brutally arrested simply in order to disencumber herself of a confederate. Marie Antoinette had rashly yielded to the promptings of the hatred instilled into her by her mother. Her thoughtless and clumsy action served only to deprive her of the protective mantle of sovereignty. By yielding to an impulse of ordinary feminine spite, she exposed herself to the onslaught of general detestation.

Now, at length, it became possible for the Queen's secret adversaries to make common cause. Marie Antoinette had tempestuously thrust her hand into a serpent's nest of mortified vanities. She should not have forgotten that Louis Cardinal de Rohan bore one of the oldest and most distinguished names in France. She should have remembered that he was related by ties of blood to the other great lines of the feudal aristocracy, and above all was near of kin to the Soubises, the Marsans, and the Condés. Of course all the members of these puissant families felt it to be a personal affront that one of their order had been arrested in the King's palace as though he were a common pickpocket. The higher clergy, likewise, were outraged. Was it to be expected that they should make no protest when a cardinal, an eminence, dressed in full canonicals, was seized and conveyed to prison by a swashbuckler when on the point of saying Mass? Complaints were lodged at Rome, the centre of ecclesiastical authority. Another powerful group whose interests were touched was that of the freemasons, for not only had their patron the Cardinal been imprisoned, but the gendarmes had likewise hurried off to the Bastille the great Cagliostro, worshipful master of a lodge and one of the gods of the godless craft. In a word, a fine chance now opened for the throwing of stones which would break the stained-glass windows protecting throne and altar from the inclemencies of the weather. It was a case for rude measures, since the matter was of supreme interest to the common folk, who as a rule were excluded, not only from the festivals, but also from the piquant scandals of the world at court. At length the canaille was to have a fine sight. A real, live cardinal, wearing a scarlet soutane, was to be publicly accused, as central figure of a galaxy of rogues and swindlers, of thieves and forgers. Best of all, in the background but plainly visible, was the arrogant "Austrian woman"! What more amusing topic could there be for the conquistadors of the pen, for the pamphleteers, the caricaturists, the newspaper reporters (in those days when the periodical press was just beginning to become a power), than the scandal of the "handsome cardinal"? Neither in Paris nor the world over had even the balloon ascent of the brothers Montgolfier, whose invention opened a new sphere to mankind, attracted so much attention as did this trial instituted by a Queen which by degrees became metamorphosed into a trial of the Queen herself.

Just before the proceedings began, the speeches for the defence were freely printed without censorship, the bookshops were stormed by would-be purchasers, and the police had to regulate the crowds. Not Voltaire's, not Rousseau's, not Beaumarchais's immortal works had, in the course of decades, secured so extensive a circulation as did these pleadings in the course of a single week. Seven thousand, ten thousand, twenty thousand copies, were torn from the hands of the hawkers. In the foreign embassies, the staffs had to spend day after day making up packets which would convey without loss of time news of the latest scandal at Versailles to brother members of the trade union of ruling princes. For weeks the trial was the chief topic of conversation, and the maddest suppositions were accepted as truth.

The proceedings were attended, not only by the curious from Paris and its suburbs, but by persons who had come by hundreds from the provinces—noblemen, bourgeois, and lawyers. The handicraftsmen of the capital forsook their work to see the show. The infallible instinct of the populace guided them in this matter. What was on trial was not simply one particular misdemeanour, a petty imbroglio in itself; for from it ran invisible threads to Versailles. It involved the monstrosity of the lettres de cachet, of arbitrary arrest; squandering of money by the court; mismanagement of the State finances. A shaft could now be aimed at all these abuses. For the first time the whole nation was able, through a casual rift in the screen, to secure a glimpse into the secret world of the unapproachable. The trial was not merely a trial about a diamond necklace, but was one in which the extant governmental system was being put to the test; for the indictment, if pressed home, would challenge the behaviour of the ruling class, would damage the Queen, and therewith the institution of monarchy. "What a magnificent, what a fortunate affair! A cardinal disclosed as a thief, and the Queen implicated in a most unsavoury scandal. . . . The crozier and the sceptre are being bespattered with mire! What a triumph for the ideas of liberty!"

The Queen did not as yet suspect that her hasty gesture had thus sown the dragon's teeth. But when a building is ruinous, when it is rotten to its foundation, the withdrawal of but one nail from the wall will sometimes suffice to bring the whole structure crashing to the ground.

In the court-house, Pandora's box was gently opened. The contents had a disagreeable smell. One thing, at least, was advantageous to the Valois, namely that her husband had been able to get clear away to London with what remained of the necklace, so that no fragments of this "exhibit" remained for production before the judges. Each of the rogues and dupes could endeavour to shift the possession of the invisible object to another of the band, and thus leave open the implication that perhaps, after all, the necklace was still in the Queen's jewel-case. The Valois, who foresaw that her distinguished associate would, if possible, make her pay the shot, had, in order to make Rohan look ridiculous, and in order to avert suspicion from herself, accused Cagliostro (perfectly innocent in this matter) of the theft, and had forcibly dragged him into the trial. She stuck at nothing in the effort to clear herself. When asked how she accounted for her sudden command of wealth, she shamelessly declared that she had been His Eminence's mistress, and that everyone knew how liberal-handed was this kindly cleric! In fact, matters looked black for the Cardinal, until at length the authorities were able to lay hands upon the Valois's accomplices, Rétaux the secretary and "La Baronne d'Oliva," the little modiste, and their evidence threw a much needed light upon the situation. There was one name which was carefully kept out of the proceedings both by the prosecution and by the defence, that of the Queen. Not one of the accused, not even the Valois (who was to sing a different tune in later years) had any ill to say of Marie Antoinette, and the adventuress repudiated as an abominable slander any suggestion that the Queen had received the necklace. Yet the very fact that they were all in a tale, that they all spoke with so much reverence of the Queen, worked by contraries upon public opinion, so that among the sceptical majority the idea was more and more widely expressed that the word had been passed round to "shelter" Marie Antoinette. Soon a whisper became general that the Cardinal had magnanimously taken the blame upon himself. Those letters which, by his orders, had so swiftly and so discreetly been committed to the flames—had they really been forgeries, after all? No smoke without a fire! Surely there had been something, though no one could be specific in any accusation, something amiss with the Queen's behaviour. Although in truth the proceedings cleared up the matter for all reasonable minds, mud had been thrown and some of it stuck. Just because her name was not impugned, Marie Antoinette was invisibly arraigned before the tribunal alongside the other accused.

Judgment was to be given on May 31, 1786. Since five in the morning huge crowds thronged the square in front of the Palace of Justice. There was not room for them all upon the left bank, so that even the Pont Neuf and the northern shore of the Seine were packed with persons waiting impatiently to hear the verdict. Large numbers of mounted police were on hand to maintain order. Already when the four-and-sixty judges were driving to the court-house, the passionate exclamations of the spectators must have sufficed to convince them of the importance of their decision; but a yet more decisive warning in this respect was awaiting them in the anteroom of the great hall of deliberation, in the "grande chambre." Ranged there in a double row, apparelled in mourning, were nineteen members of the Rohan, Soubise, and Lorraine families. They made obeisance as the judges walked by, but not one of them uttered a word or stepped forward out of the line. Their dress and their demeanour conveyed enough. This silent adjuration that the court should, by its decision, maintain the honour of the Rohans, must have had a powerful effect upon the councillors, most of whom themselves belonged to the high nobility of France. Before they began deliberating, they knew that the populace and the nobles, that the whole country, was anticipating the Cardinal's acquittal.

However, the deliberations lasted for sixteen hours. From six in the morning until ten in the evening the Rohans and a mob of ordinary mortals to the number of tens of thousands were kicking their heels in the streets. The judges had a complicated and far-reaching question to settle. It was easy enough to deal with the problem of the arch-adventuress, with that of her confederates, and with that of the modiste. No need for harsh measures against the last, who was a pretty little woman, and had not really known what she was doing that evening in the grove of Venus. The serious matter, the difficult matter, was that of the Cardinal. All were agreed that he must be acquitted, for the evidence had made it perfectly clear that he was a dupe and no cheat. Where the judges differed was as concerned the form of acquittal, since upon this, grave political issues turned.

The royal party insisted, not without reason, that the acquittal must be accompanied by a reprimand for "criminal presumption." Nothing less than this could account, in their view, for Rohan's belief that a queen of France would give him a secret rendezvous in a dark thicket. His Eminence's lack of due respect for the Queen's sacred majesty must, claimed the accusers, be expiated by a humble and public acknowledgment of guilt in this respect before the grande chambre, as well as by the resigning of his official posts. The other faction, that of those who were antagonistic to the Queen, demanded that the affair should be non-suited. The Cardinal had been humbugged, and was therefore blameless. An acquittal of this sort would have a sting in its tail. For, were it but admitted that the Cardinal had reasonable ground for supposing the Queen capable of such unseemly and secret practices, the latter's light-mindedness would have been pilloried before the world. Here was a thorny issue to decide. If Rohan's behaviour were at least censured as disrespectful to the Queen, Marie Antoinette would have been compensated for the misuse of her name; but if he were unreservedly acquitted, this would imply a moral condemnation of Her Majesty.

The judges, the rival factions, the populace (inquisitive and impatient) knew this well enough. It was obvious that the decision would decide something far more important than the particular case which was the ostensible matter at stake. It was no private concern that was under discussion, but the grave political issue, whether the Parliament of Paris still regarded the Queen's person as sacred, as inviolable, or as subject to the laws of the State just like that of any other French citizen, male or female. For the first time the red dawn of the coming Revolution was reflected in the windows of that building which contained, not only the Palace of Justice, but likewise the Conciergerie, the sinister prison from within whose walls Marie Antoinette would, eight years later, be hurried to the scaffold. The beginning of her doom and the end took place under the same roof. Moreover, the Queen would in due time be called to account in the very hall where the Comtesse de Lamotte-Valois had now to answer for her sins.

The judges debated for sixteen hours, the conflict of interests being no less strenuous than the conflict of opinions. The royalist party and the anti-royalist as well had set all possible influences at work, including the potent influence of money. For weeks the members of the Parliament of Paris had been subjected, not only to persuasions, not only to threats, but likewise to bribery and corruption. In the streets people were singing:

> Si cet arrêt du cardinal
> Vous paraissait trop illégal,
> Sachez que la finance
> Eh bien
> Dirige tout en France,
> Vous m'entendez bien!

Now at length the contemptuous indifference which, for years, the King and the Queen had manifested towards the Parliament of Paris was bringing vengeance in its train. There were many among the judges who opined that it was time to read the autocracy a lesson. By six-and-twenty votes against two-and-twenty (so nearly balanced were the respective parties!), the Cardinal was acquitted "without a stain upon his character"; so was his friend Cagliostro; and so was the "Baronne d'Oliva," the little modiste of the Palais Royal. The minor confederates, too, were let off lightly, banishment being thought sufficient punishment for them. It was the Valois and her husband who had to pay for all. He was sent to the galleys. She was sentenced to be flogged, branded with a "V" (voleuse), and imprisoned for life in the Salpétrière.

But one of those indirectly implicated in the affair, one who had not appeared in the dock, was also given a life-sentence through the Cardinal's acquittal—Marie Antoinette. Thenceforward she was pitilessly exposed to the shafts of calumny, to the hatred of her enemies.

From the steps of the Palace of Justice, the news of the acquittal was enthusiastically shouted to the assembled crowd. So loud were the acclamations that the noise was heard on the northern bank of the Seine. "Long live the Parliament; long live the Cardinal," rose the cry, instead of the customary "Long live the King!" The judges found it hard to protect themselves against rough manifestations of affectionate delight. They were vigorously embraced; the market-women kissed them; flowers were strewed in their path. As for the acquitted, they made a triumphal progress. Ten thousand, at least, followed the Cardinal to the Bastille, where he had still to spend a night; masses, continually reinforced, jubilated around the walls of the ancient fortress. Cagliostro was likewise idolized, and the metropolis would have been illuminated in his honour had it not been for a police prohibition. Here was a notable sign of the times when the whole nation devoted itself to extolling two men who had done nothing more for France than to inflict a deadly blow upon the prestige of the Queen and of the monarchy!

Vainly did Marie Antoinette try to hide her despair. The whip-lash on her face had struck too painful, too public a blow. Her ladies found her in tears. Mercy reported to Vienna that her distress was "greater than seemed reasonably justified by the cause." It was instinct rather than intelligence which made the Queen recognize that she had sustained an irremediable defeat. For the first time since she had assumed the crown she had encountered a power stronger than her own will.

Yet the King was still a last court of appeal. By taking energetic measures he could have saved his wife's honour and could have intimidated the members of the opposing faction. Had Louis and his spouse been resolute, the insurgent Parliament of Paris might have been rudely disbanded. That was the course Louis XIV would have followed, and perhaps even Louis XV. But Louis XVI lacked courage as well as determination. He did not dare to take steps against the Parliament, being content (hoping to compensate Marie Antoinette in some measure for her humiliation) to rusticate the Cardinal and to banish Cagliostro from the country. These were but half-measures, which angered the Parliament of Paris without effectively challenging its usurpation of authority, and affronted the representatives of justice without re-establishing the Queen's honour. With his customary weakness he chose a middle course—which in politics is invariably futile. Therewith he entered upon a steep descent, so that, in the conjoined destinies of husband and wife, there now began to be fulfilled the curse that weighed upon the Habsburgs, the doom which Grillparzer embodied in immortal strains:

> It is the doom of our great ruling line
> To rest inert at some poor half-way house
> Deaf to the call for strenuous endeavour.

The King was incapable of strenuous endeavour, of decisive action. The judgment of the Parliament of Paris was a judgment against the Queen and the monarchy, and was therefore the opening of a new epoch.

The same laodicean behaviour was shown by the royal party in its treatment of the Valois. Here, also, there were two possibilities open. The chief criminal might have been spared her cruel punishment, and this exercise of clemency would have made a good impression. Or, on the other hand, the sentence might have been carried out with the utmost possible publicity. But in this instance, too, as the result of inward hesitation and perplexity, a middle course was chosen. The scaffold was erected in the open, so that the populace was led to anticipate the barbarous spectacle of a public branding; the windows of the adjoining houses had been let at fancy prices; but at the last moment the court was alarmed at its own courage. At five o'clock in the morning, an hour when few witnesses were likely to be on hand, thirteen of the myrmidons of the law dragged the culprit, who was screaming and struggling and trying to strike her conductors, to the steps of the Palace of Justice, where the sentence to flogging and branding was read aloud to her. But they had a raging lioness to deal with. Seized with a fit of hysterics, the woman began yelling at the top of her voice, shouting invectives against the King, the Cardinal, and the Parliament of Paris, so that all the sleepers in the neighbourhood were awakened. She panted for breath, spat, kicked, and it was necessary, instead of baring her shoulder in a seemly manner, to tear the clothes from the upper part of her body in order to expose it to the branding-iron. At the moment when the hideous deed was being done, the agonized creature struggled convulsively, so that all her nudity was disclosed to the onlookers, and the fiery "V" was imprinted upon her bosom instead of upon one of her shoulders. With a beast-like howl, she bit the executioner savagely through his jerkin, and then collapsed in a dead faint. Like a corpse she was carried off to the Salpétrière where, as the sentence directed, she was to spend the rest of her life, clad in sackcloth with nothing but sabots for footwear, and nourished only on black bread and lentils.

Scarcely had the abominable details of this punishment become generally known when public sympathy veered round in favour of Madame Lamotte. No more than thirty years before, as we can read in Casanova's memoirs, when the half-wit Damiens had slightly wounded Louis XV with a penknife, the courtiers and court ladies of France assembled to gloat for four hours over the poor wretch's tortures and horrible death—to see his right hand being consumed in a slow fire, to watch how his flesh was torn off with red-hot pincers, melted oil, lead, and resin being then poured into the gaping wounds, while at last, when his hair had been turned white by the prolonged agony, he was torn in sunder by four horses. Since then, however, philanthropy had become the fashion, and "good society" was full of compassion for the "innocent" Valois. Here was a new and perfectly safe way of forming front against the Queen, by manifesting compassion for the "victim," for the "unfortunate." The Duchess of Orléans initiated a public collection in her behalf; the nobility sent gifts to her in the penitentiary; day after day fine carriages were in waiting outside the Salpétrière. To visit this convicted and punished thief became the "dernier cri." With astonishment, the abbess in charge of the institution recognized among these kind visitors one of the Queen's best friends, the Princesse de Lamballe. Had this lady come on her own initiative, or (as was promptly whispered) under secret instructions from Marie Antoinette? Anyhow, the ill-judged visit threw a distressing shadow upon the Queen's connexion with the affair. Was Marie Antoinette's conscience pricking her? Did she want to come to some sort of secret understanding with her "victim"? Naturally gossip upon these lines was rife. When, a few weeks later, the Comtesse de Lamotte-Valois was mysteriously enabled to escape from the Salpétrière by night and to seek refuge in England, it was universally believed in Paris that the Queen had effected this jail-delivery of her "friend" through gratitude to the Valois for having, in court, magnanimously kept a still tongue concerning Marie Antoinette's participation in the necklace affair.

In reality Madame de Lamotte's escape had been planned and effected by King Louis's affectionate relatives to enable them to stab the Queen in the back. It was not merely done in order to give colour to the rumours about an understanding between Marie Antoinette and the adventuress. There was a bolder and more effective game than that to play. Once safely across the Channel, the Valois could adopt the part of accuser, could have the most abominable calumnies printed; and could also, since innumerable persons in France and elsewhere were greedy for "revelations," earn extensive and ill-gotten gains. On the very day of her arrival, a London printer offered her large sums. In vain did the French court, which had at length recognized the sinister import of calumny, try to avert the poisoned arrows, sending Madame de Polignac, the Queen's favourite, to buy Madame de Lamotte's silence at the price of two hundred thousand livres; for this talented and unscrupulous cheat played double as before, accepting the hush-money, and then going to press, once, twice, thrice, and yet again, with her memoirs, penned and repenned in perpetually new and more fabulous forms.

These memoirs contained all that could gratify a scandal-loving public's lust for sensation. The trial before the Parliament of Paris was described as a sham-fight, the poor Comtesse de Lamotte-Valois having been sacrificed in the basest possible way. She declared, of course, that the Queen had ordered the necklace and had received it from Rohan, and that she herself, innocent of offending, had confessed to the alleged crime from friendship for Marie Antoinette and in order to refurbish the latter's tarnished honour. As to the way in which she had first entered into friendly relations with the Queen, this was accounted for by the unabashed liar in the manner that would best please irreconcilable enemies. There had been a Lesbian intimacy between the pair!

It mattered nothing that most of these falsehoods were obviously absurd to every unprejudiced eye. For instance, Madame de Lamotte declared that Marie Antoinette, when still an archduchess of the

House of Habsburg, had had a liaison with Cardinal de Rohan, then ambassador in Vienna. All persons of good will could reckon up on their fingers and thus satisfy themselves that Marie Antoinette was living as Dauphiness in Versailles long before de Rohan had become French ambassador to Austria. But persons of good will had become rare, so far as Marie Antoinette was concerned. The public at large read with delight the dozens of musk-scented letters from the Queen to Rohan, as published by the Valois in her memoirs; and appetite for stories about the Queen's sexual perversions grew by what it fed on.

One foul lampoon followed another, each outdoing the last in lasciviousness. Ere long there was published a "List of All the Persons with Whom the Queen Has Had Debauched Relations." This contains no fewer than four-and-thirty names of persons of both sexes: dukes, actors, lackeys, the King's brother and his groom of the bedchamber, Madame de Polignac, Madame de Lamballe, and "toutes les tribades de Paris," including a number of street-walkers who had been whipped out of the town.

But this list of four-and-thirty persons by no means exhausts the tale of Marie Antoinette's reputed lovers, those ascribed to her by the artificially stimulated opinion of the drawing-room and the gutter. When once the erotic fantasy of a whole city, of a whole nation, has become inflamed about a woman, be she empress or film-star, queen or opera-singer, her supposed excesses and perversions grow like an avalanche—for the crowd, with simulated indignation, participates in an orgasm of fancied lust. Another libel, *La vie scandaleuse de Marie Antoinette*, speaks of a vigorous pandour who, before she left the Austrian imperial court, was wont to appease the almost unappeasable "fureurs utérines" (the graceful title of a third pamphlet) of the thirteen-year-old girl. In *Bordel Royal,* a fourth dainty title, there was an account of the Queen's "mignons et mignonnes," enriched by numerous pornographic copperplates, showing Marie Antoinette in "poses plastiques" with various partners.

Louder and louder rose the chorus of hatred; ever more detestable grew the lies, which were believed because people wanted to believe them. Within two or three years after the necklace affair, Marie Antoinette's reputation had been damaged beyond recall. She was regarded as the most lascivious, the most depraved, the most crafty, the most tyrannical woman in France; whereas Madame de Lamotte, a condemned and branded felon, was looked upon as guiltless and virtuous. Directly the Revolution began, the political clubs wanted to take the refugee under their protection, so that the diamond-necklace affair might be retried—but this time before the Revolutionary Tribunal, with Madame de Lamotte-Valois as accuser and Marie Antoinette in the dock. It was only the sudden death of the adventuress (who, in a paroxysm of delirium of persecution, flung herself out of a window in the year 1791) which prevented this remarkably successful cheat from being brought back in triumph to Paris, and from being received with honour by a decree that she had "done good service to the Republic." Had it not been for this trick played by fate, the world would have witnessed an even more grotesque comedy of justice than the necklace trial before the Parliament of Paris, for the Valois would have been a loudly acclaimed spectator at the execution of the Queen she had so grossly calumniated.

CHAPTER XVII

The People and the Queen Awaken

THE historical significance of the necklace trial lies in this, that it threw the searchlight of publicity upon the Queen's person and upon the windows of the palace of Versailles—and in troublous times, extreme visibility is always dangerous. Dissatisfaction, so long as it remains vague and general, is a passive quality. If it is to become actively combatant, if it is to manifest itself, it must be able to concentrate itself upon a human figure, which may be the banner-bearer of an ideal, or may be a target for stored hatred—as was, symbolically, the scapegoat of the Bible. That mysterious entity "the people" can only think anthropomorphically, in terms of this or that individual. Abstract concepts lie, in truth, beyond the range of its understanding, so that it cannot vent its energies in punishment of a fault unless it perceives a guilty person. For a long time ere this the French people had been dimly aware of injustice, impinging upon it from some unknown source. For a long time it had subserviently bowed its head and hoped for better times. When each new Louis mounted the throne, it had enthusiastically shouted and waved flags, submissively paying the dues and performing the corvées demanded by the feudal seigneurs and imposed by the Church. But the more patient it was, the harder grew the pressure, and the more greedily did taxation suck its blood. In the wealthy land of France, barns and garners were empty; the tenant-farmers were impoverished; bread was scarce upon the most fertile land and under the finest skies in Europe. Someone, surely, must be to blame? If, for most, there was too little bread, this must be because the minority gluttonously consumed too much. If the many found their duties too heavy to perform, this must be because the few had arrogated to themselves too many rights. By degrees the country became filled with that dull disquiet which is always the antecedent of clear thinking and directed search. The bourgeoisie, its eyes opened by such writers as Voltaire and Jean Jacques Rousseau, began to judge matters for itself, to blame, to read, to write, to win self-knowledge. There were flashes preluding the great storm; homesteads were plundered, and even the lords in their châteaux were menaced.

These preliminary flashes had been slight, few, and far between; but now came two vivid outbursts of lightning: the diamond-necklace trial was one; Calonne's revelation concerning the deficit was the other. The comptroller-general of the finances, hampered in his attempts at reform and perhaps influenced also by a secret enmity to the court, was the first man in this position to publish a clear budgetary statement. Thereby it was made generally known what had hitherto been carefully hushed up, namely that during the twelve years of Louis XVI's reign the sum of twelve hundred and fifty millions of livres had been borrowed. The announcement was fulminating in its effect. Such vast loans seemed incredible. Who had spent this money, and for what? The trial before the Parliament of Paris gave the answer. Poor devils who worked ten hours or more a day to earn a few sous learned that in certain circles jewels worth a million and a half or more were lightly given as tokens of affection, and that palaces were bought for ten or for twenty millions while the populace was half-starved. But since everyone knew that the King, a kindly simpleton, modest in his tastes, reasonable in his desires, could have had no part in this preposterous expenditure, all the animus resulting from the disclosures was, naturally enough, directed against the dazzling, the spendthrift, the light-minded Queen. There was the explanation! Everyone knew, now, why the State debts had been piled up to so monstrous a figure, why paper money was continually depreciating in value, why bread became dearer and dearer and the burden of taxation heavier. It was because this harlot who was their Queen had had the walls of one of her rooms at the Trianon studded with brilliants, because she had secretly sent her brother Joseph in Austria a hundred gold millions to help him carry on his war, and because she had lavished pensions and sinecures upon her bedfellows male and female. The general misfortune had found a cause for itself, bankruptcy grew aware of its origin, and the Queen acquired a new name. Through the length and breadth of the land she was spoken of as "Madame Déficit." It was as if she had been branded between the shoulders with this stigma.

The thundercloud had burst. A hailstorm of pamphlets and polemics, a drenching rain of defamatory writings, proposals, and petitions was discharged. Never before had there been such an outburst of sermonizing in France, now that the people had begun to awaken. The volunteers who had returned from the American War of Independence, finding their way back to their native villages, told even the stupidest of their compatriots about a democratic country in which there was neither court nor king nor nobility, but only citizens, equal in station and endowed with like freedoms. Had not Rousseau's *Le contrat social* declared in plain terms, had not the books of Voltaire and Diderot shown in a more subtle and refined way, that a monarchical system was not the sole divinely willed method of government, nor yet the best of all possible methods? The days of dumb and passive and submissive veneration were over. Once the King's divine right had been openly questioned, the nobles, the bourgeoisie, and the lower classes acquired a new confidence. What had been whispered in the freemasons' lodges and muttered in the local parliaments became loudly vocal, and at length developed into a thunderous roar. The electrical tensions of the time were being discharged. A note of alarm was sounded by Mercy in his reports to Vienna.

"What intensifies the evil to an enormous degree is that people's minds are growing more and more excited. One may say that, by slow degrees, the agitation has extended to all classes of society, and that it is this ferment which has encouraged Parliament to persist in its opposition. You would hardly credit the audacity with which, not merely in the privacy of their homes, but in the public streets, people express opinions concerning the King, the princes, and the ministers of State. All their actions are criticized. The wasting of money by the court is depicted in the darkest colours, and everyone insists upon the need for summoning the States-General, as if the country were without a government. No repressive measures could put a stop to this licence of speech. So universal has become the fever, that even if offenders were to be imprisoned by thousands no headway would be made against the malady, for the only result would be to inflame the anger of the people to the utmost, and a revolt would inevitably ensue."

The widespread discontent had no further need of mask or of caution, but found frank expression, so that even the outward forms of reverence were disregarded. When the Queen appeared in her box at the theatre for the first time after the close of the diamond-necklace trial, she was greeted with such loud hisses that thenceforward she thought it best to keep away. Madame Vigée le Brun had intended to exhibit her portrait of Marie Antoinette in the Salon but it seemed almost certain that this picture of "Madame Déficit" would be made the occasion for violent antagonistic demonstrations, so the speaking likeness was withheld from the public gaze. In the boudoirs, in the Gallery of Mirrors at Versailles, wherever she went, Marie Antoinette could not but be aware of the detestation with which she was regarded, for it was now shown to her openly and face to face. As a final and still more insulting demonstration came a report from the lieutenant of police in which that official, of course wording his advice as civilly as possible, explained in somewhat involved terminology that it would be better if at this juncture Her Majesty would keep away from Paris, since the authorities felt that, in the event of a visit, they might find it impossible to prevent undesirable incidents. The pent-up excitement of the whole country was being spurted as from a fire-hose against one individual, and the Queen, whipped at length into wakefulness by the scourgings of this universal hatred, shaken out of her customary indifference, exclaimed in despair to those few who still remained faithful to her: "What do they want of me? . . . What harm have I done them?"

This violent thunder-clap was requisite to startle Marie Antoinette out of her arrogant indifference, out of her hitherto invariable mood of "laisser-aller." Being thus awakened, she began to realize where she had gone astray, and, her nervous energy being directed into new channels, she made a hasty endeavour to atone for the worst of her errors. Instantly she cut down her expenditure. Mademoiselle Bertin was dismissed. Economies amounting to more than one million livres a year were effected in the wardrobe, the housekeeping expenses, and the stables. The gaming-tables disappeared from her drawing-room. A stop was put to some additions and embellishments that were going on in the palace of Saint-Cloud; some of the other palaces were sold as speedily as possible; a number of sinecures were cancelled; and, above all, order was taken in respect of the public money wasted upon her favourites at Trianon. For the first time Marie Antoinette's ears were open. She had begun to ignore the old power, the fashion set by society, and was trying to guide her actions in accordance with the new power, that of public opinion. Her first attempt in this direction brought her a good deal of disagreeable enlightenment as to the real feelings of many whom she had regarded as her friends, of many upon whom (to the detriment of her own reputation) she had for years upon years been showering benefits—since these blood-suckers showed little sympathy for reforms that were effected at the cost of their own appetites. "It is intolerable," declared one of these toadies, "to live in a country where one cannot be sure of possessing tomorrow what one owned yesterday!" But Marie Antoinette showed herself firm of purpose. Now that her eyes had been opened, she could see much better. Conspicuously she withdrew from the disastrous company of the Polignacs, to resume close ties with her former counsellors, Mercy, and Vermond (who had long ere this been dismissed). It seemed as if, by the belated recognition, the daughter wanted to do justice to her dead mother's old-time exhortations.

"Too late!" was, however, the answer to all her endeavours. The puny efforts at reform remained unnoticed amid the general tumult; the hurried retrenchments were no more than drops in the ocean. The court, greatly alarmed, had to recognize that such casual measures as this would no longer be of any avail, and that a new labour of Hercules would be requisite to balance the finances. One minister after another was summoned to try his hand at the job, but none of them could suggest anything more than temporary palliatives, of the kind with which (since history repeats itself) post-war finance has made so many of the countries of Europe too painfully familiar: gigantic loans, which ostensibly paid off the previous ones; reckless and excessive taxation; the withdrawal of gold from circulation and a frantic use of the printing-presses to create what for a time would masquerade as money; in a word, preposterous inflation. Since, however, the roots of the malady lay deeper than in any mere defect of circulation; since the trouble was due to an unwholesome distribution of substance because all wealth was accumulated within the hands of a few dozen feudal families; and since the finance doctors did not dare (as yet) to take the requisite surgical measures—the enfeeblement of the State treasury assumed the proportions of an incurably chronic disorder. With his usual sagacity, Mercy was able to put his finger upon the centre of the evil.

"When waste and unthrift deplete the royal treasury, there arises a cry of despair and of terror. Thereupon the finance minister has recourse to disastrous measures, such as, in the last resort, that of debasing the gold currency or the imposition of new taxes. Thus for the moment funds are secured, embarrassment is relieved, and, with incredible levity, the authorities leap from gloom to a sense of the utmost security. However, in the last analysis, it is certain that the present government is worse than that of the late King in respect of disorderliness and extortion. Such a condition of affairs cannot possibly continue much longer without a catastrophe resulting."

The nearer the approach of collapse, the more uneasy became the court. At length those concerned were beginning to grow aware that it would not suffice to change one minister for another, since nothing but a change of the whole system could avail. When bankruptcy was imminent, it was realized at headquarters that the desired saviour need not necessarily be a member of one of the best families; but that, before all, he must be (and this was an entirely new idea in the French monarchy) popular—that he must be a man who would inspire confidence in the unknown and dangerous entity termed "the people."

There was such a man to be had, a man already known at court, for, though he was only of bourgeois origin, his advice had already been sought in case of need. His advice had been sought, though he was not merely a bourgeois, but a foreigner, a Swiss, and, still worse, a heretic, a Calvinist. The ministers had not been greatly pleased by having to rub shoulders with the outsider, and they had been quick to rid themselves of him because, in his *Compte rendu,* he had allowed the nation to see too far into their witches' cauldron. Greatly annoyed by such unceremonious treatment, the peppery man had responded by sending in his resignation upon an offensively small half-sheet of notepaper. Louis XVI had found this disrespect unpardonable and for a long time he had declared, had even sworn, that nothing would ever induce him to recall Necker.

Never again? But as far as Necker was concerned it had become a question of now or never. He was the man of the moment. The Queen

had at length realized how essential it was (for her own sake in particular as well as for that of the institution of monarchy in general)
to appoint a minister capable of taming the wild beast, public opinion.
She had an obstacle within herself to overcome too, for his predecessor
as minister for finance, Loménie de Brienne, who had so swiftly become unpopular, had been her selection! Was she to make herself
responsible for another appointment, and thus perhaps for another
failure? Since her irresolute husband still hung in the wind, she made
up her mind, and grasped at the dangerous Necker as a sick man will
grasp at a remedial dose of poison. In August 1785 she summoned
Necker to her private room and devoted her powers of persuasion to
appeasing him. Necker was able to enjoy a double triumph: that of
being not merely sent for but urgently implored by a queen; and that
of being demanded by the whole nation. "Long live Necker!"—"Long
live the King!" Both were shouted that evening in the galleries of
Versailles and in the streets of Paris as soon as the appointment of
the Swiss financier was announced.

Only the Queen lacked courage to join in the acclamations for she
was overwhelmed with anxiety as to the responsibility she had undertaken when, with inexperienced hands, she had thus grasped the rud-
der of State. Besides, an inexplicable foreboding filled her with gloom,
her instinct being stronger than her reason. She wrote that same day
to Mercy: "I tremble at the thought that Necker's recall has been my
work. It seems to be my fate to bring misfortune, and if some devilish
machination should make him fail like his predecessors, or if he should
do anything to impair the King's authority, I shall be hated even more
than I am hated now."

"I tremble at the thought."—"You will pardon me my weakness."
—"It seems to be my fate to bring misfortune."—"I have such urgent
need, at this juncture, of the support of so good and faithful a friend
as yourself."—Such words had never before been used by Marie
Antoinette. We hear a new tone, the voice of one who has been
shaken to the depths, and we are no longer listening to the light and
easy laughter of a spoiled young woman. Marie Antoinette has eaten
the bitter fruit of the tree of knowledge, has lost the confident gait
of the sleep-walker, for they only are fearless who do not know that

danger threatens. She has begun to understand what a price those must pay who occupy exalted positions. She has learned the burden of responsibility, has begun to feel the weight of the crown which hitherto has pressed as lightly on her brow as a fashionable hat made by Mademoiselle Bertin. Her gait has become hesitating now that she is aware of the volcanic ebullitions that are going on beneath the thin and fragile crust of the earth. She would rather go back than forward! There has been a complete change in Marie Antoinette's attitude. She, who up till now has always been happiest amid a turmoil, seeks tranquillity and retirement. She avoids theatres, shuns masked balls, keeps away from the King's council chamber, and can only breathe easily when she is in her children's nursery. Into that room, resounding with merry laughter, the plague of hatred and envy cannot find its way. She feels more secure as a mother than as a queen. There is a further mystery which this disillusioned and disappointed woman has too late unveiled; for the first time her feelings have been profoundly stirred to the depths by a man, who is able also to be her spiritual intimate, the friend of her soul. All might still go well with her could she but live quietly within a narrow circle, no longer challenging fate—that enigmatic adversary whose might and malice she is beginning to understand.

But now, when her heart craves for calm, the barometer of the times points to storm. At the very hour when Marie Antoinette is eager to atone for her faults and to withdraw into the background, a pitiless will, overmastering her own, drives her forward to become one of the central figures in the most tumultuous scenes of history.

CHAPTER XVIII

The Decisive Summer

NECKER, to whom in this time of intense financial stress the Queen had entrusted the helm of State, steered a resolute course in the teeth of the storm. He did not timidly shorten sail, he did not tack, for he knew that half-measures would be of no avail. Nothing could help but the turning of public confidence into an entirely new direction. During the last years of the old regime, Versailles ceased to be the centre of interest. The nation no longer believed in the King's promises or in his paper money; it had ceased to hope anything from a parliament of nobles or an assembly of notables. If credit was to be consolidated and anarchy averted, a new authority must be created, were it only for a time. A severe winter had hardened the hearts and stiffened the backs of the common people. The towns were crowded with refugees from the starving countryside, and at any moment the hungry masses might begin to riot. Though he hesitated too long, as usual, at the twelfth hour the King decided to summon the States-General, and this, in the new times that were dawning, meant an appeal to the whole population of France. Acting on Necker's advice, Louis—in order from the outset to counterbalance the power of the first estate and the second, the nobility and the clergy, in whose hands privilege and wealth were concentrated—decided to double the number of representatives of the third estate. As a result (it was supposed) the forces would be equally balanced, and in the end the decisive authority would remain in the hands of the monarch. The court believed that the summoning of the States-General, soon to become the National Assembly, would lessen the King's responsibility while strengthening his authority.

The people at large held other views. It was the first time in France that "common folk" had thus been called in council, and they knew well enough that an appeal was being made to them, not out of kindness, but in despair. A tremendous task was being laid upon the nation, yet at the same time it was being given an opportunity which might never recur, and which must therefore be turned to the utmost account. A flame of enthusiasm ran from town to town and from village to village; the elections became popular festivals; and public meetings were inspired by a sort of religious frenzy. As always before a violent hurricane, nature fashioned a resplendent sunrise. At length the actual work could begin when, on May 5, 1789, the States-General met at Versailles, which thereby became, not merely a King's palace, but the capital, the brain, heart, and soul of the whole realm of France.

Never before had the little town contained so many persons as during those spring days of the year 1789. The ordinary population was four thousand. France had sent two thousand delegates; and to these newcomers were superadded countless visitors from Paris and a hundred other places, eager to watch the historical spectacle. A bag full of gold pieces was needed to hire a room, and a handful of ducats could secure no more than a sack of straw as sleeping accommodation. Hundreds—latecomers or less well supplied with funds—had to camp in open doorways. During the night before the opening ceremony, although there were heavy showers of rain, crowds were waiting throughout the night, drawn up in double lines, to watch the procession of deputies. Food prices were trebled or quadrupled, the influx having exceeded all expectations. What took place in those momentous days was symbolic. This tiny provincial town had room for only one sovereign of France, and not for two. In the long run one of them would have to cede place—the monarch or the National Assembly.

To begin with, however, it seemed as if everything would pass off harmoniously, as if the summoning of the States-General were to mark a reconciliation between King and people. On the fourth of May the church bells pealed early in the morning. Before the deliberations opened, God's blessing was invoked upon the deputies for the exalted task they were about to undertake. Half Paris had flocked to Versailles, that people might be able to tell their children and their grandchildren about this day which was to inaugurate a new era. Costly tapestries were hanging from the window-sills and above them protruded heads in serried masses; even to the chimneys, clustered human beings were clinging like bunches of grapes, for, at deadly risk, people were determined to watch the great procession. A wonderful sight, in-

deed, was this march past of the estates. For the last time the court
of Versailles was flaunting its manifold splendours, in the endeavour
to convince the populace that it was the true seat of majesty, and to
emphasize the divine right of kings. At ten o'clock in the morning
the royal train left the palace, headed by pages in bright liveries and
falconers with their birds on their wrists. Then, slowly and majesti-
cally, there followed the royal chariot, gleaming with gold, drawn by
horses gaily caparisoned and with plumes waving above their heads.
The King's elder brother sat on His Majesty's right, his younger
brother on the box, and on the back seat were the young dukes of
Angoulême, Berry, and Bourbon. Shouts of "Long live the King!"
greeted this first equipage, the jubilation of the crowd being in painful
contrast with the silence which fell upon the assembled multitude as
the second vehicle, that containing the Queen and the princesses,
drove by. A like silence hailed the other carriages, in which the remaining members of the royal family drove by on their way to the
church of Notre Dame, where the three estates, each of the two thousand deputies holding a lighted candle, were awaiting the court, ready
to form in line and follow the royal progress through the town.

The chariots pulled up in front of the church. The King, the Queen,
and the other members of the court descended to encounter an unwonted sight. They were, of course, familiar with the aspect of the
representatives of the nobles' estate, had seen them often enough on
festal occasions, decked out as now in silken cloaks trimmed with
gold lace, wearing hats adorned with huge white feathers; nor was
there anything startlingly new in the splendid apparel of the clergy,
the scarlet vestments of the cardinals, the violet cassocks of the bishops.
These two estates, the first and the second, had for centuries been
faithful to the throne, and had been ornaments at every royal festival.
—But this sombre crowd of men in designedly simple black coats
whose general impression of darkness is relieved only by white neck-
cloths, these strangers wearing three-cornered hats; who are these
that form a solid block in front of the church? What thoughts are
hidden behind their unfamiliar and inscrutable faces, whose expression is bold, enlightened, and even severe? The King and the Queen
appraise the opponents who, made strong by numbers, refrain from
servile obeisances and from shouts of acclamation, but stand their

ground in a virile silence, regarding themselves as possessed of equal rights with the proud and ornate, the privileged and famous, members of the first and second estates, as equally entitled to undertake the work of renovation. In their gloomy habiliments, and with their serious and impenetrable aspect, do not they look more like judges than devoted advisers? We may well suppose that at the initial encounter with the third estate the King and the Queen must have shuddered with a prevision of their impending fate.

But at this first meeting there was no passage of arms. An hour of harmony was to precede the opening of the inevitable struggle. Grave of mien, the two thousand deputies, candles in hand, strode, between the lines of the French troops and the Swiss guards, from Notre Dame de Versailles to the cathedral of Saint Louis. The bells pealed, the drums rattled, the uniforms glittered; but the solemn chanting of the priests may have helped to turn people's thoughts from military display to higher things.

At the head of the long train marched the last who would soon be first, the deputies of the third estate, in two parallel files. They were followed by the estate of nobles, while the clergy brought up the rear. When the last representatives of the third estate were passing there were loud outbursts of applause from the assembled populace. This display was called forth by the sight of the Duke of Orléans, a renegade from his order, for, guided by demagogic calculation, he had decided to function as one of the elected of the third estate instead of taking the place in the procession to which he was entitled as a member of the royal family. Not even the King, marching behind the baldachin beneath which the Archbishop of Paris in a surplice embroidered with brilliants was carrying the host, was received with so much vociferation as the head of the junior branch of the royal house who had cast in his lot with the people and was openly challenging autocracy. Some of the spectators, wishing to underline their opposition to the court, chose the moment when Marie Antoinette drew near to raise shouts, not of "Long live the Queen!" but of "Long live the Duke of Orléans!" Realizing that this was a deliberate affront, Marie Antoinette turned pale, was obviously near to fainting, and found it difficult to show a semblance of composure for the remaining steps of her path of humiliation. Next day, at the formal opening of the States-General, further contumely awaited her. Whereas the entry of the King had been greeted with loud cheers, a frosty silence hailed the coming of Marie Antoinette. Not a lip moved, not a hand stirred to welcome her.

"Voilà la victime," whispered Mirabeau to his nearest neighbour. Gouverneur Morris, an American who had no personal concern in the matter, tried to induce his French friends to soften the blow by a shout of acclamation. But his attempted intervention was fruitless. "The Queen wept," wrote this son of a free nation in his diary, "and not a single voice was raised on her behalf. I would gladly have raised mine had I been French, but I had no standing-ground here." For three hours the Queen of France had to sit as if in the dock facing the representatives of the people without having received any tokens of respect. It was not until the close of Necker's almost interminable speech, when she stood up in order to leave the hall with the King that a few of the deputies, sympathizing with her in this extremity, raised scattered cries of "Vive la Reine!" Touched by the demonstration, Marie Antoinette acknowledged it with a bow, and thereat the whole audience joined in the greeting. But, as she returned to her palace, Marie Antoinette was under no illusion. She knew well enough how marked a difference there had been between this hesitant and compassionate salutation and the cordial outbursts of popular affection which had stirred her childish heart during the days of her first coming to France. She realized that she had been excluded from the great reconciliation, and that a life-or-death struggle had begun.

All those who saw her during these days were struck by Marie Antoinette's disquiet. Even at the opening of the National Assembly, Madame de Staël noticed that, though the Queen was splendidly attired in a violet-white-and-silver gown, her head surmounted with ostrich plumes, so that she looked both majestic and beautiful—she had a depressed and unhappy expression which seemed entirely new in a woman who had always been cheerful and coquettish. The fact was that Marie Antoinette had found it hard to make these necessary public appearances, for her thoughts were elsewhere. While she was thus on parade, in his little bed at Meudon her eldest son, the six-year-old Dauphin, was dying. The year before she had lost one of her four children, Princess Sophie Béatrix, who died when only eleven months old. Now for the second time death was visiting the royal nursery. The first signs of rickets had been manifest in the Dauphin a year earlier. "I am most uneasy about the health of my eldest boy," she wrote to Joseph II in 1788. "His growth is somewhat awry, for he has one leg shorter than the other, and his spine is a little twisted and unduly prominent. For some time, now, he has been inclined to attacks of fever, and he is thin and weakly." Thereafter, for a while, there had been misleading signs of improvement, but it was not long before the sorely tried mother lost all hope. The solemn procession before the opening of the States-General was the last spectacle the dying lad was to enjoy. Wrapped in a warm cloak and lying upon a heap of cushions (he had long since grown too weak to stand), from the veranda of the royal stables he watched his father and his mother and the gaily clad notables pass by. Within a month he was dead and buried. Throughout the intervening period, Marie Antoinette's mind was wholly absorbed in her own sorrows, with thoughts of the oncoming of this irremediable loss, and nothing, therefore, can be more preposterous than the frequently resuscitated legend that at this time she was engaged from morning till night intriguing against the National Assembly. During those days there was no fight in her. What combativeness she might have shown was paralysed by the pangs of imminent bereavement superadded to the distresses caused by the manifestations of public opprobrium. Not until later, fighting a lone and desperate campaign for bare life and for the royal position of her husband and her second son, could she rally her forces to a last resistance. For the nonce she had no energy left, and the energies of a Titan would have been requisite to change the march of destiny.

For at this juncture the course of events had become that of a raging torrent. Within a few days the two privileged estates, the nobility and the clergy, were at daggers drawn with the third estate; and soon the latter, balked of its will by the higher orders in the Assembly, had declared itself alone to be the true National Assembly, and had, on June 28, 1789, taken the famous Oath of the Tennis Court not to dissolve until the will of the people had been fulfilled and a constitution granted. Thus it defied the royal decree of dissolution! The court, terrified at the spectre of the sovereign people which it had itself conjured up, torn this way and that by the dictates of asked and unasked advisers, prepared one day to yield to the third estate, and siding next day with the privileged caste, vacillating hopelessly at an hour when clarity and resolution were the primary needs—the King was at one moment ready to comply with the promptings of the military braggarts, who proposed to drive the canaille home at the sword's point; and at the next willing to give ear to Necker, who persistently favoured yielding and conciliation. Louis would lock up the third estate in the meeting-hall, and would then timidly retreat from this bold position as soon as Mirabeau declared "The National Assembly will give way only to the point of the bayonet."

But the popular determination grew in proportion as the court became increasingly irresolute. Betwixt night and morning the dumb "people" had acquired a voice through the granting of freedom of the press; in hundreds of pamphlets it was clamouring for its rights; in inflammatory articles it was giving vent to its furious spirit of revolt. In the Palais Royal, under the protection of the Duke of Orléans, there assembled day after day thousands upon thousands of agitators, shouting, screaming, urging one another on to the last extremity of fanatical violence. Persons previously unknown, persons whose mouths had been stopped for years and for decades, suddenly discovered a lust for public speaking and for pamphleteering. Hundreds of ambitious and hitherto unoccupied individuals realized that the hour was propitious. It seemed as if everyone were reading, discussing, engaged in political propaganda. Arthur Young declared that each hour witnessed the issue of a new pamphlet, that thirteen had appeared on the day he was writing, sixteen the day before, two-and-twenty within the previous week; and he added that nineteen among twenty of them were on behalf of liberty—this meaning that the writers were advocating the abolition of privileges, not excepting the privileges of the monarch. The royal authority was crumbling and being washed away like a child's sand-castle by the rising tide. For hundreds of thousands of persons the words "people" and "nation" had within a few weeks become, no longer the almost senseless stringing together of a few letters, but quasi-religious ideas that were the embodiment of omnipotence and supreme justice. In the army, both officers and privates were being swept into the irresistible movement; the officials of the State and of the towns became aware that this ebullition of popular energy was depriving them of their prestige; and even the National Assembly, drawn into the current, had lost the initiative of the first significant days. The advisers in the royal palace grew ever more anxious, and, as usually happens with those who are not sure of themselves, they tried to mask their fears by making forcible gestures. The King, deciding once more to use the strong hand, got together the few regiments that could still be considered loyal and trustworthy, garrisoned the Bastille with them, and then, trying to convince himself of his own strength, threw down the gauntlet to the nation on July 11, 1789, by dismissing Necker, who alone was popular among the ministers of State, and ordering him to leave the kingdom.

The days that immediately followed were signalized by events that have graven themselves in history, and yet there is one contemporary document in which they have left scarcely a trace, namely the diary penned by the simple and unsuspecting Louis. The entry of July 11th is only: "Nothing. Departure of Monsieur Necker." On July 14th, when the Bastille was stormed, and when the fall of this ancient fortress signalized the final destruction of his power, the entry is even shorter. Only the one word: "Rien." This signified that His Majesty had not gone out hunting, had not brought down a stag, so that nothing noteworthy had occurred. True, in Paris people took another view, and the whole French nation continues, a hundred and forty years later, to celebrate this fourteenth of July as the birthday of its consciousness of freedom. On the morning of July 12th the tidings of Necker's dismissal reached Paris, and had the effect of a spark in a powder-barrel. In the Palais Royal, Camille Desmoulins, one of the political intimates of the Duke of Orléans, jumped on to a bench, brandished a pistol, shouted that the King was planning a new massacre of Saint Bartholomew, and called the people to arms. The answer was a general rising; military posts were seized, arsenals were plundered, barricades were erected. On July 14th twenty thousand men marched against the Bastille, the detested stronghold of feudalism; within a few hours the place had been taken, and the governor's

head was ornamenting the point of a pike. No one ventured any
further resistance to this elemental outbreak of popular wrath. The
troops, not having received any definite orders from Versailles, withdrew from Paris, and that evening the metropolis was illuminated
to celebrate the victory. Yet at Versailles, only just over ten miles
from the gates of the capital, the court might have been in another
hemisphere. The troublesome minister had been dismissed. Now
things would go on comfortably as before; Louis would be able to
enjoy his usual sport next day. Still, the news was disquieting, after
all. Messenger after messenger came to the National Assembly, to
report disturbances in Paris, the plundering of the arsenals, the attack
on the Bastille. The King listened to the news, but did not make up
his mind to do anything active. After all, what was this tiresome
National Assembly for? Let it look to the matter! There was no
change in the time-honoured routine of his daily life. As usual, the
easy-going, phlegmatic, uninterested man went to bed at ten o'clock.
If any further tidings came to hand, they could very well keep until
morning. He slept the sleep of the just, soundly, heavily, untroubled
by these happenings of worldwide importance. Yes, for part of the
night. But they were unreasonable, impudent, anarchistic times! So
lacking in respect were they, that they did not hesitate to disturb a
monarch's slumbers. The Duc de Liancourt came galloping to Versailles, with fuller news about the uproar in Paris. On arrival, the
Duke was informed that His Majesty had already gone to bed, was
asleep. The messenger insisted that His Majesty must be awakened,
and was at length admitted into the royal bedchamber. He reported:
"The Bastille has been taken by storm, the governor has been murdered! His head, on the point of a pike, is being carried in triumph
through the streets!"

"You are bringing me news of a revolt," said the unhappy sovereign
in alarm.

The bearer of evil tidings unhesitatingly amended his master's
phrase: "No, Sire, it is a revolution."

CHAPTER XIX

Friends Desert

MANY have made mock of Louis XVI because, thus startled out of his sleep on July 14, 1789, by the news of the fall of the Bastille, he did not instantly grasp the import of what was then (in the political sense) substantially a new word—revolution. But, as Maeterlinck writes in *Wisdom and Destiny:* "It is easy for those who are wise after the event to see what ought to have been done when time has brought full knowledge of what was really taking place." Neither the King nor the Queen was aware that their world was being devastated by an earthquake, but they did not stand alone in their lack of insight. Who among their contemporaries perceived in these opening hours the immensity of the drama upon which the curtain had just been rung up; who even among those who were the pioneers of the Revolution? The leaders of the new movement of the people— Mirabeau, Bailly, and Lafayette—had not the remotest notion how, in defiance of their own wishes, the forces they were unchaining would shoot onward to a mark far in advance of the goal they had contemplated; for in 1789 the very men who, a few years later, were to be the most bloodthirsty of the revolutionists, Robespierre, Marat, and Danton, were still convinced royalists.

It was only thanks to the French Revolution that the term "revolution" acquired that far-reaching, turbulent, and historical meaning which attaches to it today. Time was needed for it to gain the peculiar stamp which was lacking to it in 1789. The paradox which was so disastrous to King Louis was, not that he could not understand the Revolution, but the very opposite, that, though a man of mediocre capacity, he earnestly endeavoured to understand. When Dauphin, when no more than a timid youth, Louis XVI had been fond of reading history, and nothing had made a profounder impression on him than his having introduced to him the famous David Hume, for a time an attaché at the British embassy in Paris, and author of *The History of England,* whose publication had begun in the year of

Louis's birth. This book had been the lad's favourite reading. He had conned and reconned the chapter in which Hume described the revolutionary movement directed against Charles I, which culminated in the King's execution. There can be no doubt that the lesson of what had happened to the unlucky Stuart monarch must have gone home to the heir of the Bourbon throne.

When, at the close of the eighteenth century, there began in France a movement akin to that which had ravaged England a hundred and fifty years before, it seemed to Louis XVI, reading and re-reading Hume, that he might learn to guide his footsteps by recognizing the mistakes of his unhappy predecessor. Hume could tell him what a king ought not to do in such circumstances! Where Charles had tried the strong hand, he would be gentle and pliable, and would thus (so he hoped) escape the crowning disaster. Yet this very attempt to read the riddle of the French Revolution by the light of English analogies was disastrous, seeing that circumstances were so utterly different. For in decisive moments of history, a ruler must not act in accordance with arid recipes or be guided by the endeavour to follow precedents which can never be wholly applicable to a new situation. Nothing but the prophetic insight of genius can discover the saving principle in the present situation; nothing but a hero's creative impulse can tame the wild and confused energies of the elemental. Nor will anyone be enabled to ride out a storm by the expedient of furling sail, for if he does this his ship will be at the mercy of the winds and the waves.

Therein lay the tragedy of Louis XVI. He wanted to gain understanding of what to him was incomprehensible by studying history as if it had been a school-book, and to safeguard himself against the Revolution by timidly abandoning all that had been kingly in his behaviour. It was otherwise with Marie Antoinette. She did not go to books for counsel, nor yet, in any considerable measure, to men or women. Even in times of the utmost peril, it was not her way to look before or after; calculation and combination were alien to her spontaneity of character. Her human strength rested entirely upon instinct. Now this instinct of hers rose from the outset in revolt against the Revolution. Born in a royal palace, brought up to believe in divine right, convinced that her privileges as a ruler were unchallengeable, she regarded any claim of her subjects to rights of their own as no more than an unwarrantable manifestation of impudence by the mob. One who demands unlimited freedoms and rights for himself is, indeed, the last person in the world to concede privileges and rights to others. For her the matter did not seem open to discussion. Like her brother Joseph she said: "Mon métier est d'être royaliste." Her place was above, that of the populace was below; she would not stoop, and the people must not try to rise. From the time when the Bastille was stormed until she perished on the scaffold, she remained convinced that her position as absolute ruler was not open to question. Never for a moment did she, as far as her innermost feelings went, come to terms with the new movement, and "revolution" seemed to her nothing more than a euphemism for flat rebellion.

Yet this arrogant, this unqualified condemnation of the Revolution, did not (at any rate to begin with), as far as Marie Antoinette was concerned, imply the slightest hostility towards the people. Having spent her childhood in the more genial atmosphere of Vienna, the Queen regarded "le bon peuple" as comprising a mass of persons who were rather stupid, but thoroughly good-natured. She was certain that in due time the kindly crowd would turn away in healthy disillusionment from the agitators and spouters, would come back to its allegiance, would put its trust once more in those who knew what was best for it, in the hereditary ruling house. Her hatred was reserved for the "factieux"; for conspirators, agitators, demagogues of the political clubs, street orators, career-hunters, and atheists, who, in the name of confused ideologies or in pursuit of self-interest, wanted to persuade the worthy populace to renounce its loyalty to the throne and the altar. "Un amas de fous, de scélérats," a lot of idiots and rascals, such was her description of the deputies of twenty million Frenchmen. Those who had listened but for a moment to Korah and his company were for her anathema; those who were willing to make terms with the innovators were suspect. Lafayette, for instance, who tried to save her life and that of her husband and her children at the risk of his own, had no word of thanks from her; it would have been better to perish than to be rescued by this vainglorious aspirant

to popular favour! Never, not even in prison, did she show honour
by so much as a request, either to her judges (whose rights as judges
she challenged, and whom she stigmatized as executioners), or to any
one of the deputies. She was uncompromising in her defiance. From
the first moment to the last, Marie Antoinette regarded the Revolution
as nothing more than a filthy sea of mud, to which the sluices had
been opened by the basest passions of humanity. She had not the
remotest understanding, either of its historical justification or of its
constructive will, being concerned only to maintain with the utmost
resolution her own divine right as ruler.

Let us not deny that this lack of understanding was Marie Antoinette's supreme defect. Since she was no more than an average
woman, narrow-minded where political issues were concerned, having
neither the will nor the training that would have made her competent
to see beneath the surface of the abstract world or to grasp conceptual
relationships, nothing but the immediately human aspect of things
close at hand could appeal to her. Seen at close quarters and contemplated as the expression of our fallible humanity, every political
movement looks confused and muddled. Invariably an ideal becomes
caricatured as soon as its mundane realization is attempted. How
could Marie Antoinette be expected to do anything but judge the
Revolution by what she thought of the personalities who were its
leaders? And, as always happens in days of convulsive change, the
loudest and most conspicuous were by no means the sincerest and the
best. How could the Queen be otherwise than suspicious when the
members of the aristocracy who were the first to espouse the cause
of liberty were men of dubious reputation, heavily burdened with
debt, and the most corrupt among their order—such men as Mirabeau
and Talleyrand? How could Marie Antoinette believe the cause of
the Revolution to be great, to be honourable, to be moral, when she
saw that Philip, Duke of Orléans, who was avaricious, covetous, apt
for unsavoury intrigue, posed as an enthusiast on behalf of the new
doctrine of fraternity? What could she think of the revolutionary
movement when the National Assembly chose as its favourite Mirabeau, a man both corrupt and obscene, spawn of the nobility, one
whose manifold transgressions had earned him numerous terms of
imprisonment, and who had subsequently made his living as a spy?

Could a religion be divine which set up its altars to such as he? Was it reasonable to ask her to believe that fishwives and prostitutes who raged through the streets carrying human heads on pike-points were really the vanguard of a new humanity?

Because she could see nothing but outbursts of uncontrolled violence, Marie Antoinette could not believe in the slogan of liberty; because she saw only individual human beings, she had no inkling of the glorious ideal which, invisible and impalpable, animated this savage and world-shaking movement. Hidden from her eyes were the great humanist and humanitarian achievements of a new development from which we derive the most magnificent principles of our mutual relationships. Freedom of religion, opinion, and the press; freedom of occupation and the right of public meeting; the revolution which engraved equality of classes, races, and creeds, upon the tables of the law which have become the modern heritage; the revolution which swept away the shameful vestiges of the Middle Ages, the rack, the corvée, and slavery—never could she discern these spiritual aims behind the crude uproar and tumult of the streets, and never did she try to understand what was afoot. All that she could catch a glimpse of amid the limitless turmoil was chaos. Veiled from her sight were the heralds of a new order which was to arise out of these horrible convulsions. From the first day till the last, therefore, she hated both leaders and led with the fervour of a defiant heart. The upshot was inevitable. Since Marie Antoinette was unjust to the Revolution, the Revolution was unjust to Marie Antoinette.

The Revolution was the enemy—such was the Queen's standpoint. The Queen was the chief obstacle in its path—such was the fundamental conviction of the Revolution. With their infallible instinct, the masses of the people regarded the Queen as their essential, their fundamental adversary; and from the outset the fury of the campaign was concentrated upon her person. Louis XVI counted for nothing, either good or bad. This was well known to the stupidest peasant in the villages, to the youngest children in the streets. He could be so thoroughly frightened by a few musket-shots that he would be ready to accede to any demand. Clap the red bonnet of revolt upon his head, and he would wear it without protest. Order him to shout: "Down with the King! Down with the tyrant!" and, though himself King, he would make no demur. There was one person left in France to defend the throne, one vigorous will to stand firm against the Revolution. As Mirabeau put it, the Queen was "the only man at court." Anyone, therefore, who was on the side of the Revolution must necessarily be against the Queen. It was at her that all guns were aimed.

In the opening phase of the Revolution, the revolutionary pamphleteers began to make it plain that Marie Antoinette was their target, and to describe Louis XVI as the true father of his people, as good, virtuous, noble-minded, though, unfortunately, infirm of purpose, and "misled." If only the royal philanthropist could get his own way, there would be perfect peace between the King and the nation. It was the Austrian woman, the foreigner from Vienna, guided by the counsels of her brother, in the toils of her lovers of both sexes, arbitrary, tyrannical—it was she who stubbornly resisted such an excellent understanding. She was continually hatching new plots in order to lay Paris in ruins by summoning troops from abroad. With devilish cunning she was trying to persuade the officers to fire their cannon upon the defenceless people. Thirsting for blood, she lavished wine and money on the soldiers to spur them on to the crime against which Camille Desmoulins had uttered his famous warning on the fourteenth of July: "A Saint Bartholomew of the patriots." Surely it was time that the King's eyes should be opened! Fundamentally, the adversaries entertained like thoughts of each other. Marie Antoinette considered that the people were good, but were misled by the "factieux." The people, on the other hand, thought the King good, but egged on to mischief and blinded by his wife. The real struggle lay between the revolutionists and the Queen. While Marie Antoinette became more and more the object of popular hatred, and the target for calumny and invective, she herself grew increasingly stubborn. One who is resolutely leading or steadfastly resisting a great movement, has his energies stimulated by opposition. Now that she was faced by a world in arms, the Queen's childish arrogance was transformed into pride, and the powers which had previously been frittered away upon trifles underwent concentration to endow her with a vigorous character.

This belated development of Marie Antoinette's forces could, however, take effect only in the defensive, for one whose ankles are shackled cannot march forward to meet the foe. Marie Antoinette's fetters were riveted upon her by the timidity of poor Louis. Smitten on the right cheek by the storming of the Bastille, next morning he humbly offered the left cheek to his assailants. Instead of flying into a rage, instead of blaming and chastising, he promised the National Assembly to withdraw from Paris the troops that were perhaps still ready to fight in his behalf—thus repudiating the defenders of the Bastille who had fallen for his sake. By refraining from a single word of censure upon those who had murdered the governor of the Bastille, he recognized the Terror as the legitimate power in France. His weakness was a justification of revolt. In gratitude for this abasement, Paris was ready enough to crown the accommodating ruler with flowers, and to give him (though only for a brief space) the title of "Restaurateur de la liberté française." At the gates of the capital, Bailly, president of the third estate and of the National Assembly, and mayor of Paris, welcomed him with the ambiguous words: "Paris has achieved the reconquest of its King." Subserviently Louis XVI pinned to his hat the tricolour cockade which the populace had adopted as a sign of rebellion against his authority, failing to realize that the acclamations of the multitude were not really uttered for his sake but in order to exult that their own strength had made their sovereign into their subordinate. On the fourteenth of July, Louis XVI had lost the Bastille; on the seventeenth, he threw the handle after the hatchet, cast aside his dignity, and made so profound an obeisance to his adversaries that the crown dropped from his head.

Since the King had made this sacrifice, Marie Antoinette had to follow suit. She was constrained to disavow those whom (with good reason) the new ruler, the people, hated most; to dissociating herself from her friends and playmates, the Polignacs and the Count of Artois, who were to be banished for ever from the realm of France. Had it not been forced upon her, the Queen would have been little troubled by this severance, since for a long time she had ceased to find her former light-minded associates congenial. But now, in the hour of parting, she felt cordial once more towards these companions of years that had seemed so happy and so free from care. She had shared in their follies; Madame de Polignac had known all her secrets and had helped her in the upbringing of her children. Now that the sometime favourite was being sent into exile, how could the Queen fail to recognize that farewell was also being said to her own untroubled youth? The nonchalant hours were passing away beyond recall. The porcelain and alabaster world of the eighteenth century had been shattered by the hard fists of the revolutionaries, and in the world now being fashioned there would be no place for delicate and refined enjoyment. The days that were dawning would be rough even if great, would be murderous even if mighty. The silver chimes of the Rococo were silent, and the joys of Trianon had vanished into the limbo of the past. Vainly trying to fight down her fears, Marie Antoinette found it impossible to say a personal farewell to her friends. She kept her chamber, being afraid that she could not maintain her composure before the public eye. In the evening, however, when in the courtyard below the carriages for the Count of Artois and his children, for the Duke of Condé, the Duke of Bourbon, Madame de Polignac, the ministers of State, and the Abbé Vermond were waiting— were waiting for all those who had been the companions of her youth—snatching up a pen she hastily scribbled a few lines to Madame de Polignac: "Adieu, dearest of friends. What a dreadful word 'good-bye,' but I have to say it. Here is the order for the horses. I have only strength left to send you my love."

Henceforward there is this undertone of melancholy in all the Queen's letters. Next day she wrote to Madame de Polignac: "I do not try to put into words the sorrow I feel at being separated from you, but I hope that you reciprocate my sentiments. I am fairly well, although shaken by this succession of blows. We are environed by hardships, misfortunes, and ill-starred persons—to say nothing of those who have been sent away. Since all are deserting us, I am in truth happy to think that those in whom I am chiefly interested have had to depart." Yet as if unwilling that her old friend should detect her in a weakness, as if she knew that a royal demeanour was the only thing remaining to her as a relic of her power as Queen, she went on to say: "You may be sure, however, that adversity has not lessened my strength or my courage. These I shall never lose. My troubles will teach me prudence. It is in such moments as the present that one learns to know people, and becomes enabled to distinguish between those who are and those who are not truly attached."

A silence of death now surrounds this Queen whose taste it has always been to live amid turmoil. The great flight, the great desertion, has begun. Where are her former friends? They have vanished like the snows of yester-year. Those who used to resemble clamorous children round a table laden with Christmas presents—Lauzun, Esterhazy, Vaudreuil—where are they, the partners at cards, those who danced with her and who rode with her in the park of Versailles? There has been a "sauve-qui-peut." They have left in disguise, not this time masked for a fancy-dress ball, but muffled up to the eyes for fear of being lynched by the populace. Evening after evening another carriage drives through the gilded gateway, never to return. Fewer and ever fewer footsteps sound in the wide halls. No theatre-going, no dances, no receptions! Only Mass every morning, and thereafter to spend hours in the private cabinet, listening to the tedious reports and suggestions of the ministers, who are at their wits' end. Versailles has been deserted by those whose first thought is for their own safety.

At this juncture, when the Queen had been forsaken by those whom the world believed to be her closest friends, there emerged from the darkness the man who had in very truth been her friend all along, Axel Comte de Fersen. So long as it brought power and glory to be accounted a favourite of Marie Antoinette, this exemplary lover, mind-ful of the honour of the woman he adored, had remained in the background, thus sheltering the most precious secret of her life from the eyes of the curious and from the tongues of scandalmongers. Now, when to appear in public as a friend of the maligned woman brought no advantage, no honour, no respect, no envy, when it needed courage and self-sacrifice—now Marie Antoinette's only true lover and the only man she truly loved stepped boldly forward to her side, and therewith made his entry upon the stage of history.

CHAPTER XX

The Friend Appears

THE name and the personality of Axel de Fersen were long enveloped in mystery. He was not referred to in the before-mentioned scandalous chronicle of Marie Antoinette's lovers male and female. We find few allusions to him in ambassadorial dispatches or in the reports of his contemporaries. Fersen was not one of the familiar guests in Madame de Polignac's salon. His tall, grave figure was never among those in the limelight. Thanks to this retiring dis-position, owing to this prudent reserve, he never became a mark for the malicious shafts of the court clique; and, for the same reason, he long escaped the notice of historians, and it seemed likely enough that the Queen's love-story would remain for ever shrouded in dark-ness. But during the latter half of the nineteenth century a romantic tale began to gain currency. In a Swedish castle there had been pre-served under seal numerous packets of Marie Antoinette's private letters. At first little credence was given to this improbable report. Then there appeared a printed edition of the private correspondence, and, although the letters had been barbarously pruned of intimate details, the book was enough, at one stroke, to thrust the previously unknown Scandinavian noble into the most distinguished place among the friends of Marie Antoinette. These letters modify our whole out-look upon the character of a woman hitherto regarded as light-minded. They show a spiritual drama splendid and perilous, an idyll partly in the shadow of the King's court and partly in that cast by the menacing guillotine, one of those soul-stirring romances which per-haps can only be penned by history herself. We see, as we read, two persons who are wholly devoted to each other, compelled by duty and by caution to hide their secret, again and again torn apart and again and again moving irresistibly towards one another from widely separated constellations; one of them the Queen of France, and the other a member of the minor Swedish nobility, a junker from the North. The background to these two human destinies is a world falling into ruin, an apocalyptic era, a universe in flames—and the picture is all the more moving because the truth of the relationship between the pair can only be deciphered from the faded handwriting upon crumbling pages of manuscript.

This love drama did not open with pomp and circumstance, but quite in the Rococo style of the day. A youthful Swede, the son of a senator, was at the age of fifteen sent, accompanied by a tutor, to make what was then known as the Grand Tour. He was to spend three years travelling in the chief countries of Europe, and perhaps even in our own day this is the best way of acquiring the elements of a cosmopolitan education. In Germany, Axel studied polite letters and the science of war; in Italy, medicine and music; in Geneva, he paid the indispensable visit to the oracle of contemporary wisdom, to Monsieur de Voltaire, the Sage of Ferney. Wrapped in an embroidered dressing-gown, the wizened old man gave him a cordial welcome, and therewith bestowed upon Fersen a spiritual accolade. Now the youth was eighteen, and needed only the final polish which could be gained nowhere else than in Paris. There he would learn the art of elegant conversation, there his manners would acquire a courtly polish, and there the education of a young nobleman of the eighteenth century would be completed. Thus perfected, he could become an ambassador, a minister of State, or a general. The summits of life would have been opened to him.

To the advantages of blue blood, high personal standing, shrewdness and commonsense, wealth, and the nimbus of a distinguished foreigner, there were added in Axel de Fersen's case the exceptional merit of being a remarkably good-looking man. Upright, broad-shouldered, muscular, he was a typical Scandinavian in build, virile without being stout or massive. In his portraits, we cannot help being charmed by his frank expression, his regular features, his thoughtful eyes, surmounted by well-arched and thick black brows. Add to this a broad, finely shaped forehead, and warm red lips—which knew the value of silence. Here was a man to arouse both the love and the trust of a passionate woman. Fersen does not, indeed, seem to have shone as a conversationalist, as a wit, as an amusing companion; nevertheless, his somewhat dry and homely intelligence was set off by sincerity and natural tact. As early as 1774, King Gustavus III's ambassador in Paris reported to his royal master: "Of all the Swedes who have visited this city during my term of office, Fersen has secured the best reception in the great world."

There was nothing morose or fastidious about this young gentleman; the ladies believed him to have a "cœur de feu" beneath an icy exterior. He did not forget to amuse himself in Paris, becoming a regular attendant at court balls and at the receptions held in the best houses. In the course of these relaxations, he had a strange adventure. One evening, on July 30, 1774, at the Opera ball, where the "monde" and the "demi-monde" rubbed shoulders, a slender young woman who moved as if on wings and was richly apparelled, accosted him without introduction, and, under cover of her mask, opened a lively conversation. Fersen, flattered by being thus singled out, responded in kind. The conversation assumed a gallant tone. He found the lady to be endowed with a stimulating personality, and perhaps had begun to entertain fancies of a night that would be signalized by "bonne fortune." He could not, however, fail to be struck by the fact that he and his partner had become encircled by ladies and gentlemen who were exchanging eager whispers, and were regarding the pair with lively attention. When, at length, the situation began to grow embarrassing, the young woman who had been flirting with him thought best to remove her mask. It was Marie Antoinette! Forsaking the tedious couch of her sleepy spouse, the Dauphiness had driven off to the Opera ball and had entered into conversation with this handsome stranger. Such an incident was unprecedented in the court annals of France, and Marie Antoinette's attendant ladies did their utmost to ensure that it should not attract too much attention. Surrounding the escapee, they promptly conducted her back to her private box. But what could be secret at Versailles? There was much whispering, much astonished conversation about the Dauphiness's breach of etiquette in thus showing favour to an unknown cavalier. It seems likely enough that next morning Mercy may have written a distressful letter to Maria Theresa, to which the response may have been the sending of a special courier from Schönbrunn to convey one of those censorious epistles to the "giddy-pated" daughter, telling her it was time for her to put an end to her unspeakable "dissipations," and to cease from entering into conversation with unintroduced strangers at these abominable masked balls.

However that may be, Marie Antoinette had had her own way; the young man had pleased her, and she had made the fact plain to him. Thenceforward the youthful Swede, though by no means of outstanding rank or position, was always a welcome guest at Versailles balls and receptions. Are we to suppose that, as an immediate sequel of the acquaintanceship begun under such favourable auspices, the pair conceived a passion for one another? We do not know. It was not very long certainly, before an important event put an end to what can have been nothing more than an innocent flirtation, for the death of Louis XV made the little princess Queen of France. Two days later, perhaps in consequence of a plain hint, Axel de Fersen left for his native country.

The first act was over. It had been nothing more than a prelude to the real drama. A young man and a young woman, both of them eighteen years of age, had met, and had found favour in one another's eyes, voilà tout—a ballroom friendship, an innocent boy-and-girl love affair. The matter had not gone far beneath the surface; the depths of feeling had not been stirred.

The second act did not begin until four years later, when, in 1778, Fersen returned to France. His father had sent him to look for a rich wife, specifying among possible brides, a certain Miss Reyel in London and Mademoiselle Necker, daughter of the Genevese banker, in later days known to the whole world as Madame de Staël. But Axel Fersen had no penchant for matrimony; and his reasons are obvious enough. Immediately after his arrival in Paris, the young man presented himself at court. Would anyone there remember him? The King gave him a rather sullen nod; the courtiers paid little heed to the unimportant foreigner; no one vouchsafed him a courteous word. But the Queen, directly she caught sight of him, cried impetuously: "Ah, c'est une vieille connaissance"—Hullo! here's an old acquaintance. She had not forgotten him, this handsome northerner, and her interest in him promptly revived, by no means the flame of a fire of straw. She invited Fersen to her parties, and she overwhelmed him with kindnesses. Just as at the opening of their ac-

quaintance, when they met at the Opera ball, Marie Antoinette had
been the more forthcoming of the twain, so now. It was not long
before Fersen wrote to his father: "The Queen, the most amiable
princess I have ever met, was good enough to ask after me. She
inquired of Creutz why I did not attend her Sunday card-parties,
and when she was informed that one day I had arrived for a reception
which had been put off, she actually made me her excuses." It certainly was a remarkable sign of favour when this arrogant young
woman, who would give duchesses the cut direct, who for four years
had refused to say a word to Madame Dubarry, and who for seven
years had totally ignored Cardinal de Rohan, apologized to the young
foreigner because he had paid a fruitless visit to Versailles. "Every
time I attend one of her card-parties, she makes a point of speaking
to me," wrote Axel a few days later. In defiance of etiquette the
"amiable princess" requested the young Swede to come to Versailles
in his Swedish uniform for (the whim of a woman in love) she was set
upon seeing how it suited him. It need hardly be said that "le bel
Axel" complied with her desire. The old, old story had begun again.

It was a dangerous game for a Queen to play, for her who was
the centre of a court where she could not escape being watched by
a thousand eyes. Marie Antoinette had to be more cautious than in
the days of her first acquaintanceship with Fersen, for she was no
longer the princess of eighteen, whose vagaries could be excused on
the ground of her being still in her teens. She was four-and-twenty,
and Queen of France. But her senses had been stirred. At length, after
seven deplorable years, the previously incompetent husband, Louis
XVI, had fulfilled his conjugal duties, had consummated the marriage. She, a woman of charm and refinement, what must she feel
when she compared her dull and corpulent spouse with the handsome
stripling to whom her heart had gone out in love? Without her
being fully aware of it, she began to betray her passion by the kindnesses she heaped upon Fersen and by the way in which she blushed
or looked confused when he entered the room. As so often before,
Marie Antoinette's sympathies ran away with her, for neither in
liking nor in disliking could she put on false pretences. One of the
court ladies reported that, Fersen having unexpectedly entered the

room, the Queen began to tremble in the sweetness of her alarmed delight. On another occasion, so the story ran, when she was sitting at the clavecin singing an aria from *Dido* before the assembled court, at the words, "Ah, que je fus bien inspirée quand je vous reçus dans ma cour," her blue eyes, usually so unimpassioned, turned enthusiastically and tenderly towards the chosen of her heart. Gossip was rife upon the matter. To courtiers and court ladies the most private love affairs of their royal masters and mistresses are matters of supreme importance, and they were all asking one another whether the Queen would make Fersen her lover, and how, and when. Marie Antoinette herself, in fact, was probably the only member of her circle who did not yet fully realize that Fersen could win the Queen for his mistress if he were bold enough or light-minded enough to grasp what was ready for his hand.

But Fersen was a Swede, and (a man through and through) endowed with the peculiar characteristics of his race. Among these northerners a strongly romantic disposition may go hand in hand with a tranquil and sober understanding. He was quick to perceive that the situation was untenable. No one knew better than he that the Queen was in love with him, and he, in his turn, both loved and honoured this charming young woman. Honouring her as he did, it would have seemed to him a breach of principle to turn the passion of the senses to account in a way which could not fail to promote malicious gossip about Marie Antoinette. If the pair were to go to an extreme in their love-making a terrible scandal would ensue, for the King's wife had already been compromised more than enough by the platonic favours she had shown to the young foreigner. On the other hand, to play the part of a Joseph; to reject, with chaste pride, the offered embraces of a young and beautiful and beloved woman—for such a role Fersen was too ardent and too young. Being a fine fellow, he therefore took the best course open to a man in these ticklish circumstances, speedily putting thousands of miles between himself and the lady to whom his presence was a danger, enrolling himself as Lafayette's aide-de-camp in the French contingent that was fighting on the side of the American insurgents. Thus did he cut the tangle which was threatening to become tragical in its complications.

Concerning this departure of the lover we have an unchallengeable document, in the form of an official dispatch from the Swedish ambassador to Gustavus III which gives historical warrant for the conviction that the Queen was in love with Fersen. Here is an excerpt: "I have to report to Your Majesty that young Fersen is so much in the Queen's good graces that this has roused suspicion in certain quarters. I must admit that I myself believe she has a fondness for him. The signs I have seen are too plain for any doubt on the subject to remain in my mind. Young Count Fersen has, in these circumstances, behaved in the most exemplary way, not only in respect of his modesty and his reserve, but also in that he has made up his mind to go to America. He has put an end to all danger by his departure; and it cannot but be admitted that to have withstood such a temptation signifies him to be endowed with a resolution hardly to be expected at his age. During the last days before he left, the Queen could not keep her eyes off him, and, when she looked at him, they were filled with tears. I would ask Your Majesty to be good enough to keep this matter to yourself and to Senator Fersen. When the favourites at court heard of the Count's intended departure, they were delighted, and the Duchess of Fitz-James said to him: 'What, Sir, are you leaving your conquest in the lurch?'—'Had I made one, I should not leave it in the lurch. I am going away because I wish to, and without any regrets.' I think Your Majesty will admit that this reply indicates a prudence and power of self-restraint beyond the man's years. Moreover, the Queen now shows much more self-control and prudence than of yore."

The defenders of Marie Antoinette's virtue are continually waving this document as the banner of her lily-white innocence. Fersen, they say, decided at the last moment to restrain an adulterous impulse. With amazing power of renunciation, the two lovers said farewell to one another, and their ardent passion remained "pure." The ambassador's dispatch, however, does not carry as much weight as this, or give any definitive proof, for all it shows is that in 1779 there had been no intimate relations between Marie Antoinette and Fersen. There were years still to come in which this passion would be more perilous. We have only reached the end of the second act, and are still far from the most complicated phases of the entanglement.

We come to the third act, that in which Fersen returned. After four years' voluntary exile, having landed in June 1783 at Brest with the American auxiliary corps, he hastened to Versailles. While in America he had remained in touch with the Queen by letter, but love craves for bodily presence. They must not again be severed; at length they must be settled in close proximity, so that they could see one another's dear faces whenever they pleased! Obviously upon the Queen's instigation, Fersen promptly applied for the command of a French regiment; but his father, the thrifty old Swedish senator, regarded his son's behaviour as inexplicable. Why should Axel want to stay in France? Being now an experienced soldier, being the heir to an ancient name, being regarded with great affection by Gustavus III, almost any position was open to him in Sweden. "Why stay in France, of all countries in the world?" asked the angry and disappointed father again and again. "To marry an heiress, Mademoiselle Necker, with her Swiss millions," was the most plausible fiction the son could coin for a reply. A private letter to his sister of the same date disclosed that marriage was the last thing he had in mind, and laid his heart bare. "I have determined never to marry. It would be unnatural. . . . I cannot belong to the one woman to whom I should like to belong and who loves me, so I will not belong to anyone."

Is not that plain enough? Is there need to ask who was this "one woman" who loved him and whom he could never marry—"elle," the pronoun he uses in his diary to denote the Queen? Decisive things must have happened, or he would not have ventured to acknowledge, either to himself or to his sister, Marie Antoinette's fondness for him so frankly as he does. When he writes to his father of "a thousand personal reasons which I cannot commit to paper," of a thousand reasons which keep him in France, behind this thousand there is one reason which he will not declare in so many words, namely the Queen's wish to keep her chosen friend near her. For who was it that was "gracious enough" to take the affair in hand, to secure the appointment of Fersen as commander of a French regiment, who but the Queen, though she was not wont to concern herself about military nominations? And who was it that, in defiance of use and wont, informed the King of Sweden that the commission had been granted? The news did not come from the appropriate person, the commander-in-chief, but was conveyed in a letter penned by Marie Antoinette's own hand.

During these or the following years the intimacy between Marie Antoinette and Fersen probably reached its climax. For two years indeed the young man, much against his will, had to accompany King Gustavus as aide-de-camp when the monarch was on his travels, but in 1785 Axel returned to France. During his absence there had been a decisive change in Marie Antoinette. The affair of the diamond necklace had almost created a solitude around her, and had diverted her thoughts from trivialities to essentials. She had withdrawn from the giddy circle of the spiritually untrustworthy, of the amusingly treacherous, of the spoiled children of gallantry; and, disillusioned and sorrowful, weary of her worthless associates, she was in search of a true friend. Now that she had become an object of general dislike, she had increasing need for a trustworthy associate who would regard her with tenderness and love. She was a mature woman, no longer satisfied to waste her time looking at herself in the mirror of general admiration. She wanted to give herself wholeheartedly to a man with a straightforward and resolute spirit. Fersen, on his side, being of a splendidly chivalrous disposition, loved her all the more heartily now that she was calumniated, maligned, persecuted, and threatened. He, who had shunned her favour when she was idolized by the world and surrounded by a thousand flatterers, ventured at length to love her when she was lonely and in urgent need of help. "She is most unhappy," he wrote to his sister; "and her courage, which is admirable beyond compare, makes her yet more attractive. My only trouble is that I cannot compensate her for her sufferings, and that I shall never be able to make her as happy as she deserves." The more unfortunate she became, the more she was forsaken, the more profoundly she was troubled, the more vigorous became his virile determination to make up to her for everything by his love. "Elle pleure souvent avec moi, jugez si je dois l'aimer." The more imminent the catastrophe, the more stormily and the more tragically were the two drawn together: she in the hope of finding in his love one last happiness that should outbalance such innumerable disappointments; he hoping by his self-sacrificing and chivalrous affection to provide a substitute for her lost kingdom.

Now that what had been no more than a superficial attraction of the flesh had become a union of two spirits, now that flirtation had ripened into love, they both did their utmost to conceal their relationship from the world. To avert suspicion, Marie Antoinette arranged that the young officer should hold his command, not in Paris, but in Valenciennes, near the Netherland frontier. When summoned to the palace (even in his diary he did not say by whom), he was careful to hide the real aim of his journey from his friends, so that no one should know of his presence at Trianon and therefore cast aspersions on the Queen. "Never let anyone learn that I write to you from here," he exhorts his sister in a letter headed "Versailles." He goes on: "Except when I am writing to you, I date all my letters from Paris. Farewell, I must go to the Queen."

Fersen never frequented the society of the Polignacs nor mixed with the other members of the Queen's intimate circle; he took no part in the skating expeditions, the dances, the card-parties. Let the pseudo-favourites of Marie Antoinette parade their intimacy with her, for that would help to conceal the true secret from the court. They ruled during the day, but Fersen's realm was the night. They paid homage and chattered; Fersen was loved and maintained silence. Saint-Priest, who was privy to the affair and who knew everything connected with it (except that his own wife was madly in love with Fersen and wrote him passionate love-letters), reports in that confident way which makes his testimony peculiarly valid: "Fersen went three or four times every week to Trianon. The Queen, unattended, did the same, and these assignations gave rise to gossip notwithstanding the modesty and reserve of the favourite, who never plumed himself on his position and was the most discreet of the Queen's friends."

Still, during the five years that followed Fersen's travels with King Gustavus the lovers could enjoy no more than stolen and fleeting hours in one another's company, for, although her ladies-in-waiting were devoted and courageous and trustworthy, Marie Antoinette could not afford to run grave risks. Not until 1790, shortly before the parting, could Fersen, with the happiness of a passionate lover, report that at length he had spent a whole day "avec elle." It was only betwixt night and morning, in the shadow of the park, or perhaps in one of the Hameau cottages which were out of sight of the windows of Trianon, that the Queen could meet her lover. In the groves of Versailles and in the winding paths of Trianon, the garden-scene of *Figaro* with its delicately romantic music played itself out to an end. But already, preluded by the harsh pulsations of the *Don Giovanni* music, there was sounding outside the door the heavy, stony, crushing tread of the Commander. The third act was passing out of the delicacy of the Rococo into the grandiose style of the revolutionary tragedy. Not until the final act, shuddering with the reek of blood and of violence, would come the crescendo, the despair of the farewell, the ecstasy of destruction.

Only when the Queen was in uttermost peril and when her so-called friends had fled, did he come forward, the man who had discreetly effaced himself during the days of happiness and good fortune, the true, the only friend, ready to die with her and for her. The more his beloved was threatened, the more resolute did he become. Little, now, recked the pair of the limits set by convention between a Habsburg princess, a queen of France, on the one hand, and a Swedish junker, on the other. Day after day Fersen visited the palace. The Queen's correspondence passed through his hands. Every resolve was discussed with him before it was put into effect. The most difficult tasks, the most dangerous secrets were confided to him. He alone knew Marie Antoinette's intentions, her sorrows and her hopes; he alone witnessed her tears, her hesitations, and her unfathomable sadness. At the very moment when all had forsaken her, and when she had lost all, the Queen found what she had vainly sought throughout her life—a sincere, an upright, a virile and courageous friend.

CHAPTER XXI

Was He or Was He Not?

THIS much, at any rate, is now beyond dispute, that Axel de Fersen was not, as was so long believed, a mere accessory, but was the chief figure in Marie Antoinette's spiritual romance. We know that his relationship to the Queen was not a mere flirtation, but an enduring love, equipped with all the insignia of love's power, with the fiery mantle of passion, the splendour of courage, the unstinted greatness of feeling. One last uncertainty persists as to the form of this love. Was it, as in the nineteenth century people were fond of saying, a "pure" love—a term by which, basely enough, was meant a love relationship in which a passionately loving and passionately loved woman prudishly refused the gift of her body to the loving and the beloved man? Or was it, in the sense of those who still cherish the puritan tradition, a "criminal" love—that is to say in our sense a love without chill reserve, a love which boldly gave and boldly took all? Was Axel de Fersen no more than the cavaliere servente, the romantic worshipper of Marie Antoinette; or was he really and physically her lover? Was he or was he not?

"No! Certainly not!" exclaim, with suspicious haste and irritability, certain royalist-reactionary biographers, whose one desire it is that at all costs the Queen, "their" Queen, should be regarded as "pure" and as safeguarded against any "degradation."—"He loved the Queen passionately," contends Werner von Heidenstam with enviable certainty, "without ever having this love besoiled by fleshly thoughts, this love worthy of the troubadours and of the knights of the Round Table. Marie Antoinette loved him without ever for a moment forgetting her duties as wife, her dignity as Queen." A fanatic of this sort finds it inconceivable, or protests against anyone's entertaining the thought, that the last queen of France could have been false to the "dépôt d'honneur which all or almost all the mothers of our kings had bequeathed to her." For God's sake, therefore, let there be no inquiry into the matter, no discussion of this "affreuse calomnie" (Goncourt), no "acharnement sournois ou cynique" for the disclosure of the true state of affairs! The fanatical defenders of Marie Antoinette's "purity" warn us off the course directly we approach the question.

Must we comply with their wishes, with their commands? Must we, finger on lips, pass over the inquiry whether Fersen continued, for all the years of their acquaintanceship, to regard Marie Antoinette only "with an aureole round her head," or whether he really and effectively loved her as a man loves a woman? Are we not right in saying that anyone who "chastely" evades this question misses the core of the problem? We do not know a human being until the last secrets of the heart have been revealed; and above all we do not understand the character of a woman until we understand her love-life. In such a relationship as this, which is intimately connected with one of the great movements of history—where a passion held in leash for years was not something which had a merely casual bearing on the lives of those concerned but was a matter which stirred their souls to the depths—the question as to the actual form in which their love found expression is neither idle nor depraved, but is a decisive element in the composition of the spiritual likeness of the woman about whom this book is written. No painter can paint a portrait with his eyes half closed. Let us face the issues, therefore; let us closely consider the situation and the documents that bear on it. We may well hope that a frank inquiry will enable us to solve the riddle.

Here is the first question! Even supposing the champions of the bourgeois code of morality are right, even though Marie Antoinette were to be accounted blameworthy if she gave herself unreservedly to Fersen—who among us has the right to cast a stone? Let us consider the personality of those who have unhesitatingly declared that the Queen became his mistress. Among her contemporaries there were three, all men of mark, not eavesdroppers, but thoroughly well-informed persons, who may be supposed to have written or spoken with full knowledge and a due sense of responsibility: Napoleon, Talleyrand, and Saint-Priest the minister of State; the last-named a daily witness of what was going on. All three of them say without reserve that Marie Antoinette was Fersen's mistress. Saint-Priest, who had the most direct acquaintance with the situation, gives precise details. By no means hostile to the Queen, thoroughly matter-of-fact, he tells of Fersen's secret nocturnal visits to Trianon, Saint-Cloud, and the Tuileries. He declares that Madame de Polignac was privy to the liaison, regarding it with no disfavour, seeing that the Queen's affection had been given to a foreigner who would not derive any personal advantages from Marie Antoinette's passion for him. It is amazing to find even the most rabid champions of the Queen's "virtue" disregarding such testimony, and speaking of Napoleon and Talleyrand, likewise, as calumniators!

Now comes a second question. Which among the contemporaries of the affair who were eye-witnesses of what went on can be found to stigmatize as a falsehood the statement that Fersen was Marie Antoinette's lover? Not a single one. No, the remarkable feature in the case is that those who must have been most intimately acquainted with what was happening, and whose position made it necessary for them to be discreet, seem to have carefully avoided the mention of Fersen's name. Mercy, for instance, a meticulous observer, and profoundly interested in the Queen's doings, never mentions the Swedish count in his official dispatches. The familiars of the court make frequent mention of "a certain person" to whom letters have been conveyed, but the name of this person is withheld. For a whole century there was a conspiracy of silence, and the first official biography explicitly omitted to say a word about Fersen. How can we avoid gathering the impression that a "mot d'ordre" had been issued to shun any reference to a man who marches disturbingly athwart the romanticist legend of the martyred Queen's immaculate chastity?

For a long time, therefore, historical students were faced with an insoluble enigma. Everywhere they encountered ground for serious suspicion; and yet everywhere the decisive documentary proof had been carefully shuffled out of sight. The available material did not justify a plain yes or no. Forse che si, forse che no—perhaps, perhaps not. That is all that historians could venture to say, since they lacked definitive proof.

Yet where strictly factual research reaches its bourne, imagination, with soaring pinions, can still do useful and in a sense trustworthy work; where paleography fails us, psychology has a word to say—for we know that the probabilities unveiled by psychological study are often nearer the truth than the crude "truth" of documents and facts. Were we exclusively dependent upon documents in our study of history, how narrow, how poverty-stricken, how full of gaps would this science be! The unambiguous, the manifest, is the domain of science; the polyvalent, the ambiguous, that which needs interpretation and illumination, is the realm of the poietic imagination. When we are short of materials for proof that would be accepted as valid in a law-court, there still remain boundless possibilities for the psychologist. Feeling can tell us more about a man or a woman than can all the documents in the world.

Still, let us return to the documents. Axel de Fersen, though romantically inclined, was an orderly person. He wrote up his diary with the utmost regularity and precision. Morning after morning he carefully noted the weather, the barometric reading of the day, and the political and personal pressure as well as the atmospheric. In addition to this diary, he had a correspondence book in which he recorded the letters received and sent under the appropriate date. He also had a memorandum book in which he made notes of his plans; and he carefully filed his correspondence. In short, he was one of those men who are treasure-trove for the historian. When he died a violent death in 1810, he left behind him an accurate record of all the details of his life—a record of incomparable value for those who love "hard facts."

Well, what was done with this treasure? Nothing! This seems strange enough at the first glance. Its existence was carefully, nay timidly, concealed by Axel's heirs. No one was granted access to the archives, no one was told anything about them. At long last, half a century after Fersen's death, one of his successors, a certain Baron Klinkowström, published the correspondence and part of the diaries. But the correspondence was incomplete. A number of Marie Antoinette's letters, entered in the correspondence book as received from "Josephine," had disappeared. Vanished, too, were Fersen's diaries recording the incidents of the most decisive years. Strangest of all, in the published letters we find passage after passage represented merely by dots. Someone, it is evident, must have played the censor in dealing with these literary remains. But whenever correspondence is thus "edited" or destroyed by those of a later day, we cannot free ourselves from the suspicion that inconvenient facts have been obscured in pursuit of some etiolated ideal aim. However, we must not prejudge the case. Let us preserve our calm, let us maintain our sense of justice. Look into the matter dispassionately!

Passages are omitted from the letters, and have been replaced by dots. Why? Klinkowström informs us that they had been deliberately made illegible in the original. By whom? "Probably by Fersen him self," quoth Klinkowström. "Probably!" But why? Klinkowström, obviously at a loss for a plausible answer, says that presumably these erased lines had contained political secrets or undesirable remarks made by Marie Antoinette concerning King Gustavus III. Since Fersen showed all these letters (all?) to the King, it is likely (likely!) that he had himself erased the objectionable passages. A very remarkable story! A great many of the letters were written in cipher, so Fersen can only have read transcripts to the King. Why, then, should he take the trouble to mutilate the originals and to render them unreadable? Is not this a highly suspicious circumstance? Still, as aforesaid, let us go on considering the matter without prejudice.

The essential thing is to undertake a closer scrutiny of the excisions. What is the first thing that strikes us? We find that the dotted passages are almost always at the beginning or the end of a letter, so that there is no opening address, or there is a gap after the word "Adieu." For instance, we read: "Je vais finir"—signifying "I have done with business and politics, and am now going on to . . ." Going on to what? In the mutilated publication nothing follows but dots, dots, dots. When there is an omission in the middle of a letter, we always find it in a place where political matters are not in question. Let me give another example: "Comment va votre santé? Je parie que vous ne vous soignez pas et vous avez tort. . . . Pour moi je me soutiens mieux que je ne devrais." Will anyone in his sane senses imagine that the elided passage can have related to politics? Again, when the Queen is writing about her children, "Cette occupation c'est mon seul bonheur . . . et quand je suis bien triste, je prends mon petit garçon," nine hundred and ninety-nine persons out of a thousand will fill in the gap with the words "since you left me," and not with some sarcastic observation concerning the King of Sweden! It is impossible to accept Klinkowström's embarrassed assertion. Obviously what has been suppressed is not a political secret but a secret which concerns the intimate sentiments of human beings. Well, after all, there is a way of unriddling such riddles. Micro-photography makes it easy for us to decipher passages in letters which have thus been rendered illegible by "pigeons' nests." Let us examine the originals!

Here we are faced with a fresh surprise. The originals no longer exist! Down till about 1900, for more than a century, they were kept in good order and condition in the Fersens' hereditary seat. Then they were destroyed. Baron Klinkowström, a strictly moral man seems to have been haunted by the spectre that a day might come when the passages that had been rendered illegible might be read; and so, shortly before his death, he burned Marie Antoinette's letters to Fersen. It was an act of vandalism worthy of Herostratus, not only senseless, but, as we shall learn, ineffective. However, Klinkowström wanted, at any cost, to keep Fersen's relations with the Queen shrouded in mystery, to foster a legend in place of disclosing irrefutable truths. He could die (so he imagined) with an easy conscience, since Fersen's "honour" and Marie Antoinette's "honour," had been safeguarded by committing the letters to the flames.

But, to quote a well-known saying, this auto-da-fé was worse than a crime, it was a blunder. For, first of all, the destruction of evidence is itself evidence of a guilt-complex; and, secondly, as every criminologist knows, when proofs are hastily annihilated it nearly always happens that some damnatory item is left undestroyed. Alma Sjöderhelm, an able investigator, looking through the documents that had survived, discovered a copy made by Fersen of one of Marie Antoinette's letters, which seems to have escaped Klinkowström's notice because it was a transcript and not in the Queen's handwriting. Thus we have a full text of one, and therewith the key to all, of the mutilated letters. We can guess, now, we can more than guess, what the mealy-mouthed editor had cut out of those that he published, for in this epistle likewise there is, towards the close an "Adieu" which is followed, not by erasures or dots, but by loving words: "Adieu, le plus aimant et le plus aimé des hommes."

We understand, at length, why the Klinkowströms, the Heidenstams, and the other purity fanatics (who probably had access to more documents of this kind than will ever become known to posterity), showed so much affect whenever an unbiased attempt was made to study the Fersen case. For one familiar with the tones of the human heart there can be no doubt that a queen who addresses a man so boldly and in such sublimely unconventional terms, must long before have granted him the last proof of her love. The one line that has come down to us makes good for all those that were cancelled. Had not the cancellation in itself been sufficient proof, persons endowed with insight, persons capable of true feeling, will be fully convinced by these words that have escaped the hand of the destroyer.

But there is more to come! In addition to this rescued letter, we have knowledge of a scene in Fersen's life which is characterologically decisive. It occurred six years after the Queen's execution. Fersen had been chosen by the Swedish government to attend the Congress of Rastatt as its representative. Bonaparte, however, bluntly informed Baron Edelsheim that he would not negotiate with Fersen, who was a royalist, and who, moreover, had slept with the Queen. The Corsican, who was wont to call a spade a spade, did not say that the man to whom he took exception had been "on intimate terms" with Marie Antoinette, but challengingly and almost offensively declared: "Fersen s'est couché avec la reine." It never occurred to Baron Edelsheim that it was incumbent upon him to defend Fersen, to protest against this charge, for he, likewise, took the relations between the pair as a matter of course. He therefore answered with a smile that he had thought these stories dating from the "ancien régime" were over and done with, and had no further bearing upon contemporary politics. Then he went to Fersen, and related the whole conversation. What did Fersen do? Or, rather, what should we have expected him to do if Bonaparte's remark had been a falsehood? Would he not at once have defended the dead Queen against the accusation? Would he not have angrily denounced the calumny? This upstart little Corsican general, who used so derogatory a term in speaking of a lady who had beyond question been Fersen's intimate friend—would not the Swedish nobleman have challenged him forthwith to a duel? Can a straightforward and upright man allow anyone to say a woman was his mistress when she was nothing of the kind? Now or never was Fersen's chance, nay his duty, to use his naked sword for the destruction of a rumour which had long been current.

What did Fersen actually do? Alas, he was silent. Taking up his pen, he soberly recorded in his diary the whole conversation between Edelsheim and Bonaparte, not excepting the accusation that he had "slept" with the Queen. He made no comment; did not add a word in this private communing with himself to mitigate the force of an assertion which, in the opinion of his biographers, was "an infamous and cynical" accusation. Substantially, therefore, with lowered head, he admitted that the statement was true. When, a few days later, the British newspapers got wind of the incident, and, in connexion with it, dilated "upon him and the unhappy Queen," he wrote of this publicity: "Ceci me choqua." That was Fersen's only protest, which was no protest at all. This was one of the many cases in which silence says more than speech.

Thus we see that what the pusillanimous have so strenuously endeavoured to hide, namely that Fersen was Marie Antoinette's lover, was never denied by the lover himself. There are dozens upon dozens of confirmatory details. For instance, on one occasion when he had been seen in public in Brussels with another lady-love, his sister implored him to be more careful, for if she ("elle") were to hear anything of the matter she would be deeply wounded—and with what right, one must ask, if she had not been his mistress? Again, there is a passage in the diary where Fersen mentions having spent the night in the Queen's rooms at the Tuileries, and this passage has been erased, though it is still decipherable. Once more, giving evidence before the Revolutionary Tribunal, a housemaid testified that a gentleman had frequently left the Queen's bedroom secretly by night. These incidents are, of course, only given weight by the fact that they fit into the general picture. Disparate elements would be unconvincing if they were not in keeping with the character of the whole. An individual's behaviour is only explicable as the outcome of his whole personality for every "voluntary" action is the expression of the circumscribed causality of a person's whole nature. In the last analysis, therefore, the question as to whether the relationships between Fersen and Marie Antoinette were those of a passionate intimacy or remained within the limits regarded as seemly and conventional must be decided in accordance with the general spiritual make-up of the woman concerned. We have, therefore, details apart, to inquire which sort of behaviour, a liberal self-surrender or a timid renouncement, would have been logically and characterologically in conformity with the Queen's disposition.

One who contemplates the matter from this standpoint will not hesitate long. Despite her many weaknesses, Marie Antoinette had one great strength: her unrestrained, unreflective, truly sovereign courage. Thoroughly straightforward, incapable of pretences, she flouted the conventions hundreds of times in matters of much less importance, indifferent to the gossip which might be going on behind her back. Even though she only achieved true greatness in the most formidable and decisive moments of her fate, she was never petty, never timid; she never subjected her will to the formalities of "honour," or "morality" to the pettifogging restrictions of court life. Are we to suppose that in the case of the one man whom she dearly loved this valiant woman would suddenly have played the prude, the timid and "faithful" wife of her Louis, to whom she had been wedded only for reasons of State and with whom she was not bound by any ties of love? Can we believe that in so apocalyptic a time, when the bonds of discipline and order had been torn in sunder, that in the intoxicating agitation of imminent death and amid the menaces of a terrible destruction, she would have sacrificed her passion for the sake of a social prejudice? Can we believe that she, whom no one could hinder and no one could control, would have forced herself to abstain from the most natural, the most womanly expression of feeling for the sake of a phantom, of a marriage which was the mockery of true marriage, out of respect for a man who had never shown himself to be a real man, and for the sake of a moral obligation which had always been odious to the untamed instincts of her impetuous nature?

If people want to believe the incredible, no one can prevent them. But it is not those who frankly ascribe to Marie Antoinette boldness and inconsiderateness where the one great love passion of her life was concerned that deform her image; those who thus err are they who would represent a fearless woman as a coward, a brisk woman as a dullard, an impulsive and impetuous woman as one paralysed by caution and consideration—as one who would not venture the last hazard but would fight down her most natural promptings. To those who have the capacity for picturing a character as a unity it must be indubitable that Marie Antoinette, not only with her mind which had suffered such manifold disappointments, but also with the body which had so long been robbed of its rights, became the lover of Axel de Fersen.

And what about the King? Whenever a marriage bond is broken, it is the third party, the dupe, the deceived, who becomes (according as our sympathies range) an object of compassion or a figure of fun: and a goodly number of the attempts to obscure the lineaments, to round the corners of this triangle may have been made in the interests of Louis XVI. In reality, however, Louis XVI was by no means deceived, was not a ridiculous cuckold, for there can be no doubt that he was aware of the intimate relations between Fersen and his wife. Saint-Priest says in plain terms: "She found ways and means of making him acquainted with the fact that she had a liaison with the Comte de Fersen."

This assertion is in conformity with our general picture of the situation. Nothing was more uncongenial to Marie Antoinette than hypocrisy or misrepresentation. To have betrayed her husband behind his back while pretending that she was still devoted to him both in body and in mind would have been foreign to her temperament; and we cannot in her case suppose that there can have possibly existed the common but always unclean form of triangle in which a wife goes on cohabiting with her husband while, without his knowledge, she enjoys, whenever opportunity permits, the embraces of a lover. There can be no question that as soon as her intimate relationship with Fersen began (it was probably in the later years of her married life, between the fifteenth and the twentieth), Marie Antoinette ceased to be Louis's wife except in name. We should assume this on characterological grounds, but the supposition is confirmed by a letter from her brother the Emperor who, by means which have not come to our knowledge, had learned that his sister, after the birth of her fourth child, wished to withdraw from her husband's embraces —the date coinciding with that at which we have good reason to believe her intimate relations with Fersen began.

For those, then, who like to look facts in the face, the situation is perfectly clear. Marie Antoinette, wedded for reasons of State to an unloved and by no means attractive man, had for many years repressed her need for love in favour of conjugal obligations. But as soon as she had given birth to two sons, so that dynastic duties had been fulfilled by the provision of heirs who were indubitably of Bourbon blood, she felt that she had done all that morality, the State, law, and family ties had a right to demand of her. At length she was free. Having devoted nearly two decades to the fulfilment of political obligations, during the last and tragically convulsive hours this sorely tried woman felt entitled to enjoy her pure and natural right, to give herself at length to the man whom she had long adored, the man who was everything to her, friend and lover, confidant and companion, as courageous as herself, and ready to requite sacrifice with sacrifice.

How pitiful seem the sophisticated hypotheses about the sweetly virtuous Queen, as contrasted with the intelligible forthrightness of her behaviour; and what a poor figure do those cut who make such a to-do about defending the royal "honour" of this woman. How lacking they are in courage and in spiritual dignity. For never is a woman more honourable and nobler than when she gives free rein to the unerring sentiments and instincts which have been animating her for years; never is a queen more queenly than when she shows herself a true woman.

CHAPTER XXII

The Last Night in Versailles

NEVER in the ancient realm of France had the seed ripened so swiftly as in this summer of the year 1789. The golden grain swelled on the tall stalks; and still more swiftly, manured with blood, sprouted the impatient seed of the Revolution. With a stroke of the pen, an end was put to the neglect of decades, to the injustice of centuries; other Bastilles were stormed, the fortresses in which the rights of the French people had been prisoned by their kings. On the fourth of August, amid universal jubilation, the ancient (though invisible) stronghold of feudalism fell. The nobles had to renounce corvées and tithes, the princes of the Church must forgo their rents and their revenues from the salt tax. Serfdom was abolished. The third estate became supreme. The press was declared free. The Rights of Man were proclaimed. During this one summer, all the dreams of Jean Jacques Rousseau were fulfilled. In the meeting-place of the Assembly, the windows rattled, now because of shouts of exultation, and now because of the disputes among the excited deputies. A hundred paces away the buzzing as of a great hive of bees was plainly audible. A thousand paces farther yet, in the huge palace of Versailles, the chillness of dismay prevailed. With alarm the court looked from the windows towards this noisy guest who, though summoned only to give advice, had arrogated the role of ruler. It was like the fiend conjured up by the magician's apprentice. How was he to be sent home again? How could the spectre be laid? The King, in his perplexity, could get no help from his councillors, whose advice was contradictory. To Marie Antoinette and to Louis it seemed best to wait until the storm had blown itself out. Let them remain quietly in the background; let them gain time; then, in the end, all would come right.

But the Revolution had to make headway, since otherwise it would be in danger of becoming silted up—for a revolution is necessarily a movement, a flow. Stagnation would be its doom, retrogression would put an end to it; it must demand more and ever more concessions in order to maintain itself; it must conquer if it would avoid being conquered. The drums for this unceasing march were beaten by the newspapers, the gutter-snipes of the revolution, which ran, shouting ecstatically, in front of the real army. Freedom had been given to the written and the spoken word; and freedom, in its first exuberance, is always fierce and unmeasured. Ten, twenty, thirty, fifty journals appeared. Mirabeau founded one of his own, so did Desmoulins, so did Brissot, so did Loustalot, so did Marat; and since, on the hunt for readers, they outvied one another in the extravagance of bourgeois patriotism, their clamour swelled into a roar which was heard throughout the country.

Each of them tried to be louder, to be more savage and unrestrained than the others. The louder, the better; make the court the target of universal hatred! The King was planning treason; the government was interfering with the supplies of grain; foreign regiments were being sent for to suppress the Revolution and to dissolve the Assembly by force; a new massacre of Saint Bartholomew was imminent. Wake up, citizens! Wake up, patriots! Rataplan, rataplan, rataplan! By day and by night, the newspapers beat the big drum, spreading fear, distrust, rage, bitterness, into millions of hearts. And behind the drummers there was already standing the hitherto invisible army of the French people, equipped with pikes and sabres, and inspired with overwhelming wrath.

For the King, things were going too quickly; for the champions of the Revolution, too slowly. Louis, being cautious and stout, could not keep step with the vehement advance of the new ideas. Since Versailles continued to hesitate and to postpone, so Paris must rush forward. The cry of the revolutionary newspapers was that there must be an end of this tedious parleying, this insufferable bargaining between King and people. "You have a hundred thousand, two hundred thousand fists; there are muskets and cannon in the arsenals; get them out, ready for use; fetch the King and the Queen from Versailles; take your destinies into your own hands!" At the headquarters of the Revolution, in the Duke of Orléans's abode, the Palais Royal, the word was given. Everything had been prepared, and the Marquis de Huruge, one of the deserters from the court, was ready to command the expedition.

But there were underground passages communicating between the palace of Versailles and the metropolis. Patriots in the clubs were kept informed by the servants, whom they had bribed, concerning all that went on in the palace; and the palace, in its turn, had secret agents in Paris and knew everything about the proposed attack. Versailles decided to take a strong line, and since French soldiers were not to be trusted to act against their fellow-citizens, a Flemish regiment was summoned for the protection of the palace. On October 1st, the troops marched from their cantonments to Versailles, where the court had prepared to give them a cordial reception. The great opera hall had been arranged for a banquet. Although Paris was suffering from a scarcity which bordered upon famine, there was to be no lack here of wine and good food. Loyalty, like love, often depends upon the stomach. In order to stimulate the soldiers' enthusiasm for their ruler, the King and the Queen, the latter leading the Dauphin by the hand, visited the banqueting-hall. It was an unprecedented honour!

Marie Antoinette had never learned the useful art of winning people to her cause by shrewdness, by calculation, or by flattery. Still, nature had equipped her, both in mind and body, with a considerable measure of dignity which produced a good impression upon anyone who saw her for the first time. It was fleeting, but none could escape it. On the occasion of this entry, she looked both dignified and lovable, a handsome woman, only thirty-four years of age. Officers and men rose from their seats, drew their swords, and raised a shout of welcome to King Louis and his wife. The Queen walked up and down the room. She wore a bewitching smile. Like her autocratic mother, like her brother, like almost all the Habsburgs—like the Austrian aristocracy in general—she had an extraordinarily affable manner, and, notwithstanding her invincible arrogance, she could be courteous and forthcoming to ordinary folk in the most natural way possible, without producing in them any feeling that she was "condescending." It was long since she had heard an enthusiastic "Vive la Reine!" and the sound gladdened her heart. The sight of this gracious, this truly royal lady, as, accompanied by her children, she moved round the great banqueting-table and behaved as if she had herself been the guest of those whom she was entertaining, aroused a rapture of loyalty both in officers and in men. At this moment, every one of them was ready to die for Marie Antoinette. The Queen, too, was profoundly moved. The wine of so hearty a welcome was intoxicating. It restored her confidence. France still knew the meaning of loyalty; the throne was still secure.

On October 2nd and 3rd, however, the drums of the patriotic journals were rattling once more. Rataplan, rataplan, rataplan; the Queen and the court were scheming to assassinate the people. They had made the soldiers drunken with red wine that these armed men might shed the red blood of fellow-citizens; servile officers had trampled upon the tricolour; lickspittle songs had been sung—and the mischief had been wrought by the challenging smiles of the Queen. Patriots, have a care! Paris is about to be attacked; regiments are already on the march. To arms, citizens, for the last decisive struggle! Assemble, patriots. Rataplan, rataplan, rataplan!

Two days later, on October 5th, there was a tumult in Paris. There was a tumult, and how it came to pass remains one of the impenetrable mysteries of the French Revolution. For this tumult, spontaneous though it may seem to have been at the first glance, was in truth remarkably well organized, was a political master-stroke. The shot was fired from the right quarter and hit the bull's-eye. Obviously, then, cunning brains and practised hands were at work. The most outstanding feature of the affair was worthy of the able psychologist Choderlos de Laclos, who, in the Palais Royal, was directing the Duke of Orléans's campaign. The King was to be brought from Versailles to Paris, not by an army of men, but by an army of women. Men who undertake such a deed can be shot down as rebels. Any well-drilled soldier will fire at a man upon the word of command. But when women play a leading part in a popular riot, the authorities look upon them only as poor creatures driven by despair. The sharpest bayonet finds the armour of a woman's soft breast invulnerable. Besides, those who were fomenting the revolt knew that a man so timid and sentimental as Louis would never give the order to fire upon women. The first move in the game, therefore, was to fan the excitement to fever-heat. Next (and here again we do not know through whose instrumentality) the supply of bread to Paris must be held up for two days, since nothing can compete with hunger as a stimulant of popular wrath. Thirdly, when all was ripe, let women, not men, take the field!

It was, in fact, a young woman (and rumour declares that she was wearing valuable rings) who, on the morning of October 5th, broke into a guardroom and seized a drum. Behind her, in a trice, there ranged themselves a vast number of women, clamouring for bread. The riot had begun, and speedily men dressed up as women mingled with the crowd, to give it the prearranged impetus in the direction of the Hôtel de Ville. Within half an hour, the place had been stormed, pistols and pikes and even two cannon had been seized, and then there suddenly appeared as if from nowhere a leader, Maillard by name. This young revolutionist took command of the disorderly and chaotic mass, organized it into an army, and incited it to march on Versailles; ostensibly to demand bread, though really in order to bring the King to Paris. Too late, as usual, Lafayette, commanding officer of the National Guard, appeared upon the scene, mounted on his white charger. (It was always the fate of this distinguished laggard, sincere and honourable, but maladroit, to turn up the day after the fair!) His duty of course was, and he earnestly tried to accomplish it, to prevent the march on Versailles; his men, however, would not obey orders. There was nothing left for him but to lead the National Guard as rear-column of the army of women, thus giving revolt a cloak of legality. Enthusiastic champion of liberty though he was, he knew that today he was playing a sorry part. He rode gloomily westward in the trail of the revolutionists, symbol of cool and calculating reason fruitlessly endeavouring to overtake (after having vainly attempted to control) the splendidly illogical passion of an elemental storm.

Not until noon did the court of Versailles hear a word about the approach of the thousand-headed danger. In accordance with his daily custom, the King had had one of his hunters saddled and had ridden off into the woods of Meudon; and the Queen had early in the morning, unaccompanied, walked over to Trianon. Why should she stay at Versailles, the huge palace whence those who had been her most intimate friends had long since fled or been sent to exile, and where, close at hand, in the National Assembly, day after day the "factieux" were volleying new and ever more hateful accusations against her? She was weary of this bitterness, of this struggle in the void; she was weary of human beings, and weary of her queenship. She would get a few hours' rest and quiet, away from political chatter, in the lovely park where the foliage was beginning to assume the warm tints of the fall. She would pick the last flowers in the beds before chill winter came to destroy them; perhaps she would feed the chickens, and the Chinese goldfish in the little pond. After that she would rest, remote from the turmoil and disorder; would do nothing, would want to do nothing, but sit at ease in the grotto, simply attired, with an open book beside her on the bench, open but unread—her heart attuned to the weariness which overcomes nature in autumn.

There sat the Queen upon the stone bench in the grotto (forgetting, perhaps, that it used to be called "the Grotto of Love"), when she saw one of her pages coming, a letter in his hand. She went out to meet him. The letter was from Saint-Priest, and it reported that the mob was marching on Versailles. The Queen would do well to return to the palace instantly. Snatching up her hat, wrapping her cloak round her, she hastened thither with her youthful and springy gait—so swiftly, one may presume, that she never looked back towards the Little Trianon and its "natural" landscape which had been constructed with such careful art. How could she foresee that never again would she see these pleasant meadows, these gentle hillocks, with Cupid's Temple and the pond; that she was bidding farewell for ever to her Hameau, her Trianon?

At Versailles Marie Antoinette found the nobles and the ministers of State in hopeless perplexity. So far, nothing but vague rumours of the march from Paris had arrived, brought by a servant who had managed to get away in advance of the mob. Subsequent messengers had been intercepted by the women. Now at length came a horseman, who sprang from the saddle and ran hot-foot up the marble staircase: Fersen. At the first tidings of peril, he had galloped off to Versailles, circumventing the army of women—the "eight thousand Judiths" as Desmoulins emotionally called them—determined to be at the Queen's side in the moment of danger. At length the King also appeared at the council. Messengers had found him in the forest close to the Porte de Châtillon, and had had to disturb him at his favourite amusement That evening his diary would record with annoyance that he had had a poor day's hunting, with the comment "interrupted by events."

Well, he had to return, disconcerted and alarmed; and at length, after possible measures of defence had been neglected, and when, in the general confusion, no one had thought of blocking the progress of the revolutionary vanguard by closing the bridge at Sèvres, a council was held. There were still two hours; there was still time for energetic action. One of the ministers proposed that the King should mount his horse and lead a troop of dragoons and the Flemish regiment against the undisciplined masses; the mere sight of him thus attended would compel the horde of women to retreat. Those of a more cautious temperament, however, held that it would be better for the King and the Queen to leave Versailles immediately and to betake themselves to Rambouillet, for this withdrawal to a safe distance would counter-mine the crafty and malicious attack upon the throne. But Louis, hesitant as ever, found it impossible to make up his mind either to one expedient or to the other. It was his invariable practice to let events take their course instead of trying to guide them.

The Queen stood, biting her lips, amid the perplexed men, not one of whom was really and truly a man. Her instinct told her that forcible resistance would be successful, that the mob would scatter, terror-stricken, at the first shedding of blood. "Toute cette révolution n'est qu'une suite de la peur." But how could she take the responsibility for meeting force by force? Below, in the courtyard, the horses had been put to. In an hour the royal family with the ministers of State and the members of the National Assembly, who had sworn to follow the King wherever he went, could be safe at Rambouillet. Still Louis pro-crastinated, was unwilling to give the sign. His ministers grew more and more urgent, especially Saint-Priest, who said: "Sire, if you let them take you to Paris tomorrow, you will lose your crown." Necker, who was more interested in maintaining his own popularity than in upholding the monarchy, was opposed to the Rambouillet scheme; so poor Louis, a pendulum devoid of will, swung unceasingly from one side to the other. The hours drew on towards evening, and the horses pawed the ground impatiently, made even more restless by the heavy rain which had begun to fall. For hours the lackeys had been waiting by the carriage doors, and still the council of indecision went on.

At length there came a confused murmur of many voices from the Avenue de Paris. The army of women was close at hand, their skirts drawn up over their heads as a protection against the downpour. Stamping onward in their thousands, the amazons of the market-place drew nigh. The vanguard of the Revolution was in Versailles. The opportunity for decisive action, whether by resistance or by flight, had been lost.

Drenched to the skin, cold and hungry, their shoes filled with mud and squelching at every step, the women marched up to the palace. These six hours had been no pleasure-trip, even though the drinking-saloons on the wayside had been stormed, and the raiders had been able now and again to warm the cockles of their heart with a tot of brandy. Their voices were hoarse with cold and wet and fatigue as well as with anger; and what they shouted was anything but friendly towards the Queen. Their first visit was to the National Assembly. It had been in session since early that morning, and many of the deputies, those who were doing their best to prepare the way for the Duke of Orléans, were not taken by surprise by this march of the women.

The first demand the newcomers made of the Assembly was for bread, it having been arranged that to begin with not a word was to be said about removing the King to Paris. A deputation of the women was sent into the palace, accompanied by Mounier, the president of the Assembly, and by some of the representatives of the third estate. The six selected women made for the entrance, where the lackeys politely opened the doors for these dressmakers, fishwives, and street-walkers. With every conceivable honour the uncanny deputation was escorted up the marble staircase into the halls which, heretofore, had only been open to the blue-bloods of France. Among the deputies who accompanied the president of the National Assembly was a tall, rather corpulent and genial-looking man about whose appearance there was nothing to attract particular attention. His name, however, gives his first encounter with King Louis peculiar significance. It was Dr. Guillotin, professor of anatomy at the University of Paris and representative of that city, through whose instrumentality an improved form of the instrument subsequently called by his name was adopted by the revolutionists as a "humane killer."

Good-natured Louis received the ladies in so friendly a fashion that their spokeswoman, a young lady who sold flowers (and probably something more) to the habitués of the Palais Royal, actually fainted from embarrassment. She was sedulously cared for. The worthy father of his country put his arm round the terrified girl, promised the gratified members of the deputation bread in plenty and everything else they wanted, and even placed his own carriages at their disposal to save them the trouble of the long walk back to Paris. Everything seemed to have gone off swimmingly; when the deputation went downstairs it was received with cries of rage by the general body of the women, who had, meanwhile, been worked upon by the secret agitators among them. Their representatives must have been bribed, or at any rate must have allowed themselves to be fobbed off with lies! "We have not tramped for six hours from Paris, through a cloud-burst, in order to go home again with gnawing stomachs and empty pledges. We shall stay here until we can take back the King and the Queen and the whole band with us to Paris, where we can keep them under close observation and teach them not to play any more tricks on us." The women crowded into the meeting-hall of the National Assembly to sleep there—except for a few of them, professional prostitutes (of whom Théroigne de Méricourt was one). These latter sought custom from among the soldiers of the Flemish regiment. Stragglers of questionable character continued to swell the army at Versailles. Sinister figures, dimly lit by the oil lanterns, prowled round the railings.

On the first floor, the court was still deliberating. Would it not be better, after all, to flee? But how could the carriages make their way through the excited crowd? Too late! Towards midnight, drums were heard in the distance. Lafayette was coming. He, too, paid his first visit to the National Assembly, and his second to the King. Although, with honest devotion, and a profound obeisance, he said: "Sire, I have come to bring you my head in order to save Your Majesty's," no one gave him any thanks, least of all Marie Antoinette. The King declared that he no longer desired to leave Versailles or to remove out of touch with the National Assembly. Everything seemed settled. Louis had given his word, Lafayette and the armed forces of the people were on hand to protect him; and so the members of the Assembly went home to bed, while the National Guard and the insurgents sought shelter from the drenching rain in the barracks and the churches, in doorways and under arches. Light after light was extinguished, and Lafayette, after making a final round to inspect his sentries, likewise went to bed, at four in the morning, in the Hôtel de Noailles—although he had pledged himself to watch over the King's safety. Marie Antoinette and Louis retired to their separate chambers, never dreaming that this was the last night on which they would lay themselves down to sleep at Versailles.

CHAPTER XXIII

The Hearse of the Monarchy

THE authorities of the old regime, the monarchy and its guardians the aristocrats, had gone to bed. But the Revolution was young. The hot, the uncontrollable blood of youth coursed through its veins. It needed no rest. Impatiently, it awaited the day and the deed. Round the camp-fires, in the streets and in the roads, were many of the combatants of the Paris rising, who had found no shelter. It was difficult to say why they were staying in Versailles instead of being on their way home to Paris, since the King had agreed to their demands and had pledged his royal word. But a subterranean will held the restless swarm together and controlled its actions. Secret instructions were conveyed from group to group, and at five in the morning, when the palace was still shrouded in darkness and in sleep, a considerable number of the insurgents, under cunning guidance, made their way through the chapel court and halted beneath the windows of the palace. What did they want? Who were the leaders? Who was urging the raiders towards a goal which had been well considered, although it was still unknown to many of the tools? The main instigators were behind the scenes. There can be little doubt, nevertheless, that the Duke of Orléans and the Count of Provence had arranged matters to suit their own ends, and that it was for a good reason that on this eventful night they were not in the palace beside their lawful King. However this may be, suddenly a shot was fired, one of those provocative shots that are always fired when a collision is intended. Instantly there rushed up from all sides hundreds upon hundreds of the insurgents, armed with pikes and mattocks and muskets; the regiments of women and of men disguised as women. The assault had a definite and preconcerted aim. "To the Queen's apartments!" How was it that the fishwives of Paris, the market-women, who had never before been to Versailles, could find their way so easily to their goal in this vast palace with its dozens of staircases and hundreds of rooms? There were some with them who knew the way, and the human wave rushed up the steps leading towards the Queen's private suite. A few of the bodyguard tried to bar the entrance. Two of them were cut down and barbarously murdered. A big, bearded man hacked their heads off, and within a few minutes the bleeding trophies were flaunted on pike-points.

But the victims had gained the object of their self-sacrifice. Their death-cries had roused the palace. One of the three guardsmen had escaped, though wounded, and, hastening up the stairs, he shouted at the top of his voice: "Save the Queen!"

This cry did actually save her. One of the ladies-in-waiting, terror-stricken, burst into Marie Antoinette's room to warn her. Though the guard had hastily barricaded the doors, they were being broken down by crowbars and axes. There was no time for the Queen to put on shoes or stockings. She slipped a petticoat over her nightdress and drew a shawl round her shoulders. Thus, barefooted, her stockings in her hand, with beating heart she ran along the corridor leading to the Œil de Bœuf and on through this wide chamber to the King's apartments. Alas, the door was barred! The Queen and her ladies beat upon it with their fists, but it remained inexorably closed. For five minutes, five interminable minutes, while the hired assassins were breaking into one room after another, stripping the coverlets from the beds and searching the cupboards, the Queen had to wait until a servant within heard the knocking and opened the door. At length, Marie Antoinette could take refuge in her husband's suite, and at this moment the governess brought the Dauphin and the little Princess. The family was reunited, their lives had been saved. But nothing more than their lives.

There had also awakened the sleeper who, above all, ought not, on this momentous night, to have surrendered to the embraces of Morpheus—Lafayette, thenceforward often spoken of by the contemptuous nickname of "Général Morphée." He realized soon enough the mischief that had been done by his slackness and credulity. Only by prayers and petitions, and no longer with the authority of a commander, was he able to save from slaughter those of the bodyguard who had been taken prisoner by the mob; and only with the utmost difficulty was he able to clear the invaders out of the palace. Now, when the danger was over, there appeared on the scene, carefully shaved and powdered,

the Count of Provence and the Duke of Orléans; and, strangely
enough, the excited crowd made way for them respectfully. It was
possible to open a royal council. After all, what was there left to
discuss? The multitude, ten thousand in number, held the palace like
a thin nutshell in its grimy and bloodstained fists. No longer was
there any chance of escape. There could be no question of parleying
between victors and vanquished. As with one voice, the masses beneath the windows shouted the demand which yesterday and today
had been secretly impressed upon them by the agents of the clubs.
"Le Roi à Paris! Le Roi à Paris!" The window-panes rattled under
the reverberation from these menacing voices, and the portraits of the
King's ancestors hanging on the walls of the palace shook as if in
alarm.

At the commanding exclamation, the King glanced questioningly
towards Lafayette. Should he obey? Or, rather, had he any choice
but to obey? Lafayette lowered his eyes. Since yesterday this idol of
the populace knew that he was no longer an object of worship. Louis
still hoped to procrastinate. In order to keep the raging mob from
proceeding to extremities, in order to throw at least a crust to those
who hungered for a plain acknowledgment of their triumph, he
resolved to appear upon the balcony. Hardly had the worthy fellow
presented himself when the crowd below broke out into loud acclamations! The populace always acclaimed the King when he had been
conquered. After all why should they not rejoice when a sovereign
bared his head before them, and nodded in friendly fashion down
towards the courtyard where two of his defenders had just been
slaughtered? He was a phlegmatic creature. No moral sacrifice came
hard to him. If, after he had first humiliated himself, the women of
Paris had quietly returned to their homes, it is likely enough that a
few hours later he would have tranquilly mounted his horse and gone
hunting as usual, in order to make good for having yesterday been
"interrupted by events." But the crowd was not yet satisfied with its
triumph, and, already intoxicated by success, craved for hotter and
more fiery wine. The Queen, arrogant, harsh, impudent, the immalleable Austrian woman, must also show herself! She, too, she above all,
must bow her neck beneath the invisible yoke. Louder and more

savage grew the cries, fiercer the stamping of feet. There was a universal shout: "The Queen, the Queen to the balcony!"

Marie Antoinette, pale with wrath, biting her lips, did not stir. What palsied her limbs and took the colour from her cheeks was not dread of the musket-shot that might be awaiting her, not fear of volleyed stones and abuse, but pride, an inherited, imperturbable sense of personal dignity. Hers was a head which had never before been bowed before an inferior. All present looked at her with embarrassment. It could not be long before the unanswered shouts would be followed by missiles thrown at the windows. Lafayette advanced to her side, and said: "Madame, it is indeed necessary that you should do this in order to placate the people."—"In that case I shall hesitate no longer," answered Marie Antoinette, giving a hand each to her son and her daughter. Head erect, her mouth firmly set, she appeared upon the balcony. She appeared, not as a petitioner, not as one seeking a favour. She looked like a soldier marching to the attack, firm of will, ready to die without flinching. She appeared, but she made no sort of obeisance. Yet her very defiance had an appeasing influence. There were two streams of force encountering one another in the glances of the Queen and the glances of the people, and so profound was the tension that for a whole minute perfect silence prevailed in the courtyard. No one could foretell how this tension would be resolved; whether the silence would be broken by a howl of wrath or by a shot; whether the immobility of the crowd would find issue in a shower of stones. At this juncture Lafayette, who always kept his presence of mind on great occasions, stepped up to her side, bowed profoundly, and kissed her hand.

Thereon a most surprising thing happened. Again there was a universal shout, but this time came the words: "Long live the Queen! Long live the Queen!" Without themselves knowing why, the very people who had, a few minutes before, been delighted by the King's weakness were now enchanted by the unyielding pride of this woman who had shown that she would not woo their favour with a false smile or a cowardly greeting.

When she re-entered the room, all surrounded Marie Antoinette and congratulated her as one who had escaped from deadly peril. But she had been disillusioned too often to be deceived by this belated acclamation of the populace: "Long live the Queen!" There were tears in her eyes as she said to Madame Necker: "They will compel us, the King and me, to go back with them to Paris, while they carry in front of the heads of our bodyguards, on the tops of their pikes."

Marie Antoinette was right. The people would no longer be satisfied with a mere greeting. It was ready to shatter this great house into fragments rather than budge from its demands. Not for such a trifle as a Queen's gracious gesture had the clubs put this gigantic machine in motion, not for a trifle had these thousands marched for six hours through the rain. Within an hour or two, the mood of the women from Paris was once more threatening; within an hour or two the National Guards who had come to protect the royal family showed themselves more than half inclined to join the masses in storming the palace. At length, therefore, the court gave way. Notes were thrown from the balcony and out of the windows to inform those beneath that the King had decided to remove with his family to Paris. That was what the rabble wanted for the moment. The soldiers and their officers mingled with the people; there were mutual embraces, joyful shouts; flags were waved. The pikes bearing the decapitated heads were sent off to the metropolis. The menace they conveyed at Versailles was no longer needed.

At two o'clock in the afternoon the huge gilded gates of the palace grounds were opened. In a calash drawn by six horses, the King, the Queen, and their children drove forth to leave Versailles for ever. A chapter of French history, a millennium of monarchical autocracy, had been closed.

It was in pitiless rain and amid the blasts of a furious wind that, on October 5, 1789, the Revolution had surged out of Paris to fetch the King. The victory of the revolutionists on October 6th was greeted by a radiant day. The atmosphere had the mellow clarity of autumn; the skies were blue; no breeze stirred the gold-tinted leaves on the trees. One might have fancied that nature was holding her breath to watch the unique spectacle of a people carrying off its King. For it was, indeed, a remarkable sight, this return of Louis XVI and Marie Antoinette to their capital! It was at one and the same time a funeral parade and a festival procession, the burial of a monarchy and the carnival of a horde. Strangest thing of all was the new fashion in etiquette! No longer, now, were there gaily clad outriders in front of the King's carriage, no longer were there on either hand falconers upon iron-grey horses and mounted guardsmen wearing tunics trimmed with gold-lace, no longer did nobles in glittering attire accompany the King's chariot. Instead, a dirty, disorderly rout encompassed the melancholy calash as it drifted along like a dismasted ship. First came the National Guards in ragged uniforms, not keeping their ranks, but arm-in-arm, pipes in mouth, laughing and singing, each of them carrying a loaf of bread upon the point of his bayonet. Among them or following them were the women, sitting astride of the cannon, riding pillion behind complaisant dragoons, or striding afoot, arm-in-arm with workers and soldiers, as if on their way to a dance. The calash was followed by carriages and carts filled with sacks of flour from the royal stores, guarded by cavalrymen. Now in front, now in the rear, shouting with delight and swinging a sabre, pranced Théroigne de Méricourt, the leader of the amazons. Amid this turbulent crowd, the calash drove on its way, conveying, closely packed together, Louis XVI, the weakling who now occupied the tottering throne once stablished so firmly by Louis XIV, and Marie Antoinette, the unhappy daughter of Maria Theresa, with their children and the governess. At the same funereal pace followed the carriages of the royal princes, the other members of the court, the deputies to the National Assembly, and those few friends who had remained loyal—the powers of the old regime, torn from their moorings by the forces of the Revolution, which today was for the first time showing its irresistible strength. The hearse of the monarchy took six hours to drive at a foot's pace from Versailles to Paris. From the houses that lined the way, people flocked out to see the show. But these spectators did not raise hats or curtsy in salutation of the sovereign rulers who had sustained so shameful a defeat; they merely stared open-mouthed, every one of them wanting to contemplate the King and the Queen in their abasement. The women of Paris, leading the way, shouted triumphantly to such onlookers: "We are bringing back the baker, the bakeress, and the bakerling. We shall no longer go hungry now!"

Marie Antoinette, listening to these yells of hatred and scorn, leaned back as far as she could into the recess of the carriage, to avoid seeing and being seen. Her eyes were downcast. She probably thought from time to time, during the interminable drive, of the countless other drives when she sped gaily and swiftly along the same road with her friend Madame de Polignac beside her in a cabriolet, setting out to a masked ball, to the Opera, or to a supper-party, from which they would not return till day was dawning. Probably, too, she looked up from time to time to watch among the accompanying horsemen one who was muffled to the eyes in his cloak in order to escape recognition—Fersen, her only true friend. Maybe, however, she was so extenuated by fatigue as to think and see very little while the wheels tediously turned, and she was being conveyed slowly, slowly, towards her doom.

At length the hearse of the monarchy pulled up at the gates of Paris, where the funeral of the court was to receive its formal consecration. By the flickering light of torches, Bailly, the mayor, welcomed the King and the Queen, and extolled the beauty of the day on which Louis had become the subject of those who had hitherto been his subjects. "What a splendid day, on which the Parisians are at length able to have Your Majesty and his family in their city." Even Louis felt this prick through his elephantine hide, for he answered curtly: "I hope, Sir, that my sojourn in Paris will bring peace, harmony, and obedience to the laws." Tired out though these royal captives must have been by this time, they were not yet to be allowed to repose. They must drive to the Hôtel de Ville, that the city might gloat over its prey. Reporting the King's words: "It is always with pleasure and confidence that I find myself among the inhabitants of my good town of Paris," Bailly omitted the word "confidence." With remarkable presence of mind, the Queen detected the omission. Recognizing how important it was, by insisting upon this word "confidence" to demand a pledge from the rebellious people, she said in a loud voice that His Majesty had also expressed his confidence. "You hear, gentlemen," said Bailly, pulling himself together. "This is even better than if my memory had not betrayed me."

Now the royal pair were led to the window. Torches were placed close to them on either side, so that the populace could recognize that they were not dressed-up puppets, but in very truth the King and Queen who had been brought from Versailles. The people, intoxicated by its unexpected triumph, was in a generous mood. It was long since so hearty a shout of "Long live the King, long live the Queen!" had been uttered as that which now resounded across the Place de Grève. Thereafter, Louis XVI and Marie Antoinette were allowed to drive to the Tuileries without military escort, at length to seek rest after this terrible night, and to meditate into what an abyss it had plunged them.

The dusty carriages drew up in front of a dark and neglected pile of masonry. Since the building of Versailles palace more than a century before, the French court had forsaken the Tuileries. The rooms had been dismantled, the furniture removed, beds and lights were lacking, the doors would not shut properly, the night air struck chill through the broken window-panes. By the glimmer of borrowed candles, a sort of camp was hastily improvised for the royal family fallen from heaven like Lucifer. "How ugly everything is here, Mamma," said the poor little Dauphin, four and a half years old, who had grown up amid the sheen of Versailles and the Trianon, and was used to brilliant candelabras, glittering mirrors, splendid decorations. "My son," replied the Queen, "Louis XIV used to live here, and liked the place well enough. You must not be more exacting than he was." As for King Louis the Indifferent, he made no complaint about his uncomfortable lodgings. With a yawn he said sleepily: "Let us all shake down as best we can. For myself, I am content."

But Marie Antoinette was not content. Never would she regard this house to which she had not come of her own free choice as other than a prison; never would she forget in how humiliating a fashion she had been brought hither. She wrote to Mercy: "What has happened during the last four-and-twenty hours seems incredible. No description of it could be exaggerated; and, indeed, whatever could be said would fall short of what we have seen and suffered."

CHAPTER XXIV

Self-Awareness

IN THE year 1789 the revolution was not yet aware of its own strength, and was still at times alarmed at its own boldness. Such was the case now. The National Assembly, the Paris municipal council, the bourgeoisie in general, being fundamentally loyal to the monarchy, were outraged at the exploits of the amazons who had delivered the King defenceless into their hands. From shame they did everything possible to gloss over the illegality of this brutal manifestation of force, setting themselves with one voice to describe the rape of the royal family as a voluntary change of residence! With touching simplicity they vied one with another in scattering roses upon the tomb of monarchical authority, secretly hoping the flowers would hide the fact that on October 6th the monarchy had died and had been buried. Deputation followed deputation to announce loyalty. The Parliament of Paris sent three of its members; the municipal council presented its respects; Bailly, the mayor, making obeisance to Marie Antoinette, said: "The town is delighted to see you in the palace of our kings; it hopes that the King and Your Majesty will be so good as to make it their habitual residence." No less respectful were the Grande Chambre, the University, the Council of Finance, the Crown Council, and, finally, on October 20th, the whole National Assembly. Day after day a mob thronged the streets in front of the Tuileries shouting: "Long live the King! Long live the Queen!" All did their best to inform the monarch of their joy at his "voluntary change of residence."

But Marie Antoinette, incapable of false pretences, and Louis, ever ready to follow his wife's lead, stubbornly resisted these attempts to throw a rose-coloured light upon offensive actualities. The line they took was natural enough, however foolish politically considered. "Through ignoring where we are and how we came here, we have been enabled to be fairly satisfied with the attitude of the populace, especially this morning," wrote the Queen to Mercy. In truth she neither could nor wished to forget. She had been too profoundly humiliated. She had been brought by force to Paris. Versailles had been stormed, and some of her bodyguard had been murdered without the National Assembly or the National Guard stirring a finger to prevent what was going on. She was prisoned in the Tuileries, and the whole world should know how the divine right of a king had been challenged. Unceasingly both she and Louis emphasized their defeat. The King abstained from his favourite sport of hunting; the Queen refused to visit the theatre; neither of them would appear in the streets; they never went out driving, and they sedulously refrained from doing anything that might have once more made them popular in Paris. The result of this segregation was to create a growing and dangerous prejudice against them. Because the court insisted that it had been subjected to constraint, the people grew more convinced of its own power; and because the King was continually declaring himself to be the weaker party, he became so in reality. It was not the populace, it was not the National Assembly, but the King and the Queen who digged invisible trenches round the Tuileries. In a foolish mood of defiance they, whose freedom had not been seriously contested except in regard of the one matter of their removal from Versailles, immured themselves behind walls of their own building.

Still, while laying such emotional stress upon its view that the Tuileries was a prison, the court was determined that the prison should be regally equipped. Within the next few days vast quantities of furniture were brought from Versailles. Carpenters and upholsterers were at work from morning till night. Ere long there had been assembled at the new palace the whole staff of the old one, except in so far as some of them had already fled to foreign parts. The servants' quarters at the Tuileries were crowded with valets, lackeys, coachmen, and cooks. The old liveries glittered afresh in the corridors; the splendours of Versailles were reproduced, and even the rigid ceremonial of the former palace was translated to the new abode. The only difference was that the bodyguard of noble birth had been dismissed, and Lafayette's National Guard, a bourgeois force, stood on watch in front of the doors.

All the same, the royal family occupied no more than a small number of the vast expanse of rooms in the Tuileries and the Louvre, for there were to be no more parties, there was to be no needless display. The only part of the Tuileries set in order for the royal family was that which gave upon the gardens, the part burned in 1871 during the days of the Commune and never rebuilt. On the first story were the King's bedroom and reception-rooms, with a bedroom for his sister, another for each of the children, and a small drawing-room. On the ground-floor were Marie Antoinette's bedroom, a reception-room, a dressing-room, a billiard-room, and the dining-room. The two stories were connected, not only by the original staircase, but by a new flight of steps built for the occasion. This led from the Queen's apartments on the ground floor to those of the Dauphin and the King; and only the Queen and her children's governess had keys of the door which commanded the entry to this stairway

To those who ponder these arrangements it will become plain that Marie Antoinette had deliberately isolated herself from the rest of the family. She lived and slept alone, her bedchamber and her boudoir being so placed that she could receive visitors whenever she pleased without their having to use the main entrance and the public stairway. The object of these arrangements will soon become plain, and the advantage the Queen was to derive from being able to betake herself unobserved to the upper story while herself safeguarded against observation by servants, spies, National Guards (and, perhaps, the King). Though prisoned, she would passionately maintain the vestiges of personal liberty until her last breath.

This ancient palace, with its dark passages (which had even by day to be lighted by smoky oil lamps), with its winding staircases, its crowded servants' quarters, and above all with the ever-present National Guards as standing witnesses of the omnipotence of the people, was by no means an agreeable residence; and yet the royal family, crowded together by fate, was able to lead a more tranquil, more intimate, and perhaps more comfortable life than in the pompous stone box at Versailles. After breakfast, the Queen had the children brought down to her; then she went to Mass, and thereafter remained alone in her room until the midday meal which the family ate in common. Then she played a game of billiards with her husband, this being the best exercise available to make up for the hunting he would so much have preferred. Thereafter, while the King read or dozed,

Marie Antoinette repaired to her own room, to converse with her intimate friends: with Fersen, the Princesse de Lamballe, or others. After supper, the family gathered in the big drawing-room: the King's brother the Count of Provence with his wife, who were quartered across the river in the Luxembourg; the old aunts; and one or two faithful friends. At eleven o'clock the lights were extinguished, and the King and the Queen retired to their separate rooms. This orderly, quiet, petty-bourgeois existence was undisturbed by any change, any display. Mademoiselle Bertin, the dressmaker, was rarely summoned; the reign of the jewellers was over now that the King had to keep his money for more important purposes, for bribery and for secret political service. The windows, as aforesaid, gave upon the gardens, where autumn was now far advanced, and the leaves had fallen from the trees. Time, which of old had run too slowly for the Queen, was swift in its passing. She could at length enjoy the tranquillity which hitherto she had always shunned; could, for the first time in her life, find opportunity for serious and lucid reflection.

Quiet is a creative element. It assembles, it purifies, it arranges the internal energies; it brings once more together what riotous movement has dissipated. Just as in a bottle which has been shaken, if you place it on the table the contents will settle, the heavy severing itself from the light, so in a mingled disposition do calm and thoughtfulness make certain elements of the character more plain. Having been brutally thrust back upon herself, Marie Antoinette began to discover her own personality. She came at length to recognize that for one whose chief equipment had been the levity of her character, nothing had been more disastrous than the ease with which fate had dropped the best of its gifts into her ready hand. She came to understand that this unmerited profusion had given rise to an inward impoverishment. Too soon and too abundantly had advantages been heaped upon her, high birth and a still higher position having been accorded without any effort on her part, with the result that she had been led to fancy that she need make no effort, need only let things run their course, and then all would be well. The ministers of State thought, the populace laboured, the bankers paid out money for her convenience; she, a spoiled child of fortune, had accepted these boons heedlessly and without gratitude. Now, when it had become incumbent upon her to defend her crown, her children, her very life, against the mightiest upheaval in history, she looked within for powers of resistance, and discovered unutilized reserves of intelligence and activity. At last there had come a regeneration. "Tribulation first makes one realize what one is"—this touching phrase, a sign that the writer had been profoundly shaken, now appeared in one of her letters. For two decades no warnings, not those of her mother nor those of her friends, had had any effect upon this defiant spirit. Sorrow and suffering were her first teachers, the only possible ones for a woman otherwise unteachable.

With the coming of misfortune, there began a new epoch in her inner life. But misfortune cannot transform a character, for it does not introduce any new elements from without; it can only develop the rudiments of what has already long been present. We should be foolish to suppose that, during these final years of trouble, Marie Antoinette had, of a sudden, grown intelligent, active, energetic, and vital. The germs of these qualities had existed in her from the first; and only through a strange inertia, through her having been one of the spoiled children of this world, had it happened that such essentials of her personality had remained undeveloped. Hitherto she had played with life and had never wrestled with it; but now, in face of so formidable a challenge, her energies answered the call to arms. Marie Antoinette had only begun to think seriously now that serious thought had become imperative. She worked because she was compelled to work. She rose to a higher level because she was called upon to do so, and because if she failed to do so she would be crushed by inexorable forces.

That was why a complete transformation both of her outer and of her inner life occurred in the Tuileries. The woman who for twenty years had never been able to hear an envoy patiently to the end of his say, who had never read a letter or a book attentively, who had cared for nothing beyond cards, sport, the fashion, and other trifles, now changed her writing-table into that of a chancellor, her room into a diplomatic cabinet. Taking the place of her husband (whom everyone thrust contemptuously aside as an incurable weakling), she held council with the ministers and ambassadors, watching over their undertakings and revising their dispatches. She learned to write and to read cipher and excogitated a remarkable technique for secret communications that she might be able through diplomatic channels to parley with her friends in foreign parts. Sometimes her letters were written in sympathetic ink, or news was smuggled into and out of Paris in chocolate boxes or by using a numerical system referring to words in the newspapers. Everything must be made plain to the initiated while remaining incomprehensible to prying eyes. All this she was able to do unaided, with spies at the doors and even in her own rooms. A single intercepted and deciphered letter would bring ruin upon her husband and her children. At these unfamiliar tasks she toiled to the pitch of exhaustion. "I have been writing until I am completely tired out," she says at the end of one of her letters; and in another: "I can no longer see what I write."

Here is an additional and extremely significant indication of her spiritual metamorphosis. Marie Antoinette had at last realized the importance of trustworthy counsellors, and was no longer so foolish as to believe herself capable of deciding difficult political problems without trouble at the first glance. Whereas hitherto she had always listened to Mercy with a suppressed yawn, and had drawn an obvious breath of relief when the door closed behind the grey-haired "pedant," now, ashamed of her previous behaviour, she sought the advice of this devoted and much-experienced man. "The more unfortunate I am, the stronger grows my attachment to my true friends." Such are the affectionate words in which she writes to her mother's old confidant. Again: "I am looking forward so much to the moment when I shall be able to see you freely and to assure you of the feelings which you have every right to expect from me—feelings which will last to the end of my life."

At the age of thirty-four she had at length become aware why fate had chosen her for a remarkable position: not to vie with other pretty, coquettish, intellectually commonplace women for the snatching of the brief triumphs of fashion; but to show herself worthy of her position as queen and as Maria Theresa's daughter, to prove her mettle before the eyes of her contemporaries and before the judgment-seat of posterity. Her pride, which had hitherto been no more than the childish arrogance of a spoiled girl, now impelled her to devote herself to the task of being great and bold in a great epoch. She no longer strove for personal ends, for power or for private happiness. "As far

as we personally are concerned, happiness is over and done with whatever the course of events may be. I know that it is the duty of one
king to suffer on behalf of the others, and we are fulfilling that duty
well. I hope that some day the fact may be recognized by them all."
Too late, Marie Antoinette had grasped in the very depths of her
soul that she was destined to become a historical figure, and this need
for transcending the limitations of her own time intensified her forces
to an extreme. For when a human being begins to plumb his own
depths, when he has determined to dig into the inmost recesses of his
own personality, he discovers in his own blood the shadowy powers
of his ancestors. The fact that she had sprung from the House of
Habsburg, that she was descendant and heiress of an ancient imperial
line, that she was daughter of Maria Theresa, lifted this weak and
unsteady woman as if by magic above her previous limitations. She
felt it incumbent upon her to be "digne de Marie Thérèse," to be
worthy of her mother, and "courage" became the leit-motif of her
progress towards imminent destruction. Again and again we find such
declarations as that "nothing can break my courage"; and when news
came from Vienna that her brother Joseph, on an agonizing deathbed,
had maintained his composure to the last hour, she felt prophetically
that she, too, was foredoomed to die bravely, and she replied with
the most self-confident saying of her life: "I venture to declare that
he died in a way worthy of myself."

This pride, waved before the world like a banner, cost Marie Antoinette more, no doubt, than most people imagined. For fundamentally
this woman was neither proud nor strong, was not a heroine, but of
a thoroughly feminine disposition, formed for self-sacrifice and tenderness and not for struggle. The courage she displayed was displayed
only to make others courageous, for she herself no longer believed in
the coming of better days. Directly she was alone, fatigue and dis-
couragement overtook her; she lowered the flag she had defiantly
hoisted before the world. Fersen says that he almost always found her
in tears. These hours of love spent together by the friends who had
at length come together and who loved one another so tenderly were
far from being hours of gallant wooing, for Fersen, though himself
touched to the quick, had to devote his best powers to overcoming his

mistress's unhappiness; and it was precisely her misfortune, her sorrow, which aroused the deepest feelings in the lover. Writing to his
sister he said: "She often weeps and is extremely unhappy. How
devoted I am to her!" The closing years were too harsh for the woman
who had been so ready to believe in good fortune. "We have seen
too much horror and too much bloodshed ever to be happy again."
Hatred continually raised its head against her, and she had no one
left to defend her but her own conscience. "I defy the universe to
show that I have done anyone a wrong," she wrote to her sister. Again:
"I expect an upright judgment from the future, and this helps me to
bear my sorrows. As for those who refuse it to me now, I despise
them too much to trouble about them." Yet once more she groaned:
"How with such a heart can one live in such a world!" We cannot
but feel that often and often in her despair she had but a single desire,
for the end to come! "If what we are now doing and suffering could
be counted upon to make our children happy at some future day!
This is the wish I still allow myself to cherish."

The thought of her children was the only one which Marie Antoinette now ventured to associate with the word "happiness." For
instance: "If I could be happy, I should be made happy by these two
little beings. . . . I am alone in my own room the whole day. My
children are my sole resource, and I have them with me as much as
possible." Again: "When I am more sad than usual, I have my little
boy brought downstairs." The love of the mother who once looked
at the world so light-heartedly, had turned passionately to concentrate
itself on the two children that were left to her. She was especially
fond of the second Dauphin, who was well-grown, cheerful, clever,
and gentle, "un chou d'amour" as she fondly wrote of him. But, as
with all her other feelings, so likewise even in her maternal affection
she retained the power of clear vision. Although she idolized her little
boy, she was determined not to spoil him. "Our affection for him
must not lack an element of severity," she wrote to the governess;
"we must not forget that we are bringing him up to be a king." The
lady to whom these instructions were penned was Madame de Tourzel,
who had replaced Madame de Polignac as the Dauphin's instructress.
The Queen, when appointing this lady to her position, gave her a

description of the little boy which is inspired by a psychological insight and spiritual intuition hitherto lacking to Marie Antoinette. The document throws so much light upon the mother's own character that I quote it in full.

"In two days my son will be four years and four months old. I need not say anything about his bodily development, his general appearance, for in these respects you have merely to look at him for yourself. His health has always been excellent, but while he was still in his cradle it became plain that his nerves were extremely sensitive, and that any unusual noise startled him. His teething was somewhat delayed, but did not give rise to any trouble at first. Later on, however (I think it was when he was cutting the sixth) he had a convulsive seizure. Since then he has had several attacks of convulsions; one during the winter of 1787-1788, and the other when he was inoculated with the smallpox. The latter was no more than a trifling disturbance. Owing to the undue nervous susceptibility to which I have already referred, any unexpected or unusual noise frightens him. For instance, he is afraid of dogs when they bark at him. I have never forced him to play with these animals, for I believe that in proportion as his intelligence develops his timidity will disappear. Like all children who are vigorous and in good health, he is very thoughtless, extremely scatter-brained, and subject to violent fits of anger; but he is a good boy, and most affectionate when his thoughtlessness does not get the better of him. His self-esteem passes all reasonable bounds, but still, if he is carefully guided, even this may be turned, in due time, to good account. Until he has got quite at home with a new acquaintance, he knows how to keep control of himself, and is even able to swallow his impatience and his wrath in order to seem gentle and lovable. He is to be depended upon when he has given his word; but he is extremely indiscreet, being always ready to repeat whatever he has heard. Often enough, without any intention to tell a falsehood, he embroiders it with his imagination. This, indeed, is his chief fault, and the one which it is, above all, essential to correct. For the rest, let me reiterate, he is a good boy; and through kindliness mingled with firmness (which must, of course, be kept within reasonable limits), you will be able to guide him in whatever direction you think best. But harshness will arouse a spirit of revolt, since he has a great deal of character considering his age. To give you an example, since he was quite a tiny tot, he has always found it extremely difficult to ask for pardon. He will do and will say almost anything you want after having been naughty—but as for saying 'I am sorry,' he will only do that after you have taken an infinite deal of pains, and he will do it with tears of vexation in his eyes. It has been my way with my children to make them confide in me, so that, when they have been naughty, they will come and tell me about it themselves. I was able to achieve this by assuming an air of being distressed rather than angry at what they had done. I have also taught them to understand that my 'yes' or my 'no' is irrevocable; but I have never failed to give them reasons for my decision (reasons within the bounds of their understanding) so that they might realize that I was not being guided by a mere whim. My little boy does not yet know how to read, and he is slow to learn, being too inattentive to give his mind seriously to the matter. He has absolutely no conception of the exalted position he occupies, and it is my strong desire that he should continue to be simple-minded in this respect, for our children learn all too soon into what rank they have been born. He is extremely fond of his sister. Whenever anything gives him pleasure—whether it be some excursion, or a present that has been given him—his first instinct is to ask that she shall have a like indulgence. He is of a cheerful temperament; and it is essential to his health that he should spend a great deal of his time in the fresh air."

Comparing this maternal epistle with the young wife's earlier letters, it seems hard to believe that they were penned by the same hand; for the new Marie Antoinette is as remote from the old one as unhappiness is from happiness, despair from overweening confidence. It is upon soft and malleable minds, upon persons who by nature are inchoate and pliable, that unhappiness stamps its imprint most clearly. In this case, a character that seemed unstable as water acquired the fixity, the firmness of ice. "When will you at length become your true self?" had been, again and again, the distressful question of Maria Theresa. Now, when the hair on her temples was beginning to turn grey, Marie Antoinette was developing into her true self.

This complete transformation is witnessed by the only portrait of the Queen that was painted during her residence in the Tuileries

Kucharski, a Polish artist, sketched it, but the flight of the royal pair to Varennes prevented its completion. Nevertheless, it is the finest of the likenesses that have come down to us. The full-dress-parade picture by Werthmüller and the drawing-room portraits by Madame Vigée le Brun aimed at impressing the observer by costly gowns and stage effects intended to show that the lady represented on the canvas was Queen of France. She was depicted in a huge hat with ostrich plumes, brilliants sparkled upon her brocade attire; she was posed in front of her satin-upholstered throne. Even when portrayed in fancy-dress (as a mythological heroine or as a country-girl), she was shown by one indication or another to be a modern lady of high rank, nay, the highest lady in the land, the Queen. Kucharski's sketch, however, discards these meretricious devices. We see no more than an exceptionally beautiful woman seated on a stool and gazing forth dreamily into the void. She looks somewhat weary and depressed. There are no artifices; the days for that are over. Restlessness and the search for amusement have given place to repose, vanity has been substituted by simplicity. The hair, already sprinkled with white, is plainly dressed; the gown which shows her well-shaped neck and shoulders is no longer stylish; nothing in the portrait suggests an attempt to create an impression. She does not smile; her eyes do not challenge the on-looker; though her beauty is still remarkable, it is a gentle, a maternal, an autumnal beauty. Passing from desire to renunciation, as "une femme entre deux âges," no longer young but not yet elderly, no longer desirous but still desirable, she dreams, she dreams, she dreams. All the other portraits are what is now termed "narcissistic." We see in them a woman in love with herself, who has flashed before the painter's astonished eyes, posing only for a moment in the midst of a run, a dance, a laugh, to resume her follies the instant the sitting was over. Kucharski shows us a woman who has achieved tranquillity and loves it. At length this half-finished sketch discloses to us a human being. In it alone, among all the life-size portraits, the miniatures, the pastels, the statues, the ivory carvings, we for the first time discern that Marie Antoinette, Queen of France, had a soul.

CHAPTER XXV

Mirabeau

FIGHTING a desperate struggle against the revolution, the Queen had hitherto set her trust in only one ally—time. "Nothing but forbearance and patience can be of any avail." Time, however, is an untrustworthy, an opportunist ally, who ever espouses the cause of the stronger, contemptuously leaving in the lurch those who do not fight strenuously in their own behalf. The Revolution marched onward inexorably. Week by week it gained thousands of new recruits in the capital, among the peasantry, in the army; and the Jacobin Club speedily became the fulcrum of a lever which was to subvert and make an end of the monarchy. At length the King and the Queen began to realize the danger of their isolation, and looked hither and thither in search of assistance. Honoré Gabriel Riquetti, Comte de Mirabeau, sent as deputy to the National Assembly by the third estate of Aix-en-Provence, "the Lion of the Revolution," both dreaded and admired, was ready, had been known since September to be ready (in a measure, and at a price), to espouse the King's cause. "Let them know in the palace," he wrote to a go-between, "that I am rather on their side than against them." So long as the court was still at Versailles, it felt itself firmly seated in the saddle; and the Queen was not yet prepared to recognize the importance of this man who was better fitted than anyone to guide the Revolution, being the very spirit of revolt, the human embodiment of the will to liberty, insubordination, and anarchy. The other members of the National Assembly, worthy and well-meaning intellectuals, shrewd lawyers, convinced democrats, thought in idealistic terms of order and reorganization. None but Mirabeau among these deputies was a man for whom chaos in the State seemed a way of escaping from the chaos within his own self. His volcanic energy (which he once proudly spoke of as the energy of ten) needed a worldwide storm to give adequate scope for its development. In a condition of ruinous decay alike as regards his moral, material, and family relationships, he needed to sow ruin in the State in order to have a chance of recovery from personal disaster. The previous outbursts of his daimonic nature—pamphlets, seductions of women, duels, and manifold scandals—had been inadequate safety-valves for his impetuous temperament, which had not been tamed even by a sojourn in many of the prisons of France. His uncontrolled spirit needed wider spaces and mightier opportunities. Like a bull kept too long in a stall and then accorded the spurious freedom of the arena and roused to fury by the banderillas of disdainful picadors, with lowered head he charged and overthrew the rickety barriers of the estates. The National Assembly was terrified when his thunderous voice was for the first time heard at its deliberations, and it bowed itself beneath his imperious yoke. Strong of will as well as an extremely able writer, Mirabeau, a mighty smith, was able within a few minutes to fashion the most difficult laws, the most dauntless formulations. His overwhelming flood of eloquence swept the Assembly into his wake, and had it not been for the distrust aroused by his questionable past, had it not been for the unconscious self-defence of order against this emissary of chaos, from its first opening the twelve hundred deputies would have had but one head, but one ruler.

However, this stentorian advocate of freedom was not himself free. Debts tied him hand and foot, a network of unsavoury lawsuits hampered his every movement. Such men as Mirabeau can only live, can only work, when they squander their resources. He needed unconcern, lavish display, full pockets, clinking gold, an open house, secretaries, women, assistants, servants. Only when surrounded by abundance could he develop his own plenty. To win freedom in the sense which to him was all-important, the man dunned by a thousand creditors was willing to sell himself to the highest bidder, offering his services to Necker, to the Duke of Orléans, to the Count of Provence, and at length to the court. But Marie Antoinette, who detested no one so much as she detested renegades from the nobility, believed herself while she was still at Versailles strong enough to dispense with the venal favours of this "monstre." In answer to the overtures of the go-between, the Comte de La Marck, she said: "I trust we are not yet so unfortunate as to be reduced to the painful necessity of seeking help from Mirabeau."

Matters had come to a worse pass now, and Mirabeau's help was indispensable! Five months had intervened, and five months are a long time in days of revolution. Through the instrumentality of Mercy, the Comte de La Marck was informed that the Queen was ready to negotiate with Mirabeau, or, in plain words, to buy his services. Fortunately it was not yet too late, and Mirabeau instantly snapped at the golden bait. His eyes glistened with greed when he heard that Louis XVI was ready to give him four promissory notes, each of two hundred and fifty thousand livres, the whole sum of one million to become payable when the sittings of the National Assembly were ended—"provided that," said the thrifty and cautious King, "he has by then done me good service." Directly the tribune realized that his debts were to be paid by a stroke of the pen, and that within a month he was to receive six thousand livres, being weary of the unceasing attentions of bailiffs and sheriff's-officers, he manifested "an intoxication of delight whose violence was a surprise to me" (Comte de La Marck). With the same fervour, the same passion, that he was accustomed to use in persuading others, he now persuaded himself that he alone could and would save, at one and the same time, the King, the Revolution, and the country. Having money in his pocket, Mirabeau, who had been the raging lion of the Revolution, remembered that he had always been an ardent royalist! On May 10, 1790, he signed a receipt for the sale of himself by pledging himself to serve the King with "loyalty, zeal, activity, energy, and courage." Here is what he wrote in addition:

"I professed monarchical principles in days when all I could see in the court was its weakness, and when, knowing neither the spirit nor the thoughts of Maria Theresa's daughter, I could not count upon this august auxiliary. . . . I served the monarch when I knew that from a king who, though just, was misled, I could expect neither advantages nor recompense. What, then, shall I do now, when the trust felt in me has raised my courage and when the recognition vouchsafed to me has transformed my principles into duties? I shall henceforward be what I have always been, the defender of monarchical power regulated by the laws, and the champion of liberty as guaranteed by monarchical authority. My heart will follow the road which reason has already pointed out to it."

Despite the tribune's emphasis, both parties to the agreement knew well enough that the pledge was not an honourable one, but one which, like an owl or a bat, would shun the clear light of day. It was therefore understood between them that Mirabeau would never visit the Tuileries, but would send his advice to Louis by letter. In the public eye, the Count had to remain an ardent revolutionist while working in the National Assembly on behalf of the King's cause—a shady deal by which neither gained anything and in which neither of the partners trusted the other. Still, Mirabeau set to work as agreed, writing letter after letter of advice to Louis, though these letters were in truth addressed to Marie Antoinette. It was his hope to make himself understood by the Queen, for he was quick to realize that Louis XVI counted for nothing. In his second note we read:

"The King has but one man to support him—his wife. The only safeguard for her lies in the re-establishment of the royal authority. It pleases me to fancy that she would not care to go on living without the crown on her head; and of this much I am certain, that she will not be able to save her life unless she saves her crown. The moment will come ere long when she will have to see what a woman and a child can do in the saddle; this has been essayed before in her family; but, meanwhile, she must show moderation, and must not believe herself able, whether by the aid of chance or by the aid of intrigue, to overcome an extraordinary crisis through the instrumentality of ordinary men and ordinary measures."

Obviously Mirabeau was putting himself forward as the extraordinary man who would help the court out of its terrible dilemma. He hoped with a trident of brave words to calm the stormy waters no less easily than he had made them turbulent. In his overweening self-confidence, he foresaw himself as simultaneously president of the National Assembly and first minister of the King and the Queen. But he deceived himself. Not for a moment did Marie Antoinette dream of giving this "mauvais sujet" effective power. The average human being is instinctively suspicious of those who are daimonic; and the Queen was incapable of grasping the splendour of the way in which this man of genius transcended conventional morality, for he was the first and the only person of the kind she encountered in the course of her life. His bold changes of front were thoroughly uncongenial to her, and the titanic passion of his nature alarmed her without pleasing her. Her secret intention, therefore, was to pay off and dismiss the savage, violent, immoderate, uncontrollable, incalculable man as soon as she should no longer have need of him. She had bought him; and, for the time being, he was to work diligently for money that was hard to come by, was to give advice, as he was well able to do. She would read letters from him, act upon whatever in them was not too eccentric, too foolhardy, and there would be an end of the matter. When the deputies were about to vote upon important matters he would be a useful agitator; he could keep the court informed about what was going on; in the National Assembly, he could be used as a peacemaker on behalf of the "good cause"; and, being himself venal, he could certainly be instrumental in the corruption of others. Let the lion roar his loudest before his colleagues, while led in leading-strings by the court. Such were the Queen's thoughts concerning Mirabeau, who was too great to be measured by an ordinary yardstick; but never for an instant did she give her confidence to one whom she certainly found useful at times, but whose "immorality" seemed odious to her, and whose genius was, from the first hour to the last, beyond the bounds of her comprehension.

It was not long before the honeymoon of the initial enthusiasm began to wane. Mirabeau perceived that his letters only helped to fill the royal wastepaper-basket instead of stimulating a spiritual fire. Nevertheless, whether from vanity or from the covetous desire to earn the promised million, the tribune continued to besiege the court with his adjurations. Becoming aware that his written recommendations bore no fruit, he determined upon a last venture. His experience in political life and in his countless love-affairs had shown him that he was even more effective with the tongue than with the pen, indeed far more effective, for his personality radiated an electrifying influence. He therefore was perpetually urging his emissary the Comte de La Marck to procure him an opportunity for a conversation with the Queen. He believed that an hour's talk would be enough to dispel her suspicions; that, like so many other women, she would conceive an admiration for him. An audience—one would suffice—such was his reiterated demand. Being full of self-approbation, he did not for a

moment believe that the first interview would be the last. No one
who had once made his acquaintance but would be eager to follow
it up!

For a long time Marie Antoinette was deaf to these proposals. At
length, however, she gave way, and arranged to receive Mirabeau on
July 3rd in the palace of Saint-Cloud.

It need hardly be said that the meeting had to be a secret one. By
one of the ironies of fate, Mirabeau was accorded what the Cardinal
de Rohan, poor fool, had been accorded only in semblance, an
assignation in a shady grove. At midsummer, 1790, there was a last
brief respite from detention at the Tuileries. As Axel de Fersen
learned during this period, there were plenty of well-hidden spots in
the park of Saint-Cloud. "I have found a place," wrote the Queen to
Mercy, "which, though not as convenient as it might be, is suitable
for the proposed meeting, and free from the inconveniences of the
gardens and the château." The time chosen was Sunday morning at
eight, an hour when the court was asleep, and when the park was
deserted. Mirabeau, who was doubtless considerably excited about the
matter, spent the night at his sister's house in Passy. Early next
morning he was driven to Saint-Cloud, his nephew, suitably disguised,
acting as coachman. Having left the carriage as well ambushed as
possible, Mirabeau pulled his hat down over his eyes, cloaked his face
like a conspirator, and entered the park by one of the lesser gates
which had expressly been left unlocked. Soon he heard a light footfall
upon the gravel. The Queen appeared, unaccompanied. Mirabeau was
about to make an obeisance, but as soon as Marie Antoinette caught
sight of his face, deeply pitted with smallpox, seamed by the violence
of his passions, framed in an untidy mat of hair, at once powerful and
brutal, an involuntary shudder passed across her countenance. Mirabeau did not fail to notice these signs of alarm, with which, in other
women, he had long been familiar. All members of the fair sex were
the same, even the gentle Sophie Voland had shrunk back in alarm
when she first caught sight of him. But, as with Medusa, his hideous-
ness exercised an invincible attraction. Invariably, hitherto, he had
been able to transform initial fear into astonishment, into admiration,
and, often enough, into passionate affection.

We do not know what took place at this rencounter between Mirabeau and Marie Antoinette. Since there were no witnesses, the reports of the conversation, not excepting that of the omniscient lady-in-waiting Madame Campan, are purely suppositious; are, to put it more bluntly, fables. This much only has transpired, that it was not Mirabeau who bent the Queen to his will, but the Queen who bewitched Mirabeau. Her exalted position, with its nimbus of royalty; her natural dignity and the quick understanding which, at a first interview, she always manifested to a degree that was not confirmed by a closer acquaintance with her—these things exerted an overwhelming charm upon Mirabeau's inflammable and in many respects generous nature. Courage always aroused his sympathy. On leaving the park, still in a condition of marked agitation, he grasped his nephew's arm and said with characteristic fervour: "She is great, noble, and unfortunate; but I shall save her." In that one hour's conversation, Marie Antoinette had transformed a man who was both vacillating and venal into a resolute champion of her cause. "Nothing shall stop me, I would rather die than fail to fulfil my promises," he wrote to the Comte de La Marck.

The Queen did not, so far as is known, say or write a word to anyone about this meeting. No expression of gratitude or confidence ever passed her lips. She did not wish to see Mirabeau again, nor did she ever pen a line to him. She had not entered into an alliance with him, but had merely received the assurance of his devotion. She had given him her gracious permission to sacrifice himself in her behalf.

Mirabeau had given a pledge, or, rather, two. He had sworn fealty both to the King and to the nation. While a fierce struggle was going on between the twain, he was chief of staff to both sides. Never has a politician played more dangerous a role, nor has any ever played it so brilliantly to the end. Wallenstein, compared with him, was no more than a bungler. Considered merely as an expenditure of bodily energy, Mirabeau's achievement during these dramatic weeks and months was unparalleled. He delivered speeches in the National Assembly and in the clubs; he carried on agitation, parleyed, received numberless visitors, read, worked in his study; writing in the middle hours of the day reports and proposals for the National Assembly and in the evening his secret dispatches to the King. Three or four secretaries were simultaneously trying to keep pace with the rapids of his torrential eloquence—but all this was not enough to appease his inexhaustible energy. He wanted still more work, more danger, more responsibility; and he wanted, over and above, and simultaneously, to live and to enjoy. Like a rope-dancer he kept his balance on a perilous perch, leaning now to the right and now to the left, devoting both the basic powers of his extraordinary nature to the service of either cause; both his brilliant political insight, and the fierce passion of his inflammatory temperament.

So lightning-swift were thrust and parry, so impetuous were the movements of his rapier, that no one could tell whether he was fighting for the King or for the people, against the new powers or against the old; and perhaps, in his most enthusiastic moods, he himself did not know for which cause he was fighting.

In the long run, however, so contradictory a position becomes untenable. Suspicion was rife; Marat said that the Count had sold himself to the enemy; Fréron threatened him with lynching (à la lanterne!). "More virtue and less talent!" was the shout raised against him by his fellow-members in the National Assembly. Mirabeau, however, in his intoxication, knew no fear. His debts being the talk of Paris, he marched confidently forward towards the promised wealth. What did he care because people were amazed at his new and lavish expenditure, because there was much gossip, much questioning, as to the sources from which he could have drawn the means which enabled him to give such costly banquets, to buy Buffon's library, to hang diamonds round the necks of opera-singers and harlots. He was as indifferent as Zeus to the storms, since he himself was their lord. If anyone took him to task, he answered with the bludgeon of his wrath, with the lightnings of his mockery—a new Samson fighting the Philistines. An abyss beneath his feet, environing suspicion, deadly peril stalking in his rear, were but agreeable stimulants, now that at last he felt himself in his true element. His incomparable energies blazed heavenward during these last decisive days when his fire was about to be extinguished for ever. At length, at length, to this scarcely credible being there had been allotted a task proportional to his genius: to arrest the inevitable, to stop the march of destiny. With formidable strength, with overwhelming frenzy, he hurled himself into events, endeavouring, a lone man fighting against myriads, to reverse the rolling of that revolutionary stone which he himself had set in motion.

Marie Antoinette, straightforward by disposition, lacked the political insight which would have enabled her to understand and to sympathize with the foolhardiness of this fight on two fronts, the grandeur of a position so amazing in its duplicity. The bolder Mirabeau's memorials to Louis, the more sulphureous the reek of his counsel, the more did the sobriety of her understanding revolt against his extravagances. The tribune's guiding principle at this juncture was that Satan should cast out Satan, that the Revolution by its excesses should annihilate anarchy. Since for the moment conditions could not be improved, it was necessary to adopt his notorious "politique du pire," deliberately to make them worse—like a physician who by means of irritant measure intensifies the crisis in order to hasten recovery. His designs, though amoral, were clairvoyant. The popular movement was not to be arrested but mastered. The aim was not to be in direct conflict with the National Assembly; but, instead, the populace was to be secretly incited to send the National Assembly to the devil. To hope for the immediate coming of tranquillity and peace would be a mistake; for, on the contrary, the flames of injustice and dissatisfaction were to be fanned throughout the country until, in the end, there would arise a universal demand for order, for order of the old kind. Those who desired to re-establish the royal authority should shrink from nothing, not even from civil war.

The Queen trembled at the thought of such bold measures as Mirabeau advocated with a flourish of trumpets: "Four enemies are advancing at the double; taxation, bankruptcy, the army, winter. We must take the bull by the horns; or, rather, we must prepare for coming events by guiding them. In two words, civil war is not certain, but perhaps expedient." She wrote protestingly to Mercy: "How can Mirabeau, or any other reflective being, possibly suppose . . . above all just now, it could be auspicious for us to instigate a civil war? . . . His scheme is crazy from beginning to end." By degrees her lack of confidence in the amoralist who was ready to have re-

course to all means however dreadful, became insuperable. Vainly did
Mirabeau try "to shake the court out of its lethargy by a thunder-
clap." Louis, Marie Antoinette, and their other advisers would not
listen to him. At length, angered by their mental inertia, he began to
feel a contempt for the "royal bétail," for the sheep who were submissively being driven to the slaughter. He realized that the court
was incapable of effective action, and that he was fighting for its
cause in vain. But trouble was his element. Himself foredoomed to
early destruction which was now close at hand, about to drink the
black wine of death, almost his last words were a despairing prophecy:
"Excellent but weak King; unfortunate Queen! Contemplate the
terrible abyss into which your vacillation between too blind a confidence and too exaggerated a suspicion has swept you! There still
remains one possible effort for you and for the others. If you renounce it, or if it fails, a funeral pall will cover this realm. What will
be its fate? Whither will the dismasted ship drive, shattered by the
lightning, at the mercy of the storm? I do not know. But should I
myself escape the general shipwreck, I shall be able, in my retirement,
to say with pride: 'I exposed myself to disaster in the hope of saving
them. But they did not want to be saved.'"

They did not want to be saved. Does not the Bible tell us: "Thou
shalt not plough with an ox and an ass together"? The court, cumbrous and conservative, could not keep step with the great tribune,
fiery, hasty, fretting against bit and bridle. Marie Antoinette, being a
woman of the old world, could not understand Mirabeau's revolutionary inclinations; the straightforwardly simple was alone within her
mental grasp; the neck-or-nothing policy of this brilliant political
adventurer was incomprehensible to her. Yet to his last hour Mirabeau
went on fighting, partly from mere lust for battle, partly from pride
in his own foolhardiness. One against a multitude, mistrusted by the
people, mistrusted by the court, mistrusted by the National Assembly,
he twisted the three of them round his fingers even while he worked
against them. With a body ravaged by his excesses, with a frame
racked by fever, he returned again and again to the arena, once more
imposing his will upon the twelve hundred of his fellow-deputies,
until at length, in March 1791, when for eight months he had been

playing double, serving both the King and the Revolution, death touched him on the shoulder. He gave one more speech; almost to the very end he went on dictating to his secretaries; during the last night of his life he slept with two opera-singers—and then his mighty strength was annulled. Huge crowds had assembled outside his house, waiting to learn when the heart of the Revolution ceased to beat; and his body was followed to its resting-place by three hundred thousand persons. The Pantheon, converted to new uses by the Revolution, was to be a fitting shrine for the ashes of those who had done good service to their country. The mortal remains of the great tribune were to stay there while eternity ran its course.

But how pitiful a word is "eternity" in such stirring times! No more than two years later, when Mirabeau's double dealings with the King had come to light, what was left of his corpse was snatched from its distinguished tomb and thrown contemptuously into the pit dug for carrion from the knacker's yard.

For the moment, however, there was general consternation at Mirabeau's premature death. Only the court was unperturbed, for reasons still known to itself alone. We can confidently discredit Madame Campan's foolish tale that, when the news was brought, Marie Antoinette's eyes filled with tears. Nothing is more improbable, for we can hardly doubt that the Queen must have heaved a sigh of relief at the dissolution of what to her had been an uncongenial partnership. The man was too great to serve, too venturesome to obey. The court had feared him when alive, and feared him even after he was dead. While he was in the death-agony, a confidential agent from the palace came to his house and rifled his desk of compromising letters, so that for the time being a veil was drawn over the alliance of which both parties were ashamed—Mirabeau because he served the court, and the Queen because she allowed him to serve her. Yet when Mirabeau died, there died the last man who was perhaps capable of mediating between the monarchy and the people. Thenceforward Marie Antoinette and the Revolution confronted one another with none between them to temper their mutual animosity.

CHAPTER XXVI

Preparations for Escape

THE death of Mirabeau meant the loss to the monarchy of its only second in the fight against the Revolution. Once more the court stood utterly alone. There were two plain possibilities, resistance or capitulation. As usual, the court wobbled, choosing the most unlucky course, the middle course of flight.

Mirabeau had already pondered the question whether it might not be well for the King, in the hope of re-establishing his authority, to withdraw from the defenceless position enforced on him in Paris. Prisoners cannot wage war. Those who wish to carry on an effective fight must have their arms free and a firm standing-ground beneath their feet. But the tribune had insisted that if this expedient were adopted the King must not steal away in secret, for that would be to compromise the royal dignity. "A king," he said, "does not run away from his people"; and, yet more emphatically, "a king must live in full daylight, in order to establish his kingship openly." His proposal was that Louis XVI should go out driving into the suburbs, where a cavalry regiment which had remained loyal would await him. Then, on horseback, surrounded by these soldiers, he should join his army, and, as a free man, treat with the National Assembly. But for such a course a man in the full sense of the word was needed, and never had Louis XVI been one to adopt bold measures. He toyed with the idea, indeed, taking advice in this quarter and in that; however, in the end, he preferred immediate comfort to his throne and the chance of saving his life.

Now that Mirabeau was dead, Marie Antoinette, weary of perpetual humiliations, energetically adopted the notion. She was not alarmed by the risks the flight entailed, being only distressed because to abscond in such a fashion seemed beneath the dignity of a queen. Still, since the situation grew worse from day to day, she wrote to Mercy:

"There is no middle course. Either we must stay where we are beneath the sword of the 'factieux' (and, consequently, must be of no

account any longer) if they retain the upper hand; or else must be
fettered beneath the despotism of persons who declare themselves well
intentioned, but who do and will continue to do us harm. Such is the
outlook upon the future, and perhaps the moment which awaits us
is nearer than I think, unless we ourselves take the initiative, unless
we guide public opinion by our own strength and by the course we
ourselves adopt. Believe me that what I am now telling you is not
dictated by any fantastic notion, nor yet by disgust with our position
or by an impatient desire to act. I am fully aware of the dangers and
the various unpleasant possibilities which loom at this juncture. But
I see on all hands such terrible eventualities that I would rather perish
while seeking a means of salvation than allow myself to be crushed
and annihilated in a condition of absolute passivity." Since Mercy,
sober-minded and cautious, writing from his safe retreat in Brussels,
continued to offer objections, she expressed herself even more emphatically, in a clear-sighted letter which shows that this woman, formerly
characterized by so much levity, had come to recognize how disastrous
had been her fall: "Our position is horrible, so horrible that those
who have not had it actually under their eyes cannot form any
idea of it. If we remain here, we have no alternative but to do blindly
all that the 'factieux' demand, or else to perish under the sword which
is perpetually suspended over our heads. Believe me that I do not
exaggerate our risk. You know that I have always done my utmost to
exercise forbearance, trusting in time, and in the hope that public
opinion may change; but today everything is different. If we would
escape destruction, we must take the only path open to us. We are
far from being so blind as to believe that this plan is free from danger;
nevertheless, if we must perish, let us do so gloriously, and having
done our best to fulfil our duty, to maintain our honour, and to comply with the dictates of religion. I believe the provinces to be less
infected by this corruption than the capital; but it is always Paris that
gives the tone to the kingdom. . . . The clubs and the secret societies
lead France whithersoever they will. The decent folk and those who
detest the present posture of affairs (there are plenty of them) have
fled the country or are in hiding, because they are the weaker party
and have no common platform on which to rally their forces. If only
the King could show himself freely in a fortified city, the number of

malcontents who would disclose themselves would be amazing—persons who, up till now, have done no more than groan almost inaudibly. The longer we wait, however, the less support we shall find. The republican spirit gains ground day by day among all classes; the troops are becoming infected, and it will be impossible to count upon them should we delay."

Danger threatened from another quarter than the Revolution. The French princes, the Count of Artois, the Prince of Condé, and the other émigrés—unheroic individuals, but full of braggadocio—were rattling sabres in their safe retreat across the frontier. Intriguing at all the courts, they were endeavouring, by brave words, which entailed no risk, to distract attention from their cowardice in taking flight. They travelled from place to place trying to spur on the Emperor and the kings to make war against France, without considering that by these futile demonstrations they were involving the lives of Louis XVI and Marie Antoinette in deadly peril. "The Count of Artois is very little concerned about his brother and my sister," wrote Emperor Leopold II. . . . "He never seems to think of the danger to which his projects and his attempts expose them." These "heroes" disported themselves in Coblenz and in Turin, keeping a good table, and telling all and sundry how they thirsted for the blood of the Jacobins. The Queen was hard put to it to restrain their follies within bounds. Were it only to take the wind out of their sails, Louis and Marie Antoinette must escape from Paris. The King must be free to hold in check the extremists in both camps; the ultra-revolutionists and the ultra-reactionaries; the fanatics in Paris and the fanatics over the border. The King must be free, and his only way to freedom was a distressing one—flight.

The details of the arrangements for escape were left in the Queen's hands, and it was natural that she should entrust their practical working-out to one from whom she had nothing to hide and in whom she had absolute confidence, namely Fersen. Had he not said: "I live only to serve her"? He was the one friend left to her. It was his task, therefore, to undertake what would be possible only by the devotion, not solely of all his energies, but even life itself. The difficulties were wellnigh insuperable. The first step was hard enough, to escape from a palace round which the National Guards were posted as sentries, and where almost every servant was a spy. Next the refugees would have to traverse a hostile city, and for this stage of their journey various precautions were requisite. As for travel through the countryside, that would be rendered possible only by negotiation with General Bouillé, the one who had (in secret) remained loyal to the King. The plan was that squadrons of cavalry should be spread out along the road as far as Châlons, on the way to the frontier fortress of Montmédy, so that, should the royal carriage be recognized or pursued, the King and the royal family could instantly be protected. Since a pretext was needed for the strange-seeming movements of soldiers, an Austrian army corps had to be concentrated on the imperial side of the frontier to give Bouillé some sort of justification for what he was about. The requisite correspondence, a considerable amount, had to be conducted with the utmost caution, for most of the letters leaving France were opened, and, as Fersen said: "All would be lost if there were the tiniest breath of suspicion." Another difficulty was that the flight would demand the expenditure of vast sums of money, and both the King and the Queen were almost penniless. Attempts to secure a few millions on loan from Emperor Leopold, from other rulers in England, Spain, or Naples, and from the court bankers, proved fruitless. In this matter, as in the rest, Fersen, a foreigner, and a man of moderate rank, had to come to the rescue.

But Fersen's passion for his mistress quadrupled his energies. He worked as it were with ten heads, twenty hands, though with only one self-sacrificing heart. In the daytime or after dark he spent hours with the Queen, making his way furtively into the palace that he might discuss details. He carried on a correspondence with the foreign princes and with General Bouillé; he selected the most trustworthy among the nobles, who, disguised as couriers, were to accompany the flight; and he also decided which among them were to carry letters to the frontier and back again. He ordered the carriage in his own name; he procured forged passports; he supplied funds by mortgaging his estate to two ladies, one Russian and one Swedish, for three hundred thousand livres in each case; and, in the last resort, he actually borrowed three thousand livres from his own steward. Piece by piece, he brought the necessary disguises into the Tuileries, and smuggled the Queen's diamonds out of the palace. By day and by night, week after week, he wrote, negotiated, planned, travelled hither and thither, in continual peril, and that of the deadliest; for if one mesh of the net he was spreading over France were to break, if one of those in the plot were to turn informer, if a single letter were to be intercepted, his life would pay the forfeit. He did not count the cost. Bold, clear-sighted, indefatigable, an unobtrusive hero working behind the scenes, he played his part in one of the great dramas of history.

Even now there was hesitation. The King, always a procrastinator, continued to hope that some lucky turn in events would spare him the distress and the trouble of thus absconding. But it was of no avail. The carriage was ordered, funds had been laboriously gathered together; the escort provided by General Bouillé was posted in detachments along the route. Only one thing more was needed—a manifest excuse, a sort of moral justification for a flight which was, after all, not easy to provide with a seemly colour. In one way or another the world must be convinced that the King and the Queen had not (as a schoolboy would put it) run away in a blue funk, but had been actually compelled to leave by the Terror. To furnish this pretext, the King announced to the National Assembly and to the town council of Paris that he wanted to spend Easter week at Saint-Cloud. Instantly, as the court had hoped and expected, the Jacobin press raised a clamour that the proposed visit to Saint-Cloud must be to hear Mass read and to receive absolution from a priest hostile to the Revolution. Furthermore, said the papers, there was grave danger that the palace outside the fortifications of Paris would be the starting-point for an escape of the royal family. The inflammatory newspaper articles had their due effect. On April 19, 1791, when the King was about to enter his carriage for the drive to Saint-Cloud, huge crowds assembled, whipped up by Marat and the clubs, and he was forcibly restrained from leaving the Tuileries.

The public exhibition of the fact that the King was a prisoner in his own palace was precisely what the Queen and her advisers had wanted. It was now made plain to the world that Louis XVI, alone among Frenchmen who had not been in due form sentenced as criminals, was not granted the liberty of driving a few miles in order to enjoy a breath of fresh air. Ostentatiously, therefore, the members of the royal family seated themselves in the carriage, and waited for the horses to be put to. The mob, however, with which the National Guards had fraternized, would not allow the beasts to be taken out of the stables. At length the professional "saviour," Lafayette, appeared upon the scene, and, as commanding officer of the National Guard, ordered that the King should be allowed free passage. No one heeded the general. He commanded the mayor of Paris to hoist the red revolutionary banner as a warning; Bailly laughed in his face. Then Lafayette tried to address the populace, and was shouted down. Anarchy had entered into its own.

Meanwhile, what time the unhappy commander was imploring his troops to obey him, the King, the Queen, and Princess Elisabeth sat quietly in the carriage amid the shouting mob. The yells and the coarse invectives, left Marie Antoinette unperturbed. In truth she was pleased to see how Lafayette, the champion of freedom, the darling of the people, was now disgraced before his own spoiled children. She would take no part in this dispute between the rival factions, both of which she loathed. It was agreeable to her to watch the tumult raging around her, for it gave unmistakable proof that the authority of the National Guard no longer counted, that anarchy was supreme in France, that the canaille could insult the royal family without punishment, and that therefore the King was morally entitled to flee from Paris. For two hours and a quarter the farce endured, until at length Louis ordered that the carriage should be wheeled back to the coach-house, explaining that the excursion to Saint-Cloud had been abandoned. Thereupon, as usual in moments of triumph, the crowd which had just before been spewing abuse, underwent a sudden change of mood, acclaimed the King and the Queen, and expressed its delight with its "rulers," while the National Guard promised to protect the royal pair. Marie Antoinette, however, knew how much this protection was worth, and answered, so loudly that she could be heard far and wide: "Yes, we count on your devotion. Still, you must admit that we are no longer free." She had good reason for speaking in a loud tone. Ostensibly addressed to the National Guard, the words were really meant for Europe at large.

If, next evening, action had followed inconspicuously upon attention, if effect had speedily followed cause, then insult and indignation, thrust and counterthrust, would have occurred in natural and successful sequence. If two simple, light, inconspicuous carriages, one of them bearing the King with his son, the other the Queen and her daughter with presumably Madame Elisabeth as well, had driven away, no one would have paid any attention to these ordinary vehicles conveying to all appearance ordinary persons. The royal family would have made its way to the frontier without attracting remark. The King's brother, the Count of Provence, departing without ostentation, made good his escape.

Even when only a finger's breadth separated life from death, the royal family would not infringe the sacred laws of the royal household; even when a journey was so hazardous an adventure, immortal etiquette must come as travelling companion. Here was the first vital error: it was decided that the five principal persons in the drama should occupy one of the carriages, the whole royal family, the father, the mother, the sister, and the two children, the very group which was known even in the smallest of French villages thanks to a hundred copperplate engravings. But this was not enough. Madame de Tourzel, mindful of her oath never to let the royal children out of her sight for a moment, must form a sixth member of the company. In a carriage thus grossly overloaded, it was naturally impossible to drive fast, although every quarter of an hour, perhaps every minute, counted. Then came a third mistake: it was inconceivable that a Queen should dress and undress herself, so there must be two ladies-in-waiting in a second carriage, this swelling the tale of the escapees to eight persons. Since, moreover, the coachman, the outriders, and the lackeys must be persons of trust, and, no matter whether they knew or did not know the road, must be of noble birth, the six were more than doubled, and the number was yet further increased by Fersen and his coachman. A goodly company for a secret journey! Fourth, fifth, sixth, and seventh mistakes: fine clothes must be brought along, so that the Queen and the King could appear at Montmédy in gala dress and not in travelling rig. Consequently a couple of hundredweight, packed in brand-new trunks, was piled upon the already overburdened carriages, this meaning, not merely a further slackening of pace, but an additional means of making the procession conspicuous.

What should have been a secret flight, had become a royal progress.

But the greatest of all the mistakes was this. If the King and the Queen had to drive for four-and-twenty hours, even to get out of hell, they must drive comfortably. A new carriage was ordered, exceptionally wide, exceptionally well-sprung; a carriage which stank of fresh varnish and of wealth; a carriage which, whenever the horses were changed, could not fail to arouse the curiosity of postilions, posting-masters, and ostlers. Lovers are not apt to be far-sighted when the comfort of the women they love is at stake, and Fersen naturally wanted Marie Antoinette to have everything as gorgeous, as beautiful, and as luxurious as possible. According to his specifications, reputedly for a certain Madame la Baronne de Korff, a monumental structure was built, a sort of little warship on four wheels, to provide accommodation, not only for the six members of the royal family together with the governess, the coachman, and the servants, but in addition for all thinkable conveniences: a silver dinner-service, a clothes-press, a cupboard for comestibles, and a close-stool for the bodily needs from which not even kings are exempt. A wine-cellar was built into the framework and duly stocked, for everyone knows that monarchs are thirsty souls. To crown the absurdity, the vehicle was lined with a light-coloured damask. One wonders, in fact, that the designer had omitted to have the fleur-de-lis conspicuously embossed upon the carriage doors. Being equipped as heavily as a hoplite, so ponderous and luxurious an equipage needed, if it were to be driven at a reasonable pace, at least eight and usually twelve horses. This signified that, whereas a light post-chaise with two horses would be delayed only five minutes at a posting-station, here the supply of a new relay occupied about half an hour, so that four or five hours were wasted on the stages of a journey when every few minutes counted for life or for death. To compensate the blue-blooded "servants" and outriders for having to be clad as menials for four-and-twenty hours, they were decked in brilliant, perfectly new, and therefore conspicuous liveries, which contrasted markedly with the plain attire deliberately chosen by the King and the Queen. Attention was further drawn to the affair by the fact that in every little town the carriage was about to traverse there suddenly appeared—in peace-time—a squadron of dragoons, ostensibly on the look-out for a "monetary convoy." Then, to crown all, as the supreme folly, the Duc de Choiseul had chosen as liaison officer between the various contingents, the most impossible of creatures, Figaro in person—the King's hairdresser, the divine Léonard, an excellent man at his own job, which was not that of diplomacy, and who, even more than the King, true to his lifelong role, was eminently calculated to complicate an already hopelessly involved situation.

There was one excuse for this absurdity. State ceremonial in France had no precedent for a King's flight. A royal baptism, a coronation, how the King or the Queen went to the theatre, His Majesty's clothing at the hunt, which shoes and which buckles he and his gracious spouse should wear at receptions or parties, at Mass, or at the card-table—such details, and a hundred others of equal importance, were prescribed by ceremonial routine. But precisely how a king and a queen should flee in disguise from the palace of their ancestors was 'not mentioned in the tables of the law. Here, free improvisation was necessary. Precisely because the court had never come into touch with the realities of life, at its first contact with them it was perforce impotent. When the King of France had to dress as a menial in order to escape from his people, he could no longer be lord of his own destiny.

After interminable delays, June 19th was fixed upon for the flight— not too soon, for a net of secret negotiations, spread so wide and held by so many hands, may tear somewhere at any moment. Like the crack of a whip there sounded amid ominous whispers an article by Marat in "L'Ami du Peuple," announcing a plot to carry off the King. "The idea is to remove him forcibly into the Low Countries, on the pretext that his cause is that of all the kings of Europe. . . . Are you imbeciles, that you take no steps to prevent the flight of the royal family? Parisians, stupid that you are, I am weary of saying to you over and over again that you should have the King and the Dauphin in safe keeping; that you should lock up the Austrian woman, her brother-in-law, and the rest of the family. The loss of one day might be disastrous to the nation, might dig the graves of three millions of Frenchmen." A remarkable prophecy, uttered by a man whose morbid suspicion endowed him with keen insight; and only in this respect was he wrong, inasmuch as "the loss of one day" was to be disastrous, not to the nation, but to the King and the Queen. Disastrous to them because, once again, at the last moment, Marie Antoinette postponed the flight of which the minutest details had already been prepared. Vainly had Fersen tired himself out in order to have everything ready for June 19th. For weeks and months in succession, he had concentrated his energies upon this undertaking. Not only, in his nightly visits to the Queen, had he brought hidden under his cloak the various articles of clothing that were needed for the escapees' disguise, but, in countless letters to General Bouillé, he had specified the various points at which the dragoons and hussars were to wait for the King's carriage. Himself taking the reins, on the road to Vincennes he had made trial of the post-horses engaged for the flight. All those concerned had been allotted their parts; the mechanism had been perfected down to the tiniest cog-wheel.

But, at the last moment, the Queen countermanded the arrangements. One of her ladies of the bedchamber, who had a liaison with a revolutionist, was suspect. As it happened, on June the 20th this woman was to have a day off, so Marie Antoinette thought it essential to wait twenty-four hours longer. A sinister delay! Fresh orders had to be sent to Bouillé, the cavalrymen must be instructed to off-saddle, and there was a superadded nervous tension for Fersen and for his beloved, whose sensibilities were already strained to breaking-point. At length, however, this last day of waiting had gone by. To avert suspicion, in the afternoon the Queen with her two children and her sister-in-law Elisabeth went for an expedition to the pleasure-gardens of Tivoli. On her return, with her usual dignity and precision she gave the commandant her instructions for the ensuing day. There was no sign of excitement in her behaviour, nor, of course, in that of King Louis, for he was one of those who are said to have "no nerves." At eight in the evening, Marie Antoinette retired to her own apartment and dismissed her ladies. The children were put to bed, and then the elders of the royal family, unconcerned to all seeming, assembled for supper in the great salon. A shrewd observer might perhaps have noticed that the Queen was continually looking at the clock, as if she was tired out and wanted to go to bed. In reality, she had never been more wakeful, more fully in possession of her senses and ready to meet her fate, than on this momentous evening.

CHAPTER XXVII

The Flight to Varennes

O N THE evening of June 20, 1791, not even the most suspicious onlooker could have detected that anything unusual was afoot in the Tuileries. As always, the National Guards were at their post; as always, the servants male and female had been dismissed to their supper; and in the great salon, as was customary, sat the King with his brother the Count of Provence and the other members of the royal family, some of them playing backgammon and others engaged in quiet conversation. Was there anything remarkable in this, that at about ten o'clock the Queen should break off what she was saying, and leave the room for a moment or two? We all have occasion to do so from time to time! None of the domestics followed her, and when she entered the corridor it was empty. There Marie Antoinette stood for a while holding her breath as she listened to the footfall of the sentry in the garden; then, hastening to her daughter's bedroom, she knocked gently. The girl awoke with a start and called to the assistant governess, Madame Brunier, who was on duty that night. The latter came, and, although astonished at the Queen's incomprehensible command to dress the princess at once, naturally offered no objection. While "Madame Royale" was being dressed, the Queen went to wake the Dauphin. Pulling aside the curtains of the damask canopy, she whispered to him: "Come, darling, you must get up. We are going on a journey, to a fortress where there are plenty of soldiers." Heavy with sleep, the little prince murmured that he must have his sword and his uniform, for he would be one of the soldiers. "Quick, quick, we must get away as soon as possible," said Marie Antoinette to the chief governess, Madame de Tourzel, who had long been in the secret, and who now dressed young Louis in girl's clothes, explaining to him that they were going to a masked ball. The two children were noiselessly led down the private staircase into the Queen's room. There a surprise, a joyous one, awaited them, for when their mother opened the cupboard let into the wall there stepped forth an officer of the bodyguard, a certain Monsieur de Malden, whom the indefatigable Fersen had smuggled into the palace. All four now hastened to the private exit, where no sentry was posted.

Opening the door, the Queen looked forth, unaffrighted as ever at such moments. From the shadow of one of the waiting carriages there emerged a man dressed as a coachman, and he, without a word, took the Dauphin by the hand. It was Fersen, who since early morning had been working like a galley-slave. He had got the postilions ready, had arranged for the three bodyguards to masquerade as couriers, and had posted them in their places. He had secretly conveyed out of the Tuileries the necessaries for the journey, had got the carriages together, and once, during the afternoon, had consoled the Queen when he found her in tears. Again and again, in disguise for the most part, but once in his ordinary dress, he had hastened through the streets of Paris to perfect his arrangements. Now he was risking his life by leading the Dauphin of France out of the King's palace, and he asked for no other reward than the thanks of his mistress who was thus entrusting herself and her children to his care.

The four shadows, Fersen, Malden, and the two children, vanished into the darkness; while the Queen, as if she had merely gone away to write a letter, returned to the salon and resumed an indifferent conversation. Meanwhile Fersen took the children across the great square and got with them into an old-fashioned fiacre, where, while awaiting their parents' coming, they promptly fell asleep. The Queen's two ladies-in-waiting had already been sent ahead to Claye in another carriage. At eleven came the most critical hour. The Count of Provence and his wife, who were also to escape that night, left the palace as usual. The Queen and Madame Elisabeth sought their apartments. To avoid arousing suspicion, Marie Antoinette had herself undressed by her lady's maids, and told them to bespeak the carriages next morning for a drive. At half past eleven, knowing that Lafayette's invariable visit to the King must be over, she ordered the lights to be put out, this being the signal for the servants to go to bed.

The instant the door had closed behind the maids, the Queen jumped out of bed and dressed as quickly as she could, putting on a simple gown of grey silk, and a black hat with a violet veil thick enough to make her face unrecognizable. Going down the little flight of steps leading to the private door, where a confidant was awaiting her, she crossed the dark Place du Carroussel. All was going on splendidly when, by an unlucky chance, there came the light of torches, a carriage with outriders, the carriage of Lafayette who had convinced himself by his inspection of the Tuileries that everything was in perfect order. The Queen hastily withdrew into the shade of a doorway, and so close to her passed Lafayette's carriage that she could have touched the wheels. However, no one noticed her. A few steps farther on, and she reached the fiacre which contained all that she loved most on earth—Fersen and her children.

It was not so easy for the King to get away. First of all he had to receive Lafayette, on the commandant's nightly visit, which lasted so long this time that even the thick-skinned Louis began to lose patience. Again and again he jumped up from his chair and went to the window, as if to look at the sky. At length, towards half past eleven, the unwelcome guest departed. Thereupon Louis XVI retired to his bedroom, where he had to engage in the last desperate struggle with the etiquette in which he was perpetually enmeshed. Ancient custom decreed that His Majesty's valet must sleep in His Majesty's chamber, a string tied round his wrist, so that a pull upon his cord of communication would instantly awaken the servant. If, therefore, Louis was to get away, the first thing the poor man had to do was to escape from his own valet! The King allowed himself to be undressed as usual, got into bed, and had the curtains drawn on both sides as if he were settling down for the night. Really what he was waiting for was the moment when the attendant retired into the neighbouring closet to undress, and then, seizing his opportunity (assuredly a feat worthy of Beaumarchais!) Louis jumped out from behind the curtain, and fled barefooted in his nightgown through the other door into his son's forsaken bedroom, where there had been laid out for him a simple suit of clothes, a roughly made wig, and (a further shame) a lackey's hat. Meanwhile the faithful valet had tiptoed back into the royal bedchamber holding his breath lest he should awaken his master, whom he supposed to be asleep behind the curtains, and carefully attached the end of the pull-cord round his wrist. Clad only in a nightgown, barefooted, there stole down the staircase Louis King of France and Navarre, carrying on one arm the grey coat, the wig, and the lackey's hat. On the ground floor was waiting for him, hidden once more in the wall-cupboard, the guardsman Monsieur de Malden, who was to show His Majesty the way. Having dressed as quickly as possible, the King, unrecognizable in the bottle-green coat and with the lackey's hat upon his exalted head, strode across the deserted court-yard of his palace. The National Guards, who at this hour were not very much on the alert, failing to recognize him, let him pass without protest. Then it seemed that the worst difficulties had been overcome, and by midnight the family was assembled in the fiacre. Fersen, dressed as a coachman, mounted the box, and drove the King, Marie Antoinette, and their children across Paris.

He had fully half of the great city to traverse. But Fersen, a man of rank, was not used to driving himself through these labyrinthine streets. That task was ordinarily left to his coachman. Besides, as a last precaution (an undesirable precaution), instead of driving forth-with to the meeting-place, he thought it better to visit the Rue Matignon once more, in order to make sure that the great chariot should start. It was not until two in the morning, instead of at mid-night as previously arranged, that he conducted his precious charge through the gates of Paris. Two hours, two irrecoverable hours had been lost. Beyond the barrier, the brand-new chariot ought by now to have been waiting for them, but, alas, it was not to be found! More time was wasted until, at length, it was discovered, with four horses in the traces, and with its lamps veiled. Fersen drew up his fiacre beside the chariot, so that the royal family could transfer itself to the latter without (dreadful thought!) having to soil their footgear with French street-mud. It was not until half past two that the other horses could at length be harnessed to the cumbrous vehicle. Fersen did not spare the whip, and in half an hour they had reached Bondy, where an officer of the guards was awaiting them with eight fresh post-horses. Now the Queen had to say farewell to her lover, and this was a painful duty. Most unwilling, naturally enough, was Marie Antoinette to leave the only friend in whom she really trusted, but the King had expressly declared he did not wish Fersen to accompany them any further. We do not know why the stipulation had been made. Perhaps Louis did not wish to appear before his own intimates with this too-intimate friend of his wife in attendance; but it may well have been that he entertained a kindly thought for Fersen, and did not wish the foreigner who had done so much for them to run any further risk. All we know with certainty is that Fersen himself tells us: "Il n'a pas voulu." Besides, it had been arranged that, after the royal family had got safely across the frontier, Fersen was to visit them. The good-bye was only for a short time. Fersen, therefore, when the early dawn of midsummer was already breaking, rode once more round the chariot to see that all was well, and, in a loud voice, to deceive the uninitiated postilions, called out: "Adieu, Madame de Korff!"

Eight horses can pull better than four, so the huge chariot now made good progress along the grey strip of road. Its occupants were in a good mood; the children had had their sleep out; even Louis was more lively than usual. Jokes were exchanged about the false names under which the various travellers were passing. Madame de Tourzel was supposed to be the lady of the party, and represented herself as Madame de Korff; the Queen, "Madame Rochet," was the governess of Madame de Korff's two girls; the King, in his lackey's hat, was Durand, the steward. Madame Elisabeth was the lady's maid. The family felt much more at ease in this roomy and comfortable carriage than, for a long time, they had felt in their palace, watched over by a hundred servants (most of whom were in the pay of the Revolution) and by six hundred National Guards; nor was it long before Louis XVI's inseparable companion, a healthy appetite, began to make its presence known. The liberally stocked food-baskets were opened, and a hearty breakfast was eaten off silver platters; the bones of the chickens and the empty wine-bottles were disposed of through the carriage windows; the worthy guardsmen were not forgotten. The children, delighted by this strange adventure, played merrily; the Queen responded to their chatter with a light heart; and the King was glad to avail himself of an unwonted opportunity for learning a little about his own realm. With a map upon his knees, he followed the progress of the journey, from town to town, from village to village, from hamlet to hamlet. The fugitives began to feel that they were safe. At the next change of horses, except for the ostlers at the posting-station everyone was in bed, for it was only six in the morning, and no one troubled to ask Baroness Korff for her papers. Subsequent relays were obtained without difficulty, and, as the day wore on, the party was approaching Châlons-sur-Marne, for they had now covered a hundred miles since leaving Paris. Could they but get safely through Châlons, surely all would be well, seeing that, less than half an hour's drive beyond, at Pont-de-Somme-Vesle, there was waiting for them the first squadron of cavalry, under the command of the young Duc de Choiseul. Châlons at last, and it was four o'clock in the afternoon. Neither malice nor suspicion animated the crowd which assembled round the posting-station. It was natural that when travellers in a great hurry were passing through from Paris many in this country-town should like to ask the postilions what was the latest news from Paris in these moving times. Some would want to send a letter or a package to the next posting-station. Besides, even more in the old times than today, country folk like to pass the time of day with strangers, and are interested at the sight of a fine chariot.

It was a glorious summer day, work was nearly finished, and what could there be better to do than to have a crack with the passers-by? People who knew something about coach-building were quick to per-ceive that the vehicle was something quite out of the ordinary; then there was such a lot of baggage; the travellers must certainly be of high rank, and were probably refugees. The main impulse of the crowd was curiosity, conjoined with a wish to gossip. Strange, how-ever! Why on this hot midsummer afternoon, after so long a drive, did the whole six of them remain seated in their carriage as if glued there, instead of stretching their legs a little, instead of getting out, as might have been expected, to drink a glass of wine and have a friendly chat? Why did these gold-laced servants assume the airs of people of importance? There must be something queer about the whole matter! One of the spectators stepped up to the posting-master, and whispered into his ear. The official seemed much concerned, but did not interfere, and let the chariot drive on its way unmolested, Still (no one knew how it came about), within half an hour the town of Châlons was buzzing with the report that the King and the royal family had just driven through on their way eastward.

The travellers, however, suspected nothing. Tired though they were, they were glad at heart, since it could not be long before they would be met by Choiseul and his hussars. Then there could be an end to this mummery and concealment. The menial-looking hats could be thrown away; the false passports could be torn up; at length Louis and Marie Antoinette could have their ears tickled once more with shouts of "Long live the King! Long live the Queen!" Madame Elisabeth was continually thrusting her head out of the window, hoping to be the first to greet Choiseul; the outriders were expecting from moment to moment to see the scabbards of the cavalrymen's sabres flashing in the light of the setting sun. At length a horseman appeared in the road, but only one, a lonely officer of the guard.

"Where is Choiseul?"

"Gone."

"And the rest of the hussars?"

"Not one of them here."

The refugees' hearts fell. There must have been a hitch somewhere. Night was at hand. How terrible seemed the risk of driving on unguarded into the darkness. But a fugitive can neither turn back nor stand still. For him there is only one path—forward. The Queen tried to console her companions. Although the hussars had failed to meet them at the appointed spot, there would certainly be dragoons in Sainte-Mènehould, only two hours' drive farther. Then all would go well. These two hours seemed longer than the rest of the interminable day.

But on arrival at Sainte-Mènehould another disagreeable surprise awaited the escapees, for again there was no escort. The cavalrymen had stayed a long time in the little town, had, in fact, spent the whole day in various inns, and, bored by the delay, had drunk freely and had let their tongues wag, so that the populace had grown suspicious. In the end their commanding officer, misled by a confused message from Monsieur Léonard the court hairdresser, had thought it better to send his men out of the town along the eastward road in charge of a subaltern, and to stay unattended to receive the royal party.

Here was the chariot at last, imposing vehicle with its eight-in-hand team, followed by the carriage-and-pair, a startling apparition enough to these worthy provincials, after the strange events of the day. First of all a lot of dragoons, loitering in their town with no ostensible object; now the great chariot and the smaller carriage, with postilions in smart liveries. Mark how devotedly, how reverently, the commandant of the cavalrymen was greeting these remarkable travellers. Nay, reverence was too feeble a term. The man was subservient, keeping his hand at the salute all the time he was speaking to them. Drouet, member of the Jacobin Club and an ardent republican, Drouet, the posting-master, opened his eyes wide and set his wits to work. "These must be émigrés," he thought; "blue bloods; perhaps I ought to have them arrested!" Rejecting so extreme a course, on the quiet he told his post-boys to moderate the pace of the convoy as much as they could, and thereupon the chariot rolled sleepily onward, filled with the no-less sleepy and no-less mysterious passengers.

Within ten minutes of the departure, rumour had done its work. Perhaps someone had brought the news from Châlons, or maybe the instinct of the populace had hit the mark. Anyhow, the belief was rife that the royal family had passed through the town. A clamour was raised, the commanding officer of the dragoons realized the danger, and, having now summoned his men back to Sainte-Mènehould, wanted to gallop after the chariot and provide it with an escort. His impulse came too late. The populace raised objections. The dragoons, plied with wine, fraternized with the people and refused to obey orders. A few stalwarts sounded the call to arms, and, amid the tumult, there was one man ready to decide upon prompt action. Drouet the posting-master, himself an ex-cavalryman who had seen active service, had a horse saddled, and, with one companion, galloped away by a short cut to reach Varennes in advance of the cumbrous chariot. There the suspect travellers could be held to account, and if King Louis were really among them then God have mercy on him and his throne! As has happened a thousand times in history, the course of events was turned by the action of one energetic man.

Meanwhile the chariot was making its way along the winding road to Varennes. Its inmates were tired out by their long day's drive beneath a midsummer sun. The children had gone to sleep; Louis had folded up his maps and put them away; the Queen held her peace. One more hour, one last hour, and the party would have a trustworthy escort. But now came a fresh surprise. At the place where the next change of horses had been arranged for, a little short of Varennes, no horses were in readiness. Groping in the darkness, the outriders tapped at the windows of the posting-station, and were answered from within by angry voices. The two officers who had had instructions to wait here had been led by Monsieur Léonard the fore-runner to believe that the King was not coming after all. This court hairdresser was a muddle-head, and one should not entrust Figaro with so important a mission. The officers had gone to bed, and their sleep was as momentous to the King as had been Lafayette's sleep in the early morning of October 6th nearly two years before. Well, there was nothing for it but to drive on into Varennes with the tired horses, in the hope that there a relay could be found. At the gate of the city, however, a couple of young fellows stopped the first outrider with a peremptory "Halt!" In a trice both the carriages were surrounded and accompanied into Varennes by a considerable number of youths. Drouet and his companions, who had arrived ten minutes earlier, had dragged the revolutionary youths out of beds and pot-houses.

"Your passports!" said someone.

"We are pressed for time, and you must not delay us," replied a woman's voice from the carriage.

It was the reputed "Madame Rochet" who spoke—the Queen, the only one to retain her presence of mind in this moment of deadly peril. But it was futile to resist. They had to drive to the nearest inn, which, by one of the ironies of history, bore the sign "Au Grand Monarque." In waiting was the mayor, a shopkeeper by trade, bearing the tasteful name of Sauce. He examined the passports. A petty bourgeois, secretly a royalist, and afraid to mix himself up in so troublesome an affair, he gave a hasty glance and said: "The papers are in order." He was for letting the carriages proceed on their way.

Young Drouet, however, feeling the pull of the fish on his line, thumped the table and shouted: "It is the King and his family, and if you let him escape to a foreign land you will be guilty of high treason." So threatening a tone was enough to intimidate a man of Sauce's mettle. Besides, the revolutionists aroused by Drouet and his mates were sounding the tocsin, lights were flaming in the windows, the town was buzzing like a wasps' nest. A larger and ever larger crowd had gathered round the carriages. As for whipping up and driving away without heed to the wishes of the populace, this was not to be thought of, since no fresh horses had been put to.

The worthy mayor, to escape from his embarrassment, informed the travellers that in any case it was too late for them to proceed on their journey. Madame la Baronne de Korff and her company could put up for the night in his house. By morning, thought the shrewd fellow, matters would be cleared up, and he himself would have escaped taking a dangerous responsibility upon his shoulders. Hesitatingly, but aware that there was nothing better to be done, and in the hope that the missing dragoons would turn up by morning, the King accepted the invitation.

In an hour or two, surely, Choiseul or Bouillé would be here! Louis XVI, therefore, wearing his inappropriate wig, went quietly into Monsieur Sauce's house, and his first royal action was to ask for a bottle of wine and some bread and cheese. "Is it the King? Is it the Queen?"—such were the whispers that went round. Varennes was so far away from the court which till recently had been unapproachable that not one of these subjects of his had ever seen their King's countenance except upon the coins of the realm. It was necessary to summon a nobleman who lived hard by before anyone could be certain whether this remarkable traveller was really no more than Baroness de Korff's lackey, or His Majesty Louis XVI, the Most Christian King of France and Navarre.

CHAPTER XXVIII

The Night in Varennes

ON THIS June 21, 1791, Marie Antoinette, in the six-and-thirtieth year of her life and in the seventeenth year of her reign, for the first time entered the house of a French bourgeois. That was the only interruption of her progress from palace to palace and from prison to prison. She had first to pass through the shop, smelling of rancid oil, sausage, and spices. Then, by a sort of companion-ladder, the royal party—Madame la Baronne de Korff as ostensible chief, the Queen as governess, and Louis as a bewigged servant—mounted to the first story, where there were two rooms, a bedroom and a parlour, low-ceilinged, poor-looking, and dirty. In front of the door were promptly stationed two sentries, very different from the noble and gaily uniformed guardsmen at Versailles, for they were peasants armed with pitchforks. The eight visitors, the King, the Queen, Madame Elisabeth, the two children, the governess, and the two maids had all to find accommodation as best they could in this narrow space. The children, tired out, were put to bed, and quickly fell asleep, watched over by Madame de Tourzel. The Queen, dropping into an easy-chair, lowered her veil, for no one should be able to boast of having seen any signs of anger or bitterness in her face. Louis, how-ever, began to make himself at home, sitting down to table and cut-ting himself a big slice of cheese. No one uttered a word. After a while, however, there came the clattering of horses' hoofs in the streets, and loud shouts from the crowd: "The hussars! The hussars!" Choiseul, who had been following a false scent, had at length found the trail, and now arrived on the spot. Drawing his sword and calling to his men to follow, he forced a way through the mob and took possession of the front of the house. The good hussars, being Germans, understood barely a word of what their leader said, but he had at least enough command of their tongue to cry aloud to them: "Der König und die Königin." Anyhow, he could give them orders by signs, and, at the sword's point, they drove back the populace until, for a time, the carriage was unencumbered.

Meanwhile the Duc de Choiseul made his way upstairs and unfolded a plan of escape. He could spare seven horses. Louis, Marie Antoinette, and the rest of their company were to mount and ride away with all speed, guarded by the troop of hussars, before the National Guard of the neighbourhood had been mustered. Then, saluting, he said: "Your Majesty, I await your orders."

But Louis XVI had never found it easy to issue commands and had never been the man for quick decisions. Could Choiseul be quite certain that during the escape the Queen, Madame Elisabeth, one of the children, might not be hit by a bullet? Would it not be better to wait until the dragoons quartered in the various inns had been assembled? These parleyings occupied several minutes, precious minutes. There sat the old regime, in a sordid little room, hesitating, hesitating. The Revolution, however, the hasty and vigorous spirit of the younger generation, was in no mood to wait. Summoned from the neighbouring villages by the tocsin, the National Guard, the bourgeois or citizen militia, was quickly gathered together; a few ancient pieces of artillery had been dismounted from the walls, and barricades had been erected in the streets. As for Choiseul's soldiers, scattered hither and thither among the crowd, they had been four-and-twenty hours in the saddle riding hither and thither upon what appeared to them an aimless errand. They were ready enough to drink and to fraternize with the people. The streets became more and more closely thronged. As if an intuition that the hour was of supreme importance had spread electrically throughout the countryside, the peasants, cottagers, shepherds, manual workers of all kinds, were flocking into the town. Even palsied old women were limping in on crutches, eager to see the King—and now, when Louis had no choice but to acknowledge his identity, the hot-bloods of Varennes were determined that he should not continue his eastward journey. Every attempt to harness fresh horses was resisted by overwhelming force. "Back to Paris, or we will shoot him in his carriage," shouted fierce voices to the outriders—and, to intensify the excitement, to heap clamour upon clamour, the tocsin was once again sounded. Then came a new exciting incident on this dramatic night. A carriage drove in by the road from Paris, and in

it were seated two of the commissaries dispatched that morning by
the National Assembly along all the main roads to overtake the King
whithersoever he might be going. This pair had been lucky enough
to find the spoor. Their arrival as official representatives of the power
of the people was greeted with yells of delight. Now Varennes was
freed from responsibility, and the bakers, the shoemakers, the tailors,
and the butchers of a little country town were no longer called upon
to make one of the vital decisions of history. The messengers of the
National Assembly, the supreme popular authority, would settle what
had to be done in this emergency. Triumphantly, they were escorted
to Sauce's house; they entered the shop and climbed the companion-
ladder in search of the King.

By now the dreadful night had drawn to a close; the sun had risen
a couple of hours ago; it was half past six in the morning. One of the
two commissaries, Romeuf, was pale of countenance, embarrassed, since
he had little liking for his task. As Lafayette's aide-de-camp he had
often kept watch over the royal pair in the Tuileries, and had conceived a liking for Marie Antoinette, who was invariably gracious to
underlings. Both she and King Louis had often addressed him in
friendly tones; and in the bottom of his heart Romeuf had but one
desire that morning—to help the fugitives to escape. As fate would
have it, however, his companion on the expedition was a certain Bayon,
an ambitious fellow as well as an ardent revolutionist. Romeuf, as soon
as he realized that they were on the right trail, had secretly done his
utmost to delay the hunt, whilst Bayon, like a hound on a hot scent,
had pushed eagerly forward, dragging his leashed companion along.
Now it was incumbent upon the latter, for all his embarrassment, to
present to the Queen the National Assembly's decree commanding
that the flight of the royal family should be stayed. Marie Antoinette
could not conceal her surprise: "What, Monsieur, you? I should not
have expected it of you!" Romeuf stammeringly explained that Paris
was in a condition of wild excitement, and that the King's return was
necessary in the interests of the State. The Queen impatiently turned
away, aware that something sinister underlay this idle chatter. At
length King Louis took the decree and read it. It was to the effect that
his rights had been suspended by the National Assembly and that the
messengers bearing this mandate were instructed, should they over-

take the royal family, to do everything in their power to hinder the continuance of the journey. True, the words "flight," "arrest," "imprisonment," were sedulously avoided; but for the first time it was made plain by the Assembly that the King was no longer a free agent, and was subordinate to the will of those who had been his subjects. So much was clear enough even to Louis the heavy-witted.

Yet he made no protest, being content to say sleepily: "There is no longer a king in France." Thereupon, absent-mindedly, he tossed the decree on to the bed in which the children were still sleeping. The action, however, roused Marie Antoinette out of her stupor. When her pride was touched, when her honour was threatened, this woman who in petty circumstances was herself petty, and where superficialities were concerned was herself superficial, was fired by a dignity appropriate to the occasion. Snatching the missive in which the National Assembly arrogated to itself the right of disposing of herself and her family, she crumpled it up and threw it contemptuously on to the floor, saying: "I will not have my children soiled by contact with this document."

Romeuf and Bayon, petty officials, were horrified at the desecration. To put an end to the scandal, Choiseul hastened to pick up the decree. All in the room were greatly perturbed; the King by his wife's rashness, and the two envoys by the painful situation into which that rashness had thrust them. There was a general sense of indecision. At this juncture Louis made a proposal which was outwardly one of compliance with the Assembly's order, but behind which craft lurked. He would like the commissaries, he said, to allow them two or three hours' rest before starting on the return journey. They must see for themselves how weary the children were. After two such terrible nights and a long, long journey time must be given for repose. Romeuf saw what was in the King's mind. Within two hours Bouillé's cavalry squadrons would be on hand, quickly followed up by infantry and artillery. Since he wanted to save the monarch, he raised no objection—after all, his commission had merely been to stop the journey. Well, he had done so. But Bayon, the other commissary, was no less quick of apprehension, and made up his mind to answer cunning with cunning. Seeming to agree for the moment, he made his way as if indifferently down the steps, and out through the shop into the street. When the crowd surrounded him, eagerly asking what had been settled, he sighed sancti-

moniously, and replied: "They don't want to start yet. . . . Bouillé
will be here soon, and they will wait for him." The fat was in the
fire! The revolutionists were not going to allow themselves to be humbugged! "To Paris! To Paris!" shouted the crowd. Under the menace
of these cries, which could be plainly heard within, the town councillors, with poor Sauce at their head, urged the King to start immediately on the return journey, for otherwise they could not guarantee his
safety. The hussars had been dispersed, were wedged singly amid the
crowd or had fraternized with the populace. The chariot was jubilantly
turned round and got ready, the horses being put to so that there
should be no excuse for further hesitation.

Now began a humiliating attempt to postpone departure. Bouillé's
men could not be far off; every minute gained might save the monarchy; though by the most unworthy means, let all be done that could
be done to delay the return to Paris. Even Marie Antoinette had to
curb her pride. Turning to the shopkeeper's wife, she implored help.
But the poor woman was afraid for her own husband's safety. With
tears in her eyes she said that it was terrible to be forced to refuse
hospitality to a king, to a queen of France, but she had her children
to think of, and, were she to comply, it would cost poor Monsieur
Sauce his life. (In actual fact, the shopkeeper had already done more
than enough, and ere long had to pay with his head for having helped
the King, during that dreadful night, to burn a few private papers.)

Louis and Marie Antoinette tried one unlikely expedient after another, while the time ran on and Bouillé's cavalrymen failed to put in
an appearance. At length, when everything was ready for the start,
Louis XVI—who must have sunk low before he could demean himself
to play such a part in such a comedy—said he was hungry. Surely no
one would refuse to give a king a reasonable meal? No one would
refuse! But they were quick about the preparations. The King forced
down a few mouthfuls, whilst Marie Antoinette contemptuously thrust
the plate aside. No further pretext for postponement could be thought
of. Then came a new, a last incident. The family was already at the
door when one of the ladies-in-waiting, Madame Neuveville, fell down
in a pretended epileptic fit. The Queen imperiously declared that she
would not move a step before a doctor had arrived. Well, since every
soul in Varennes was on the alert, the doctor came before Bouillé and

the cavalrymen. He gave the malingeress a calmative potion, and thereupon the curtain had to be rung down upon the tragi-comedy.

With a sigh the King led the way down the steep steps. Marie Antoinette followed him, on the arm of the Duc de Choiseul. She alone realized what this return journey meant for them all. Still, amid her own troubles, her thoughts turned to her friend. When Choiseul arrived her first words had been: "Do you think that Fersen has escaped?" With a real man by her side even this detestable "homecoming" would have been endurable; but it was hard to remain strong when her only companions were faint-hearts and weaklings.

The royal family got into the chariot. They still entertained hopes of the coming of Bouillé with his men. But there was no sound of galloping hoofs, and only the threatening murmur of the crowd could be heard. At length the great equipage started. There were six thousand persons surrounding it. All Varennes was accompanying its prey on the first stage of the journey; and now mingled rage and fear gave place to open triumph. Amid the strains of revolutionary songs, environed by the proletarian army, the unhappy ship of the monarchy sheered away from the reef on which it had struck.

Twenty minutes later, a cloud of dust swept along the highroad eastward of Varennes, dust raised by the hoofs of many horses, for squadron after squadron of cavalry was galloping into the town. At length they had come, Bouillé's men, so long and so vainly desired! If the King could have succeeded in putting off his departure for half an hour more, he would have been in the midst of a loyal army, and the revolutionists who were now rejoicing would have had no option but to slink away to their homes. When Bouillé heard that His Majesty had yielded, he withdrew his troops. Of what use, now, the shedding of blood? Besides, he knew well enough that the fate of the monarchy had been decided by the weakness of the monarch; he knew that Louis was no longer King and Marie Antoinette no longer Queen of France.

CHAPTER XXIX

Return to Paris

A SHIP sails faster when the sea is calm than when the waves rage high. The chariot had driven from Paris to Varennes in twenty hours; the return was to last three days. Drop by drop and to the dregs had the King and the Queen to drink the bitter cup of humiliation. Worn out by two sleepless nights, without a chance to change their clothes (except for the King, whose shirt was so befouled with sweat, that he borrowed another from a soldier) the six of them sat huddled together in the carriage which felt like an oven beneath the fiery sun of late June. The road would have been dusty in any case; now in every town and every village the dust was kicked into the air in clouds by the trampling feet of those who assembled to gloat over the sad home-coming of the royal laughing-stocks. The six hours' drive from Versailles to Paris had been a pleasure trip compared with this one. The coarsest invectives were defiantly hurled at the home-comers. Better, then, to shut the windows, and, in spite of the suffocating heat, to escape in this way the continual molestation by offensive words and looks. The faces of the unhappy travellers were plastered as if with flour; their eyes were reddened with want of sleep and with the irritation of the dust; they were not allowed to draw down the blinds for long at a time, since, at every posting-station, some jack-in-office, a mayor or what not, thought fit to deliver a lecture to the King and on each occasion he had to give an assurance that it had never been his intention to quit France. At such times Marie Antoinette was more successful than Louis in maintaining a semblance of dignity. At one of the halts, when food was brought them, and they lowered the blinds to have their meal in peace, the crowd outside raised a hubbub, and shouted that they must be drawn up. Madame Elisabeth wanted to give way, but the Queen emphatically refused. She let the people outside rage as they pleased, and not until a quarter of an hour had elapsed, so that it could no longer seem that she was obeying a command of the rabble, did she herself raise the blinds, throw the chicken-bones out of the window, and say: "We must maintain a proper bearing to the last."

Evening had come; they were back at Châlons, and were to pass the night there. Rest was what they now needed above all. The burghers were awaiting their arrival on the farther side of a stone triumphal arch—the very arch which had been erected twenty years earlier when, as a youthful maiden, Marie Antoinette had arrived on her way from Vienna to Paris, driving in the glass coach, acclaimed by the people. The motto carven on the frieze was "Perstet æterna ut amor"—May this monument be as everlasting as our love! Love, however, is more perishable than good marble and ashlar. "Surely it must have been a dream," thought Marie Antoinette, "that beneath this arch, long ago, the nobles received me in festal array, that the streets were illuminated in my honour, and thronged with welcoming crowds!"

Now the best she could hope for was cool and perhaps compassionate civility—so much would be agreeable after the volleyings of hatred to which she had been exposed. She could enjoy the refreshment of a change of clothes and could get a good sleep.

Next morning, however, another hot and seemingly interminable day of pilgrimage had to be endured. The nearer they drew to Paris, the fiercer became the animosity of the populace. The King asked for a moist sponge, to clean the dust from his face, and thereupon an official mocked him, saying: "That's what you gain by travelling!" When, after leaving the carriage for a minute or two to stretch her legs, the Queen mounted the steps again, a woman hissed at her: "Take care, little one, you will soon look on other steps than those!" A nobleman who greeted her in passing was torn from the saddle, stabbed, and pistolled. The King and the Queen at length began to realize that it was not Paris alone which had succumbed to the "error" of the Revolution, for the new seed was sprouting vigorously in every field throughout the country. Maybe, however, they no longer had strength left to grasp the issues. Their sensibilities must have been dulled by fatigue. They were sitting worn out in their carriage, almost indifferent to what fate might bring, when mounted couriers arrived from Paris to tell them that three members of the National Assembly were on the way to safeguard the journey of the royal family. Their lives would be saved, at any rate, though little else.

The carriage was halted in the open road, for now the three deputies, Maubourg the royalist, Barnave the bourgeois lawyer, and Pétion the Jacobin, were at hand. The Queen herself opened the carriage-door. "Messieurs," she said, in considerable excitement, extending her hand to the three of them, "I hope you will see to it that no disaster happens, that those who have accompanied us will not be sacrificed, that their lives will not be attempted." With the tact customary to her on great occasions, she sounded the right note. It was not becoming for a Queen to ask protection for herself; but an appeal on behalf of those who had served her faithfully was on another plane altogether.

The Queen's energy and dignity disarmed the deputies and overcame their patronizing attitude. Even Pétion, the Jacobin, admits in his Report that these vigorous words made a strong impression on him. Having imposed silence on the crowd, he informed the King that it would be better if two of the delegates from the National Assembly were to take their places in the carriage, since their presence would safeguard the royal family against further peril. The best thing would be for Madame de Tourzel and Madame Elisabeth to transfer to the other carriage. The King, however, replied that he would rather they should be crowded a little and thus make room for the deputies without breaking up their party. In haste, therefore, the following arrangements were made. Barnave sat between the King and the Queen, the latter having taken the Dauphin on her lap. Pétion sat between Madame de Tourzel and Madame Elisabeth, the former lady holding the little princess between her knees. Thus there were now eight persons in the chariot instead of six; the representatives of the monarchy and those of the people cheek by jowl, and it can be said beyond question that never were the royal family and the deputies of the National Assembly so close together as during these hours.

What happened thereafter in the carriage was the most natural thing in the world. To begin with, of course, there was the utmost antagonism between the two poles, between the five members of the royal family and the two representatives of the National Assembly, between the prisoners and their jailers. Marie Antoinette, for the very reason that she was now under the protection of these "factieux" and at their mercy, looked through them as if they did not exist, and maintained an obstinate silence. She would not let them suppose that a queen of France could woo their favour. The deputies, in their turn, did not dream of showing servility or even of exchanging a few courteous words. If anything were to be said during the journey it must be in the form of a lecture to the King, something that would show His Majesty that the members of the National Assembly, free and incorruptible, were very different from lickspittle courtiers. Both parties, then, were determined to keep their distance!

It was in this mood that Pétion the Jacobin (later president of the Convention and one of the leaders of the Girondists) took the offensive. He concentrated his attention on the Queen and aimed his little lecture at her, since she was the proudest of the royal family and it would be a special triumph to shake her equanimity. He was well aware, he explained, that the royal family had left the neighbourhood of the Tuileries in an ordinary fiacre, and that this had been driven by a man of Swedish nationality named . . . named . . . Pétion hesitated, as if he were unable to recall the name, and asked the Queen what this Swede was called. Here was a stab with a poisoned dagger, to question Marie Antoinette about her lover in the King's presence. But she parried the thrust, saying: "Do you think I am likely to know the name of a hackney-coachman?" The confined space within the carriage was tense with anger as a result of this first clash of arms.

Then a trifling incident brought about a relaxation. The little prince had jumped down from his mother's knee. His curiosity had been aroused by the two strange gentlemen. Fingering a brass button on Barnave's official uniform, he laboriously spelled out the inscription: "Vivre libre ou mourir." Of course the two commissaries were delighted that the future king of France should in this way become acquainted with one of the fundamental maxims of the Revolution. The ice had been broken, and by degrees a friendly conversation ensued. Balaam, who went forth to curse, remained to bless. Each party found the other, on closer acquaintance, much less objectionable than had been supposed. Pétion and Barnave having had no personal experience of the private life of "tyrants," had imagined these latter to be unapproachable, swollen with self-conceit, arrogant, stupid, impudent; and they had believed that all human qualities must be stifled in the clouds of incense prevailing at court. The two revolutionists were astonished to find that, among themselves, the members of the royal family were much like other human beings.

Even Pétion, who aped the manners of Cato the Censor, reported as follows: "I could not fail to notice a pleasing simplicity and family affection. There were no kingly and queenly airs, but an easy intercourse tinged with homely good feeling. The Queen called Madame Elisabeth 'little sister,' and Madame Elisabeth responded in kind. Madame Elisabeth addressed the King as 'my brother'; the Queen dandled the prince on her knees. The little girl, though rather shy, played with her brother. The King looked on with a gratified air, but he seemed rather obtuse."

The representatives of the Revolution were amazed to see these royal children no less sportive than their own youngsters at home; and it dawned on them as a distressing fact that they themselves were much better dressed than the ruler of France, whose underlinen was dirty. The barriers were down. When the King drank, he civilly offered Pétion his own glass. Then came an incident which, to the astonished Jacobin, seemed almost beyond the bounds of possibility. The Dauphin, in his childish phraseology, announced that he wanted to pass water. Thereupon the King of France and Navarre himself unbuttoned the lad's breeches and held the silver chamber-pot while the performance was going on. These "tyrants" were men and women, of one flesh with the plebs!

But the Queen, no less, had been shaken out of her preconceptions. After all, the "scélérats," those "monstres" of the National Assembly, were good fellows with excellent manners. They were not bloodthirsty, they were not uneducated, and they were far from stupid. On the contrary, they were more conversable than were the Count of Artois and his companions. Before the strangely assorted party had been three hours on the road, the two sides, dropping their mask of harshness and arrogance, had begun to woo one another's favour. The Queen introduced political topics, hoping to convince the revolutionists that the royal circle and the aristocracy were not so narrow-minded and spiteful as the people (misled by the newspapers) supposed. The deputies, on their side, wished to make it clear to the Queen that she was in error if she supposed the aims of the National Assembly to be identical with those vociferated by Marat in "L'Ami du Peuple." When the talk turned to the question of establishing a republic, Pétion grew cautious and evasive. Old as kingship is the experience that the air of courts can confuse the senses of even the reddest of revolutionaries; and it would be difficult to discover a more striking example than Pétion's Report of the way in which a vain man may have his head turned by the proximity of inherited Majesty.

After three nights disturbed by such terrible anxieties, after three days' driving through intense heat in a crowded carriage, after all the excitement and humiliation, it was only to be expected that the ladies as well as the children should have become utterly exhausted by fatigue. Madame Elisabeth fell into a doze, and her head drooped to a resting-place on her neighbour Pétion's shoulder. Thereupon the conceited idiot promptly conceived the notion that he had made a conquest, with the result that his Report contains words which have pilloried the writer for the ridicule of subsequent generations.

"Madame Elisabeth looked at me mournfully, with that languid air which misfortune gives and which arouses a lively interest. Our glances met from time to time with a sort of mingled understanding and attraction; night was drawing on; the moon began to diffuse its soft illumination. Madame Elisabeth took Madame [the little princess] upon her knees, and after a time she placed the girl half on her knee and half on mine. . . . Madame fell asleep. I stretched out my arm, Madame Elisabeth slipped hers within mine, so that mine was in contact with her armpit. I felt the movements of her body, and the warmth which passed through her clothing. She seemed to me more deeply stirred. I perceived a relaxation in her demeanour; her eyes glistened with moisture; a kind of voluptuousness tinged her melancholy. I may be mistaken, for it is easy to confound the manifestations of misfortune with those of pleasure; but I believe that if we had been alone, that if, by some enchantment, the others had vanished, she would have slipped into my arms and would have given herself up to the promptings of nature."

More serious than the erotic fantasies that whirled through the brain of "handsome Pétion" was the effect of the dangerous spell of Majesty upon his companion Barnave. Thirty years of age, a young lawyer who had recently come from the provinces to Paris, this revolutionary idealist was delighted that a queen, that the Queen of France, should mod-

estly invite him to explain the fundamental principles of the Revolution, the notions cherished by himself and his comrades in the clubs.
What an opportunity for inducing her to respect these sacred principles,
and perhaps winning her over to constitutionalist views. He spoke
ardently, and was intoxicated by his own eloquence. That was no new
thing; but what surprised him was that this reputedly thoughtless
woman (what a calumny to call her "superficial") should listen attentively, understandingly, interpolating now and again a shrewd objection. With her Austrian amiability, with her apparent readiness to be
influenced by his discourse, Marie Antoinette worked a spell upon one
who was simple-minded and credulous by nature. He became convinced that she had been unjustly treated, scandalously maligned. She
had the best intentions in the world; and if only someone were always
at hand to give her appropriate hints, matters would go for the best
in France!

The Queen gave him to understand that she was greatly in need of
such a counsellor, and that she would be most grateful to him if in
future he would help her inexperience. That should be his task, henceforward to keep this unexpectedly perspicacious woman acquainted
with the true wishes of the people; and, on the other hand, to convince
the National Assembly of the purity of her democratic inclinations.
During detailed conversations held in the archiepiscopal palace of
Meaux, where the travellers made a prolonged stay, Marie Antoinette
was able by her blandishments to enlist Barnave in her service. Thus
did the Queen achieve what none could have anticipated, a huge political success as the outcome of the flight to Varennes. While, in their
rolling prison, her husband and her sister-in-law could think only of
heat and discomfort and fatigue, she was busily winning a last victory
for the royal cause.

The third day of the return from Varennes was the hottest and most
uncomfortable of all. At length, however, the procession reached the
gates of Paris. Since the crowd that had assembled for a sight of
the recaptured "rulers" must not be disappointed of their spectacle, the
King and the Queen were not allowed to drive straight back to the
Tuileries from the Porte Saint-Denis, but were compelled to make
a detour along the boulevards. Neither acclamations nor abuse greeted

their passing, for bills had been posted announcing that anyone who should shout "Long live the King!" would be an object of public contempt, and at the same time declaring that any who should openly revile the prisoners of the nation would render themselves liable to a flogging. The carriage that followed the royal chariot, however, had something that resembled the "royal progress" of earlier days, being received with the wildest jubilation, for in it sat the man whom the populace had to thank for the triumph it was now enjoying—Drouet the posting-master, the bold huntsman who cunningly and fiercely and tenaciously had tracked the quarry.

The last moment of the return, the short traverse between the chariot and the gates of the palace, was the most dangerous. Since the royal family was safeguarded by the presence of the deputies, and the popular wrath needed a victim, the fury of the multitude vented itself upon the three innocent bodyguards who had helped to "kidnap" the King. They were dragged from the box, and for a second or two it looked as if the Queen would once more have to see bleeding heads brandished on pike-points in front of the entrance to her palace; but the National Guards hastened to the rescue, and, at the point of the bayonet, cleared the mob out of the way and rescued those who were about to be lynched. Then the door of the chariot-oven was opened. The King, dirty, tired, dripping with sweat, was the first to step out. The Queen followed. At once there were dangerous murmurs of hatred directed against the "Austrian woman." Swiftly she tripped after her heavy-footed husband through the gates, the children followed, and the dreadful journey was over. Within, the lackeys were waiting, drawn up in line. The table was set as usual for the evening meal. All the rules of precedence were observed. The travellers who had returned might have fancied their journey had been no more than a dream. In reality, however, these five days had done more to shake the foundations of the monarchy than the previous five years of reforms, for prisoners are no longer crowned rulers. The King had fallen to a much lower plane, and the Revolution had risen much higher.

The tired man did not seem much perturbed about the matter. Indifferent as usual, he was indifferent even to his own fate. In his customary firm handwriting he noted in his diary no more than this: "Left Meaux at half-past six. Reached Paris at eight, without halting on the way." That was all Louis XVI had to say about one of the profoundest humiliations of his life. Pétion confirms the impression of imperturbability in his Report: "The King was as phlegmatic, as calm, as if nothing had happened. . . . One might have believed that he had returned from the hunt."

To a woman as proud as Marie Antoinette, the torment of this futile expedition must, however, have been almost overwhelming. Yet, being wholly woman—and a woman in love—even in Malebolge, with the self-sacrifice of a belated and invincible passion, she could think only of her lover and that he might be unduly anxious about her. Amid the perils that environed her, she was chiefly concerned about his compassionate anxiety. "Let me reassure you; we are still alive," she wrote. "I exist . . . but I have been terribly uneasy about you, and it distresses me to think how much you will suffer if you get no news of us. Will Heaven grant that this letter reaches you? Do not write to me, for that would expose us to needless risks; and, above all, do not return hither on any pretext. It is known that you were mainly instrumental in getting us away, so that all would be lost if you should reappear. We are kept under watch day and night, but I care nothing about that. . . . Do not be troubled in your mind, I shall get on all right. The Assembly wants to treat us gently. Adieu. . . . I shall not be able to write to you again."

She found it impossible, however, to be left at this juncture without a word from Fersen. Next day, therefore, she wrote once more, in ardent and tender phrases, asking for news, appeasement, and love: "I can only tell you that I love you, though really I have not even time for that. I am well. Do not be uneasy about me. I crave so much to know that you, too, are well. Write to me in cipher . . . and get your valet to pen the address. Let me know whither I am to address my own letters, for I cannot live without writing to you. Farewell most loved and most loving of men. All my heart goes out to you."

"I cannot live without writing to you"—never before had the Queen uttered such a cry of passion. But in truth very little of the Queen was left in her, stripped as she had been of her sometime royal power. All that remained to her was her womanly love, of which no one could deprive her. It was this feeling, this passion, which gave her the strength to fight resolutely in defence of her life.

CHAPTER XXX

Reciprocal Deception

THE flight to Varennes opened a new phase in the history of the Revolution, for its outcome was the birth of a republican party. Down till July 21, 1791, the National Assembly had with one accord been royalist, being composed as it was exclusively of noblemen and bourgeois. But now, when fresh elections were at hand, there came treading on the heels of the third estate, of the bourgeoisie, the fourth estate, the proletariat, the elemental mass of the population, of which the bourgeoisie was no less terrified than the King had been terrified of the bourgeoisie. Full of anxiety and with belated concern the possessing classes began to contemplate the daimonic forces they had unchained, and were eager, with all convenient speed, to establish a con-[stitution which would hold the scales between the power of the King and that of the people. Forbearance must be shown towards Louis XVI if his consent to such an arrangement were to be gained, and the moderates, therefore, were able to ensure that the King should not be reproached for the flight to Varennes. By their instrumentality it was bruited abroad that Louis had not quitted Paris of his own will, but had been "kidnapped." When, shortly afterwards, on the Champ de Mars, at a public meeting, the Jacobins brought forward a proposal that the King should be forced to abdicate, Bailly and Lafayette, the leaders of the bourgeoisie, had the multitude dispersed by a charge of cavalry and by musketry fire. The Queen, however, kept under close watch and ward in her own palace, with the National Guard scrutinizing her every movement and not even allowing her to have her doors locked—was not deceived as to the value of such belated attempts at saving some vestiges of the royal power. Instead of the old cries "Long live the King!" there were now frequently heard beneath her windows shouts of "Long live the Republic!" She knew full well that the proposed republic could only be established through the destruction of herself, her husband, and her children.

Moreover, it soon became plain to her that the most disastrous outcome of the Varennes affair was, not so much her own failure to get clear away with Louis, as the fact that her brother-in-law the Count of Provence had made good his escape. Scarcely had the future Louis XVIII arrived safely in Brussels than he openly rejected the subordinate position which had always been uncongenial to him, declaring himself regent of France and legitimate representative of the monarchy so long as King Louis XVI was a prisoner in Paris. Secretly, meanwhile, he did everything in his power to ensure that his brother should be kept in duress. Writing from Brussels, Fersen said: "There has been the most unseemly joy manifested because the King was taken prisoner; the Count of Artois is positively radiant."

Now this precious pair of brothers felt themselves firmly seated in the saddle, they who so long had been compelled to tow in Louis's wake; they could indulge in orgies of sabre-rattling, could incite the other powers of royalist Europe to make war upon a France infected with the virus of republicanism. If, thanks to their machinations, Louis XVI, Marie Antoinette, and (it was to be hoped likewise) the little Dauphin should perish—perhaps after becoming in name Louis XVII—so much the better. At one stride, they would be two stages nearer the throne, and "Monsieur," the Count of Provence, would at length be able to style himself Louis XVIII. Unfortunately for the King, the Queen, and their little boy, the other sovereigns of the western world were only too ready to listen to the younger brothers' promptings. It was of no moment to them, as champions of the monarchical idea, which among the Louis might be seated on the French throne; the essential thing was that the revolutionary poison should be eradicated from Europe, that the "French epidemic" should be stifled in the germ. Gustavus III wrote with cynical coldness: "Although I am greatly interested in the royal family of France, I am still more interested in the public welfare, in the special interests of Sweden, and in the cause of all kings. For these latter reasons it is desirable that the French monarchy should be re-established, no matter whether Louis XVI, Louis XVII, or Charles X should occupy the throne, provided that the monster of the Riding School [the National Assembly] be laid low." Gustavus was merely voicing the opinion, tacit or disclosed, of his brother sovereigns. The maintenance of monarchical authority was their supreme concern, whereas they were indifferent to the fate of the present wearers of the crown in France. This indifference cost Marie Antoinette and Louis XVI their lives.

It was against the twofold danger from within and from without, against republicanism in France and against the bellicose intrigues of her brothers-in-law beyond the frontier, that Marie Antoinette had to fight—a superhuman task, and one utterly beyond the powers of a woman who had been forsaken by her friends. What was needed for success in so titanic an endeavour was a genius combining the qualities of an Odysseus and an Achilles, bold and collected, a new Mirabeau; but only assistants of the second and third grade were available, so to these, in her utmost necessity, the Queen had recourse. On her way back from Varennes, Marie Antoinette had been quick to notice that Barnave's head had been turned by a few flatteries in the mouth of a queen. Knowing that this lawyer from the provinces had considerable influence in the National Assembly, she resolved to take advantage of his weakness.

She wrote to him to the effect that since her return from Varennes she had been thinking much about the keenness of his intelligence, and that she felt she could derive great advantage from a correspondence with him. He could rely upon her discretion, for, where the general interest was at stake, she was always ready to bow to necessities. After this preamble, she became more specific: "Things cannot be left as they are. Something must be done. But what? I do not know. It is to you that I address myself in the hope of finding out. Our discussion must have shown you that I am acting in good faith, and I shall continue to do so. This is the sole advantage left to us, and one of which no one will be able to deprive me. I believe you to be endowed with good intentions. So are we; and, whatever people may say, we have always had them. Let me, then, work hand in hand with you. If you will discover a means of interchanging ideas, I shall reply with frankness as to whatever may be within my power, and shall shrink from no sacrifice where the public welfare is concerned."

Barnave showed this letter to his friends, who were simultaneously delighted and alarmed, and decided, after considering the pros and cons, that henceforward they would hold secret parleyings with the

Queen—since Louis XVI counted for nothing. Their first demand from Marie Antoinette was that she should induce her brothers-in-law to return to France, and should do her utmost to persuade her brother the Emperor to recognize the French constitution. Appearing to comply, the Queen wrote to Leopold in terms suggested by these advisers, making only one reservation—as to her inability to yield in any matter where her honour or her gratitude might be involved. These political tutors believed themselves to have found in Marie Antoinette an attentive and thankful pupil.

The worthy fellows deceived themselves grossly! In reality the Queen had not the slightest intention of being guided by the counsels of these "factieux." Her only object in the negotiations was to gain time until her brother should have summoned the "armed congress" which had long been desired, and which now seemed imminent. Like Penelope tricking the suitors, she destroyed every night the work she had with her new friends' aid done during the previous day. The prescribed letter to Emperor Leopold was secretly countermanded by a dispatch to Mercy: "On the 29th I wrote you a letter, and have no doubt that you will have detected that it was not in my usual style. I thought it expedient to yield to the wishes of the party chiefs here, who drafted the letter for me. Yesterday, the 30th, I wrote in a different sense to the Emperor. This fraud would be a humiliation to me were it not that I have good reason to hope my brother will realize that in my present position I have no choice but to do and to write whatever is demanded. . . . It would be unjust to deny that, although they hold fast to their opinions, I have always found them extremely frank, persons of strong will, and inspired with a genuine desire to restore order through re-establishing the royal authority. . . . Nevertheless, however good their intentions, their notions are extravagant, and we could never find them acceptable." She added that it was essential for the Emperor to be convinced that no word in the letter of the 29th had been an expression of her true opinions or of her way of looking at things.

It was a sinister double game that Marie Antoinette was playing; a dishonourable game, since, for the very reason that she had now begun to meddle with politics, she found it necessary to lie, and to lie boldly.

While unctuously assuring her aides in the Assembly that in her correspondence with them she had no hidden thoughts, had no private ends to gain, she was simultaneously writing to Fersen: "You need have no anxiety! I shall not allow myself to be misled by these 'enragés.' If I have interviews with some of them, or enter into relationships with them in any way, it is only in order to make use of them; and I loathe them too much to make common cause with them, whatever the circumstances." Ultimately she did not fail to realize the iniquity of thus cheating persons who were well disposed towards her and who, in the end, were guillotined for having espoused the royal cause. She saw clearly enough that her conduct was immoral; but unhesitatingly she thrust responsibility for this misbehaviour upon the times, upon circumstances, which had forced her to play so deplorable a part.

"Sometimes," she wrote in great distress of mind to Fersen, "I cannot understand myself, and have to ask myself again and again whether it is really I who am speaking. Still, what am I to do? These things have become necessary, and I assure you that our position would be even worse than it is if I had not been prompt to take such a line. At any rate we can gain time thereby, and time is our first need. You can imagine what a delight it will be to me if the day ever comes when I can be myself once more, and can make it plain to all these rascals [gueux] that I never became their dupe!" Such was the one consolation to her pride, that she could dream of being free at some future day, no longer compelled to play the sordid game of politics, to diplomatize, to lie. Inasmuch as, being a Queen, she believed this unrestricted freedom was hers by divine right, she felt justified in fooling to the top of their bent all those who wished to restrict her God-given privileges.

Nevertheless it was not only the Queen who was cheating, for in this crisis just before the Revolution reached its climax all the partners in the great game were cheating one another. No more conspicuous examples of the amorality of secret policy, of secret diplomacy, can be found than those which are revealed by a study of the interminable correspondence of the sovereign princes, the ambassadors, and the ministers of State during those troublous times. They were all working underground against one another, all mining and countermining, and each of them was seeking to grind an axe of his own. Louis XVI was trying to humbug the National Assembly; which, on its side, was waiting until the republican idea had gained sufficient ground for the deposition of the King to be an easy matter. The constitutionalists dissembled by making Marie Antoinette believe they still possessed a power which had long since slipped from their hands; but she gave as good as she got, inasmuch as she was scandalously deceiving them by treating behind their backs with her brother Leopold. Nor was the latter playing a straight game with his sister, inasmuch as he had made up his mind not to risk a soldier, not to spend a taler, in her behalf—being engaged at the moment in negotiations with Russia and Prussia concerning a second partition of Poland. While Frederick William II, King of Prussia, was discussing with Leopold II the arrangements for an "armed congress" against France, his ambassador in Paris was simultaneously financing the Jacobins and dining with Pétion. The royal émigrés were clamouring for a fight, not in the hope of helping their brother Louis XVI to keep his throne, but in the expectation that war would enable them to mount it sooner. Amid all such paper gymnastics, Gustavus III, the Don Quixote of monarchy, who really cared for none of these things, was gesticulating in the hope of being taken for a new Gustavus Adolphus, the saviour of Europe. The Duke of Brunswick, who was to lead the army of the coalition against France, was in treaty with the Jacobins, who were offering him the throne of that kingdom. Danton and Dumouriez were both playing double. The rulers were no more unanimous than were the revolutionists. Brother betrayed sister, king betrayed people, the National Assembly cheated King Louis, one monarch humbugged another, all were lying against all, unanimous only in respect of one desire, that each wanted to gain time for the pursuit of his private aims. Each of the fishermen expected to hook the biggest fish in the troubled waters, and every one of them was furthering the general sense of insecurity. They played with fire while hoping to escape getting their own fingers burned. Persistently trying to hoodwink one another, the Emperor, the kings, the princes, and the revolutionists created an atmosphere of general distrust (like that which poisons the world today); and, in the end, though they had not directly purposed anything of the kind, they involved five-and-twenty millions of men in the cataract of a war which lasted for five-and-twenty years.

Meanwhile, regardless of these petty tricks, the storms of the epoch continued to rage, for the tempo of the Revolution would not comply with the "temporizing" of the old diplomacy. It was essential to come to a decision. At length the National Assembly finished its draft of a constitution and laid the document before Louis XVI. The King must give an answer. Marie Antoinette knew that this "monstrueuse" constitution, as she called it in a letter to Catherine of Russia, denoted "a moral death infinitely worse than bodily death, which frees us from our troubles." She knew, likewise, that in Coblenz and at the courts King Louis's acceptance of the constitution would be regarded as a deliberate sacrifice of his own cause, and would perhaps be stigmatized as the outcome of personal cowardice; but so low, by now, had the royal power sunk that even she, for all her pride, advised bowing before the storm.

"Our journey two months ago proves, even more than there was need, that we do not hesitate to risk our persons when the general welfare is in question. In view of the position here, however, it is impossible for the King to refuse his consent. You must believe in the truth of what I say, since it is I who say it to you. You know my character well enough to believe that it would incline me rather to noble and courageous action. Still, what good can there be in exposing oneself to certain and needless peril?" Yet when the pen was already prepared for the signing of the capitulation, Marie Antoinette told Mercy that in his innermost heart King Louis (one deceiving another and being himself deceived) had no thought of keeping his pledge to the people. "As regards the acceptance of the constitution, it is impossible that any thinking person can fail to see that, whatever we may do, we are not free. But it is essential that we should give the monsters who surround us no cause for suspicion. However things turn out, only the foreign powers can save us. We have lost the army; we have no more money; there exists within this realm no power to restrain the armed populace. The very chiefs of the Revolution are no longer listened to when they try to talk about order. Such is the deplorable position in which we find ourselves. Add to this that we have not a single friend, that all the world is betraying us: some because of hatred, and others because of weakness or ambition. I myself am reduced to such a pitch that I have come to dread the day when we shall be given a semblance of freedom. At least, in view of the impotence to which we have been condemned, we have no reason to reproach ourselves." Then, with remarkable sincerity, she goes on: "You will find my whole soul in this letter. Perhaps I am wrong, but that seems to me the only means of keeping things going. I have done my best to hear what persons belonging to both sides have to say, and I have formed my own opinion by studying theirs. I cannot tell whether my advice will be followed. You know the person with whom I have to deal. When one believes him persuaded into accepting any course, a single word, a trifling argument, may make him change his mind and his purpose without warning. That is why a thousand things I should like to do can never be undertaken. To conclude, whatever happens, continue to give me your friendship and your affection. I need them; and I ask you to believe that, into whatever misfortunes I may be plunged, though I may yield to circumstances, I shall never consent to do anything unworthy of me.

"Tribulation first makes one realize what one is. My blood courses through my son's veins, and I hope that a day will come when he will show himself worthy of being the grandson of Maria Theresa."

These are great and touching words, but they do not succeed in hiding the sense of shame from which an essentially straightforward woman was suffering because crooked courses had been forced upon her. In the bottom of her heart she knew that such dishonourable behaviour was less worthy of her royal position than would have been a voluntary renunciation of the throne. She had no choice, however. "It would have been nobler to refuse," she wrote to Fersen; "but refusal was impossible in the circumstances. I should have preferred the acceptance of the constitution to be more simply worded and briefer, but it is our misfortune to be surrounded exclusively by scoundrels. Let me assure you once more that the scheme which has been adopted is the least undesirable of several. Besides, the follies of the princes and of the émigrés have forced our hand; and, in accepting, it was necessary to leave no doubt that the acceptance was made in good faith."

By this dishonest and consequently impolitic pseudo-acceptance of the constitution, the royal family won breathing-space. That was the sole (and, as we shall soon see) the cruel reward of its duplicity. The mutual deceivers drew a breath of relief, each feigning to believe the other's lies. For a fleeting moment, the storm-clouds were scattered. Once more, though illusively, the sun of popular favour shone upon the Bourbons. As soon as, on September 13, 1791, the King had announced that next day, in the presence of the National Assembly, he would solemnly pledge himself to observe the constitution, the National Guards who had been watching the Tuileries were withdrawn, and the gardens of the palace were thrown open to the public. The imprisonment was over, and (so most people were only too ready to believe), the Revolution likewise. For the first time after weeks and months, and also for the last time of all, Marie Antoinette heard enthusiastic shouts of "Long live the King! Long live the Queen!"

Months before this, however, many, both ostensible friends and declared enemies, on the hither side and the farther side of the frontier, had sworn that their vital thread should soon be cut.

CHAPTER XXXI

The Friend's Last Appearance

THE most tragical hours in the declining years of Marie Antoinette's short life were not those when storms were manifestly raging, but the deceptive interludes of fine weather. Had the Revolution come like a landslide, had it crushed the monarchy with the overwhelming and sudden violence of an avalanche, giving no time for reflection, hope, or resistance, it would have been less painful to the Queen than the agony long drawn out which she actually had to suffer. Again and again, between the hurricanes of events there were periods of calm. Five times, ten times perhaps, the royal family had good reason to believe that peace had at length been re-established, that the fight had been fought to a stable conclusion. The Revolution, however, is like the rising tide. After each wave there is a reflux, in which the force of the onslaught seems exhausted, but the decline is followed by another and yet another and more destructive advance. Those who are threatened by the flood can never know whether the last wave has been the strongest, the most decisive.

After the acceptance of the constitution the crisis seemed to be over and done with. Revolution had become the law of the land, unrest had been, so to say, crystallized! Came a few days, a few weeks, of illusory wellbeing, a period of fallacious euphoria. There were cheers when the King and the Queen were seen in the streets, shouts of jubilation when they appeared at the theatre. Marie Antoinette, however, had long since lost the simple credulity of youth. Returning to the Tuileries from a drive through the illuminated town, she said with a sigh to Madame de Tourzel: "How sad it is that a sight so beautiful should give rise only to feelings of melancholy and disquiet!" Having been too often disillusioned, she would no longer tolerate the veil of illusion. Writing to Fersen she said: "Things are perfectly quiet for the moment, to all seeming, but this tranquillity hangs by a thread. The people is just what it has ever been, ready to commit atrocities. We are told that it is on our side, but I have no faith in the assurance, at any rate as far as I personally am concerned. I know how much such assurances are worth! Speaking generally, one has to pay for popular favour, and the crowd only loves us while we yield to its whims. Things cannot go on much longer like this. There is no more safety in Paris than there was before, and perhaps even less, since people are getting accustomed to see us humiliated." In fact the newly elected National Assembly was a great disappointment. The Queen regarded it as "a thousand times worse than the other." One of its first decisions was that the King should no longer be spoken of as "His Majesty." Within a few weeks, the leadership had passed into the hands of the Girondists, who outspokenly favoured the establishment of a republic; and the rainbow, the sacred symbol of reconciliation, was speedily hidden by new storm-clouds. The struggle was renewed.

It was not, however, merely to the progress of the revolutionary movement that the rapid deterioration in the position of the King and the Queen had to be ascribed. The conduct of their own relatives was mainly at fault. The Count of Provence and the Count of Artois had established their headquarters at Coblenz, and from this safe retreat they waged war against the Tuileries. It suited their purpose marvellously that the King, under constraint, had accepted the constitution, since this gave a specious justification to the reiterated assertions of journalists in their pay that Marie Antoinette and Louis XVI were cowards who had sought safety by abandoning the cause of the monarchy, and that they themselves were the true defenders of that sublime institution. Little did they care that they were staking their brother's life by the game they were playing. Vainly did Louis XVI implore, nay command, them to return to Paris, and thus to dispel the justified suspicions of the people. The legacy-hunters spitefully declared that such utterances as this could not be the expression of the true will of the captive King. At Coblenz, being well away from the fighting front, they could assume the heroic role without any risk to their own precious skins.

Marie Antoinette was infuriated by the pusillanimity of the émigrés, "contemptible men who proclaim their attachment to us and who only do us harm. . . . It is their conduct which has brought us into the position wherein we now find ourselves. .... Well, what can you expect? In order to escape having to do what we wish, they continue to proclaim that we are not free agents (which is true enough); that, consequently, it is impossible for us to say what we really think; and that they are therefore compelled to do the precise opposite of what we ask." Vainly, through Mercy's instrumentality, did she beg her brother the Emperor to keep within bounds her brothers-in-law and the other émigrés. The Count of Provence outstripped her messengers, to represent that all the Queen's commands were issued "under constraint," and everywhere the bellicose royalists took the same view. Gustavus III returned unopened the letter in which Louis XVI announced his acceptance of the constitution; and Catherine of Russia showed even more contempt for Marie Antoinette by writing that it was a pity to have no better hopes than for a wreath of roses. In Vienna the Count of Provence let weeks elapse before he sent his brother a confused reply to the effect that the powers were waiting until circumstances should take a turn which might enable them to derive some advantage from the anarchical situation in France. No one offered effective help. No one honestly tried to discover what the captives in the Tuileries really wanted. The two French princes, the other émigrés, all the "royalists" of Europe, continued to play a double game—at the cost of the unhappy King and Queen of France.

What were Marie Antoinette's true wishes and designs? The French revolutionary leaders (being ever ready, like political partisans in general, to ascribe deep-laid schemes to their adversaries) believed that the Queen, that the "comité autrichien" in the Tuileries, was organizing a crusade against the French people, and many historians of later days have shared this view. In actual fact Marie Antoinette, who had entered the paths of diplomacy only because of the promptings of despair, never had a clear idea or a consistent plan. With admirable self-sacrifice, with a diligence which in her case was astounding, she sent letter after letter in all directions; she composed and revised memorandum after memorandum; she negotiated and advised: but the more she wrote, and the more of her writings at this period we read, the less plain does it become what political notions she cherished. She had some vague scheme for an armed congress of the powers, a half-measure, neither hot nor cold but laodicean, which must avoid trying to intimidate the revolutionists by threats and must be equally careful to do nothing which could affront French national sentiment. As to the how and the when of this congress, her mind was hazy. She did not think logically. Her violent movements, her abrupt cries of alarm, recall those of a drowning man whose struggles serve to plunge him deeper into the water. She would insist that the only course open was an attempt to win the confidence of the people; and in the same breath, in the very same letter, she would write: "There is no longer the faintest possibility of reconciliation." She declared herself opposed to war, foreseeing clearly enough what would ensue: "On the one hand we should have no choice but to take up arms against the foreign invaders; and, on the other, we should be suspected of bad faith and of being in league with them." Yet soon she wrote that "nothing but armed force can set things right again"; and, "without foreign aid we shall be able to do nothing." She tried "to induce the Emperor to feel that insult and injury are being done him. Let him show himself at the head of the other powers with an imposing force, and I can assure you that the revolutionists here will shake in their shoes. There is no reason for being anxious as to our safety; it is this country which is inciting to war." A few days later, the opposite view was urged, and she wanted to arrest the movement against the republicans: "An attack from without would put our heads under the knife." In the end it was impossible for those with whom she was corresponding to gain a consistent idea of her wishes. The chancelleries, which were far from being inclined to lavish funds upon the holding of an "armed congress," and which, if they sent armies to the frontiers would only do so in order to wage war with the prospect of annexations and indemnities, derided the notion that they should mobilize merely "for the sake of the King of France."

"What," wrote Catherine of Russia, "are we to think of persons who are continually championing two conflicting outlooks?" Even Fersen, the staunchest of the staunch, the man who might really have been supposed to know Marie Antoinette's intimate thoughts, was unable to ascertain what the Queen hoped for, war or peace; whether she had reconciled herself to the constitution or was trying to trick the constitutionalists with vain hopes; whether she was cheating the Revolution or the rulers of Europe. All that the poor, tortured woman really wanted was to live, to live, to live, and to escape humiliation. Inwardly she suffered more than anyone suspected, for duplicity was intolerable to her straightforward disposition. Again and again her loathing of the part she was forced to play found expression in a cry of anguish. For instance, writing to Mercy, she said:

"I do not know what attitude to adopt or what tone to assume. Everyone accuses me of dissimulation, of falsehood; and (naturally enough) no one can believe that my brother can take so little interest as he does in his sister's terrible position, so that he is perpetually exposing her to danger without saying a word to her about the matter. Yes, he exposes me to danger, and a thousandfold more than he would if he were to take effective action. Hatred, mistrust, and insolence are the three motive forces at work in this country. People are insolent because they are in such a dreadful fright, and because, at the same time, they do not believe that an attack will be made on them from across the frontier. Nothing could be worse than for us to stay as we are, since we can no longer expect any help from time or from within the country."

There was only one person who realized that these movements now in one direction and now in another, all these orders and counter-orders, were but signs of hopeless perplexity, and that Marie Antoinette could not possibly save herself unaided. He knew that she had no one standing shoulder to shoulder with her, for Louis XVI was too irresolute to count. Even her sister-in-law, Madame Elisabeth, was far from being the ideally faithful, the God-given companion of royalist legend. "My sister is so indiscreet, surrounded by schemers, and (above all) held in leading-strings by her brothers across the frontier, that we find it impossible to converse with one another except at the risk of quarrelling from morning until night." Again, more explicit and terser, comes a cry from the soul: "Our family life is a hell —can only be thus described, with the best intentions in the world!"

More and more evident did it become to Fersen, now far away, that no one could help her but a person who possessed her full confidence; not, therefore, her husband, nor her brother, nor yet any of her relatives by blood or by marriage, but only himself. A few weeks before, she had conveyed a message to him through the instrumentality of Count Esterhazy, assuring him of her inviolable love: "If you write to him, tell him that neither many leagues nor many countries separate our hearts. I become more strongly assured of this truth day by day." Again: "I do not know where he is. It is a torment to have no news of those whom one loves, and not to know where they are living." These last words of ardent affection were accompanied by a gift, a gold ring on which were graven three lilies with the inscription: "Faint-heart he who forsakes her." This ring, explained Marie Antoinette to Esterhazy, had been made to fit one of her own fingers, and had been worn by her for two days before she sent it, so that the chill gold might bear with it the warmth of her own blood. Fersen wore his mistress's ring on his little finger, and the inscription "Faint-heart he who forsakes her" made its daily appeal to his conscience, urging him to hazard all for the woman he loved. Indeed, so profound was the despair now breathed to him in her letters, that he felt impelled to perform heroic deeds in her behalf; and he resolved, since he could not keep closely in touch by correspondence, to seek out the Queen in Paris, in that city where he had been placed under a ban, and where, if he were discovered, he would unquestionably be put to death.

Fersen's announcement of this intention terrified Marie Antoinette. It was impossible, she said, for her to accept so heroic a sacrifice. Since she was truly in love with him, she loved his life more than her own, and more even than the unspeakable comfort and happiness his proximity would have given her. She therefore wrote to him under date December 7, 1791: "It is absolutely out of the question that you should come here at this juncture; your coming would risk our happiness. You can believe that I feel this strongly, since I have so great a longing to see you!" But Fersen would take no denial, replying: "It is essential to extricate you from the present position of affairs." In collaboration with the King of Sweden, he had elaborated a new plan of escape. Despite her protest, his lover's clairvoyance showed him how much she craved for his coming, and what an intense relief it would be to her lonely spirit to be able to converse with him freely and unrestrainedly after the caution and secrecy of their correspondence. In the beginning of February 1792, therefore, Fersen made up his mind that he would wait no longer, but would return to France in order to see Marie Antoinette.

The resolve was almost suicidal. The chances seemed a hundred to one against his ever being able to get away unscathed, since in France at this juncture the revolutionists lusted for his blood. There was a warrant out for his apprehension; he had been declared an outlaw; should anyone recognize him his shrift would be short. Yet Fersen had determined that, instead of looking for some secure hiding-place in the purlieus of Paris, he would make his way to the very heart of danger, to the Tuileries, watched day and night by twelve hundred National Guards, to the palace where every groom, every footman, every waiting-maid, every coachman, among the multitude of servants knew him personally. It seemed to him that now or never was his opportunity of showing his devotion to his beloved. "I live only to serve you," he wrote to her on February 11th, just before starting on one of the boldest journeys, just before beginning one of the most fool-hardy enterprises, in the history of the Revolution.

Wearing a wig, provided with a false passport at the foot of which he had forged the signature of the King of Sweden, he set forth ostensibly as part of a diplomatic mission to Lisbon—representing himself to be the servant of his own orderly, who was his sole companion. As luck would have it, neither his person nor his papers were closely scrutinized, and on February 13th he reached Paris safely at half past five in the evening. Although he had in the city a lady-friend who was prepared to offer him harbourage at whatever peril to herself, Fersen, on quitting the post-chaise, made direct for the Tuileries. Since night had fallen, darkness favoured him. By an extraordinary piece of good luck, the private entrance, of which he had a key, was un-guarded. He effected his entry unobserved. After eight months of cruel severance, eight months during which the world had changed, Fersen and Marie Antoinette were together for the last time.

There have come down to us in Fersen's handwriting two accounts of this memorable visit, one an official report and the other a memo-randum intended for private use. The reader can detect notable dif-ferences between the two, and the fact confirms the opinion we have previously formed as to the intimate nature of the relationships between this Swedish junker and the Queen of France. In the official report he informs the King of Sweden of the day and hour of his arrival in Paris, and goes on to say that he saw Their Majesties (note the plural!) that same evening, and again on the next evening. Fersen knew his royal master to be a gossip, and had therefore worded his missive in a way which would safeguard the Queen's honour. In his private journal, however, he wrote: "Went to see her; made very anxious because of the National Guards; she is comfortably installed." Note that he writes "her" and not "them." Thereafter in the diary follow two words which have been written over with pen-and-ink coils by the prudish hand of the successor who tampered with the diary, and who designed to make them unreadable. Fortunately, however, it has been possible to decipher them. They are "resté là"—stayed there. The late-revealed conclusion of the sentence, brief and clear, makes evident to posterity what happened on that Tristan night. Fersen was not received by "Their Majesties" as he reported to the King of Sweden, but by Marie Antoinette alone, in her private apartments. It would have needlessly multiplied the danger to visit and to leave King Louis's rooms that same night, since the corridors were patrolled by the National Guards. But Marie Antoinette's private quarters were on the ground floor, and they consisted only of a bedroom and a small dressing-room. What other inference, then, is possible, than that which is so distressing to the purity-fanatics, namely that Fersen spent the night of February 13th and the whole of the next day until midnight hidden in the Queen's bedroom, the only place in the palace where he was safe from discovery by the National Guards and from the prying eyes of the servants?

Concerning the hours in which he and his mistress were alone together, Fersen, who had a fine capacity for silence, said no word even in his private journal. Anyone who chooses to do so is, therefore, at liberty to believe that this night was exclusively devoted to platonically chivalrous service and to political conversation. But those who have known the spell of ardent passion, those whose observations of themselves and others have convinced them that hot blood will run its course, can hardly doubt that, even if Fersen had not already long ere this become Marie Antoinette's lover, he must have become her lover on so fateful a night, a night which when once gone would be lost beyond recall, a night on which he had shown such splendid courage.

The first night and the next day belonged to the lovers; and, so far as we know, it was not until evening came that politics had their turn. Then, at six o'clock on February 14th, exactly twenty-four hours after Fersen's arrival, the discreet husband came to his wife's room in order to hold converse with the bold envoy. The upshot of their talk was that Louis XVI rejected the proposal to attempt escape once more, and this for two reasons: first, because the King held the practical difficulties in the way of flight to be insuperable; and, secondly, because he had pledged his word to the National Assembly to stay in Paris. In this connexion, Fersen respectfully notes in his diary: "Louis is, in truth, a man of honour."

Talking as man to man, having full confidence in Fersen, the King expounded his view of the situation as follows: "We can talk plainly to one another, since there is no interloper present. I know that people charge me with weakness and irresolution; but who has ever found himself in so difficult a position? I missed my chance of escape on the fourteenth of July, and have never had so good an opportunity since. The whole world has left me in the lurch."

The Queen had no more hope than the King that they would be able to save themselves. The best thing would be for the powers to do all that was possible, regardless of what might happen to the captives in the Tuileries. Nor ought they to be surprised if, being held prisoner, Louis were to give his assent to many things that might seem undesirable. He and Marie Antoinette were in a position which compelled them to do much that went against the grain. They might thus be enabled to gain time, but as for rescue, it could only come from outside.

Midnight struck. Every possibility had been discussed. Now came the hardest task of these thirty hours, the farewell. Fersen and his beloved tried to persuade themselves that it was not a last farewell, but in their secret hearts they foreboded the inevitable. Never again would they meet in this life! Trying to reassure his mistress, the lover promised to come again if it should prove possible to do so, and his sorrow at parting was tinged by happiness through the knowledge that his visit had been a comfort to her. The Queen accompanied Fersen to the door, which again, by good fortune, was unwatched. But the last good-byes were still unsaid, the last embraces had not yet been exchanged, when the measured tread of an approaching sentry was heard. There was no choice left; they had to wrench themselves away from one another. Fersen slipped out into the night, and Marie Antoinette fled back to her room. The lovers had seen one another for the last time.

CHAPTER XXXII

Flight into War

WHEN States and governments find that home conditions are critical and are tending to pass out of control, they are wont, following a traditional recipe, to seek relief from tension in some foreign imbroglio. For months the spokesmen of the revolution in France, hoping to escape an almost inevitable civil war, had been clamouring for war against Austria. Although, by accepting the constitution, Louis XVI had lowered his kingly status, he had for the time being safeguarded the monarchy. Simple-minded persons like Lafayette believed that the Revolution had reached its term. The Girondists, however, who were dominant in the newly elected Assembly, were at heart republican. They wanted to do away with the monarchy, and it seemed to them that a war would be the best method of bringing that about, for it could not fail to entangle the royal family in a conflict with the nation. The Count of Provence and the Count of Artois were in the vanguard of the proposed coalition against revolutionary France, and had the support of the foreign general staffs.

Marie Antoinette was well aware that a declaration of war could only do harm to her cause. Whatever its upshot, it would be disastrous to herself and her husband. If the revolutionary armies got the better of the émigrés and the Emperor and the King, it was certain that France would no longer tolerate a "tyrant" within its borders. If, on the other hand, the national troops were defeated by the King's and the Queen's relatives, beyond question the Paris mob (on its own initiative, or under due incitement) would regard the prisoners in the Tuileries as responsible. If France were victorious, they would lose the throne; if the foreign powers were victorious, they would lose their lives. Guided by these considerations, in letter after letter Marie Antoinette implored her brother Leopold and the émigrés to keep their activities within bounds; and the Emperor, cautious, hesitant, cold-blooded, and temperamentally opposed to war, did in fact discountenance the fire-breathing princes and refugees and scrupulously avoided anything that could be regarded as challenging behaviour.

Alas, Marie Antoinette's star was setting. Henceforward fate had nothing but misfortunes awaiting her. On March 1, 1792, Leopold, the pacific-minded, died after a brief illness; and a fortnight later a conspirator's pistol made an end of Gustavus III, the most ardent and the ablest champion of royalism among the monarchs of Europe. His death made war inevitable. His son and successor, Gustavus IV, only fourteen years of age, was not to be counted upon as a prop to the monarchical cause. As for the new emperor, Francis, the son of Leopold II, he had no concern for the fate of his royal relatives in France, and thought only of his own interests. He was rather dull-witted, hard of heart, this man of twenty-four, with no trace of Maria Theresa's genius. From her nephew, Marie Antoinette could expect neither understanding nor will to understand. He gave her messengers a chill reception, and was indifferent to her letters, caring not a jot that the position of affairs in France and throughout Europe involved her in a most distressing spiritual conflict, or that her life was endangered by his policy. All that he could see was a fine chance of enlarging his own power, and he therefore contemptuously rejected the demands of the National Assembly.

This suited the Girondists' book, and gave them the upper hand. On April 20, 1792, after long resistance (and, we are told, with tears in his eyes), Louis XVI was compelled to declare war upon the "King of Hungary." The armies were set in motion, and destiny took its course.

To which side did the Queen's heart turn in this war? Towards the land of her birth or the land of her adoption? Did she wish success to the French or to the foreign armies? Royalist writers, her unstinted defenders and eager to extol her every action, have gone so far as to falsify or interpolate passage after passage in memoirs and letters in the hope of concealing the obvious fact that she whole-heartedly desired the triumph of the foreign allies and the defeat of the French troops. Her attitude was unmistakable, and one who tries to conceal it is misrepresenting her. Whoever denies it, lies. Nay more, Marie Antoinette, whose primary feeling was that she was Queen, whereas only to a secondary degree did she regard herself as Queen of France, was not opposed only to those who had restricted her royal power, nor a supporter only of those who wished to strengthen her dynastic position—for she was active in the endeavour to do all in her power, legitimate or illegitimate, to hasten the defeat of France and to favour the victory of the allies. "God grant that vengeance will at length be taken for the provocations we have received from this country," she wrote to Fersen; and although she had long since forgotten her mother-tongue, and had to have letters penned in it translated to her, she added: "Never have I been more proud than at this moment to have been born a German."

A few days before war was declared, she acquainted the Austrian ambassador with the revolutionists' plan of campaign, insofar as it was known to her. To use plain terms, she betrayed it. There was not the slightest ambiguity about her position. For Marie Antoinette the Austrian and the Prussian flags were those of her friends, and the tricolour was the banner of her enemies. Beyond question most readers will say that this was flat treason, and that there is no modern land in which the law-courts would fail to condemn it as a crime. Still, it must not be forgotten that a century and a half ago the concepts of "national" and "nation," as we understand them today, could hardly be said to have come into existence; and it was not until the revolution we are now considering that they began to become generalized for Europe. Whatever may be said for the view that the Treaty of Westphalia (1648) signalized "the birth of the nations," the fact remains that the eighteenth century, to whose outlooks those of Marie Antoinette inseparably belonged, did not recognize until its last decade any other than the purely dynastic standpoint. A country belonged to its king; where the king stood, there stood the law; he who fought on behalf of the king and the monarchy was fighting for the just cause. He, on the other hand, who opposed the monarchy was a rebel, even though he were defending his own country.

The undeveloped condition of patriotism was strikingly shown in this particular war by the fact that many of the ablest and best among the Germans of that day—Klopstock, Schiller, Fichte, and Hölderlin, for instance—being enthusiasts for liberty, actually hoped for the defeat of the German troops, which were not popular armies, but armies of professional soldiers fighting on behalf of despotism. They rejoiced at the retreat of the Prussian forces, whereas in France the King and the Queen acclaimed the defeat of their own French troops as a personal advantage. On both sides of the fighting front the war was waged, not in the interests of this country or of that, but to further a spiritual idea, that of sovereignty or that of freedom. The disparity of outlook as between that time and our own cannot be better instanced than by the fact that the Duke of Brunswick, a month before he became commander-in-chief of the united German forces, had been seriously considering whether he would not prefer to lead the French troops against the Germans. We see, then, that, in 1792, the notions of fatherland and nation had not yet become clarified for the men and women of the eighteenth century. It was the war of the allied monarchs against the French republicans which brought into being popular armies, a national consciousness in this State and in that, with the result that there was a terrible struggle of nation against nation. The upshot was the birth of the idea of national patriotism which was handed down to become dominant throughout the nineteenth century.

The Parisians had no proof that Marie Antoinette longed for a victory of the foreign powers, no proof of her treasonable views and practices. But even though the masses never think logically or purposively, they have a more elemental, more animal-like flair than has any individual. They work with instinct instead of with reasoned considerations, and their instincts are almost infallible. From the outset the French people sensed the atmosphere of hostility in the Tuileries. Although it had no producible evidence, it was intuitively aware that Marie Antoinette had betrayed its army and its cause. No more than a hundred paces away from the royal headquarters, Vergniaud, one of the Girondists, was outspoken in his declamation to the National Assembly: "From this tribune whence I speak, I can see the dwelling-place in which false counsellors lead astray and deceive the King who has given us the constitution, forge the fetters with which they wish to chain us, and prepare the manœuvres that are designed to hand us over to the House of Austria. I see the windows of the palace where they are hatching counter-revolutions, and where they are contriving ways and means of thrusting us back into the horrors of slavery." In order to point out Marie Antoinette as the central mover in the conspiracies he thus denounced, he added threateningly: "Let those who dwell in the aforesaid palace realize that our constitution guarantees inviolability to the King alone. Let them know that our laws will run there without distinction among the guilty, and that there is not any head proved to be criminal which can hope to escape passing beneath the axe."

The revolutionists were beginning to understand that they could only get the better of their foes abroad by settling accounts with their enemies at home. If they were to win the great game they were playing against the world, the influence of their own King must be checkmated. Energetically, therefore, those who were heart and soul for the Revolution drummed to the assault. Once more the newspapers led the way, demanding the deposition of Louis. New editions of the notorious publication *La vie scandaleuse de Marie Antoinette* were sold in the streets to vivify the old hatred with fresh energy. In the Assembly, extremist proposals were brought forward, with the deliberate hope that the King would feel impelled to make use of his constitutional right of veto; the most notable of these schemes being one to which Louis XVI, as a devout Catholic, could never agree, namely that priests who refused to swear loyalty to the constitution should be expelled from the country. To speak plainly, a breach was provoked. In actual fact, the King asserted himself for the first time, and vetoed the measure. While still strong, he had made no use of his rights, his privileges, and his powers. Now, when his destruction was imminent, the unhappy man chose the most ill-omened of hours in which to display his vigour. The people, however, was no longer in a mood to tolerate the activities or objections of this puppet. The veto was to be the King's last word against and to his people.

In order to read the King, and above all in order to read the arrogant Austrian woman, his wife, a convincing lesson, the Jacobins, the shock-troops of the Revolution, fixed upon a symbolical day, the twentieth of June. This same day three years earlier, in the tennis court at Versailles, the representatives of the third estate had solemnly sworn that they would not yield to force, and that they would, with their own unaided powers, establish a new order in France. On June 20, 1791, the King, disguised as a lackey, had slunk out of the postern of his own palace hoping to escape from the dictatorship of the people. Now, when the anniversary of the "Serment du jeu de paume" had come round once more, he was to be reminded that he counted for nothing and the people for everything. As in October 1789 the storming of Versailles had been sedulously prepared, so now in June 1792 was the storming of the Tuileries. In 1789, however, the levying of the army of amazons had been an underground and illegal affair, carried out behind the veil of darkness. Today it was in the broad sunlight, to the sound of the tocsin, that five thousand men assembled under the command of Santerre, the brewer. The town council was in attendance, with banners flying. The National Assembly opened its doors to the levies, and Pétion, mayor of Paris, who was responsible for order in the capital, placed himself at the disposal of those who were determined to humiliate King Louis.

The march of the revolutionary columns began as a mere festival performance in front of the hall of the National Assembly. The five thousand carried huge placards bearing legends of "Down with the veto!" and "Liberty or death!" In time with the strains of the "Ça ira" they paraded along the front of the Manège. At half past three, this phase of the spectacle was over. But now came the real demonstration. For, instead of going peaceably to their homes, the huge crowd that had gathered, together with the five thousand organized demonstrators, made for the entrance to the Tuileries, doing so without express command from anyone, but thanks to the promptings of unseen leaders. The palace front was lined with National Guards, who stood there with fixed bayonets; but the court, with its customary indecision, had given no orders as to how an obviously probable invasion was to be dealt with. The soldiers offered no resistance, and the masses pushed in a steady stream through the narrow gateway. The invaders speedily made their way into the palace and up to the first story. Now there was no holding them. The doors were forced, and before anything could be done to safeguard the King the foremost were in his presence, separated only by a small body of National Guards. Now within his own dwelling Louis XVI had to take orders from his rebellious "subjects," and nothing but his imperturbable phlegm, his masterly equanimity, prevented a collision. Patiently, courteously, he complied with the most outrageous demands, obediently donning the red Phrygian cap which one of the sansculottes snatched from his own head. For three and a half hours, amid the blazing heat, without attempting to resist, he gratified the curiosity and the scorn of these hostile guests.

Simultaneously another troop of the insurgents had stormed the Queen's apartment, and it seemed not unlikely that the scenes of October 5, 1789, at Versailles, would be repeated in Paris. Since, however, the Queen was known to be in much greater danger than the King, the officers on guard had speedily summoned a number of their men, had pushed Marie Antoinette into a corner of the room, and had drawn a large table in front of her; and the National Guards were then stationed in three ranks on the other side of the table. The furious men and the still more furious women of the mob could not get at her to do her bodily mischief, but they were close enough to contemplate the "monstre" as a loathsome spectacle, close enough for the Queen to hear every syllable of their invectives and their threats. Santerre, whose only purpose was to humiliate Marie Antoinette, and to give her a thorough fright (while avoiding violence), ordered the grenadiers to draw to either side, so that the populace could have its will in the way of securing an unrestricted view of its victim. At the same time, he did his best to tranquillize the Queen, saying: "You have been misled. The people wishes you no harm. If you liked, there would not be one of them who did not love you as sincerely as you love that little boy" (pointing to the Dauphin who trembled as he pressed close to his mother). "Besides, you need not be afraid, for no one will do you any harm." But, as invariably happened when one of the "factieux" offered assistance to the Queen, she hardened her heart and stiffened her pride. "I have not been misled, I have not been deceived, and I am not afraid," she answered fiercely. "There is no occasion for fear, why should anyone be afraid who is among decent folk?" Coldly, impassively, she endured the hostile glances and the rude utterances. Not until they tried to make her put the "cap of liberty" upon her little boy's head, did she revolt, saying to the officers: "This is too much, and passes the limit of human patience." That was her only outburst. Otherwise, not for a moment did she betray alarm, not for an instant did she lose composure. After a long time, when the invaders had ceased to be really threatening in their demeanour, Pétion arrived on the scene and requested the crowd to disperse—"lest occasion should be given to doubt the worthiness of your intentions." The palace, however, was not evacuated by the "enemy" until the evening was far advanced; and when the need for putting a brave front on the matter had passed away, the Queen, the humiliated woman, at length realized the torment of her defenceless-ness. She knew that all was lost. "I am still alive, though by a miracle. The twentieth was a terrible ordeal," she wrote to Fersen. "However, do not be too anxious about me. Have faith in my courage."

CHAPTER XXXIII

Last Cries

WHEN hatred had breathed its venom into her very face, when she had seen the pikemen of the Revolution brandishing their weapons in her private room, when she had learned the impotence of the National Assembly and the enmity of the mayor and the town councillors of Paris, Marie Antoinette knew that her fate and that of her family were sealed unless help came speedily from without. Nothing but a prompt and overwhelming victory of the Prussians and Austrians could save their lives. True, in this last hour a possibility of escape opened. Old friends and unexpected new ones counselled flight and were ready to assist. General Lafayette was prepared, on the fourteenth of July when there were to be anniversary celebrations in the Champ de Mars, to head a detachment of cavalry, surround the members of the royal family, and conduct them safely out of the town. But Marie Antoinette, who still regarded Lafayette as one of the prime originators of disaster, would rather perish than entrust her children, her husband, and herself to this unduly sanguine rescuer.

For nobler reasons she rejected another proposal, that of the Landgravine of Hesse-Darmstadt, who planned to get her away from the palace—alone, since it was she who ran the greatest risk by staying on in the capital. "No, Princess," she replied. "Though I am most grateful to you for your offers, I cannot accept them. The rest of my life will be consecrated to my duties, and to those dear ones whose misfortunes I share, and who, whatever people may say, deserve every credit for the courage with which they are trying to maintain their position. . . . My only hope, the only one I allow myself to cherish, is that a day may come when what we are now doing and suffering will redound to the happiness of our children. Farewell, Princess. They have deprived me of my all, excepting only my heart, which (do not doubt it) will continue to be filled with affection for you. The sole disaster I should find it impossible to bear would be that you should fail to believe me in this respect."

The foregoing was one of the first letters which Marie Antoinette wrote with an eye to the judgment of posterity. At bottom she was fully assured that the advance of the Revolution could not be stayed, and her one remaining wish, therefore, was to keep her head high, to maintain a confident bearing to the last. Perhaps she already had an unconscious longing for a speedy and heroic death, instead of the tedious agony of sinking into a quicksand. On the fourteenth of July, when for the last time she attended the popular festival in the Champ de Mars to commemorate the storming of the Bastille, she refused to wear a coat of mail beneath her dress, whereas the cautious Louis had adopted this precaution. At night she continued to sleep unguarded, although once, at least, a suspicious figure had appeared in her bed-chamber. She had ceased, now, to go out walking in the gardens of the palace, for even this limited exercise was impossible without her hearing the strains of the popular song:

> Madame Véto avait promis
> De faire égorger tout Paris.

She slept alone, I said; but, as a matter of fact, she now slept little. Whenever a church clock struck, a shudder ran through the palace, for it might well be the first note of the tocsin that would sound for the long-since planned assault upon the Tuileries. Kept informed by its spies as to what was going on in the clubs, the secret societies, and the faubourgs, the court knew full well that it was likely to be a question of no more than a few days until the Jacobins would have recourse to the strong hand. Indeed, the reports of these spies did but betray an open secret. More and more vociferously, more and more rancorously, were the journals of Marat and Hébert clamouring for the King's deposition.

The horror of the last days of dread expectation is reflected in the Queen's letters to Fersen. Cries they may be termed rather than letters, passionate cries of alarm, shrill and almost inarticulate like those of a hunted beast. It was hard enough, now, to smuggle any communications out of the Tuileries, for the servants in the palace were no longer to be trusted, while every window and every door was watched by the revolutionists. Hidden in boxes of chocolate, rolled up beneath hat-brims, penned in sympathetic ink and in cipher (seldom written in plain script), Marie Antoinette's last letters were composed in such a fashion that their interception could work harm to no one. They referred, ostensibly, to generalities of trifling importance, to imaginary affairs. The messages the Queen really wanted to convey were generally couched in the third person as well as being in cipher. Swiftly, ever more swiftly, these last cries of distress followed hard upon one another. Even before the twentieth of June, she had written: "Your friends . . . believe the re-establishment of their fortunes to be impossible, or at any rate the prospect to be exceedingly remote. Give them, if you can, some consolation in this respect; they need it! Day by day their situation grows more dreadful." On June 23rd came a yet more urgent warning: "Your friend is in the utmost danger. His illness advances in the most alarming fashion. The doctors no longer know what to do. If you hope to' see him again, you must hasten. Keep his relatives informed concerning his desperate plight." The temperature continued to rise. Here are extracts from a missive under date June 26th: "Nothing but a prompt crisis can bring him release, and as yet there is no sign of anything of the kind, so that we are reduced to despair. Make the position known to those who have any dealings with him, for this may enable them to take the necessary precautions. Time presses."

While uttering these cries of alarm, she often conceived a new fear. Devoted to Ferson as she was, the unhappy woman (like all true lovers) was afraid that she was causing undue distress to the man dearer to her than all the world. Even in her utmost anxiety and need, Marie Antoinette thought less of her own evil fate than of the perturbation her anxious appeals would cause in the object of her affection. "Our position is horrible, but do not be too much disquieted about it. I keep up my courage, and there is something within which tells me that we shall soon be happy, shall soon be rescued. This thought sustains me. . . . Farewell! When shall we meet again in tranquil circumstances?" That was written on July 3rd. A little later, the following was dispatched: "Adieu. Do your utmost to quicken the sending of the promised help. . . . Take care of yourself for our sake, and do not be uneasy about us." Then the letters follow in brief succession.

"Tomorrow [July 22nd] there are expected eight hundred men from Marseilles, and it is said that in a week thereafter they will have got enough force together to carry out their plans." Three days later she wrote: "Tell Monsieur de Mercy that the lives of the King and the Queen are in the utmost danger, and that a single day's delay may cause incalculable disaster. . . . The band of assassins is being continually swelled by new recruits." In the last letter ever received by Fersen from the Queen, under date August 1, 1792, Marie Antoinette described the overwhelming risks of the situation with the clairvoyance of despair.

"The King's life has obviously been threatened for a long time, and so has the Queen's. The arrival of about six hundred men from Marseilles and of a number of deputies from the various Jacobin clubs has increased our anxiety, which, unfortunately, is only too well grounded. All kinds of precautions are being taken to safeguard Their Majesties, but the assassins are continually prowling round the palace; the passions of the populace are being artificially inflamed; some of the National Guards are disaffected, while the rest of them lack strength and courage. . . . For the moment our main thought must be to escape dagger thrusts, and to defeat the plans of the conspirators who swarm around the trembling throne. It is a long time since the *factieux* have taken the trouble to hide their plan of annihilating the royal family. At the two last nocturnal meetings, the only differences of opinion concerned the best means to employ for this purpose. An earlier letter will have shown you how important it is to gain even as much as four-and-twenty hours. Today I need merely repeat that affirmation, while adding that unless help arrives promptly, no one but Providence can save the King and his family."

Marie Antoinette's lover received these missives in Brussels, and we can imagine his despair. From morning till night he was doing his utmost to overcome the inertia, the vacillation, of the kings, the military commanders, and the ambassadors. He wrote letter after letter, heaped visit upon visit; with the energy of justified impatience, he urged prompt military action, a rapid advance of the troops. But the Duke of Brunswick, the commander-in-chief, was a soldier of the old school, one of those who believed that an advance must be planned in every detail months before it was begun. Slowly, carefully, systematically, in accordance with the art of war he had learned under Frederick the Great (an art long since obsolete) he posted his troops in the traditional manner; and, with the characteristic arrogance of a soldier, refused to modify his designs by so much as a hair's breadth in accordance with the wishes of politicians or other outsiders. The mobilization should take place precisely as he had arranged, and in no other way. He declared that he would not be ready to cross the French frontier before the middle of August, but that thereafter everything would go strictly according to schedule (it has ever been the dream of pigheaded generals that they will be able to carry out their plans of campaign with the precision of a sham-fight, regardless of the doings of the enemy), that thereafter there would be a quick and steady advance to Paris.

Fersen, however, racked by the cries of anguish from the Tuileries, knew that the middle of August would be too late. Something must be done to save the Queen. In the delirium of passion, the lover decided upon a course which was to prove fatal to his beloved, accelerating the attack on the Tuileries by the very measure which he had designed to hinder it. For a long time, Marie Antoinette had been asking the allies to issue a manifesto. Her idea—a sound one—was that in this manifesto they should try to draw a clear distinction between the cause of the republicans, of the Jacobins, on the one hand, and that of the French nation on the other, thus encouraging the well-disposed (those who in her sense were the well-disposed) elements of France to strike terror into the hearts of the "gueux"—the rascaldom. She urged that the foreign powers must sedulously avoid interfering with the internal concerns of France. "Be careful," she said, "not to say too much about the King, and not to arouse the impression that your main purpose is to give him support." She dreamed of a pronunciamento which would at one and the same time be a declaration of friendship for the French people and a menace to the terrorists.

But the unhappy Fersen, with terror in his own soul, aware that it might be ages before effective military help came from the allies, insisted that the manifesto should be couched in the harshest terms. He wrote a draft, got a friend to convey it to headquarters—and, as ill-luck would have it, this draft was accepted! The notorious manifesto of the allied troops to the French was as domineering as if the Duke of Brunswick's regiments had already achieved a victorious advance to the gates of Paris; it contained all the errors which the Queen, better informed regarding the situation, had hoped to avoid. There were repeated references to the sacred person of the Most Christian King; the National Assembly was berated for having illegally seized the reins of government; the French soldiers were hectoringly told to come over forthwith to the side of Louis, their legitimate monarch; the town of Paris was threatened with the severest military reprisals, with complete destruction, with "an ever-memorable vengeance," in the event of the Tuileries being stormed by the mob; a general who was essentially pusillanimous spoke in the thundering tones of a Tamerlane before a shot had been fired.

The result of these paper threats was alarming. Even those who up till now had been loyal to the King became ardent republicans as soon as they learned how dear their monarch was to the enemies of France; that a victory of the foreign troops would annihilate the acquirements of the Revolution; that the Bastille would have been stormed to no avail; that the Oath of the Tennis Court would have been taken to no purpose; and that what countless Frenchmen had sworn on the Champ de Mars would be deemed invalid. By this crazy menace, Fersen's hand, the hand of the Queen's lover, threw a lighted candle into a powder-magazine, and a mad challenge caused the wrath of twenty million persons to explode.

During the last days of July the text of Brunswick's unhappy manifesto became known in the French capital. The allied threat to raze Paris to the ground should the Tuileries be stormed was regarded by the populace as a good reason for attack. Preparations were instantly begun, and the only reason for delay was that it was thought better to wait until the six hundred Reds arrived from Marseilles. On August 6th they marched in to Paris, stern and resolute enthusiasts tanned by the southern sun, stepping bravely in time to a new marching song that within a few weeks would resound throughout the land—the *Marseillaise*, which in an inspired hour a usually uninspired officer had composed as a hymn for the Revolution. Everything was now ready for the last thrust against the crumbling monarchy. The battering-ram could be swung. "Allons, enfants de la patrie!"

CHAPTER XXXIV

The Tenth of August

THE night of the ninth to the tenth of August heralded a sultry day. There was not a cloud in the sky, where all the stars glittered brightly; no breeze stirred; the streets were quiet; the roofs shone silvery beneath the moon.

But the silence deceived no one. If the streets were deserted, this only showed that something strange, something exceptional, was being made ready. Revolution does not sleep. In the sections, in the clubs, in various dwelling-houses, the leaders were assembled. Light of foot, suspiciously quiet, messengers hastened from one district to another. The general staff of the rising, Danton, Robespierre, and the Girondists, while remaining inconspicuous in the background, were issuing orders to an illegal army, the people of Paris.

Nor was anyone asleep in the Tuileries. For days an assault had been expected. The significance of the march of the Marseillais to Paris was fully understood, and (thus ran the latest tidings) they were expected to attack next day. The windows were wide open upon this suffocating night; the Queen and Madame Elisabeth had their ears pricked for any sound. But no sound was to be heard. The gardens of the Tuileries were still as death. Through the courtyard came, now and again, the tread of a sentry, or the rattling of a sword or the stamping of a horse, for more than two thousand soldiers were camped within the precincts, and the passages were full of officers and armed noblemen.

At a quarter to one in the morning came the faint knell of a tocsin, the call to arms in a distant suburb; then there was a second, a third, a fourth alarm. Beyond doubt the rising was afoot. An hour or two more would settle the matter. Now came a roll of drums. Again and again the Queen went to the window, on the watch for visible signs of the onslaught. At length, at a little before five, the sun rose blood-red in a cloudless sky. The day promised to be intensely hot.

All had been made ready in the palace. The most trustworthy force at the disposal of the crown, the Switzers, nine hundred strong, had been assembled for the defence. They were brave, disciplined, loyal. Since six on the previous evening, moreover, the stoutest battalions of the National Guard and the best squadrons of cavalry had been stationed around the Tuileries; the sentries had been trebled; and a dozen pieces of artillery showed threatening mouths at the gate of entry. Messages had also been sent to two thousand of the nobles, and arrangements had been made to admit them up to a late hour of the night, but this had been futile, for no more than one hundred and fifty, elderly men for the most part, had answered the summons. To maintain discipline in the defensive force, the Marquis de Mandat was on hand, now commandant of the National Guard, a brave, energetic, and resolute officer, not likely to be intimidated by threats. But the revolutionists, on their side, knew how valuable Mandat would be to their adversaries, so at four in the morning they ordered him to the Hôtel de Ville. Louis was fool enough to let him go, and Mandat, although he knew what was likely to result, obeyed the command. He arrived to find a revolutionary committee in possession, and was given short shrift. Within two hours he was foully murdered, and his body sent floating down the Seine. The defensive force had been deprived of its leader, of its stalwart heart, of its vigorous hand.

For the King was hopeless as a leader. He wandered listlessly from room to room, distraught, empty-headed, waiting, waiting, waiting. The day before, it had been agreed that the Tuileries should be defended to the last, and the palace had been transformed into a fortress, or armed camp. Yet now, before the assailants had put in an appearance, vacillation began anew, and the lack of steadfastness centred in Louis XVI. He was no coward; and yet was incapable of accepting responsibility. When called upon for a decision he was always at a loss, and how can common soldiers be expected to show courage when their chief does not know his own mind? The Switzers made a firm showing, but it was otherwise with the National Guards, who were perpetually asking one another, "Shall we put up a fight or not?"

The Queen could not conceal the exasperation she felt at her husband's weakness. She made up her mind to a last effort. Her wearied nerves could no longer endure this perpetual tension, and the attitude of cowardly inertia and abasement before unceasing menace was intolerable to her pride. The experiences of the last two years had taught her that to yield and to retreat when the Revolution pressed its demands resulted only in increasing the self-confidence of the revolutionists. Now the monarchy found itself at bay on the edge of the abyss. Another step backwards, and all would be lost, even honour. Quivering with outraged pride she went in person to the spiritless National Guards, hoping to inspire them with her own determination, and to quicken their sense of duty. Maybe in this desperate hour she remembered or half-remembered what had happened to her mother long before, when Maria Theresa, the heir to the throne in her arms, had appeared before the vacillating Hungarian nobles, and, by her firmness, had won them over to her cause. Marie Antoinette knew, however, that at such a supreme moment a wife could not represent her husband, a queen could not represent the king. She therefore urged Louis XVI to hold a last review of his forces when the struggle was about to begin, and to put heart into the defence by an address couched in vigorous terms.

The idea was a good one, for Marie Antoinette's instinct in such matters was invariably sound. A few fiery words such as Napoleon, not long afterwards, was ready on suitable occasions to produce with the force of a volcanic eruption; a pledge from the King that, in case of need, he would fight to the death among his defenders; a convincing and manly gesture—this would have been enough to consolidate the crumbling battalions into a strongly buttressed wall. But who came to encourage the defenders? A cumbrous, unwarlike man, short-sighted, awkward, his hat under his arm. Having stumbled down the grand staircase, he stammered a few ill-chosen words: "We are told that they are coming. . . . My cause is that of all good citizens. . . . We should make a brave fight, don't you think? . . ." Louis's uncertain tones, his embarrassed demeanour, increased the sense of insecurity instead of diminishing it. The National Guards watched him contemptuously as he drew near. At first his words were received in silence. Then, instead of the expected "Long live the King!" came the cry, "Long live the people!" Finally, when His Majesty advanced as far as the railings, where the troops were already fraternizing with the populace, it was to hear open cries of revolt: "A bas le veto! A bas le gros cochon!" Horrified at this insolence, his supporters and ministers formed a ring round him and conducted him back into the palace. "Grand Dieu! C'est le roi qu'on hue!"—they are reviling the King—exclaimed the minister for the navy, who had been watching from one of the first-floor windows. Marie Antoinette, her eyes red-rimmed and suffused with tears, worn out by the sleepless night, had also been a witness of this pitiful scene. Turning away with desolate heart, she said to Madame Campan: "All is lost. This review of the troops has done more harm than good." The fight was over before a blow had been struck.

That morning of the last decisive struggle between monarchy and the Republic, there stood among the crowd in front of the Tuileries a young lieutenant out of a job, a Corsican, Napoleon Bonaparte, who would have laughed in the face of anyone who should have told him that on a day to come he would occupy the palace as successor of Louis XVI. Unemployed as he was, and having nothing better to do, with the insight of a man born to be a great military commander he was summing up the prospects of attack and defence. A few cannon-shots, a vigorous sally, and the canaille (as long years afterwards in Saint Helena he contemptuously termed the men from the faubourgs) would have been swept away like leaves by a besom. If King Louis had but had this little lieutenant of artillery in his service, he would have held his own against the whole of Paris. But not a soul in the Tuileries had the iron heart and the comprehensive vision of the youthful islander. "You will not fire until the assailants have fired on you" had been the only order issued to the defenders—a half-hearted measure which made defeat inevitable.

By now it was seven o'clock, and the vanguard of the rebels had arrived; a disorderly and imperfectly armed crowd, rendered danger-ous, not by military training, but by invincible determination. Some of them had already massed on the other side of the drawbridge. It could not be long before the conflict would begin. Roederer, the public prosecutor, was keenly alive to his responsibilities. An hour earlier, he had urged the King to betake himself to the National Assembly and to put himself under the protection of the deputies. Marie Antoinette had interposed, saying: "Monsieur, we have a strong enough force here, and it is time to decide which shall have the upper hand, the

King and the constitution, or the rebels." Louis, however, was as if paralysed in face of this alarming situation. Breathing heavily, looking out into vacancy, he sat in his armchair, waiting, waiting, he knew not why. His only aim was to procrastinate, since, as ever, he was unable to come to a decision. Then Roederer reappeared, wearing the scarf of office which opened every door to him, accompanied by some of the town councillors. He spoke emphatically to King Louis:

"Sire, Your Majesty has not five minutes to lose; the only place for you is in the National Assembly."

"But there don't seem to be many people in the Place du Car-roussel."

"Sire, there are vast crowds coming from the suburbs, with a dozen pieces of artillery."

One of the town councillors, a lace-maker by trade of whom the Queen had in former days been a good customer, endorsed Roederer's exhortation. Marie Antoinette promptly stopped him. (It was her wont to show temper when anyone she despised did his best to save her.) "Be good enough to hold your tongue, Sir, and not to take the words out of the public prosecutor's mouth!" Then, turning to Roederer, she went on: "Let me assure you, Monsieur, that we have a considerable armed force ready to defend us." Roederer shook his head. "Madame," he replied, "all Paris is marching to the attack; your troops are hope-lessly outnumbered; action on your part is useless; resistance is im-possible." The Queen was overmastered by her impatience; her cheeks flushed with anger; she was hard put to it to refrain from railing against these men not one of whom seemed to her truly a man. But the responsibility was too heavy for her. In the presence of the King of France, no woman, not even his wife, could give orders for battle. She waited, therefore, for the ever-irresolute Louis to decide. At length he raised his heavy head, looked Roederer in the face for a few mo-ments, sighed, and then (happy to have made up his mind at last) said: "All right, we'll go!"

Thereupon through the double row of noblemen who regarded him contemptuously, past the ranks of the Switzers without even telling them whether they were to fight or not, and through the continually thickening crowd of the populace which mocked at and even threat-ened the King, his wife, and the few stalwarts who accompanied them, walked Louis XVI out of the palace, the palace which his forefathers had built and which he was never to re-enter. They passed through the gardens, the King leading the way with Roederer; behind them the Queen on the arm of the minister for the navy, and holding her little boy with the other hand. With more haste than dignity they made their way to the covered Riding School, where in the old days the members of the court used to enjoy themselves on horseback, and where now the National Assembly, self-assured and proud, could rejoice because the King, in terror for his life, had come to seek its protection. The distance was no more than two hundred paces, but by taking them Marie Antoinette and Louis XVI bade farewell to their power and their glory. The monarchy was over and done with in France.

Yet it was with mixed feelings that the members of the Assembly regarded their sometime ruler to whom they had sworn fealty, when he came to demand their hospitality and protection. In the magnanimity of his first surprise, Vergniaud, the president, declared: "You can count, Sire, upon the loyalty of the National Assembly. We have all pledged ourselves to give even our lives to maintain the rights of the people and constituted authority." This was a far-reaching pledge, for, by the wording of the constitution, the King was still one of the two constituted authorities, and, amid the chaos which now prevailed, the National Assembly continued to act as if a legally established order was in being. It pedantically insisted upon the observance of the paragraph in the constitution by which the King was forbidden to be present in the hall during its deliberations. Since the discussion had to continue, it was agreed that the royal family should be accommodated in an adjoining room, ordinarily occupied by the reporters. "Room" was, indeed, a euphemism. The place was no more than a cubby-hole, so low that no full-grown person could stand upright; in front were two or three stools, and along the back wall a bench; an iron grating had, up till now, separated it from the hall of assembly. The grating was hastily demolished by some of the deputies with the aid of files and hammers, since it was necessary to reckon with the possibility that the mob would try to get hold of the King and the Queen by force. In this extremity, should it arise, the deputies were to stop their proceedings and safeguard the refugees in their midst. Marie Antoinette and King Louis had now to spend eighteen hours in this superheated cage —they and their children—exposed to the inquisitive, malicious, or compassionate glances of the deputies. But what made their humiliation even greater than it would have been if frank enmity or obvious hatred had been shown, was the disdainful neglect of the National Assembly. Those who had sought asylum were as little regarded as if they had been doorkeepers or ordinary onlookers. Not one of the representatives of the people troubled to come from time to time and say a friendly word to them; no one thought of devising any expedient which might have made their stay in so narrow a pen less intolerable. They were no more than an audience, ignored by the actors—although the fate of this audience hung in the balance, and was one of the topics of discussion—the scene being as phantasmal as if a man were to watch his own interment from one of the windows of his dwelling-house.

Not long after the arrival of the fugitives, a wave of excitement passed through the Assembly. Some of the deputies sprang to their feet and listened intently; the doors of the Riding School were flung open, and now there was plainly audible in the adjoining Tuileries the sound of musket shots, soon followed by the boom of artillery fire. The rabble, on breaking into the palace, had found their way blocked by the Swiss guards. In the hurry of his flight the King had, as already said, forgotten or lacked energy to give these faithful soldiers fresh orders. True to the earlier command to stand to their guns, the Switzers defended the forsaken palace, and fired several rounds. Soon, they had cleared the courtyard, had seized the cannon brought by the mob, and had thus shown that a resolute sovereign could, with their aid, have effectively defended himself. At this juncture, however, the King, doomed to lose in physical fact the head he had never had in a spiritual sense, remembered that it did not become him to ask his servants to show a courage which he himself had lacked. He therefore sent orders to the Swiss guards to cease defending the palace. Such consideration (as ever since he had mounted the throne) came too late. His irresolution or forgetfulness had already cost the lives of more than a thousand men. Unresisted, now, the furious crowd swarmed into the Tuileries. Once again the blood-red lanterns of the Revolution shone upon scenes of horror; the heads of slaughtered royalists were brandished on pike-points; not until eleven in the morning was the massacre finished. No more heads were lost on this fatal day, but only a crown.

Huddled together in their cage, the members of the royal family, not daring to utter a word, had to watch the proceedings in the assembly hall. First of all they saw their faithful Switzers, begrimed with powder, blood streaming from many wounds, rush into the Manège, followed by the victorious rebels, eager for yet more victims in defiance of the deputies. Then the loot from the palace was heaped upon the president's table: silverware, ornaments, letters, cash-boxes, piles of assignats. Marie Antoinette had to listen with compressed lips while the leaders of revolt were praised. She had to listen defenceless, mute, while delegates from the sections mounted the tribune and, in violent terms, demanded the King's deposition; and while the plainest facts were being misreported, as, for instance, that the tocsin had been sounded because of orders sent from the palace, that the Tuileries had besieged the people and not the people the Tuileries! Once again she had occasion to note the ever-recurring way in which politicians veer with a changing wind. Vergniaud, the president, who, only two hours before, had, in the name of the Assembly, declared that they would die in defence of constituted authority, now capitulated to the mob, proposing the immediate suspension of the King's executive powers, and demanding that the royal family should be transferred to the Luxembourg palace "under the protection of the citizens and the law" —which, in plain words, signified imprisonment. To save the face of the royalists among the representatives of the people, it was agreed that the Dauphin should have a tutor, but in reality no one had any more concern for either crown or king. Louis's veto, the only privilege left to him, was abolished. The National Assembly autocratically declared itself the sole and supreme legislative authority. No one dreamed of asking the assent of the tired man who sat in the reporter's box, and who was perhaps glad, at bottom, to be no longer asked. Louis XVI, henceforward, would have no need to come to any decision. Everything would be decided without consulting him.

Eight hours, twelve hours, fourteen hours—the sitting continued without a break. The five poor souls herded in the reporters' cage had not slept a wink during the previous night, and since day dawned they had lived through an eternity. The children, who understood nothing of these strange matters, had fallen asleep. The King and the Queen were dripping with perspiration. Again and again Marie Antoinette wetted her handkerchief to wash the sweat from her face; once or twice she drank a glass of iced water brought to her by some kindly hand. With burning eyes, terribly wakeful despite the extremity of her fatigue, she continued to stare into the overheated Riding School where, for hour after hour, the wordy cog-wheels were grinding out her fate. She had no appetite, and could not swallow a morsel. Her husband, in this respect, was made of tougher metal. Unconcernedly, during this long period of waiting, Louis XVI put away several meals, working his powerful jaws with as much energy and success as if he had been feeding off solid silver in his former palace at Versailles. Not even the utmost peril could disturb the workings of hunger and sleep in his unkingly frame. Gradually his eyelids drooped, and, in the very midst of the struggle which was to cost him his throne, he slumbered for an hour or more. Marie Antoinette drew away from him, retiring into the darkness of the farthest corner of their cage. At such times she always felt ashamed of this husband of hers, who thought more about his stomach than his honour, and who, amid the most terrible humiliations, could eat as heartily and sleep as soundly as if nothing were at stake. Not wishing to show her bitterness, she turned her face to the wall, and would gladly have pressed her hands over her ears to avoid hearing the debates. She alone felt to the full the abasement of their situation, and in imagination forecasted the horrors that were to come. Yet never for a moment did she lose her dignity, being greatest in the hours when she was most sorely tried. These disturbers of the peace, these "factieux," should not be gratified by so much as a tear or a sign from the Queen they were discrowning.

At length, after eighteen ghastly hours spent in the stifling little room, the King and the Queen were allowed to withdraw to what in old days had been the Convent of the Feuillants where, in one of the deserted cells, a bedroom was hastily installed for their convenience.

Marie Antoinette was able to borrow articles of clean underlinen from strangers; and, having lost her purse amid the turmoil or having forgotten to bring it with her, she secured the loan of a few gold pieces from one of her own waiting-maids. Now that she was relieved from the scrutiny of unfriendly glances, she broke her long fast. As for quiet, that was unobtainable. Paris was bubbling over with excitement; crowds rushed unceasingly past the grated windows; and from the Tuileries near by came the sound of rolling wheels. The bodies of the thousand victims of the riot were being carted away by night. The corpse of the monarchy would be conveyed to a prison-house in the garish light of day!

Next morning and the day after, the royal family had to attend the sittings of the National Assembly, being still cooped up in the same narrow pen. Hour after hour they watched and listened while the last vestiges of their power were being consumed in this smelting-oven. Yesterday the deputies had spoken of "the King"; today Danton referred to him and his wife as "the oppressors of the people," and Cloots spoke contemptuously of "individuals who pass by the name of monarchs." Yesterday there had been talk of the Luxembourg palace as a "residence" for the court, and there had been a proposal to appoint a tutor for the Dauphin; today, the word ran that Louis was to be placed "sous la sauvegarde de la nation" this being a pretentious term for imprisonment. Furthermore, the Commune, the new revolutionary municipal government which had come into being in the night of the tenth of August, refused to allow the Luxembourg or the Ministry of Justice to be used as the King's residence, saying in so many words that escape thence would be too easy. Only in the Temple would it be possible to ensure the safety of the "détenus"—the notion of imprisonment growing plainer and plainer. The National Assembly which was in truth glad to shift the responsibility, entrusted the King to the care of the Commune. This latter promised to conduct the royal family to the Temple "with all the respect due to misfortune." Therewith the matter was settled; but throughout the day and until two o'clock next morning the mill of words continued to grind, while no one had a kindly thought for the poor wretches who sat beneath the shadow of destiny and were crowded into the reporters' box.

At length, on August 13th, the Temple was ready for their reception.

During these three days a huge distance had been traversed. The progress from absolute monarchy to the organization of the power of the National Assembly had occupied centuries; from the National Assembly to the establishment of "constitutional government" had taken two years; from the constitution to the storming of the Tuileries had been a period of a few months; from the assault upon the Tuileries until the definitive imprisonment of the King required no more than three days. Nor was the imprisonment to be a long one. It began in the middle of August 1792, and in little over five months Louis XVI was to perish beneath the guillotine.

On August 13th, under Pétion's charge, the royal family was conveyed to the Temple—at six in the evening, an hour before sunset, for the populace was to enjoy the spectacle of seeing its former sovereign, and, above all, the arrogant Queen, driven off to jail. This newfashioned "royal progress" lasted two hours, since the coachman had been ordered to drive slowly and to make a long detour. In the Place Vendôme, Louis XVI was to be given the chance of glutting his eyes with the spectacle of the shattered and overthrown statue of Louis XIV, that he might convince himself of the fall, not only of his own sovereignty, but of the dynasty that had ruled France for so long.

On this same evening, when the sometime lord of France was removed from the palace of his ancestors to a prison, there was likewise a change of residence for the new master of Paris. During that same night the guillotine, which had hitherto done its fell work in the courtyard of the Conciergerie, was threateningly established in the Place du Carroussel. France was to be made fully aware that from August 13th onwards it was governed, no longer by Louis XVI, but by the Terror.

CHAPTER XXXV

The Temple

NIGHT had fallen when the royal family reached the Temple, so called because in former days it had been the Parisian castle of the Knights Templar. The windows of the main building were illuminated, for the capital was celebrating a popular festival. Marie Antoinette knew the little palace adjoining. The Count of Artois, her chosen companion in the earlier years of her married life in the happy days of the Rococo, had dwelt there. During a hard winter, fourteen years earlier, wrapped in costly furs, she had driven thither in a brightly painted sledge, drawn by horses jingling with bells, to dine with her brother-in-law. Now less amiable hosts, the members of the Commune, had invited her for a long stay; and at the door, instead of lackeys, stood armed sentries. The castle was demolished in 1811, after it had stood for nearly six hundred years, but we know its appearance from Lequeux's sketch made in September 1792. As for the great dining-hall of the palace, that is familiar to us from a celebrated picture, *Tea at the Prince de Conti's*. The picture represents a scene in the year 1774, the lad and the lass who are entertaining an illustrious company with music being Wolfgang Amadeus Mozart and his sister.

But it was in the ancient fortress, not the palace, that the Commune had determined to keep Marie Antoinette and Louis XVI prisoned. The Temple was a gloomy stronghold, standing four-square and sinister like the Bastille, with round towers at the corners, narrow windows, and a sunless inner court. It reminded onlookers of the horrors of the Middle Ages; of the Vehmgericht and the Inquisition, of witches' sabbaths and torture-chambers. Latter-day Parisians took no pleasure in contemplating this vestige from an age of brute force which lived on unused and therefore all the more eerie in the midst of a busy petty-bourgeois quarter. Symbolical, cruelly symbolical, was the choice of an outworn edifice as prison for the last representatives of a monarchy likewise outworn.

The next few weeks were devoted to making the place of incarcera-

tion secure. Numbers of small houses adjoining the towers were demolished; the trees in the courtyard were felled, that there might be no
obstacle to perpetual supervision of the prisoners; and an outer rampart
was built, so that gates in three successive walls had to be traversed
before the inner citadel was reached. Guardrooms were established
at every exit; and new barriers were set up in the passages within, to
ensure that everyone who entered or left the Temple would run the
gauntlet of seven or eight sentries. The Commune chose day after
day, by lot, four commissaries, whose business it was to visit every
room of the fortress, and who had, at nightfall, to take charge of the
keys of all the doors. Besides these officials and the town councillors
themselves, no one was allowed to enter the place without a special
permit; no Fersen or other helpful friend was to have a chance of
holding converse with the royal family; the possibility of smuggling
letters in or out had (it was believed) been done away with once for
ever.

Still harder to bear was another precaution. Late in the evening of
August 19th there came two officials with an order from the Commune
that persons other than members of the royal family were to be
removed from the fortress. It was especially painful for the Queen to
part from Madame de Lamballe who, after having got away safely to
London, had returned in order to stand beside her friend in the hour
of peril. Both women felt that they would never meet again. We may
presume that it was during this farewell that Marie Antoinette gave
the Princess, as a last token of affection, the ring found on the latter's
mutilated body after she had been murdered, the ring containing a
lock of fair hair and the tragical inscription, "A tress whitened by
misfortune." The governess, Madame de Tourzel, and her daughter,
were likewise transferred to another prison, to La Force, and so were
the King's attendants, except for one valet. Therewith the last glamour
of court life was destroyed. Louis XVI, Marie Antoinette, their two
children, and Princess Elisabeth were left to their own devices.

The dread of misfortune is usually more intolerable than misfortune
when it comes. Although their imprisonment implied a profound
humiliation for the King and the Queen, it was, at the outset, unquestionably a safeguard. The thick walls that surrounded them, the barricades in the courtyard, the sentries with loaded muskets, doubtless

prevented any attempt at flight; yet at the same time they were a protection against attack. It was no longer necessary, as it had been in the Tuileries, to listen, hour after hour, for the tocsin which might be the signal of onslaught. In their lonely dungeon, day followed day without incident, amid the calm of perfect seclusion, remote from the stir of the outer world. The town authorities provided what was requisite for the physical wellbeing of their royal captives. Though relentless in fight, the Revolution was not inhuman. Having delivered a vigorous blow, it always paused for a while to gather its forces, unaware that such interludes served only to emphasize the pitilessness of defeat.

During the first days after the removal to the Temple, the Commune did its best to make the prison comfortable. The great tower was refurnished and redecorated; one story with four rooms was assigned to the King, and four additional rooms were allotted to the Queen, Madame Elisabeth, and the children. Whenever they liked, in the daytime, they could walk in the garden; and, above all, the Commune was liberal in respect to matters upon which Louis's comfort greatly depended. There was a liberal supply of food and drink. No less than thirteen persons were appointed to minister to the pleasures of the table! At his midday meal there were at least three soups, two entrées, two roasts, four entremets, compotes, fruits, malmsey, claret, and champagne—so that in less than three months the expenses of the royal kitchen mounted up to no less than five-and-thirty thousand livres.

There was likewise an ample supply of clothing, for Louis XVI was not as yet treated as a criminal. His request for books was granted, and he received a library containing no less than 257 volumes, mostly classical Latin authors, with which he could while away the time. In fact, during this opening epoch, which was brief, the detention of the royal family was not punitive in character, so that both the King and the Queen (apart from their sense of spiritual oppression) were able to lead a fairly comfortable life. In the morning Marie Antoinette sent for her children and passed the hours until the midday meal teaching them or joining in their games. After luncheon the King and the Queen played chess or backgammon. Then, while the King went for a walk in the garden with the Dauphin, and helped the little boy to fly a kite, Marie Antoinette, who was too proud to expose herself needlessly to the gaze of the sentries, usually passed the time over needlework in her own room. In the evening, after the children had been put to bed, she and Louis would converse or play cards; and sometimes she would seat herself at the clavecin, as of old, and sing for a while—but in the Temple, cut off from the world, separated from her friends, she was for the most part too heavy-hearted for this. She talked little, being happiest when with her children or when alone. She lacked the consolations of piety, whereas Louis XVI and his sister Elisabeth, who prayed much and observed the fast-days strictly, found evil fortune less intolerable. Since she had much more character than they, her will to live was not so easily broken. Even within these thick walls her thoughts continued to turn towards the outer world; she would not abandon hope; her energies were still accumulating like water behind a dam. She, alone among the company, was in perpetual revolt against imprisonment. The others scarcely noticed it. Had it not been for the unceasing presence of armed guards, had it not been for the incessant anxiety as to what might happen on the morrow, Louis XVI the petty bourgeois and Madame Elisabeth born to be a nun would have enjoyed the life which for years they had unconsciously desired—a life of unthinking and irresponsible passivity.

But the sentries were always there. Unremittingly the prisoners were reminded that another will than their own held sway over their destinies. In the dining-room the Commune had had pasted up on the wall a large-type reprint of the *Declaration of the Rights of Man,* bearing a date which could not but be painful to the discrowned king, "In the First Year of the Republic." The brass doors of the stove bore the inscription "Liberty, Equality, Fraternity." At the midday meal there was present as an unbidden guest a commissary from the town authorities or else the commandant of the fortress. Every slice of bread was cut by an enemy hand, and carefully examined lest secret correspondence should have been introduced into the loaf. No newspapers might be brought into the quadrangle of the Temple. Everyone who entered or left the fortress was searched for papers. The doors of the rooms were locked on the outside. Neither the King nor the Queen could move a step without being shadowed by a man-at-arms; they could not exchange their thoughts unless in the presence of witnesses; and whatever they read had passed the censorship. Only in their bedrooms at night could they know the happiness of solitude.

This perpetual supervision, was it a deliberately imposed torment? Were the guardians of the royal prisoners in actual fact sadists and torturers, as depicted in the royalist chronicles? Was Marie Antoinette the victim of needless exhibitions of malice, and were the reddest of the Reds expressly chosen for this purpose? The official reports of the Commune tell another story, but they, likewise, are partisan. Great caution is needed before answering this decisive question: Did the Revolution expose the conquered King and Queen of set purpose to mortifications and humiliations? The term "revolution" is wide in its range, extending as it does by imperceptible transitions from the loftiest idealism to the utmost brutality, from greatness to cruelty, from spirituality to force; it exhibits a play of changing colours because it takes its tints from men and from circumstances. In the French Revolution, as in every other, we can plainly see that two types of revolutionists were at work: those who were revolutionists from idealism and those who were revolutionists from spite. The former, persons who had been better off than the masses, wanted to lift these to their own level, to educate and to free the crowd. The latter, who had been in poor circumstances wanted to take vengeance on those who had been happier than themselves; and, having risen to power, they sought to pay out those who had fallen from power. This twofold attitude, rooted as it is in the bipolarity of human nature, has always prevailed. During the French Revolution, to begin with, idealism had the upper hand. The National Assembly, composed of nobles and bourgeois, persons looked up to in their respective circles, wished to help the common people, to liberate the masses; but the liberated masses, when their forces had been unchained, speedily turned against the liberators. During the second phase, therefore, the radical elements, the spiteful revolutionists, gained the upper hand; men to whom power was too new a thing for them to overcome the desire to enjoy it to the uttermost. There rose to predominance many of those petty creatures whose supreme ambition it was to drag the Revolution down to their own narrow measure, to stamp upon it their own mediocrity.

Among these revolutionists from spite, Hébert, to whom the guard-

ianship of the royal family had been entrusted, was one of the most
typical and most repulsive specimens. The noblest, the most spiritual
embodiments of the revolution—Robespierre, Camille Desmoulins, and
Saint-Just—were quick to recognize Hébert for the unclean beast, for
the empty-headed spouter, he was. They knew him to be an ulcerous
growth upon the fair face of the Revolution, a morbid excrescence
which Robespierre (though too late) burned away with a red-hot iron.
A man with a bad record, openly accused of embezzlement at the
theatre, unscrupulous and unemployed, he leapt into the stream of the
Revolution as a hunted beast will jump into a river, and the current
sustained him because, as Saint-Just said, "he could change his colour
like a chameleon, in conformity with the moods and the menaces
of the time." The more the Republic became bespattered with blood,
the redder, nay the more abominable, were his writings in "Père
Duchesne," his own newspaper, the basest "rag" of the Revolution. In
the vulgarest of tones—"as if," remarked Camille Desmoulins, "the
Seine were the great sewer of Paris"—he flattered the worst instincts of
the mob, thus bringing the Revolution into discredit abroad. This
easily acquired popularity earned him lucrative posts, a seat in the
town council, and increasing power. As fate would have it, it was to
his hands that the keeping of Marie Antoinette and her husband was
entrusted.

It need hardly be said that such a man, placed as watch-dog over
the royal family, took a malicious delight in inflicting every possible
mortification upon an archduchess of Austria, a queen of France. Although in personal intercourse (posing as the ideal embodiment of the
new law and the new justice) he was cool and civil, in "Père Duchesne"
he gave vent to the mean anger roused in him by the fact that Marie
Antoinette declined to discuss matters with him; and it was the voice
of "Père Duchesne" which incessantly demanded the use of the
"national razor" for "the boozer and his whore"—the royal couple
whom citizen Hébert, deputy public prosecutor of the Commune,
was visiting politely every week. Doubtless his bark was worse than
his bite, but it was a needless humiliation of the vanquished to appoint
this most contemptible and most insincere among the patriots as
Louis's and Marie Antoinette's chief jailer. Naturally, moreover, fear
of Hébert influenced the conduct of the sentries. They were harsher

than they might have wished to be, simply because they were afraid of being regarded as untrustworthy. On the other hand, his cries of hatred in "Père Duchesne" helped the prisoners by a strange sort of recoil; for the worthy handicraftsmen and small shopkeepers who were chosen by Hébert to act as guards did not find that their experience squared with what they read in his newspaper about the "bloody tyrants," and about the "dissolute, spendthrift Austrian woman." What did the sentries actually see? A portly and simple-minded petty-bourgeois, a man just like themselves, taking his son by the hand for a walk in the garden, and amusing the little boy by measuring how many square feet there were in the courtyard. They saw him eating with a healthy appetite, sleeping soundly, and sitting over his books. Soon they came to recognize that the excellent and rather dull-witted paterfamilias had no wish to hurt a fly. It was hard to detest a "tyrant" of this sort; and had it not been that Hébert was himself constantly on the watch, the King's guardians would probably have chatted with the good-natured fellow as if he had been one of their own comrades, and would have been glad to sit down with him to play a game of cards.

The Queen, of course, was determined to keep her distance! At the dinner-table, Marie Antoinette would never utter a syllable to the man on guard; and when a deputation came to ask her if she had any wishes unfulfilled or any grievances to complain of, she answered coldly that she had neither desires nor complaints. She would rather accept all that happened than ask one of her jailers for a kindness. Yet this very aloofness in misfortune impressed the watchers, and men are always ready to sympathize with a woman in misfortune. By degrees the guardians, who were in truth fellow-prisoners of the prisoners they were set to watch, conceived a liking for the King and the royal family, and thus only can be explained the possibility of various attempts at escape. If, as the royalist memoirs tell us, the sentries were outwardly rough and emphatically republican in their demeanour, if they uttered a curse now and again and sang and whistled more loudly than they needed when on duty, it was only to hide the sympathy they felt for the prisoners. These common folk understood much better than the ideologists of the Convention that honour is due to persons in misfortune who have been dragged down from high positions; and, in actual fact, the

Queen had to suffer much less from the malevolence of the apparently rough soldiers in the Temple than she had had to suffer in former days from the malevolence of the courtiers who thronged the salons at Versailles.

But time moves on inexorably, borne forward by its giant pinions even though those prisoned behind stone walls may scarcely note its progress. There came bad news from the frontier. At length the Prussians and the Austrians had begun their advance, and, at the first clash, had routed the revolutionary troops. In Vendée, the peasants had risen in revolt; a civil war had begun; the British government had withdrawn its ambassador; Lafayette, disgusted by the radicalism of the Revolution he had helped to conjure up, had resigned his commission; food was growing scarce, and the populace was becoming restless. The most dangerous of words, "treason," was being shouted through the streets after every reverse, disturbing the whole city. At this juncture the most energetic and the most unscrupulous among the leaders of the Revolution hoisted the banner of the Red Terror, resolving that, during three days and nights of September, any prisoners whom there might be reason for regarding with suspicion should be butchered. Even Danton approved or condoned the butchery. Among the two thousand thus massacred was the Queen's friend, the Princesse de Lamballe.

The prisoners in the Temple knew nothing, at the outset, of what was going on during the terrible days in the first week of September 1792, being shut away from messengers and from the printed word. Of course, they heard the tocsin ringing, and Marie Antoinette was only too well acquainted with these brazen-voiced stormy petrels. She knew that whenever they clamoured above the roofs, a new hurricane of disaster was at hand. "What can it mean?" whispered the captives to one another. "Is the Duke of Brunswick with his troops already close to Paris? Has a counter-revolution begun?"

The sentries at the gates of the fortress were greatly excited, being better informed. Tidings had reached them to the effect that a vast crowd of the inhabitants of the faubourgs was approaching, that one of their leaders was carrying on a pike the head of the murdered Princesse de Lamballe, her hair streaming in the blast, and that her nude, mutilated corpse was also being brought along. The assassins, drunken with blood and with wine, wanted to enjoy the hideous triumph of showing Marie Antoinette these ghastly remnants of her dead friend, the bloody head and the desecrated body of the woman with whom (according to popular belief) the Queen had so long had unchaste relations. The guards sent to the Commune for reinforcements, knowing that they were not strong enough to resist the onslaught of a raging mob. But the crafty Pétion had followed his usual practice of keeping out of sight in times of trouble. No reinforcements came, and the assassins with their horrid trophies were already at the gates. Hoping to keep their fury within bounds and to avoid a murderous attack which would certainly have proved fatal to the royal prisoners, the commandant decided to admit some of the rioters into the outer court of the fortress. The crowd, like a foaming and dirty torrent, rushed through the gates.

Two of the ghouls were dragging the naked trunk by the legs, another was flaunting the intestines in the air, a third was bearing the pale head on the top of a pike. Their wish was, they explained, to mount the stairs into the tower, taking their trophies with them, that they might compel the Queen to kiss the lips of her intimate. Force could effect nothing against these maniacs, so one of the officials of the Commune tried what cunning could do. Wearing the scarf of a deputy, he demanded silence and made a speech. To appease his auditors, he began by praising them for their splendid achievements, and then went on to say that it would be better to carry the head through the streets of Paris, so that the entire population might feast its eyes upon this "trophy" as "an everlasting monument of victory." Happily his flattering tongue served his purpose, and with savage yells the murderers lurched forth into the street, to haul the headless trunk as far as the Palais Royal.

Meanwhile the captives in the tower had grown impatient. They heard the confused cries of an enraged multitude, without knowing what was afoot. They had heard similar inarticulate shouts at the storming of Versailles and at the storming of the Tuileries, and they saw that the sentries, alert at their posts and ready to ward off danger, were pale with excitement. Overcome by his uneasiness, the King asked one of the National Guards what was the matter. "Well, Sir," replied the man, "if you want to know, it is the head of Madame de Lamballe which they have brought to show you. I think you had better go to the window and let them see you, if you don't want them to come up here."

At these words there was a faint cry from the Queen, who sank in a swoon. "This was the only time in her life," we are told by her daughter, "in which she showed a lack of firmness."

Three weeks later, on September 21st, crowds were again shouting in the streets. Once more the prisoners looked forth uneasily. This time, however, the populace was not angry but delighted. The newspaper-sellers were shouting that the Convention had decided to abolish the monarchy. Next day came some of the deputies to announce to the King, no longer a king, that he had been deposed. "Louis the Last," as he was called for a time, until the name of "Louis Capet" was contemptuously bestowed on him, received these tidings as indifferently as Shakespeare's King Richard II.

What must the king do now? must he submit?
The king shall do it: must he be deposed?
The king shall be contented: must he lose
The name of king? O' God's name, let it go.

Light cannot be taken from a shadow, nor power from one who has long been powerless. There came no word of protest from the man who had been blunted to all possible humiliations, nor even a word from Marie Antoinette. Perhaps their avowed dethronement came as a relief. Henceforward they had no more responsibility either for their own destiny or for that of the State; they could neither do what they should not have done nor leave undone what they should have done; their only care in future would be for the little remnant of life that might be left to them. Their best course would be to take what pleasure was to be found in the ordinary affairs of human life: in teaching their daughter needlework or to play the clavecin; in helping their son to improve his penmanship, for he still wrote in large, stiff, childish letters—and they had often to destroy that which, in his innocence, he had written. What could this child of seven know about political happenings? He was still fond of writing the first words he had been taught, "Louis Charles Dauphin"! They solved puzzles in the latest issue of the "Mercure de France"—for now that Louis had been deposed he was allowed to read the newspapers. They strolled in the garden; or else, in their sitting-room, they noted the slow movement of the hands of the clock that stood on the mantelpiece; they watched the smoke wreaths rising above the distant roofs; they perceived the darkening tints of the autumnal clouds. Above all, they tried to forget what they had once been and to refrain from thinking about the dread possibilities of the future.

Now, so it seemed, the Revolution had reached its goal. The King had been deposed, offering no objection, and he still dwelt with his wife and children in the ancient stronghold of the Templars. But a revolution is like a rolling ball. One who mounts it and would fain guide it must foot it busily to keep his balance, must never try to arrest its motion, for there can be no safety except in unceasing advance. At the present juncture of affairs in France, every party knew this full well, and each was afraid of lagging behind the other. The Rights were afraid of the Moderates, the Moderates were afraid of the Lefts, the Lefts were afraid of their Left Wing, the Girondists were afraid of the Maratists, the leaders were afraid of the people, the generals were afraid of their own soldiers, the Convention was afraid of the Commune, the Commune of the sections: and this contagious mutual anxiety of the groups aroused a heated competition. It was the perpetual dread (shared by men of all shades of opinion) of being regarded as backward in the good cause that drove the French Revolution so far beyond its original target and gave it its torrential impetus. Its fate was to overshoot the goals it had established; to outdistance its own aims as soon as they had been reached.

At first the Revolution believed itself to have fulfilled its task by depriving the King of effective power; then, dissatisfied, it went a stage further, and deposed the monarch to establish a republic. Yet deposed and discrowned, this unhappy man, though no one could consider him personally dangerous, remained a symbol; and when the republicans were rifling the tombs of kings dead for centuries, in order to burn what had long been no more than dust and ashes, could they

be expected to tolerate even the shadow of a living monarch? The
leaders, therefore, decided that the political death of Louis XVI must
be followed up by his bodily death, for thus alone could they be safeguarded against a restoration of the monarchy. To a radical republican it seemed that the edifice of the Republic would only be stable
when its mortar had been mixed with royal blood. Ere long, vying
with the extremists for popular favour, many of the moderates began
to avow the same sentiments, and the trial of Louis Capet was fixed
for December.

In the Temple this alarming decision was announced by the appearance of commissaries to take possession of "all cutting instru-
ments"—knives, scissors, and forks. Thus the "détenu," who had
hitherto been merely kept under observation, was signalized as an
accused person. Furthermore, Louis XVI was separated from his
family. Although he still lived in the same tower, separated from them
only by one story, thanks to this cruel regulation he was no longer
allowed sight of his wife or his children. Throughout these fateful
weeks the wife was not permitted so much as one interview with her
husband, nor even to learn how the trial was going on. Newspapers
had again been cut off; she was forbidden to communicate with
Louis's defender; the unhappy woman had to pass the tense hours in
dreadful uncertainty. All she knew about her husband was that his
heavy tread could be heard as he paced up and down his room on
the floor below. This separation was an intolerable torment, and a
senseless piece of barbarity. Then, on January 20, 1793, when one of
the officials of the Commune called on Marie Antoinette and, with a
somewhat dolorous mien, told her that by an exceptional indulgence,
she was to be allowed, with her children, to visit her husband in the
lower story, she was quick to grasp what was implied. Louis XVI had
been sentenced to death; she was to see her husband, the children were
to see their father, for the last time. In view of the tragedy of the
moment, recognizing that a man who was to be decapitated on the
morrow was no longer dangerous, the four officials who had been
charged to watch this farewell meeting of husband, wife, sister, and
children, had the decency to do so only from a neighbouring room,
through a closed glass door.

There is no official report of the interview and none of the royal pair's sometime friends were present. The various printed accounts of the matter are free inventions, and so are the copperplate engravings which, conceived in the mellifluous style of the day, serve only to debase tragedy to a lachrymose sentimentalism. Who can doubt that the adieu to the father of her children must have been one of the most painful moments in Marie Antoinette's life? To what purpose, then, any attempt to depict it in darker colours? One endowed with strong human sensibilities must inevitably feel overcome with anguish when exchanging last words with a person sentenced to death. As for the man now in question, it is true that Marie Antoinette had never passionately loved him, and had long since given her heart to another, but she had lived with him for twenty years and had borne him four children. Always, even amid the storms of recent events, she had found him kindly, indulgent, self-sacrificing where she was concerned. Though they had originally been united for reasons of State, the joint misfortunes they had undergone had cemented their bond, and during the sad hours in the Temple they had drawn closer and closer together. Besides, the Queen knew well enough that before long she would have to follow him to a violent death. For her there could only be a short respite.

In these last formidable hours, that which had for most of his life been disastrous to the King, the fact that he had "no nerves," no deep sensibilities, was an advantage to him. His imperturbability, which was apt in the ordinary circumstances of life to be almost intolerable, now gave Louis XVI a certain moral grandeur. So much, at least, we have learned from the commissaries who were looking on through the glass door, that there were no tears in his eyes and that he never raised his voice. When saying farewell to his wife and children this pitifully weak man, this unworthy king, showed more strength and more dignity than ever in his life before. Quietly, as on any other evening, the condemned man rose from his chair at ten o'clock, and thus gave his family the signal to depart. Marie Antoinette did not venture to resist his plainly expressed wish, all the more because (it was a pious fraud) he told her that he would come upstairs to see her once again at seven o'clock on the following morning.

Thereafter, quiet reigned in the Templars' tower. The Queen was alone in the upper story, throughout a long and sleepless night. At

length day dawned, and therewith came the dreadful noises of preparation. She heard the gride of wheels as a carriage drew up outside the
gates; she heard footsteps coming up, footsteps going down the stairs.
Was it the confessor, a messenger from the Commune, or already those
who were to fetch the condemned man to the place of execution? In
the far distance there was a rattle of drums, for whole regiments were
being marshalled. Nearer, ever nearer drew the hour which was to deprive her children of their father and herself of the man who had been
her kindly, honourable, and considerate companion for more than two
decades. Penned in her room, with inexorable sentries stationed at the
door, the sorely tried woman was forbidden to go downstairs, and, in
her tortured imagination, suffered worse things than if she had been
in contact with the dread reality. Then, after some stir and bustle,
there was perfect stillness beneath. The King had left the building,
and was being driven away to the place of execution. Within an hour,
the guillotine had given Marie Antoinette, sometime Archduchess of
Austria, then Dauphiness, and at length Queen of France, a new name
—"Widow Capet."

CHAPTER XXXVI

Marie Antoinette Alone

THE thud of the axe was followed by a period of comparative tranquillity. In executing Louis XVI, even the extremists who now ruled the Convention had wished only to draw a blood-red line between monarchy and the Republic. For a while not one of the deputies (among whom most of those who had voted for the execution had in their secret hearts regretted having to send this weak-kneed but kindly man to a violent death) had any thought of bringing an accusation against Marie Antoinette. Without a division, without debate, the Commune agreed to supply the widow with the mourning apparel she asked for; the strictness of supervision was relaxed; and, if the daughter of the Habsburgs and her children were still kept in prison, it was only because the revolutionists felt that therewith they held a sort of hostage—something that would make it easier for them to bargain with Austria.

But they were miscalculating. The Convention greatly overestimated the strength of Habsburg family feeling. Emperor Francis, cold and obtuse, avaricious and mean-spirited, had never a thought of abstracting from the imperial treasure-house so much as a single jewel in order to ransom his aunt and his little cousins; and, besides, the Austrian militarists did their utmost to hinder negotiations for peace. It was true that, at the outset, the court of Vienna had solemnly declared the war to have been undertaken exclusively for ideal ends, and nowise in order to secure conquest or indemnities; but it is part of the essential nature of war that, however originated, it tends to become a war of annexation; and the French revolutionists, likewise, were soon ready to repudiate their ideal aims. Not in words, perhaps, but in deeds! As for the generals, they have never liked civilian interference in the conduct of war; too rarely for their taste do the nations give them a chance of showing their prowess, and therefore, when once a war begins, the longer it lasts the better they like it. Mercy, now well up in years, acting upon a hint from Fersen, reminded the court of Vienna that Marie

Antoinette, having been deprived of the title of Queen of France, had once more become an archduchess of Austria and a member of the imperial family, so that it was the Emperor's duty to claim his relative. But one imprisoned woman is of little account in a world war, one life is a trifle in the cynical game of politics! Other monarchs, too, hardened their hearts and closed their doors. Though every one of them declared himself profoundly moved by Louis's execution and Marie Antoinette's plight, they would not stir a finger to help her. Well might she repeat what her husband had said to Fersen: "Everyone has forsaken me."

Everyone had forsaken her. That was what Marie Antoinette felt when she was left alone behind the prison bars. Yet her will to live was unbroken, and this will gave her the resolution to try what self-help could do. They had taken away her crown; and, though tired and aged by her sorrows, she retained much of her old charm, she was still able to win the affection of those with whom she came into contact. The precautions adopted by Hébert and the other members of the Commune were insufficient to counteract the workings of the mysterious, the magnetic force which was radiated upon the petty-bourgeois guardians and officials brought into close proximity with the woman who had once been a great queen. Within a few weeks after Louis's execution, most of the Reds, most of the sansculottes, set to guard her had become her secret helpers; and, notwithstanding the strictness of the regulations drafted by the Commune, there were numerous breaches in the invisible wall which separated Marie Antoinette from the outside world. Thanks to the help of those who had been thus won over to her cause, messages were continually being smuggled into and out of the Temple. A gesture-language, a sort of deaf-and-dumb alphabet was used whereby, despite the alertness of the commissaries, the Queen was kept informed of the daily incidents of politics and the war; and another expedient was to employ a newsvendor to cry the latest and most important news beneath the windows of the Temple. This circle of confederates gradually enlarged to embrace more and more of the sentries and watchmen. Now at length, when Louis XVI (whose irresoluteness had been an insuperable barrier to effective action) was no longer at her side, Marie Antoinette, left to her own devices, was able to work strenuously upon a plan for escape.

Danger is like aqua fortis. Courage and cowardice, which may remain indistinguishable in the average and lukewarm circumstances of daily life, are sundered by this fiery test. The poltroons of the old regime, the more selfish among the nobility, had fled to foreign lands as soon as the King was transferred from Versailles to Paris. None but the faithful had remained, none but those in whom implicit trust could be placed, seeing that, for all who had been known as servants of the King, to stay on in Paris involved deadly peril. One of the most notable among these stalwarts was a sometime general, Jarjayes, whose wife had been lady-in-waiting at the court. To be near Marie Antoinette in this time of trouble, he left the safe harbourage of Coblenz, and, coming to Paris, he managed to let the Queen know that he was prepared to make any sacrifice in her behalf. On February 2, 1793, a fortnight after the King's execution, a stranger came to Jarjayes and made him an astonishing proposal—to help Marie Antoinette escape from the Temple. Jarjayes regarded the newcomer with suspicion, for the man's aspect was that of a thorough-going sansculotte. Most likely this was a provocative agent! However, the seeming Red handed him a note which he recognized as being beyond question in the Queen's handwriting, and which ran as follows: "You can trust the man who comes to you from me bringing this missive. His feelings are well known to me, and he has been of the same mind for the last five months."

The bearer of the note was Toulan, one of the regular guardians at the Temple, and his case is of remarkable psychological interest. On August 10, 1792, when the revolutionists had determined to make an end of the monarchy, he had been among the first volunteers for the storming of the Tuileries, and he wore a medal commemorating his deeds on that occasion. It was owing to his avowed republicanism that Toulan had been chosen by the Commune as one of the Queen's custodians, since he was believed to be peculiarly trustworthy and absolutely incorruptible. But Saul had become Paul! Touched by the misfortunes of the woman over whom he was keeping watch, he was now a devoted adherent of her whose palace he had helped to storm; and he had shown so much attachment that Marie Antoinette, in her secret communications, invariably referred to him by the pseudonym of "le fidèle." Among those who were implicated in the conspiracy to effect the Queen's escape, Toulan was the only one in whose motives avarice played no part. He was instigated by humane sentiments, and perhaps by a lust for adventure. Brave men delight in danger, and it was logical that the others, who were only seeking private gain, should find ways and means of saving their necks when the affair was blown upon, whereas Toulan's rashness cost him his life.

Jarjayes trusted the stranger, but not wholly. A letter may always have been forged, and in times of war and revolution correspondence is dangerous. The ex-general therefore asked Toulan to find a way of introducing him into the Temple, so that he could have a personal interview with the Queen. At the first glance it seemed impossible to gain an entry for an unauthorized person, a man of noble birth, into this carefully guarded tower. By liberal promises of money, however, Marie Antoinette had in the meanwhile gained new assistants, and a few days later Toulan brought Jarjayes a further note. "If you have decided to come here, the sooner the better. But for God's sake be careful to avoid being recognized, especially by the woman who is imprisoned here with us." This woman was named Tison, and the Queen's instinctive conviction that she was a spy was well grounded. The attempt to escape was, in fact, frustrated by her watchfulness and her fidelity to her revolutionary employers. For a time, however, all went well. Jarjayes was smuggled into the Temple, in a way which reminds us of a modern detective story. Every evening a lamp-lighter came into the quadrangle of the tower, for, by order of the Commune, the place had to be brightly lit since darkness might favour an escape. Now, Toulan had humbugged this lamp-lighter into believing that he had a friend who, just for the fun of the thing, wanted to see the inside of the prison. For a consideration, the lamp-lighter was to lend the friend his clothes and equipment for one evening. The story was amusing and plausible enough, the lamp-lighter pocketed his bribe, handed over the requisites, and departed to make merry over a bottle of wine. Thus suitably disguised, Jarjayes gained admission to the Temple, had a talk with the Queen, and arranged with her a bold scheme for escape. She and Madame Elisabeth, dressed as men in the uniforms of municipal councillors, and provided with stolen passes, were to quit the tower as if they had been officials of the Commune who had been holding an inspection. To get the children out of duress would prove a more difficult matter. However, as luck would have it, the genuine lamp-lighter was often accompanied on his rounds by his children. Once more, therefore, his role was to be assumed by the resolute nobleman, who, after lighting the lamps in the courtyard, would lead out the two children, poorly dressed to fit the part, as if they had been his own. Three light carriages were to be in waiting: one for the Queen, her son, and Jarjayes; another for her daughter and the second conspirator, who was called Lepitre; the third for Madame Elisabeth and Toulan. With at least five hours' start before the discovery of the flight, they hoped to be beyond pursuit. The boldness of the scheme aroused no fears in the Queen's mind. She agreed to it, and Jarjayes undertook to get into touch with Lepitre.

A remarkable role was played in the plot by this Lepitre, who had formerly been a schoolmaster, and who was talkative, stout, short, and lame. The Queen had written of him: "You will interview the new party to our plan; his looks are by no means prepossessing, but he is indispensable to us." Neither humankindliness nor yet love of adventure brought him into the affair, but the promise of a large reward—which, unfortunately, Jarjayes did not possess in hard cash, for, strangely enough, the Chevalier de Jarjayes was not in touch with the Baron de Batz, the one man of means who was active in the Parisian counter-revolutionary movement. Batz's plan and that of Jarjayes were progressing almost simultaneously but independently, and neither conspirator knew what the other was doing. Thus valuable time was lost, for funds could not be secured until the man who had been the Queen's banker under the old regime had been taken into Jarjaye's confidence. At length, after a good deal of parleying, the money was provided. Meanwhile, however, Lepitre, who as a member of the Commune had already furnished the requisite forged passports, had grown faint-hearted. It had been bruited abroad that the gates of Paris were to be closed and that carriages passing out of the city were to be searched. Lepitre was a timid fellow. Maybe, too, he had noticed that Madame Tison was on the alert. Anyhow, he refused further help, and this made it impossible to get the four captives simultaneously out of the Temple. The Queen would have to make good her escape alone. Jarjayes and Toulan did their best to persuade her, but nothing would induce her to accept this revised proposal. She would rather give up the whole thing than forsake her children! It was in moving terms that she wrote to Jarjayes assuring him her mind was absolutely made up.

"We have dreamed a pleasant dream, that is all; at the same time we have gained much by discovering a fresh proof of your whole-hearted devotion to me. My trust in you knows no limit. You will always, whatever happens, find me full of character and courage; but my son's interest is my sole guide, and however great the happiness I might feel at getting away from here, I cannot possibly consent to part from him. For the rest, I fully recognize your fidelity as shown by what you told me yesterday. Be assured I am well aware that you are thinking only of my best interests, and that the chance we are now letting slip may never return; but I should have no joy left if I were to forsake my children, and I therefore have not an atom of regret in abandoning the scheme."

Jarjayes had done his chivalrous best, and, as far as work in Paris was concerned, he could no longer be of any use to the Queen. And yet there was still one service which this loyal adherent could perform. His departure from the capital gave her a splendid chance of sending last tokens of affection to her friends and relatives abroad. Shortly before his execution, Louis XVI had wanted to send his family his signet ring and a lock of hair which his valet was to take to them as memorials; but the Commune, scenting some sinister conspiracy beneath these gifts from a man doomed to the scaffold, had confiscated the relics and had placed them under seal. Toulan, foolhardy as ever, broke the seal and brought the memorials to Marie Antoinette. Feeling that they would not long be safe in her keeping, she decided, now that a trustworthy messenger was at length available, to send the ring and the lock of hair to the Count of Provence. In this connexion, she wrote to her brother-in-law as follows:

"Since I have a faithful being, on whom I can count, I take advantage of the fact to send my brother and friend this heritage, which is to be confided to his hands alone. The bearer will inform you by what miracle we have been able to regain possession of these precious memorials. I refrain from mentioning the name of the man who has been so useful to us, but hope to be able to tell it you some day. The impossibility up till now of sending you any news, and the way in which misfortune has been heaped upon misfortune, have made us feel our cruel separation yet more keenly. I hope it may not last much longer. My warmest love, for you know that I love you with all my heart."

She wrote in similar terms to the Count of Artois. Jarjayes, however, still hesitated to leave Paris, for the valiant fellow hoped that his presence might be useful to Marie Antoinette. At length, however, his tarrying became a needless and unmeaning risk. Shortly before his departure he received through Toulan a last letter from the Queen: "Adieu. I think, if you have made up your mind to leave, the sooner you go the better. How sorry I am for your poor wife! What happiness if we can meet again ere long. Never shall I be able to show you all the gratitude I feel for what you have done in my behalf. Adieu— how cruel is the word!"

Marie Antoinette was convinced that this would be the last time she would be able to send a confidential message across the frontier. Was there no one else to whom she wished to say a word, to whom she wished to send some token of affection, than these two brothers-in-law, the Count of Provence and the Count of Artois, whom she had so little reason to thank, and whom nothing but ties of affinity had made fit guardians of her husband's legacy? Had she really no greeting to transmit to him who was the dearest in the world to her save for her children, to Fersen, of whom she had said that she could not live without news of him, to whom from the inferno of the besieged Tuileries she had sent a ring in eternal remembrance? Did not her heart go out to him when this last possibility of communication arose? It is true that the memoirs of Goguelat, which give precise information of the farewell to Jarjayes and of the messages to the two brothers-in-law, do refer to Fersen, but they mention no greeting from Marie Antoinette to her lover. Our expectation that to him, above all, she would have sent a farewell greeting is disappointed.

Nevertheless, in the end feeling triumphs over what may seem to be accurate information. Marie Antoinette, in those concluding hours of loneliness, had not forgotten her lover; and it seems probable that the duty-messages to the Count of Provence and the Count of Artois were but pretexts to cover another message faithfully conveyed by Jarjayes. But in 1823, when Goguelat's memoirs were published, the conspiracy of silence surrounding the Queen's relationship with Fersen had already begun. The most important passage in the letters had been suppressed by puritanical editors, and did not come to light until a century had elapsed. We know, now, that in actual fact never had the Queen's passion for her lover been stronger than in these moments before she perished. It will be remembered that she had sent Fersen a ring bearing the French fleur-de-lis. In like manner she had had made for her own wearing a ring adorned with the Swedish nobleman's arms, a ring which she wore constantly, so that every glance at her hand might remind her of him. Now, when Jarjayes was leaving, and there was a last chance of communication, she wished to show Fersen that all her love still went out to him. The ring could be used as a signet, so she took an impression of the arms in wax, and sent it to Jarjayes to be conveyed to Fersen. No words were needed; the token sufficed. Writing to Jarjayes she said: "The seal I enclose has nothing to do with the other matters. I want you to transmit it to the person whom you know to have come from Brussels to visit me last winter, and whom you will tell that the device has never been truer than it is now."

What, then, is the motto upon the signet ring which Marie Antoinette had had made for herself, the motto which was never truer than now? What was the device upon the only ring which, of her many trinkets, she continued to wear in prison?

The motto inscribed beneath Ferson's arms consisted of five Italian words, "Tutto a te mi guida"—Everything leads me to you.

On these five simple and heartfelt words the curtain rings down. Tutto a te mi guida.

CHAPTER XXXVII

Final Solitude

DISBURDENING! The last word has been said. Now it is easier to await the end tranquilly. Marie Antoinette has bidden farewell to the world. She no longer hopes, and no longer makes any attempt to escape. She can no longer count upon aid from the court of Vienna, no longer does she expect a victory of the French troops. Jarjayes has left the capital, and the faithful Toulan has been removed from his post as guardian, so there is no one at hand to help her. Madame Tison, the spy of the Commune, has told her employers that some of the guardians are untrustworthy. If hitherto an attempt at escape has been dangerous, now it would be foolish and suicidal.

Yet there are persons to whom danger is a lure, who love to stake the limit, whose energies are doubled and trebled when they attempt the impossible, and to whom a foolhardy adventure can alone give lust to life. Such people find it hard to breathe in the piping times of peace; tranquillity bores them to distraction; they need vent for their temperamental foolhardiness; and their ruling passion is to attempt the crazy, the absurd, the impossible. The Baron de Batz, who had stayed on in Paris, was a man of this type. Of noble blood, and wealthy, so long as the monarchy was resplendent and revered it had been his pride to lurk in the background. Why should he make obeisance to obtain a position, to win a sinecure? Nothing but peril could set him in motion. Not until the other royalists had given up the King for lost, did the Don Quixote of loyalty make heroic efforts to save poor Louis. To this dare-devil it seemed a matter of course that he should remain in the firing-line throughout the Revolution. Under dozens of aliases he stayed in hiding while carrying on his active campaign against the Reds. He devoted vast sums of money to numerous enterprises, of which the maddest, so far, had been that when the King was being driven to execution under guard of eight thousand armed men, he had drawn his sword with the cry: "Join me, friends who wish to save their King!" But no one joined him.

In all France there was no other rashling ready in broad daylight to attempt the rescue of a condemned man from a hostile city, to snatch Louis from a whole army. Finding himself unsupported, Baron de Batz vanished in the crowd before the guards had recovered from their surprise. However, this failure had not dispirited him in the least, and his only thought was to outdo so bold a venture, as soon as Louis had been executed, by staging a preposterously venturesome plan for the rescue of the Queen.

Baron de Batz had been quick to recognize the weak point of the Revolution, the poison gnawing at its vitals, the deadly evil which Robespierre was trying to excise with the guillotine—corruption. By seizing political power, the revolutionists had got control of the offices of State; and posts under government, major and minor, were paid for in money, which corrodes souls as rust corrodes steel. Nor was it only the salaries that were in question. Cash passed through the hands of officials, and stuck to their fingers. Proletarians, petty bourgeois, persons who had never before been concerned in great enterprises, handicraftsmen, clerks, agitators who had had no serious employment, could now dispose of great sums that were needed for the purchase of munitions of war, or that were received for the sale of the estates of the émigrés. There was no adequate check upon the moneys thus disbursed, and few of those concerned had the incorruptibility of a Cato or a Robespierre, few could withstand the overwhelming temptation. Obscure ties were formed between sentiment and business; and many of the revolutionary ultras, who had been eager to serve the Republic, now became no less eager to feather their own nests. Into this turbid pool of corruption Baron de Batz threw his well-baited hooks, whispering a magic word which then as today exercised a marvellous lure, a "million." There was a million at the disposal of those who would help to get the Queen away from the Temple. With such a sum the walls of the strongest dungeon can be broken down. Baron de Batz did not, like Jarjayes, deal with understrappers, with lamp-lighters and with private soldiers, but resolutely devoted himself to bribing the chiefs. Above all he made advances to important members of the town council, such as the sometime lemonade-seller Michonis, inspector of prisons, and therefore in charge of the Temple as well as of the other jails. The second string to his bow was Cortey, the military commander of the section. Thus our royalist, against whom a warrant was out and for whom the police were searching day and night, had both the civil and the military guardians of the Temple under his thumb, and at the very time when in the Convention and in the Committee of Public Safety the members were thundering invectives against "the infamous Batz," the Baron, in safe hiding, and with powerful protectors, could get on with his scheme.

A master conspirator, so splendid was his courage that, although the Committee of Public Safety had become aware that he was busily at work upon endeavours to overthrow the Republic, he calmly had himself enrolled as a private, under the name of Forguet, among the guards of the Temple, since he was determined to keep the affair under personal observation. Musket in hand, dressed in the dirty and ragged uniform of a National Guard, this millionaire aristocrat took his turn with his fellow-soldiers in doing sentry-go in front of the Queen's door. We do not know whether he had any interviews with Marie Antoinette, but there was no need for them, since Michonis, who was to earn a big share of the million, was in touch with the Queen. At the same time, thanks to Cortey's position as military commander, an ever larger number of men in the Baron's pay were introduced among the sentries. Thus there ensued one of the most amazing and improbable situations in history. A day came in the year 1793, when, in the centre of revolutionary Paris, the stronghold of the Temple (which no one could enter without a permit from the Commune and where Marie Antoinette, the detested ex-Queen of France, was supposed to be watched exclusively by devotees of the Republic) was actually under guard of a battalion of disguised royalists, whose leader was Baron de Batz proscribed in a hundred warrants issued by the Convention and the Committee of Public Safety. No writer of historical romances has ever conceived a more preposterous story.

At length it seemed to Batz that the time was ripe for his coup. The night had come when, if that coup were successful, one of the most memorable and fateful transformation scenes of history would take place, for the new king of France, Louis XVII, would be torn from the hands of the Revolution. Baron de Batz was playing at dice with fate, was playing a game of hazard which, should he win, might well result in the destruction of the Republic. When darkness fell, everything was ready to the last detail. Cortey marched into the yard at the head of his detachment, accompanied by the arch-conspirator, Baron de Batz. The military commander distributed his men in such a fashion that the exits were in the hands of the royalists recruited by the Baron. Simultaneously Michonis, the other republican official who had been so liberally bribed, was on duty upstairs in the Queen's room, and had already provided Marie Antoinette, Madame Elisabeth, and the Queen's daughter, with uniform cloaks. At midnight these three, wearing military caps and shouldering muskets, were to march out of the Temple with others of the bribed National Guards, the Dauphin in their midst. Since Cortey, as chief officer of the guard, could have the great gates opened whenever he pleased, it seemed practically certain that the little force under his leadership would be able to make its way into the street without arousing the least suspicion. As to what was to happen afterwards, Batz had arranged everything. Under a false name he owned a country house not far from Paris, a place which had never been raided by the police. There the royal family was to remain in hiding for a few weeks, until a favourable opportunity arose to get them across the frontier. Furthermore, there were a couple of vigorous and determined royalists, each armed with a pair of pistols, stationed in the street, to check pursuit if the escape should be detected.

It was nearly eleven o'clock. Marie Antoinette and the others were ready to follow their liberators at any moment. Below in the courtyard they could hear the tramp of the patrol, but this was not alarming since they knew that friendly hearts were beating beneath the uniforms of the ostensible sansculottes. Michonis was only waiting for a sign from Baron de Batz. At this juncture, however, came an alarm. Someone knocked loudly at the prison gate. Lest suspicion should be aroused, the late-comer was promptly admitted. It was Simon, the shoemaker, a steadfast and incorruptible revolutionist, a member of the Commune, who had come in haste to make sure that the Queen had not already been carried off. A few hours earlier, a gendarme had brought him a missive betraying Michonis's plans for the night, and

Simon had instantly acquainted his fellow-members of the town council with the news. They, however, were by no means ready to give
credence to so romantic a tale, for their tables were laden day after
day with hundreds of such denunciations. Besides, the story seemed
too wildly improbable. Was not the Temple guarded by 280 men,
and under the supervision of the most trustworthy commissaries?
Still, no harm would be done by entrusting Simon, instead of Michonis,
with the charge of the interior of the Temple for this one night. The
instant Cortey saw the newcomer, he realized that the game was up.
Simon, however, never guessed for a moment that Cortey was one
of the conspirators. "Since you are here," said the shoemaker, "I am
easy in my mind." Then he went upstairs to Michonis.

Baron de Batz, who realized that his plan was about to be ship-
wrecked, deliberated for a moment. Should he dog Simon up the
stairs, and blow out the man's brains? No, that would be fruitless!
The sound of the shot would instantly bring the rest of the guard
upon the scene. They were not all of them in the plot. One of the
revolutionary stalwarts must have got wind of it and betrayed it. The
Queen's escape had become impossible, and an act of violence would
needlessly endanger her life. The only thing that remained was to
get safely out of the Temple those who had entered it in disguise.
Cortey, who was sweating with alarm, quickly gathered the conspirators together into a patrol. With Baron de Batz among them, they
quietly marched out into the street. The conspirators were saved, but
the Queen had been sacrificed.

Meanwhile Simon had been furiously taking Michonis to task, insisting that the latter must instantly come to the Commune and give
an account of his doings. Michonis, who had got rid of his disguise
before Simon came into the room, remained imperturbable. Making
no objection, he followed the dangerous Simon to the sitting of the
dangerous tribunal. Strangely enough, the Commune gave Simon
rather a chill reception. He was indeed extolled for his patriotism,
his zeal, and his watchfulness, but at the same time he was given to
understand that he must have been seeing spooks. As far as appearances went, the Commune did not take the conspiracy seriously.

In actual fact, however—and this gives us a shrewd glimpse into the devious paths of politics—the town councillors took the attempt at flight very seriously indeed, but were chiefly concerned to avoid having any fuss made about the matter. This is proved by a very remarkable document in which the Committee of Public Safety directs the public prosecutor in Marie Antoinette's trial to suppress all references to the details of the great plot for the Queen's escape hatched by the Baron de Batz and his confederates, and frustrated at the last moment by Simon. The fact that there had been an attempt at escape might be mentioned, but nothing more. The Commune was afraid to let the world know how far the poison of corruption had spread among its own members and the most trusted of its employees—the consequence of this hush-it-up policy being that for many, many years one of the most dramatic episodes in history was shrouded by a veil of silence.

Nevertheless—while the Commune of Paris, the revolutionary municipal council, alarmed by the venality brought to light in the Batz affair, considered it would be better to refrain from any public trial of those who had been concerned in the plans for escape—it decided to deal more harshly than ever with the prisoner, with the bold woman who, instead of quietly accepting her fate, was fired by an invincible spirit of revolt. Measures must be taken to render such attempts impossible for the future. The suspect commissaries, beginning with Toulan and Lepitre, were dismissed from their posts, and from this time onward Marie Antoinette was watched like a criminal. One night at eleven, Hébert, the most ruthless of the town councillors, paid a visit to Marie Antoinette and Madame Elisabeth, who had long since gone to bed. Acting under instructions from the Commune, he made the fullest possible use of his authorization to effect a thorough search. It lasted five hours, every room, every article of wearing apparel, every piece of furniture, every drawer, being rigorously scrutinized.

The results of the search were, however, minimal. Nothing more was discovered than a red-leather portfolio in which were papers containing a few addresses of no consequence; a pencil-holder without a pencil; a stick of sealing-wax; two miniatures and other mementoes; an old hat that had belonged to Louis XVI. Further surprise visits, additional searches, gave no better result. Throughout the revolutionary period, Marie Antoinette had been careful to burn every scrap of writing that might incriminate her friends and helpers, so that no excuse for a prosecution could be discovered. Greatly annoyed at the lack of evidence against their redoubtable adversary, and convinced nonetheless that she must still be engaged in counter-revolutionary activities, the members of the Commune of Paris decided to assail her where she would be most sensitive—in her maternal affection. This time they hit the bull's-eye. On July 1, 1793, a few days after the conspiracy had been discovered, the Committee of Public Safety, acting upon a resolution passed by the Commune, decided that the ex-Dauphin, Louis Capet, should be separated from his mother, and confined in a part of the fortress where he would have no chance of communicating with her. Since, in these circumstances, his mother could not carry on his education, the lad, now eight years old, was to have a tutor.

Who was this tutor to be? The choice was left to the Commune, which, grateful to Simon the shoemaker for having prevented Marie Antoinette's escape, and knowing him to be a sansculotte whose principles were proof against temptation either by money or by an appeal to his sensibilities, decided that he was the very man for the job. Now Simon, though a rough fellow and a typical proletarian, was by no means the toper and the sadist of monarchical legend. Still, it was a lamentable choice. He could read and write, after a fashion; but he had certainly read little, and the only letter of his that has come down to us shows that his knowledge of spelling was elementary—but he was a Red, and in 1793 to be a Red was sufficient qualification for any office. There had been an immense decline in the spiritual level of the Revolution since, six months before, in the National Assembly, the proposal had been mooted to appoint Condorcet (philosopher and mathematician, secretary of the Academy of the Sciences, and author of the *Progrès de l'esprit humain*) tutor to the heir to the French throne. Between this man of genius and Simon the shoemaker there was a great gulf fixed. Of late, however, though the motto of the republic was "Liberty, Equality, and Fraternity," there remained scant thought of either liberty or fraternity, which had declined in value as much as the assignats. "Equality," or rather a forcible levelling-down, dominated the last, the most radical phase of the Revolution.

The deliberate aim of the Commune was that little Louis should be brought up, not to become a man of culture, but one of the uninstructed who constituted the lowest class of the population. He was to forget his high birth, for this would make it easier to ignore him.

Marie Antoinette had not had the slightest warning of this decision to remove her child from her care when, at half past nine one evening, six deputies from the Commune knocked at the gate of the Temple. The method of cruel surprise was part of Hébert's system. His domiciliary visits, his searches, his inspections, were always unannounced, and usually took place late at night. The boy had long since been put to bed, but the Queen and Madame Elisabeth were still up. The officials of the Commune entered their sitting-room, and the Queen rose with an uneasy mind, for every such nocturnal visit had brought her humiliation or evil tidings. On this occasion even the revolutionary intruders seemed more than a little embarrassed. Themselves, for the most part, fathers of families, they found it hard to tell a mother that the Committee of Public Safety had, without any apparent reason, decided to deprive her of the custody of her son.

As regards the scene which took place that night between the despairing mother and the officials of the Commune the only information available is testimony which cannot be relied upon, for it is that of the Dauphin's sister, who at the time was only thirteen years of age. Is it true, as the Duchess of Angoulême declares, that Marie Antoinette, with tears streaming down her face, implored these officials, who were merely fulfilling their instructions, to leave her son under her care? That she exclaimed they would do better to kill her than to take little Louis away from her? That the messengers from the Commune threatened (the statement is highly improbable, since they were not thus commissioned) to kill the boy and the girl if their mother continued to oppose their wishes; and that, in the end, after a tussle which had lasted for hours, they carried off the screaming and sobbing lad by brute force?

The official report of what happened contains no mention of such details, but tells us simply: "The separation was effected with all the kindliness proper to the circumstances, the officers of the people having exhibited the utmost consideration compatible with the strictness of their duties." Each report contradicts the other; both are unquestion‧

ably biased, and where the partisan spirit is at work we seldom hear
the truth. Of this, at least, there can be no doubt, that the enforced
and needlessly cruel severance from her son must have been one of
the most painful moments in Marie Antoinette's life. The mother was
deeply attached to this high-spirited, precocious, fair-haired little boy,
the boy she had wanted to bring up to be a king. It was his merry
chatter, it was his unstinted curiosity, which had made the hours in
the lonely fortress endurable. Beyond dispute, she was fonder of him
than of her daughter, who, being of a sulky temperament, mentally
inert, and in all respects insignificant, must have made much less
appeal to the liveliness and tenderness of Marie Antoinette than the
good-looking, gentle, and quick-witted youngster, who was now
snatched from her thus brutally. It was harsh almost beyond belief
that, although the Dauphin was to stay on in the Temple in a room
only a few yards from the tower occupied by his mother, she was
never to be allowed to exchange a word with him; and that she was
forbidden to pay him a visit even when he was ailing. He was quar-
antined from her as if she had been suffering from the plague. She
was actually forbidden to converse with Simon the shoemaker, the
boy's tutor, from whom she might have gleaned a little information
about her son. His seclusion from her was to be unconditional and
absolute.

After a while, however, Marie Antoinette discovered, as a trifling
and most inadequate consolation, that from one of the window-slits
in the spiral staircase she could, from the third story, get a glimpse
into the courtyard where the Dauphin often played. There she would
stand hour after hour, waiting till fortune vouchsafed her a fleeting
glance of him upon whom her affections were now centred. In this
matter, at least, her guardians were kindly, and did not interfere. The
child, who, in childish fashion, had quickly adapted himself to the
changed circumstances, never guessed, as he played merrily enough,
that his mother was spying eagerly upon him through this grated
loop-hole whose bars she may have often wetted with her tears. He
had forgotten whose child he was, from what race he sprang, and
what name he bore. Loudly and energetically he would sing the
Carmagnole and the *Ça ira,* which Simon and the other revolutionists had taught him—though, it need hardly be said, he had not the

vaguest notion of their significance. It seemed to him amusing to wear the red cap of the sansculottes. He played games with the soldiers who were set to keep watch over his mother. Not only by stone walls, but by a whole world, was the boy now separated from her. What would become of him, thought the poor woman who could no longer embrace him but could only look at him from a distance. Had not Hébert, to whose tender mercies the Convention had pitilessly entrusted her, written in his scurrilous rag the "Père Duchesne" the threatening words: "Unhappy nation! . . . This brat will bring disaster on you soon or late; for the more amusing he is, the more is he to be dreaded. The best thing would be to maroon the young serpent and his sister upon a desert island, for we must get rid of them at any cost. Besides what does a child more or less matter when the safety of the Republic is at stake?"

What does a child more or less matter? Not much to Hébert, as Marie Antoinette knew well enough. That was why she shuddered on the days when she did not see her darling at play in the courtyard. That was why she trembled in helpless rage whenever this enemy came into her room, this wretch by whose counsel her child had been reft from her and who had thereby been guilty of one of the most contemptible crimes ever known—a needless act of cruelty perpetrated upon an adversary already overthrown. It is, indeed, a black page in the story of the Revolution that it should have handed the Queen over to Hébert's charge; for even the loftiest of ideals becomes degraded and petty when, in its name, power is given to unworthy creatures capable of the basest acts of inhumanity.

Tedious were the hours and darker seemed the barred windows of the tower, now that her boy's laughter no longer brought solace to the mother's heart. No news came from without, her last helpers had vanished, there was no further means of communicating with her friends across the frontier. Marie Antoinette, her daughter, and Madame Elisabeth were a lonely company day after day; they had nothing to say to one another; the ex-Queen and her sister-in-law had ceased to hope and perhaps even ceased to fear. Though spring had passed and summer had come, they rarely went downstairs and out into the little garden, for an intense fatigue had made their limbs heavy. During these weeks of uttermost distress, the light in the Queen's countenance was extinguished. When we examine the last oil-painting made of Marie Antoinette, we find it hard to recognize the sometime queen of pastoral plays, the goddess of the Rococo; and hard even to recognize the proud, combative, and majestic creature Marie Antoinette had still been in the Tuileries. The woman of this clumsy likeness, wearing a widow's cap over her white hair, is already old, though her years number only eight-and-thirty. The sparkle has vanished from her weary eyes, and we feel that we are looking at one who is ready to answer any summons without an attempt at resistance. What had been the charm of her countenance has been effaced by a hopelessly mournful expression, and liveliness has given place to supreme indifference. Looking at it from afar, we fancy this picture of Marie Antoinette to be that of a prioress or an abbess, of a woman who no longer had any interest in the world, whose wishes were dead, and who was already living another life than ours. We see in it neither beauty nor courage nor energy; nothing but passivity. The Queen has abdicated, the woman has renounced her womanhood. The face looking forth from the canvas is that of a matron long outworn, whom no further happenings can either astonish or alarm.

In actual fact, Marie Antoinette was not affrighted when, at two o'clock one morning, there came a knocking at her door. What more harm could the world do her, now that it had taken from her her husband, her son, her lover, her crown, her honour, and her liberty? Rising from bed, she dressed, and opened her door to the commissaries. They read aloud to her the Convention's decree to the effect that the Widow Capet, since she was to be prosecuted, must be transferred from the Temple to the Conciergerie. Having listened quietly, she made no answer. She knew well enough that an accusation before the Revolutionary Tribunal was equivalent to a death-sentence, and that imprisonment in the Conciergerie was the last stage on the way to the guillotine. She made no plaint, offered no protest, did not ask for a postponement. She had not a word to say to these men who appeared with such a dread message in the night. Indifferently she submitted to having her clothes searched, to having her personal belongings taken away from her. She was allowed to keep nothing but a pocket-handkerchief and a small phial containing drops of a cordial. Then she had to make the last of many farewells, parting this time from her sister-in-law and her daughter. She had grown accustomed to such partings!

With a firm gait she walked to the door of the room and quickly down the stairs, rejecting offers of assistance. It had been needless to leave her the cordial; her heart would not fail her, since her strength came to her from within. She had long since endured the worst that fate could bring; no coming ordeal could be more grievous than had been the life of the last few months. Death, now close at hand, would be easier. She was ready, perhaps eager, to meet it. Swiftly, therefore, she sped forth from this tower of haunting memories, so swiftly that (perhaps her eyes were blinded with tears) she forgot to stoop as she passed through the low portal of exit, and knocked her forehead against the hard stone archway. Her conductors, honestly distressed, asked her whether she had hurt herself. "No," she answered unmoved; "nothing can hurt me now."

CHAPTER XXXVIII

The Conciergerie

ANOTHER woman had been called out of her bed that night, Madame Richard, wife of the governor of the Conciergerie. Instructions had been brought to her to prepare a cell for Marie Antoinette. After dukes, princes, counts, bishops, ordinary citizens, after victims of all grades and classes, the sometime Queen of France was now to pass by the same road. Madame Richard was alarmed. She was a woman of the people, she had been brought up under the old regime, and, whatever changes had taken place, the word "queen" produced its familiar reaction. A queen was a person to be revered, and now the Queen of France was to be sheltered under her roof! She searched her linen-cupboard for the finest and whitest sheets. General Custine, who was himself about to perish beneath the knife, was turned out of the little room with barred windows which had for numberless years served as council-chamber; and the gloomy place was made ready for Marie Antoinette. A folding iron bedstead, two mattresses, two straw paillasses, a pillow, a light coverlet, a basin and ewer, an old carpet hung on the wall where it was damp—she could not venture to provide more than these luxuries for the Queen. Then the officers of the ancient stone building which was more than half underground had to wait patiently for the coming of their august prisoner.

At three in the morning the noise of wheels was heard. The carriages pulled up at the gate. Now there appeared in the dark passage some gendarmes carrying torches, followed by Michonis, the lemonade-seller, who had been clever enough to escape arrest for his complicity in the Batz affair and had retained his office of inspector-general of prisons. Behind him, in the flickering light, walked the Queen, attended by her little dog, the only creature dear to her she had been allowed to bring with her to this new prison. Since the hour was late, and it would have been farcical in the Conciergerie to feign ignorance as to the identity of Marie Antoinette, she was spared the usual formalities of admission and was allowed to go forthwith to her cell. The kitchen-maid of the governor's wife, a country girl named Rosalie Lamorlière who did not even know how to write, but to whom we owe the best available information concerning the last seventy-seven days of Marie Antoinette's life, timidly followed the black-clad woman into the cell and offered to help her undress. "Thank you, child," answered the Queen; "now that I no longer have servants of my own I have become accustomed to looking after myself." She hung her watch upon a nail in the wall, to record the brief and yet long-drawn-out time that remained to her. Then she undressed and got into bed. A gendarme with a loaded musket came in, and the door was shut. The last act of the great tragedy had begun.

It was well known in revolutionary Paris, and was well known all over the world, that the Conciergerie was the place where the most dangerous of political criminals were jailed. The inscription of a name in its register of admission was tantamount to a death-sentence. From Saint-Lazare, from the Carmes, from the Abbaye, and from other jails, the inmates sometimes returned into the world of living and free men, but never—or very rarely indeed—from the Conciergerie. Marie Antoinette and the general public, therefore, could not but believe—and were intended to believe—that the transference from the Temple to the Conciergerie was the opening step of the Dance of Death. In actual fact, however, the Convention had no thought of bringing the ex-Queen, a precious hostage, to a speedy trial. Her removal to the Conciergerie was to be like the crack of a whip which might quicken up the tedious bartering now in progress with Austria. It was a threatening gesture; a means of exerting political pressure; an exclamation of "Hurry up!" Although the prosecution of Marie Antoinette had been trumpeted in the Convention as imminent, there was considerable delay. Three weeks after the dramatic nocturnal transfer to "the anteroom of death," the transfer which (as the Committee of Public Safety had desired) was greeted with a cry of horror in the foreign newspapers, no documents relating to the case had as yet been handed over to the public prosecutor; and after the first fanfare there was no mention of Marie Antoinette in the debates either of the Convention or of the Commune.

True, Hébert, the dirty watch-dog of the Revolution, barked now and again to the effect that it was time for the Austrian whore (grue) "to try on Samson's neck-tie," and for the executioner "to play at ball with the she-wolf's head." But the Committee of Public Safety, which took longer views, paid no heed to his demand "why the authorities were putting off from one day to another the fulfilment of their duty to make an end of the Habsburg tigress, and why they were troubling to look for documentary evidence, when, if she had her deserts, she would be unceremoniously chopped into mincemeat to pay for the blood she had on her conscience." Such chatter and clamour had not the slightest effect upon the Committee, whose members were keeping their eyes fixed upon the war-map. It seemed likely enough that the Austrian archduchess might be of more use to the revolutionists alive than dead, and this full soon, since the military happenings of July had been disastrous to the French armies. At any moment the allied troops might be marching on Paris, so what was the use of wasting valuable blood? It was all very well to let Hébert foam at the mouth, for this strengthened the general impression that Marie Antoinette's execution was imminent, but really the Convention held her fate in suspense. She was neither set at liberty nor was she sentenced. The sword was kept hanging over her head, in the hope of frightening the House of Habsburg and of disposing it to enter into negotiations.

Unfortunately for Marie Antoinette, the news of her removal to the Conciergerie did not disturb the Austrian chiefs. To Kaunitz she had counted as a credit entry in Habsburg political bookkeeping only so long as she had been firmly seated on the throne of France. A deposed queen, an ordinary woman fallen upon evil days, was held of no account by ministers of State, generals, kings, and emperors. Sentiment must not be allowed to interfere with diplomacy. There was but one person in Europe, and he a man without power, to whom the news of the ex-Queen's imprisonment in the Conciergerie came like a dagger-thrust in the heart—Fersen. In despair he wrote to his sister: "My dear Sophie, my one and only friend, you have no doubt learned by now about the terrible disaster of the removal of the Queen to the Conciergerie and about the decree of that execrable Convention which delivers her over to the Revolutionary Tribunal for judgment. Since I heard of the matter, I have no longer been alive, for it is not truly life to exist as I do and to suffer the pains I now endure. If I could but do something to bring about her liberation, I think the agony would be less, but I find it terrible that my sole resource is to go about begging others to help. . . . You are the only person able to share my feelings. For me all is lost. . . . My regrets will be eternal, and nothing but death will enable me to forget them. I cannot engage in any occupation, but can only think of the misfortune of this unhappy and noble princess. I even lack the force to express what I feel; I would give my life to save her and cannot; my greatest happiness would be to die for her in order to save her." Again, a few days later: "I often reproach myself for breathing pure air when I remember that she is penned in a noisome prison; this idea tears at my heart-strings, poisons my life, so that continually I veer from pain to wrath and from wrath back to pain."

These outbursts, of course, were of no avail. What did the allied general staff care for the feelings of Fersen? Was it likely they would allow him to interfere with their sagacious and sublime policy? What was there left for him to do beyond venting his anger, his bitterness, his despair, the fire that consumed him, in useless petitions, as he ran from anteroom to anteroom, begging the soldiers, the statesmen, the princes, the émigrés to bestir themselves. How, he imploringly asked, could they look on with such shameful coldness while a queen of France, a princess of the House of Habsburg, was being humiliated and murdered? Everywhere he was received with civil indifference, was fobbed off with evasive answers. He found that even Mercy, who had been so loyal to the Queen, was "icy-cold." Respectful but decisive, Mercy, though civil, was adamant as regards Fersen's attempts at intervention, and it was plain that he had a personal animus in the matter. The ambassador had never forgiven Fersen his liaison with the Queen, and Marie Antoinette's lover was the last person in the world from whom he was likely to take advice.

But Fersen was strenuous and persistent. The coldness of all these others, the coldness which contrasted so horribly with his own ardour, reduced him almost to frenzy. Since Mercy would do nothing to help, he turned to another true friend of the royal family, the Comte de La Marck, who, in the Tuileries days, before the Revolution had got into its stride, had carried on negotiations with Mirabeau. In this quarter Fersen found a humaner understanding. La Marck called on Mercy and reminded the old man of the pledge which, a quarter of a century before, he had given to Maria Theresa to the effect that he would protect her daughter to the last. Together they drafted a vigorous letter to the Prince of Coburg, commander-in-chief of the Austrian forces: "So long as the Queen was not directly threatened, it was possible to keep silence, since there was a risk of awaking the rage of the savages who surround her; but today, when she has been handed over to a bloody tribunal, is it not your duty to undertake any measures which give some hope of saving her? . . . Allow me [the letter was signed by Mercy alone] to remind you of the regret which we may all of us feel some day should we remain inactive at such a moment. Do you think posterity will be able to believe that so great a crime could be consummated only a few days' march from the victorious armies of Austria and England without any attempt being made by them to prevent it?" In a word, Mercy, incited by La Marck, demanded a prompt advance on Paris in order to strike terror into the hearts of the revolutionists. Every other military operation must be subordinated to this supremely necessary task.

But, as ill-luck would have it, the demand for a prompt move to rescue Marie Antoinette was addressed to a man who was not only weak, but also extraordinarily stupid, to one whose intelligence was that of a person who, in lower walks of life, remains an under-clerk all his days. The Prince of Coburg's answer was what might have been expected from such an individual. As if in 1793 they had still been living in the days of witch-burning and the Inquisition, the Prince loftily declared: "Should the least violence be done to Her Majesty the Queen, the Austrian authorities, having in their hands four commissaries of the Convention who were recently arrested, will immediately have them broken upon the wheel." Mercy and La Marck, both of whom were refined, distinguished, and educated noblemen, were outraged at this exhibition of wanton stupidity, and were quick to realize that negotiations with a man as feeble-minded as the Prince of Coburg could be of no avail. La Marck, therefore, implored Mercy to write instantly to the court of Vienna: "Send another messenger forthwith; make the danger clearly understood; give active expression to fears which are, unfortunately, only too well grounded. It is essential that Vienna should be made to understand how disastrous it would be for the Austrian government if, in days to come, historians could write that, no more than forty leagues from powerful and victorious Austrian armies, the august daughter of Maria Theresa perished on the scaffold without any attempt having been made to save her. It would be an indelible stain upon the record of our Emperor." Knowing the old diplomat to have become somewhat inert with advancing years, and hoping to transfuse a little fire into his veins, La Marck added as a personal exhortation: "Allow me to assure you that human judgments are so unjust that you will never be credited with the excellent sentiments your friends know you to possess if, in the present deplorable circumstances, you should fail to do your utmost, by the most forcible means at your disposal, to shake our court out of the fatal torpor from which it is now suffering."

Roused by so urgent a warning, old Mercy at length set himself energetically to work, writing to Vienna as follows: "I cannot but ask myself whether it comports with the Emperor's dignity and even with his interests, to remain a passive spectator of the fate with which his august aunt is threatened, without moving a finger in the attempt to save her. . . . Are not there special duties incumbent on him in these circumstances? . . . We must not lose sight of the fact that our government's conduct in the matter will, in due time, be judged by posterity—and we cannot but dread that the judgment will be a harsh one should it appear certain that when the Queen of France was obviously in danger of death (as she is) His Majesty the Emperor made neither efforts nor sacrifices in order to rescue her."

No answer was vouchsafed to this document, which was certainly audacious for an imperial ambassador of those days. It was filed to gather dust among the archives of the chancellery. Emperor Francis had no thought of making any move on behalf of his "august aunt." Undisturbed by the prospect of her execution, he took his daily constitutional in the Schönbrunn gardens. Coburg stayed in camp, drilling his soldiers with such unnecessary vigour that he lost more of them through desertion than he would have lost on a stricken field. All the monarchs were calm, indifferent, unconcerned. As far as the ancient House of Habsburg was concerned, what mattered a little honour more or less? Not one of the European rulers would put himself about in the attempt to save Marie Antoinette, so that Mercy scornfully declared: "They would not have tried to save her even if they had with their own eyes seen her mounting the steps to the guillotine."

Since there was to be no help from Coburg, none from Austria, none from the sovereign princes of Europe, none from the émigrés, none from the Queen's relatives, Mercy and Fersen, reduced to their own initiative, tried the last possible means—bribery. Through the instrumentality of Noverre the dancing-master and through that of an obscure financier, money was sent to Paris, and no one knows through whose fingers it trickled away. The first attempts were certainly made on Danton, who (Robespierre was right in his surmise) was generally believed to have an itching palm. There were devious channels leading, too, in the direction of Hébert. From the very nature of bribery and corruption, truth is always difficult to obtain, but it is certainly remarkable that of a sudden this spouter of venom, this man who had been clamouring like a maniac that it was "more than time for the Austrian harlot to take the last header into destruction" should now change his tune, and demand her being sent back to the Temple. Had these underground machinations any sort of success, or could they have had any? Maybe, but the golden bullets had been fired too late. At the very time when her shrewdest friends were doing their best to save her, a maladroit ally had, with the best intentions, given Marie Antoinette a final push into the abyss. Throughout life it had been her unhappy experience that those who wished her well did her more harm than her foes.

CHAPTER XXXIX

A Last Endeavour

AMONG all the prisons of the revolution, the Conciergerie, the "ante-room of death," was governed by the strictest rules. A massive stone building which dated from the Middle Ages, its walls were impenetrably thick, its massive doors were studded with iron, its windows were heavily barred, every passage was interrupted by a locked grating, and its guardians were almost as numerous as the prisoners. Over its gloomy portal might well have been written the Dantesque motto: "Lasciate ogni speranza, voi ch'entrate." For a hundred years before the Revolution, the most rigid precautions had been taken to prevent any communication between prisoners in the Conciergerie and the outer world, and since the beginning of the Reign of Terror these precautions had been intensified. No letter could be smuggled in or out; no visitors were allowed; the warders were not, as at the Temple, recruited from among amateurs, but were professional experts, familiar with the wiles of prisoners. Besides, among the latter there was a considerable proportion of persons known in French argot as "moutons" —spurious captives, stool-pigeons, professional spies, who won the confidence of their fellow-inmates in order to make the authorities acquainted with any plots that were being hatched. Where such a system had been in force for years or decades, it would seem, at first sight, futile for any individual to attempt to cope with it.

Yet there is consolation for those who are under the harrow of the collective use of force. An immalleable and resolute individual can invariably, in the long run, show himself stronger than any system. A live human being whose will remains unbroken can "drive a coach-and-six through" written or printed regulations, and this was seen in the case of Marie Antoinette. Within a few days after she had been transferred to the Conciergerie, she had been able—thanks in part to the magic of her name and position and in part to the personal dignity of her behaviour—to transform her guardians into friends, helpers, faithful servants. As far as prison rules were concerned, all that the head-warder's wife had to do for the ex-Queen was to clean out her room and provide her with rough meals. This good woman, however, cooked the most dainty food she could procure; she offered to dress Marie Antoinette's hair; every day she procured from another quarter of the town a bottle of drinking water which Marie Antoinette found preferable to that supplied in the prison. And this woman had an assistant maid who seized every opportunity of visiting the prisoner's cell to ask whether there was any little service she could do. As for the gendarmes, bearded men with clanking swords, loaded muskets, whose business it was to prevent such indulgences—what did they do? We have official records to show that day after day they brought the Queen flowers purchased with their own money, to adorn her comfortless quarters. It was among the common people, better acquainted with misfortune than the bourgeoisie, that there was so keen a sympathy for the sovereign lady who had been so much detested in her happier days. When the market-women near the Conciergerie learned from Madame Richard that a chicken or some vegetables were to be bought for the Queen, they were careful to pick out the best of their stock; and at the trial Fouquier-Tinville informed the court with anger and astonishment that Marie Antoinette had had a much easier time of it in the Conciergerie than in the Temple. In the very place where a violent death seemed imminent, humane feelings blossomed as an unconscious defence.

The reader will doubtless be astonished, in view of the Queen's earlier attempts at flight, that so important a State prisoner should have been considerately treated and one might almost say carelessly guarded in the Conciergerie. But light is thrown on the mystery when we recall that the chief inspector of prisons was Michonis, the lemonade-seller, who had been deeply involved in the plot for an escape from the Temple. The jack-o'-lantern of Baron de Batz's millions shone glitteringly even in the dark cells of the Conciergerie, and Michonis continued to play his bold double role. Every day, as in duty bound, he solemnly entered the Queen's room, rattled the bars on the windows to make sure they had not been tampered with, tested the door-fastenings, meticulously carrying out the orders of the Commune, which congratulated itself on having so trusty a republican as supervisor, as watch-dog. But as soon as the gendarmes had quitted the apartment, our worthy friend entered into conversation with the prisoner, giving her news of her children in the Temple. Moved by avarice, or perhaps by kindly feeling, he would occasionally, when making an inspection of the prison, smuggle in some inquisitive visitor; perhaps an Englishman or an Englishwoman, for it may have been he who introduced the splenetic Mrs. Atkins. It was he who brought the priest who is supposed to have heard Marie Antoinette's last confession, one of those priests who had refused to take the oath of loyalty to the Republic. He brought the painter who limned the portrait to be seen in the Carnavalet Museum. Finally, and most unfortunately, he introduced the bold fool owing to whose excess of zeal these liberties and favours were suddenly annulled.

This notorious "affaire de l'œillet" which, many years afterwards, Alexandre Dumas made the theme of one of his novels, is an obscure business. It will never be wholly elucidated, for the official reports are inadequate, and the account of it given by the principal performer has a smack of gasconade. If we are to believe the Commune and the story told by Michonis, chief inspector of prisons, the episode was of trifling importance. Michonis's tale ran to the effect that at supper, one evening, he was talking to some friends about the Queen, whom, as a matter of official routine, he had daily to visit in prison. Then a stranger, whose name he never learned, thrust into the conversation, showed a lively interest, and wanted to know whether it would not be possible, sometime, to accompany the inspector on his rounds. Michonis, being in an after-dinner mood, complied without further inquiry, having made the unknown pledge himself not to say a word to the Queen.

Now, are we to suppose that Michonis, the Baron de Batz's confidant, was really so simple-minded as he gave himself out to be? Did he not trouble to inquire as to the identity of the person whom he was to smuggle into the Queen's cell? Had he done so, he would have learned that the man was an old friend of Marie Antoinette, the Chevalier de Rougeville, one of the noblemen who on June 20, 1792, had defended the Queen at the risk of their own lives. To all seeming, Michonis, who had smoothed the way for the Baron de Batz (being well paid for his trouble), did not pry too closely into the stranger's intentions. In fact, there can be little doubt that the plot was more widespread and more mature than can be proved by the vestiges of it which have come down to our own day.

At any rate, on August 28th, the bolts on the door of the Queen's cell were shot back with a jar. Marie Antoinette and the gendarme on duty rose to their feet. The Queen was always startled anew when the prison doors opened, for any unexpected visit of the authorities might be the prelude to evil tidings—and had, for a long time now, generally been such a prelude. However, it was only Michonis, in secret a friend, accompanied this time by a strange gentleman to whom the prisoner paid no attention. Drawing a breath of relief, Marie Antoinette began to chat with the inspector, and asked him how her children were, this being always her first and most pressing inquiry. Michonis answered kindly, and the Queen grew almost cheerful. These few minutes in which the grey silence could be broken while she talked about her little boy and her daughter signified something that almost approached happiness.

Then, all in a moment, she turned deadly pale, her pallor soon giving place to a flush of excitement. She trembled, and found it hard to maintain her composure. She had recognized Rougeville, whom she had seen a hundred times at court, and whom she knew ready to run any risk. What could it signify, the unexpected appearance of this trustworthy ally in her cell. Had he some plan for her escape? Had he brought a message? She did not dare speak to him, nor even (so much afraid was she of arousing the suspicion of the gendarme and the waiting-woman) look at him significantly; and yet she could not fail to see that he was making incomprehensible signs to her. It was bewildering as well as thrilling to have in her room a messenger whose message she could not understand. Growing more and more uneasy, she dreaded lest she should betray herself. One may presume that Michonis became aware of her confusion. Anyhow, saying that he had other cells to inspect, he went out, accompanied by the stranger, but added that he would return before quitting the prison.

Left alone, Marie Antoinette sat down and tried to collect her thoughts. She resolved that when Michonis and Rougeville came back she would be more controlled and at the same time more observant. Nor had she long to wait. Again the keys jingled, again the bolts were drawn, again the two men entered. By now Marie Antoinette was in full possession of her faculties. Composedly she watched Rougeville while she was conversing with Michonis, and perceived from a sign made by the former that he had thrown something into the corner behind the stove. It was hard that she still had to wait a little while before reading the message; but as soon as the visitors had departed, she made an excuse for sending the gendarme after them "to ask something she had forgotten." She availed herself of this moment when she was free from observation to pick up what had been thrown into the corner. What? Nothing but a carnation? Ah, but there was a tiny note crushed among the petals. Opening it, she read: "Patroness, I shall never forget you, and shall continually try to find some means of showing my zeal for your service. If you need three or four hundred louis for your guardians I will bring them you next Friday."

It is not difficult to imagine the unhappy woman's feelings at this miraculous revival of hope. A royalist nobleman, defying the precautions of the Commune, had made his way into this dread and impenetrable prison, this anteroom of death. Surely rescue must be at hand? Fersen, she thought, must have spun the threads, but there must be other and more powerful helpers at work, determined to save her life when all possibility of anything of the kind had seemed over. The will to live flamed up again, courage was renewed, in this white-haired woman who had resigned herself to the inevitable.

She had courage and confidence. Her misfortune was that she had too much of both. She was quick to understand that the three or four hundred louis were intended as a bribe for the gendarme on duty in her room. All she had to do was to attend to this matter, for her friends outside would make what other arrangements were necessary. With a surge of hopefulness, she set to work. Having torn the dangerous note into tiny fragments, she proceeded to "write" an answer. She had no pen and ink, no pencil, only a scrap of paper. But necessity is the mother of invention, and, having a needle, she pricked her reply with its point, and the document is still preserved as a relic, though subsequent needle-pricks have made it unreadable. Promising a liberal reward, she gave it to Gilbert the gendarme with instructions to hand it to the stranger should he again visit the Conciergerie.

What happened thereafter is obscure. Gilbert seems to have hesitated. Three or four hundred louis were a great temptation to the poor devil, shining in his imagination like so many stars; but the axe of the guillotine had a more sinister sheen. He sympathized with the unhappy woman who had been Queen of France, but he did not want to lose his job. What was he to do? To carry out her commission would be treason to the Republic; to play the informer would be a breach of the trust the prisoner had placed in him. The worthy fellow, therefore, took a middle course, asking the advice of Madame Richard, the governor's wife. She shared his perplexity. All three possible courses—silence, betrayal of the plot, and becoming involved in so dangerous a conspiracy—seemed equally undesirable. Yet it is likely that she was open to the lure of corruption; it seems probable that whispers of Batz's millions had reached her ears.

At length Madame Richard took the same course as the gendarme. She did not inform the authorities, but at the same time she did not preserve an inviolable silence. Instead of shouldering the responsibility, she tried to pass it on, telling Michonis, her official chief, what was afoot. Michonis took fright. At this stage the affair becomes even more involved. We do not know whether Michonis had previously been aware that Rougeville was a plotter who wished to help the Queen to escape, or whether he only realized this when he heard Madame Richard's story. Was he a confederate from the outset, or had the Chevalier led him by the nose? Anyhow, the matter seemed to him too perilous now that two intermediaries were apprised in addition to the principals. Assuming the airs of the strict official, he took the paper from Madame Richard, put it in his pocket, and told her to say not a word more about it to anyone. He hoped, one may suppose, that in this way he would save Marie Antoinette from the consequences of her heedlessness, and that he would hear no more of the attempted escape. As in the plot to get the Queen away from the Temple (the plot in which Batz had been the ringleader), his policy was to "lie low" when danger loomed in the offing.

Nothing further might have been heard of Rougeville's scheme had it not been for the misgivings of the gendarme. He was uneasy in his mind. A handful of gold pieces might, perhaps, have induced him to hold his tongue, but the Queen had no money, and by degrees the risk to his own neck became his chief concern. After he had been steadfast for five days (this is the perplexing feature of the case), saying not a word to his comrades or to the authorities, on September 3rd he made a report to his superiors. Two hours later the officials of the Commune raided the Conciergerie and held a strict inquiry.

To begin with, the Queen denied everything. She said she had not recognized any visitor to the prison; and when she was asked whether she had written a letter a few days before, she answered that she had no writing materials. Michonis, too, played the ignoramus, hoping that Madame Richard, who had likewise been bribed, would hold her tongue. The latter, however, avowed having handed him the missive, so he had no choice but to produce it—having prudently made the text illegible by additional needle-pricks. At a second inquiry, held next day, Marie Antoinette ceased to feign ignorance. It was true, she said, that she was acquainted with the person who had visited her cell in Michonis's company, that he had conveyed to her a letter hidden in a carnation, and that she had replied to it. Determined, however, to sacrifice herself and to protect the man who had wanted to sacrifice himself on her behalf, she did not mention the name of Rougeville, declaring that though she knew him as an officer of the guards she had forgotten what he was called. She also magnanimously sheltered Michonis, thus saving his life. Nevertheless, within four-and-twenty hours the Commune and the Committee of Public Safety had ferreted out the name of Rougeville, with the result that the police were busily—and fruitlessly—searching Paris for the conspirator who had wanted to save the Queen and who, in actual fact, condemned her to destruction.

For there can be no doubt that this clumsy plot was disastrous to Marie Antoinette, quickening the onset of doom. Hitherto, even at the Conciergerie, she had been treated with a certain measure of consideration, but now severity was the order of the day. Such personal possessions as had been left to her were taken away; the last of her rings, the gold watch which her mother had given her before she left Austria, and even a locket in which she kept little tresses of her children's hair. Of course the needles with one of which she had pricked out the letter to Rougeville were impounded, and she was forbidden the use of candles when night fell. Michonis was cashiered as too easy-going an inspector; and Madame Richard was replaced by a new supervisor, Madame Bault. At the same time, in a decree under date of September 11th, the town council decided that the stubborn criminal must be confined in a safer cell; and since the officials of the Commune could not find one to their taste, the apothecary was turned out of his room and this was provided with double iron doors. Half of the grated window, which gave upon the court where the female prisoners exercised, was bricked up. Additional sentries were posted, and the gendarmes whose duty it now was to keep perpetual watch in an adjoining room were told that they would have to answer for the captive's escape with their lives.

Marie Antoinette had reached the last extremity of loneliness. The new wardens and gendarmes, though kindly disposed, no longer dared take the risk of saying a word to the poor woman. The watch which had ticked off the interminable hours was not there to solace her; she could do no needlework; nothing had been left her but the little dog. Forsaken, in the valley of the shadow, Marie Antoinette at length began to seek the consolation which her mother had so often commended to her. For the first time in her life she asked to be supplied with books, reading one after another with her tired eyes; and her jailers, though in this matter considerate to their prisoner, could not bring her a sufficiency. She did not want novels or plays, no light literature, no sentimentality, no love stories, which might have reminded her too keenly of past joys, but only true tales of adventure. Captain Cook's voyages, stories of shipwreck and bold journeyings, "moving accidents by flood and field," books that would snatch her thoughts away from the desolate present. These heroes of real romance were the only companions of her solitude. No one came to visit her. Day after day she heard nothing but the bells of the neighbouring Sainte-Chapelle and the grating of the key in the lock. For the rest, there was silence, perpetual silence in the little room, which was almost as narrow and damp and dark as a coffin. The lack of movement and of fresh air weakened her, and she was worn out by severe hæmor-rhages. When, at length, she appeared in court, it was an elderly woman with white hair who emerged from the long night of imprisonment into the unfamiliar glare of daylight.

CHAPTER XL

The Supreme Infamy

SHE had reached the last stage, and the end was at hand. The fates
had spun the uttermost contrasts. The woman who had been born
in an imperial palace, and then, as Queen of France, had had hundreds
of rooms in her dwelling-house, was now prisoned in a tiny basement
cell, its walls streaming with damp, and its grated window half
occluded. She who had loved luxury, she whose life had been environed with all the splendours that art and wealth could supply, had
now not even a cupboard, a looking-glass, an armchair, but only the
barest necessaries, a deal table, a stool, a folding iron bedstead. The
Queen who had had numberless gentlemen and ladies and menials
devoted to her service—ladies-in-waiting, maids of honour, lady hairdressers, two chambermaids for the night and two for the day, a
reader, a physician, a surgeon, a secretary, stewards of the household,
lackeys, cooks, pages—had now to comb her own snow-white locks.
The woman who had bought three hundred new gowns a year, had
now not even a needle with which to stitch the seams of her shabby
prison dress. She had been strong and active; she was now worn and
weary; she had been beautiful and an object of desire, but was now
pallid and prematurely old. She who had been fond of lively society
from noon till long after midnight, had to while away the lonely
hours of a sleepless dark until morning began to make the bars on the
window visible. Summer had passed, so that the gloomy cell became
more and more coffin-like, since the days were drawing in and she had
not even the solace of a candle, the only illumination of the prison-
chamber being a glimmer that came from an oil-lamp in the passage
through the fan-light over the door. Cold struck upwards from the
tiled floor. The room, which was no better than a damp cellar, reeked
of mould and corruption and death. Her health was giving way more
and more in this unwholesome environment. It seemed to her a thousand years since she had been the light-hearted Queen of the land, the
merry land of France. It was scarcely a shock to her when she was

summoned to be put on trial for her life, since for so long a time she had already endured a living death.

Thus entombed, Marie Antoinette, though in the heart of Paris, heard no murmur of the storm which that autumn was raging in western Europe. Never was the French Revolution in greater peril than during these days. Two of the strongest of the republican fortresses, Mainz and Valenciennes, had fallen; the British had occupied the chief ports; Lyons, the second capital of France, was in revolt; the colonies had been lost; the Convention was full of discord, and in Paris hunger and depression were rife. The republican government seemed tottering to its fall. Only one thing could save it: desperate courage, a suicidal challenge; the Republic could only overcome its own fear by spreading fear far and wide. "Let us put Terror on the agenda"—this dire word resounded through the meeting-hall of the Convention, and threats were relentlessly followed up by actions. The slaughter of the Girondists and of the Duke of Orléans was at hand. Countless others were delivered over to the tender mercies of the Revolutionary Tribunal. The guillotine was by now busily at work when Billaud-Varenne addressed the Assembly as follows: "The Convention has been giving a signal example of severity to the traitors who were plotting the ruin of their country; but there is still an important duty undischarged. A woman, the shame of humanity and of her sex, Widow Capet, must at long last expiate her crimes upon the scaffold. It is widely believed that she has been transferred to the Temple, that she has been secretly tried, and that the Revolutionary Tribunal has whitewashed her. How preposterous is the thought that a woman who is responsible for the death of thousands of Frenchmen could ever be acquitted by a French jury. I demand that the Revolutionary Tribunal shall pass judgment on her case this very week."

Although the proposal was not merely a request for a trial, but a prejudging of the case and a frank demand for an execution, it was unanimously adopted. Yet Fouquier-Tinville, the public prosecutor, who in general delivered blow after blow with the callousness and swiftness of a steam-hammer, now manifested a perplexing hesitation. Neither that week, nor the next, nor the next following, did he draft his indictment against the Queen. We do not know whether, in secret, men more influential than himself were holding him in restraint, or whether this being with a heart of stone, whose custom it was, with bewildering speed, to change blood into paper and paper into blood, really did not as yet possess any sufficiently incriminating documents. He wrote to the Committee of Public Safety asking for materials, and, strangely enough, the Committee, in its turn, was slow to move. At length it got together a few unimportant papers: those relating to the inquiry into the affair of the carnation; a list of witnesses; the records of the King's trial. But Fouquier-Tinville still held his hand. Probably there was lack of evidence which would give the indictment the requisite fervour of republican indignation; lack of something sufficiently incriminatory, either of the woman or of the Queen. However, at this juncture, when it seemed as if (Billaud-Varenne notwithstanding) the proceedings would be indefinitely postponed, at this eleventh hour Fouquier-Tinville received from Hébert (the embittered, the resolute enemy of the Queen) the most infamous document in the records of the French Revolution. It provided the necessary impetus, and in a trice the indictment was drafted.

What had happened? On September 30th, a letter was sent from the Temple to Hébert, a letter signed by Simon the shoemaker, the Dauphin's tutor. The opening was in an unknown handwriting, and is barely legible. It runs as follows: "Greetings. Come quickly, my friend, I have some important things to tell you, and it will be a great pleasure to see you. Today if possible. You will find me, as always, a frank and valiant republican." The rest of the missive is in Simon's own script, and, with its peculiar spelling, bears witness to this "tutor's" lack of education: "Je te coitte bien le bon jour moi e mon est pousse Jean Brasse tas cher est pousse et mas petiste bon amis la petist e fils cent ou blier ta cher soeur que jan Brasse. Je tan prie de nes pas manquer a mas demande pout te voir ce las presse pour mois. Simon, ton amis pour la vis." [Je te souhaite bien le bonjour, moi et mon épouse. J' embrasse ta chère épouse et ma petite bonne amie la petite fille sans oublier ta chère sœur que j' embrasse. Je t'en prie de ne pas manquer à ma demande pour te voir—cela presse pour moi. Simon, ton ami pour la vie.—My wife and I send you our best wishes. My love to your dear wife and to my dear little friend your daughter, not forgetting love to your dear sister. Please do not fail to come and see me—the matter is urgent. Simon, your lifelong friend.] Hébert, conscientious and energetic, promptly went to visit Simon. What he heard from the shoemaker seemed so sinister even to the tough-minded editor of "Père Duchesne" that he would not undertake the responsibility of dealing with it, but promptly summoned a committee of the whole Commune under the presidency of the mayor. Thereupon the councillors betook themselves in a body to the Temple in order to provide materials for the indictment of the Queen in the minutes of three sessions, minutes which have come down to us intact.

We have reached that episode in the history of Marie Antoinette which seems incredible, inconceivable, and which can be explained only as due, in part to the heated feelings of the time, and in part to the systematic poisoning of public opinion concerning the Queen which had been going on for years and years. The little Dauphin, who was a precocious and high-spirited child, had, a few weeks earlier, when he was still under his mother's care, injured one of his testicles with a stick. A surgeon had been called in, and had applied a spica bandage to the groin. The injury had not been serious, and one would have thought that this was an end of the matter. One day, however, after the Queen's removal to the Conciergerie, Simon or his wife discovered that the boy was practising self-abuse. Caught in the act, the child made no attempt to deny his bad habit. Taken to task by Simon, and sharply questioned as to who had initiated him into evil ways, the unhappy lad volunteered the information or was hectored into declaring that his mother and his aunt were the culprits. Simon, ready to believe anything that was wicked of the "Austrian tigress," and inflamed with righteous wrath at such viciousness on a mother's part, pushed his questions home, until he ultimately induced little Louis to say that in the Temple the two women had frequently taken him into their beds, and that his mother had had incestuous relations with him.

In normal times any reasonable person would have been extremely sceptical as to the truth of such accusations made by a lad who was not yet nine years old. However, thanks to the scurrilous lampoons circulated by the revolutionists, the conviction that Marie Antoinette was a nymphomaniac was widespread and even this preposterous assertion that a mother had enjoyed improper sexual relations with her eight-year-old son was fully credible to Hébert and Simon. To these fanatical sansculottes, the sequence of affairs seemed perfectly logical. Marie Antoinette, the whore of Babylon, the notorious Lesbian, had been accustomed day after day at the Trianon to have sexual relations with several men and several women! What, then, could be more natural than that such a bitch-wolf, imprisoned in the Temple where she could find no one else to gratify her lust, should have seduced her own innocent little son. Neither Hébert nor his friend the tutor, since both of them had their minds clouded by hatred, ever thought of doubting the youngster's accusation. All that remained was that the Queen's misconduct, her abominable lasciviousness, should be recorded in black and white, so that France at large should be made acquainted with the corruptness of the Austrian woman, for whose bloodthirstiness and depravity the guillotine would be too easy a punishment. That was why there were three sittings of inquiry, the witnesses being a boy of eight, a girl of fifteen, and Madame Elisabeth—scenes so cruel, so shameful, that we should find it hard to believe they ever took place were it not that the yellowing documents, including some in the penmanship of the two children, are still preserved in the national archives.

At the first sitting, held on October 6, 1793, there were present Pache the mayor, Chaumette the syndic, Hébert, and other members of the town council; at the second, on October 7th, we read among the signatures of those present that of a famous painter who was also one of the most unprincipled among the heroes of the Revolution—David. First of all the boy was put on the stand as witness for the prosecution. He was asked about other happenings in the Temple besides that which was now the principal concern; and the talkative little lad, without grasping the import of his utterances, betrayed the names of his mother's secret assistants, especially Toulan. Then the thorny question came up for discussion, and thereanent we read in the minutes: "Having been several times caught in bed by Simon and his wife, charged by the Commune to keep watch over him, engaged in indecent actions harmful to his health, he assured them that he had been instructed in these pernicious habits by his mother and his aunt, that on several occasions they had amused themselves by making him perform these acts in their presence, and that this had often taken place when he was lying between them. From the child's explanations, he made it clear to us that once his mother made him embrace her closely, that there was an act of copulation, the outcome of which was a swelling of one of the testicles for which he still had to wear a bandage, that his mother urged him never to say anything about it, and that this action was repeated several times. He also declared that some of the commissaries were more intimate than the others with his mother and his aunt."

In black and white, with seven or eight signatures, this monstrosity has been preserved. The genuineness of the document, and the fact that the misguided boy actually uttered the horrible charges, is undeniable. The only objection that can be raised is that the passage in which the lad of eight referred to the act of incest with his mother was not part of the original text, but had been subsequently inscribed in the margin. Thus it seems plain that the inquisitors had had certain scruples in recording the infamy. Yet no one can argue away the subscription "Louis Charles Capet" which stands beneath the declaration in the large laboriously traced, rounded letters of a child. Her own boy had actually, before these strangers, levied the basest of accusations against his mother.

As if lunacy had not gone far enough, the investigators sought confirmatory evidence by questioning the girl of fifteen, the Dauphin's sister. Chaumette asked Madame Royale "whether when she played with her brother he did not handle her improperly; and whether his mother and his aunt did not make him sleep between them." She answered, "No." Now came the most painful of scenes. The brother and the sister were confronted, to dispute in face of the inquisitors concerning their mother's honour. The little Dauphin adhered to his statement; his sister, a half-grown girl, intimidated by the reiterated inquiries of these severe-looking strangers and by such improper questions, could only take refuge in the assertion that she knew nothing about the matter, and had not seen anything of the kind. Thereupon Madame Elisabeth was summoned as third witness. The late King's sister, now nine-and-twenty, a vigorous and self-possessed young woman, was not so easily browbeaten as the innocent or timid children. As soon as the minutes of what the Dauphin had testified were given her to read, she flushed angrily, thrust the paper contemptuously aside, and said that such scandalous accusations did not need any answer. Thereupon the boy was recalled, and he unhesitatingly repeated the assertion that his aunt and his mother had misled him into these unchaste practices. Madame Elisabeth could no longer contain herself. "Ah, le monstre," she furiously exclaimed, outraged that the little brat should accuse her of such immodesty. The commissaries, however, had got what they wanted. Triumphantly Hébert carried off the report of the evidence to the examining magistrate, in the hope that the Queen's true character had at length been disclosed to her contemporaries and to posterity, that she had been successfully pilloried for time and for eternity. Patriotically throwing a chest, he declared himself ready, in the witness-box of the Revolutionary Tribunal, to sustain the charge of incest against Marie Antoinette.

This accusation brought by a boy against his own mother, being perhaps unprecedented in the annals, has always been a tough nut for Marie Antoinette's biographers to crack. Thick-and-thin defenders of the Queen have had recourse to the most preposterous attempts at explanation, or have misrepresented matters grossly in their attempts to avoid the dangerous rock. Hébert and Simon, whom they describe as devils incarnate, are supposed to have put their heads together and hatched the plot, deliberately coercing the poor little lad in order to make him bring the scandalous charge. According to the first royalist version they bent him to their will by swinging like a pendulum between kindness and cruelty, now giving him sweetmeats, and now whipping him. According to the second royalist version, which is equally discordant with our knowledge of child psychology, they had made the boy drunk with brandy before getting his testimony from him, and therefore the testimony is worthless. These unverified assertions conflict with the account given by an eye-witness of the scene, Danjon, the secretary, who does not write in any spirit of partisanship: "The young prince was seated in an armchair, swinging his little legs, for his feet did not reach the floor. Asked once more about his statements, he replied that they were true. . . ." The Dauphin's whole behaviour suggests a sort of playful impudence. The text of the report of his own evidence and of that of his sister gives no impression that he had given his testimony under constraint of any kind, but that in a childish spirit of defiance (we scent, so to say, malice and a desire for revenge), spontaneously, he had reiterated the dreadful accusation against his aunt.

How are we to explain this? There is no great difficulty nowadays, when we are much better informed than were our great-great-grand-parents concerning the mendacity of children about sexual matters. Scientific study and frequent experience in the law-courts have taught us to approach with much more understanding the spiritual and sexual aberrations of little boys and girls. Above all we must clear our minds of the sentimental view that the Dauphin had regarded his being en-trusted to the care of Simon the shoemaker as a terrible humiliation, and that he had mourned bitterly because he had been separated from his mother. Children become accustomed to a new environment with amazing speed, and it was likely enough that the boy of eight-and-a-half found the company of the rough but good-natured Simon much more agreeable than that of the two sorrowful women prisoned in the tower, who kept him at his lessons all day, and, still looking upon him as the future king of France, were continually trying to make him be-have in a manner suitable to his "high position."

Under the care of Simon the shoemaker the Dauphin could do pretty much as he pleased. He was not likely, in the hands of such a "tutor," to be plagued with lessons! He could play to his heart's content without troubling to make himself presentable. Likely enough he found it far more amusing to hob-nob with the soldiers and to learn from them to sing the Carmagnole than it had been to say his rosary with Madame Elisabeth who, besides being pious, was a bore. Every child has an in-stinctive desire to throw off the restraints imposed by a grown-up cul-ture and morality, is happier among easy-going and uncultured persons than among grave and reverend seniors. The essential anarchism of youth finds vent where there is more freedom, more irresponsibility, and less control.

The desire to ascend in the social scale does not make itself felt until the intellect awakens. Up to the tenth, and often up to the fifteenth year, almost every child belonging to a well-to-do family envies its pro-letarian schoolmates, to whom so many things are permissible which for the "respectable" are placed under taboo. With a swift metamorphosis of feeling proper to the child nature, it would seem that the Dauphin (though the sentimental biographers are loath to admit the fact) promptly broke away from the melancholy and "seemliness" of his maternal environment, to rejoice in the lower-grade but far more congenial liberty of the Simon entourage. We learn from his sister that he was fond of singing revolutionary songs. Another trustworthy witness has recorded so coarse an utterance made concerning his mother and his aunt by the Dauphin that it is really unprintable. Furthermore, we have his mother's testimony dating from four years earlier as to the youngster's tendency to give unduly free rein to his imagination, for (it will be remembered) she wrote to the governess as follows: "He is extremely indiscreet, being always ready to repeat whatever he has heard. Often enough, without any intention to tell a falsehood, he embroiders it with his imagination. This is his chief fault, and the one which it is, above all, essential to correct."

By this delineation of her little boy's character, Marie Antoinette gives us a clue to the enigma. We are assisted in our understanding by a statement of Madame Elisabeth's. Everyone knows how children, caught in a misdemeanour, incline to pass the blame on to someone else. Since they have an inkling that grown-ups are often disinclined to hold children responsible, by an instinctive impulse towards self-protection they nearly always declare themselves to have been "led astray." In the case we are now considering, the minutes of Madame Elisabeth's evidence clear up the situation. She told the committee (though most historians and biographers have suppressed mention of the fact) that her nephew had for a long time been addicted to indulgence in "plaisirs solitaires," and that she recalled having taken him sharply to task about the matter. His mother, too, often scolded him on this account. Here we are on the right track. The boy had been caught masturbating by his mother and by his aunt, and had, probably, been punished more or less severely. Then, detected by Simon in the same offence, and asked who had taught him his bad habit, by a natural association his mind turned to the earlier transgressions, and he thought of those who had punished him for his misdeeds. In the unconscious, he wanted vengeance on those who had chastised him, and, without considering the import of what he was saying, he mentioned the names of those who had punished him as the persons who had initiated him—or unhesitatingly answered in the affirmative a leading question, in the full conviction that he was speaking the truth. After that, things ran their logical course. Once involved in a web of deceit, there was no way out. Feeling, moreover, that those who were questioning him were glad to hear him slandering his mother, he was confirmed in his false statements, and cheerfully acceded to everything the commissaries might suggest. A self-preservative instinct made him cling to his tale as soon as he perceived that in this way he could escape punishment. Even persons better versed in psychology than these shoemakers, sometime actors, house-painters, and clerks, would have found it hard to avoid being misled by such plain and unambiguous assertions. In this particular instance, moreover, the investigators were influenced by a mass-suggestion. Being regular readers of "Père Duchesne," it seemed to them that the boy's accusation comported perfectly with the diabolical character of his mother, whom pornographic pamphlets circulated far and wide throughout France had depicted as a sink of iniquities. No crime, however preposterous, attributed to Marie Antoinette could seem unlikely to these victims of suggestion. They therefore devoted scant time to reflection, but, as unconcernedly as the little boy, wrote their signatures at the foot of a document containing one of the most abominable charges ever levelled against a mother.

The Queen's seclusion in the Conciergerie saved her, for a considerable time, from hearing of the charge brought against her by her own child. Not until the penultimate day of her life did the indictment make her acquainted with it. For decades she had been familiar with accusations against her honour, with the most abominable calumnies, and had never troubled to refute them. But this last indignity, this sorest of wounds inflicted by the Dauphin's tongue, came as a profound shock to her. The terrible thought went with her to the scaffold. Only three hours before she was guillotined she, usually so self-possessed, wrote to Madame Elisabeth, described as her confederate in the iniquity: "I know how much my little boy must have made you suffer. Forgive him, dear sister; remember how young he is, and how easy it is to make a child say whatever one wants, to put words which he does not understand into his mouth. I hope a day will come when he will grasp the full value of your kindnesses and of the affection you have shown both my children."

CHAPTER XLI

Preliminary Examination

Now the joint had been well larded and the public prosecutor could begin the roasting. On October 12, 1793, Marie Antoinette was summoned to the big council-chamber for her preliminary examination. Opposite to her sat Fouquier-Tinville, Herman his assessor, and a few clerks. The Queen sat alone. She had no defender, no assistant, only the gendarme who kept watch over her.

But, during these many weeks of solitude, Marie Antoinette had rallied her forces. Danger had taught her to collect her thoughts, to speak eloquently, and, better still, to be silent when silence was preferable. Her answers were surprisingly vigorous, and at the same time cautious and shrewd. Not for a moment did she lose composure. Even the most foolish or most mischievous questions failed to disturb her equanimity. At the close of her life, Marie Antoinette came to realize the responsibilities attaching to a great position. In this dark room of audience, she knew that she must show herself to be the true queen she had failed to be in the glittering hall at Versailles. Her responses here and at the Revolutionary Tribunal were given, not to a pettifogging lawyer whom hunger had driven to declare himself a Red and who had been lucky enough to be appointed public prosecutor, not to these cavalry sergeants and scriveners decked out as judges, but to the only genuine and sincere judge—history. "When will you, at last, become that which you really are?" had been the words written to her despairingly two decades earlier by her mother Maria Theresa. Now, on the edge of the tomb, Marie Antoinette began, through a surge of internal energies, to attain the dignity which heretofore had only been bestowed upon her by externals.

To the formal question, "What is your name?" she answered loudly and clearly: "Marie Antoinette of Lorraine and Austria, widow of Louis Capet, sometime King of the French, thirty-eight years of age." Meticulously determined to observe the outward formalities of legal procedure, Fouquier-Tinville went on to ask, as if he did not know, where she had been living at the time of her arrest. Without a trace of sarcasm, the Queen informed the public prosecutor that she had never been arrested, but had been removed from the care of the National Assembly and taken to the Temple. Then followed the more important questions, an accusation drafted in the emotional style of the day. She had, before the Revolution, had political relationships with the "King of Bohemia and Hungary," with the result that she had "in a terrible way" embarrassed the finances of France, "the fruits of the sweat of the people, dissipating them for her pleasures and intrigues with the collusion of nefarious ministers of State." She had "sent millions to the Emperor, funds to be used against the people which had nourished her." Since the Revolution began, she had conspired against France, had entered into negotiations with foreign agents, had induced her husband the King to exercise the veto. Marie Antoinette categorically denied these charges. But it was not until Herman brought an accusation which was very clumsily worded that the dialogue became acrimonious.

"It was you who taught Louis Capet the art of that profound dissimulation wherewith, too long, he deceived the good people of France, which never believed that wickedness and perfidy could be carried to such a pitch."

To this tirade, Marie Antoinette answered composedly:

"It is true that the people has been deceived, cruelly deceived, but not by my husband nor by myself."

"By whom, then, has the people been deceived?"

"By those who had an interest in deceiving it, whereas it was not our interest to deceive it."

At this ambiguous reply, Herman pricked up his ears. He hoped to extract from the Queen an answer which might be interpreted as hostile to the Republic.

"Who, then, in your opinion, are the persons whose interest it was to deceive the people?"

Marie Antoinette was not to be caught in this trap. She said she did not know. Her own interest had been to enlighten the people and not to deceive it.

Herman scented the irony underlying the rejoinder, and angrily exclaimed:

"You have not given a plain answer to my question."

Still the Queen stood firmly on the defensive, saying:

"I would answer in plain terms if I knew the names of the persons concerned."

After this first broil, the proceedings became more concrete. The accused was asked about the flight to Varennes. She answered cautiously, being careful to avoid anything that might incriminate her hidden friends, whom the prosecution wished to involve in the trial. It was not until Herman's next accusatory question that she responded with a vigorous parry.

"Never for a moment have you ceased to wish for the destruction of liberty; you wanted to reign at any cost, and to remount the steps of the throne over the corpses of the patriots?"

To this rigmarole the Queen replied that she and her husband had no need to "remount" the steps of the throne, since they were already established on it, and could desire nothing other than the happiness of France.

Now Herman grew more aggressive. Having realized that he could not break down the ramparts of Marie Antoinette's caution, that he could not upset her equanimity, that he could not from her answers extract "materials" for the trial, he began to assail her with more vehement accusations. She had corrupted and intoxicated the Flemish regiment, had plied the soldiers with drink, had been in correspondence with foreign courts, was responsible for the outbreak of the war, and had been instrumental in bringing about the Convention of Pillnitz. The Queen, however, corrected her accuser's facts. The declaration of war had been a decision of the National Assembly and not of her late husband. As for corrupting the Flemish regiment, she had only walked twice from end to end of the hall in which the soldiers were dining.

Herman, however, had kept his most dangerous questions for the last, those which were designed to make Marie Antoinette repudiate her own sentiments if she wished to avoid expressing hostility to the Republic. What now ensued was a sort of catechism on constitutional law.

"What interest have you in the armed forces of the Republic?"

"The happiness of France is what I desire above all."

"Do you think that kings are necessary for the happiness of the people?"

"An individual cannot decide that matter."

"No doubt you are sorry that your son should have lost a throne which he might have mounted had not the people, awaking at length to its rights, destroyed the throne?"

"I shall never regret my son's loss of anything, should his loss prove to be the gain of his country."

It will be seen that the examiner for the prosecution was not making much headway! Marie Antoinette, indeed, had shown a jesuitical skill in her answer to the last question. When speaking of her son and of France she had said that the latter was "his" country. It was "his" country just as it was that of any other Frenchman, so that, in using the pronoun, she had said nothing derogatory to the Republic; and yet, at the same time, the word could be taken as implying that it was the Dauphin's country in another sense—she had not, even in her imminent peril, sacrificed what to her was the most sacred thing in the world, the boy's right to succeed to his father's throne.

After this last crossing of rapiers, the preliminary inquiry was soon closed. The accused was asked if she wanted to name a defender for the main trial. Marie Antoinette replied that she did not know any counsel, and agreed that one or two advocates should be appointed on her behalf by the court. She knew well enough that this matter was of no importance, since at the present juncture there would hardly be forthcoming in France anyone bold enough to attempt a serious defence of the woman who had been its Queen. Whoever should dare to say a word in her favour would be likely, within a few days, to find himself in the dock.

Now that the semblance of legality had been given by this preliminary hearing, Fouquier-Tinville, who was a stickler for the formalities, could proceed to draft the indictment. His pen moved swiftly over the paper. He prepared such documents in considerable numbers day by day, and practice makes perfect. Though he had been no more than a petty provincial lawyer until the Revolution brought him to Paris and promotion, he felt that when the guillotining of an ex-queen was in question a sublimer tone was requisite than if the victim had been no more than some sempstress or milliner who had been fool-hardy enough to shout, "Vive le Roi!" The indictment, therefore, opened in stilted terms:

"An examination of the relevant documents has shown that, like the Messalinas, Brunhildes, Fredegonds, Medicis, who used to be spoken of as queens of France and whose names for ever odious will never be effaced from the pages of history, Marie Antoinette, widow of Louis Capet, has, ever since her arrival in France, been for the French a curse and a blood-sucker."

After this historical "howler" (it will be remembered that in the days of Fredegond and Brunhilde there was as yet no kingdom of France) there followed the accusations which have previously been cited. The ex-Queen had entered into political relations with a man who passed by the name of "King of Bohemia and Hungary"; she had sent millions to the Emperor; she had prompted the "orgy" when the Flemish regiment dined at Versailles; she had caused the civil war; she had been instrumental in the butchering of patriots; she had betrayed the French plan of campaign to the enemies of France.

Next came Hébert's accusation, though that firebrand's wording had been toned down a little. Marie Antoinette was "so perverted and so familiar with all crimes that, forgetting she was a mother and ignor-ing the limitations prescribed by the laws of nature, she had not been afraid to practise with Louis Charles Capet, her son, indecencies (avowed by the latter) whose very idea and whose mere name arouse a shudder."

Now there came a new and surprising charge. "She actually pushed perfidy and dissimulation so far as to print and distribute . . . works in which she herself was depicted in a most undesirable light . . . in order to lay a false scent and to persuade the foreign powers that she was being grossly maligned by the French."

Thus according to Fouquier-Tinville, the Queen had herself been the true author or disseminator of the Comtesse de Lamotte-Valois's and many other pamphlets in which she was described as a Lesbian.

These charges having been brought against her, Marie Antoinette was no longer merely a prisoner under supervision but had become an accused person.

On October 13th, this forensic masterpiece (when the ink was

hardly dry) was delivered to Chauveau-Lagarde, who had been appointed defending counsel, and who went forthwith to the Conciergerie. The lawyer and the prisoner read the indictment together,
but it was only the former who was amazed and even unnerved by its
venomous tone. Marie Antoinette, whom the preliminary inquiry had
led to expect nothing better, remained calm. Chauveau-Lagarde, however, a conscientious man, declared it would be impossible in one night
to prepare an adequate defence against so confused a miscellany of
charges. There was a chaos of documents to scrutinize and set in
order. He therefore urged the Queen to demand an adjournment of
three days, which would give him time to base his speech for the
defence upon sifted materials and closely scrutinized exhibits.

"To whom must I apply for an adjournment?" asked Marie
Antoinette.

"To the Convention."

"No, no, never."

Chauveau-Lagarde pressed his point.

"In this matter, pride is out of place, and you should not allow it to
prevent your grasping at a possible advantage. It is, in fact, your duty
to save your life if you can, not only for your own sake, but for that
of your children."

At this appeal, for her children's sake, the Queen gave way, and
wrote as follows to the president of the Convention:

"Citizen President, the Citizens Tronson and Chauveau, assigned
me by the Tribunal as defenders, have pointed out to me that only
today have they received their instructions. My trial is fixed for tomorrow, and they declare that it will be impossible for them in so
brief a time to make a proper examination of all the documents bearing upon the case. I owe it to my children to do everything in my
power to justify their mother's conduct. My defenders ask for three
days' postponement, and I hope that the Convention will grant them."

This document gives additional proof of the spiritual change which
had taken place in Marie Antoinette. She who, for most of the twenty-
odd years in which she had been Dauphiness and then Queen of
France, had shown no talent either for writing or for diplomacy, was,
in this last extremity, able to write well and with a queenly dignity.
Although she had to appeal to the Convention as the supreme author-

ity in France, she did not recognize that authority by penning a request in her own name. She applied as directed by her defenders, and expressed a hope instead of making a petition.

The Convention vouchsafed no answer. The Queen's death had long since been decided on. Of what avail, then, to spin out the legal formalities. The trial began next morning at eight, and everyone knew how it would end.

CHAPTER LXII

On Trial before the Revolutionary Tribunal

THE seventy days in the Conciergierie had made Marie Antoinette an elderly and sickly woman. Her eyes were red with weeping and sensitive to the unfamiliar light of day; her lips were pale, for during the last few weeks she had had frequent and severe hæmorrhages. She had been worn out by fatigue and hardship, and again and again the prison doctor had had to prescribe remedies for heartweakness. Today, however, when a memorable trial was to take place, she was determined that no one in court should have reasons for deriding the weakness of a queen and the daughter of an emperor. Once again, though her body was exhausted and though her feelings were numbed, she must assemble all her energies—only once more, before she went to her last rest. There were but two things left for Marie Antoinette to do on earth: to defend herself vigorously and to die with courage.

She was determined to face the Revolutionary Tribunal and those members of the public that were admitted as auditors with the dignity becoming to her station. The people must be made to realize that the woman who appeared in the dock was a scion of the House of Habsburg and, notwithstanding the decree of deposition, a queen. More carefully than of late in the Conciergerie she arranged her white locks. Then she donned a freshly starched cap of white linen, from either side of which her mourning veil fell. It was as widow of Louis XVI, the last king of France, that she was to present herself before the republican judges.

At eight o'clock, in the great hall, there assembled judges and jury, with Herman as president of the court and Fouquier-Tinville as public prosecutor. The jurors were drawn from all classes: a sometime marquis, a surgeon, a lemonade-seller, a musician, a compositor, a wigmaker, an ex-priest, and a joiner. Beside the public prosecutor several members of the Committee of Public Safety had taken their seats, in order to keep watch on the proceedings. The hall was packed. Not twice in a century has the public a chance of seeing a queen upon the stool of repentance.

Marie Antoinette entered with an indifferent air and composedly sat down. She was not, as her husband had been, granted an easy-chair, for only a hardwood seat awaited her. As for those who were to find her guilty, they were not, as when Louis XVI was solemnly tried, specially elected representatives of the Convention, but the every-day jury of the Revolutionary Tribunal. Yet the spectators looked in vain for signs of fear and excitement in the worn but imperturbable face of the accused. Upright and resolute she sat, while awaiting the formal opening of the court.

Thereupon Fouquier-Tinville rose to his feet and read the indict-ment. The Queen scarcely troubled to listen, for she had already dis-cussed the items with her lawyers overnight. Not even at the most monstrous of the accusations did she show any sign of feeling, her fingers playing indifferently upon the arms of her wooden chair "as if she had been playing the clavecin."

Now came the turn of the one-and-forty witnesses, who were sworn to give their evidence "without hatred and without fear, telling the truth, the whole truth, and nothing but the truth." Since the prepara-tions for the trial had been hurried (he really had a lot to do these days, poor Fouquier-Tinville, although the Revolutionary Tribunal had not yet got into its stride), the various charges were formulated chaotically, without any proper temporal or logical succession. At one moment the witnesses were speaking of the events of the sixth of October in Versailles, at another of what happened on the tenth of August in Paris, now of crimes committed before and now of offences perpetrated during the Revolution.

Much of the testimony, nay most of it, had little bearing on the case, and a good deal of it was ludicrous. Consider, for instance, the deposition of a serving-maid named Millot, who bore witness to having heard in 1788 how the Duc de Coigny told someone that the Queen had sent her brother Joseph two hundred millions. Still more pre-posterous was the statement that Marie Antoinette had carried pistols with the intention of murdering the Duke of Orléans. It was true that two witnesses swore to having seen remittances abroad made by the Queen, but no documents in proof of this were adduced. Nor was there extant a letter which Marie Antoinette was alleged to have sent to the commanding officer of the Switzers inquiring whether, in case of need, she could count upon his men. In fact, not a single document in Marie Antoinette's handwriting was produced in court; and as for the contents of the sealed packet containing some of her possessions which had been seized by the authorities at the Temple—there was nothing in it of an incriminatory nature. It contained locks of hair of her husband and her children; miniatures of the Princesse de Lamballe and of the friend of her childhood days the Landgravine of Hesse-Darmstadt; a notebook in which were entered the names of her washerwoman and her doctor. Absolutely nothing of any moment to the prosecution! Again and again, therefore, Fouquier-Tinville had to come back to unattested generalities; but the Queen, who was ready for this line of attack, gave even more confident answers than at the preliminary hearing.

For instance, there were such rallies of question and answer as the following:

"Where did you get the money with which you had the Little Trianon built and furnished, the place where you gave parties in which you were always the goddess?"

"The money came from a fund set apart for these purposes."

"This fund must have been a large one, for the Little Trianon must have cost enormous sums of money."

"It is possible that the Little Trianon cost immense sums, perhaps more than I should have wished. We became involved in the expenditure by degrees. Besides, no one could be better pleased than I should be if this matter were to be cleared up."

"Was it not at the Little Trianon that you saw the woman Lamotte for the first time?"

"I never saw her."

"Was she not your victim in the notorious affair of the necklace?"

"She could not have been, for I did not know her."

"You persist, then, in your denial that you knew her?"

"I am not persisting in a denial. I have spoken the truth, and I shall persist in speaking the truth."

Had there been any grounds for hope, Marie Antoinette might have entertained hope at this stage, for most of the witnesses were useless to the prosecution. Not one of those whom she had dreaded had given evidence which could do her serious harm. Her defence, her resistance, grew continually stronger. When the public prosecutor contended that through her influence she had induced the late King to do whatever she wanted, she rejoined: "To advise a course of action and to have it carried out are very different things." When, during the proceedings, the president pointed out that her declarations conflicted with those that had been made by her son, she said disdainfully: "It is easy to make a child of eight say whatever you like." When really dangerous matters came up, she replied cautiously: "I do not know, I cannot remember." Not once was Herman able to triumph over her by showing that she had spoken an untruth or by leading her into a contradiction; not once, during the long hours, did she give any occasion for the intent auditors to make an angry interpolation, to utter a cry of hatred, or to break forth in patriotic applause. The trial was dragging out its slow length tediously, ineffectively, aridly. It was time for the prosecution, if it was to give the affair the necessary impetus, to bring a decisive, a crushing charge. With this end in view, Hébert was at last called as a witness, for he was to bring the terrible accusation of incest.

Resolutely, convincingly, loudly, he uttered his charge. Speedily, however, he became aware that the very incredibility of what he alleged was undermining the force of the allegation; that no one was giving the expected response in the way of cries of horror that a mother could be so depraved, that a woman could be so inhuman. His testimony was received in silence; the auditors were pallid and perplexed. Thereupon the poor devil thought fit to introduce a psychologico-political interpretation which was probably invented upon the spur of the moment. "There seems good reason to believe," he said, "that this criminal enjoyment was not really indulged in for its own sake, through a longing for pleasure, but was an outcome of the political hope of enervating the child's physique, for his mother still amused herself with the belief that he was destined to occupy a throne, and she wished, by these machinations, to ensure that she would be able to dominate his morale."

Yet, strangely enough, even now the auditors raised no clamour, but remained disconcertingly silent. Marie Antoinette said no word, and seemed contemptuously to ignore Hébert's existence. She sat, as before, upright in her chair, and for all sign that she gave of having understood what the savage idiot had been saying he might have been talking Chinese. Even Herman, the president, seemed to ignore the accusation. He deliberately abstained from asking what the calumniated mother had to say upon the matter, for he had been quick to realize how painful an impression the charge of incest had produced on the auditors, especially the women, and was obviously inclined to shelve that part of the case for the prosecution. As luck would have it, however, one of the jurors wanted to have this particular accusation pressed, and admonished Herman with the words: "Citizen President, I must request you to call the accused's attention to the fact that she has not made any reply to Hébert's charge as regards what passed between herself and her son."

Now the president had no option. Whatever his feelings may have been, he had to put this question to the accused. Marie Antoinette raised her head proudly ("she seemed strongly moved," recorded the "Moniteur" in its otherwise dry report), answering loudly, with unspeakable disdain: "If I have made no reply, it is because nature refuses to answer such a charge brought against a mother. I appeal in this matter to all the mothers present in court."

At this passionate appeal, there was a sensation in the hall of the Revolutionary Tribunal. The women of the people among the audience, the fishwives, market-women, and so on, who were busily knitting as they listened, held their breath at the words, for they felt a strange kinship with this ex-Queen of France. In her, all their sex had been affronted. The president was silent, the juror who had last spoken was abashed; everyone had been profoundly affected by the tone of pain and wrath in Marie Antoinette's voice. Without a word Hébert retired from the witness-box, by no means proud of his achievement. Even he could not but be aware that the accusation had brought the Queen a great moral triumph in the hour of her utmost difficulty. What had been designed to abase her had uplifted her.

Robespierre, when informed of the incident that evening, was furious with Hébert. He, the only man with keen political insight among this noisy crowd of stump orators and demagogic agitators, was quick to perceive how stupid it had been to drag into the light of publicity the charge which a boy of eight, moved by fear or by a sense of guilt, had brought against his own mother. "What a fool Hébert is," he indignantly exclaimed. "It is not enough for him that Marie Antoinette should in very truth be a Messalina, for he wants to make out that she has been an Agrippina, and he has thus given her a public triumph during her last hours!" For a long time the leader of the Jacobins had been weary of this fanatic, whose vulgar demagogy, whose anarchical behaviour, served only (so he thought) to desecrate the holy cause of the Revolution. There can be little doubt that it was at this moment he made up his mind to rid himself of "Père Duchesne." The stone which Hébert had hurled at Marie Antoinette recoiled upon his own head. A few months later he was to be driven along the same dolorous road as his present victim, not full of courage as she was, but showing the white feather, so that his comrade Ronsin, likewise meat for the guillotine, said to him reproachfully: "In the days when you ought to have acted, you could only talk. Now, at least, learn to die decently."

Marie Antoinette knew that in this matter she had triumphed. Still, she had heard a voice from among the spectators, "See how proud she is," and she therefore asked her defending counsel whether she might not have assumed too much dignity in her reply. Chauveau-Lagarde consoled her, saying: "Madame, be your own self, and you will always do well."

The Queen had still another day to struggle, another day on which the trial dragged itself out, wearying both the participants and the audience; but she herself, though exhausted by the hæmorrhage from which she was suffering, and though she took nothing but a little soup at intervals, remained energetic and self-possessed. Chauveau-Lagarde writes in his memoirs: "Let the reader picture to himself, if he can, how much mental energy the Queen must have needed to bear the fatigue of so long and so horrible a sitting; on show before the populace; carrying on a combat against monsters thirsting for her blood; evading the snares set for her . . . and at the same time maintaining a demeanour worthy of herself." The court had sat more than fifteen hours on the first day. On the second, more than twelve had passed when the president at length announced that there were no further witnesses to be heard, and asked the accused whether she had anything to say in her own behalf. She answered in confident tones: "Yesterday I did not know who the witnesses were to be, nor what they were going to allege against me. Well, no one has brought forward any positive charge. I have, therefore, nothing more to say than that I was only the wife of Louis XVI, and that I had to comply with his wishes."

Thereupon Fouquier-Tinville rose to summarize the case for the prosecution. When he had done so, the two defending counsel replied—somewhat tepidly, since they could not but remember that the defender of Louis XVI, who had been ardent in his endeavours, had been claimed for the scaffold. They thought better, therefore, to appeal to the clemency of the people rather than to insist upon the Queen's innocence. Now, before President Herman put his questions to the jury, Marie Antoinette was removed from the hall. The judge brushed aside the hundred-and-one vague and irrelevant charges which had been introduced into the case, and formulated the main heads of the indictment precisely and clearly. It was the French people that was accusing Marie Antoinette, inasmuch as all the political happenings of the last five years bore witness against her. His four questions ran as follows:

"1. Is it true that there have been machinations and communications with the foreign powers and with other foreign enemies of the Republic, manœuvres and communications tending to supply these enemies with monetary help, to assist them in their invasion of French territory, and to facilitate the advance of their armies?

"2. Is it true that Marie Antoinette of Austria, widow of Louis Capet, participated in these machinations and was instrumental in maintaining these communications?

"3. Is it true that there were a plot and a conspiracy to bring about civil war in the interior of the Republic?

"4. Is it true that Marie Antoinette of Austria, widow of Louis Capet, participated in this plot and in this conspiracy?"

In silence the jurors rose and withdrew into an adjoining room. It was past midnight. The candles flickered and guttered in the overcrowded and overheated hall, and the hearts of those present flickered like the flickering flames.

As an interlude let us ask how, in strict conformity with the law, the jury ought to have decided. In the above-quoted questions, the president had disregarded the political embroidery of the trial and had reduced the accusations to one. The jury was not asked whether Marie Antoinette was an unnatural and adulterous, an incestuous, a spendthrift woman; but merely whether the ex-Queen had been guilty of treasonable communication with the foreign enemies of the Republic, whether she had desired and had done her utmost to further the victory of the invading armies and a rebellion in the interior of France.

Was Marie Antoinette proved guilty of this crime in the legal sense of the word "guilty"? Beyond question she was guilty in actual fact, from the outlook of the Republic. We know (it is impossible to deny) that she had done her utmost to keep in continuous touch with the foreign enemies of revolutionary France. She had, as the indictment declared, committed high treason, inasmuch as she had disclosed the French military plans to the Austrian ambassador; she had used all available means, whether legitimate or illegitimate, to restore throne and freedom to her husband.

In this sense, therefore, the accusers were fully justified. But (here is the weak point in the trial) her guilt had not been proved. Today we are acquainted with the documents which establish Marie Antoinette's treasonable practices against the Republic beyond a shadow of dispute; they are preserved in the State archives in Vienna and in Fersen's literary remains; most of them have been printed. However, the Queen's trial took place in mid-October 1793, and at that time in Paris not one of the aforesaid documents was in the hands of the public prosecutor of the Revolutionary Tribunal. Throughout the two days of the trial, no valid proof of treason could be laid before the jury.

Conscientious jurors, therefore, not exposed to undue influence, would have been in a dilemma. Had they followed their natural instinct, beyond question these twelve republicans would have brought in a verdict of guilty, since in their inmost hearts they must have been convinced that she was a deadly enemy of the Republic, and that she had done her utmost (after her husband's execution, if not before) to achieve for her son's sake a reconquest of the royal power. But the letter of the law was on the Queen's side, since proof of treason was lacking. As republicans, these men could not but regard the Queen as guilty, but as jurymen they were bound to observe the law, which recognizes no "guilt" other than that which has been proved in open court. In the actual state of affairs, however, these petty bourgeois had to face a dilemma of conscience which took a very different form. They knew well enough that the Convention did not look to them for a strictly legal decision. Their business was to bring in a verdict of guilty against a woman dangerous to the State. If they failed to send Marie Antoinette to the guillotine, their own heads would fall into the sack. The "deliberations" of the twelve were no more than a semblance, and if they considered their verdict longer than a minute, it was only to keep up appearances, to pretend that they were discussing pros and cons when a unanimous verdict of guilty had been decided upon before ever the trial opened.

At four o'clock in the morning the jurors filed back into the hall. Dead silence awaited their verdict. They unanimously declared Marie Antoinette guilty of the crime specified in the president's concluding address. Herman warned the auditors (thinned long since, for fatigue had driven most of them to their beds) to abstain from demonstrations. Then Marie Antoinette was brought in. She, who had been fighting for her life through two interminable days, must not enjoy the luxury of being tired! The verdict was read to her. Fouquier-Tinville demanded a death-sentence, and this, likewise, was unanimously agreed to. Then the president asked the condemned woman whether she still had any objections to raise.

Marie Antoinette had listened to the verdict and the sentence unmoved, giving no sign of fear or anger or weakness. In reply to Herman's last question, she merely shook her head, without uttering a word. Then, looking straight in front of her and amid a universal stillness she walked through the hall and down the stairs. She was weary of life and glad that her troubles were drawing swiftly to a close.

On the dark stairway, her tired eyes failed her for a moment, she missed a step, tottered, and almost fell. Lieutenant de Busne, an officer in the gendarmerie, the only man who during the trial had been bold enough to bring the accused a glass of water, now swiftly offered her his arm for support. On this account, and because he had held his hat in his hand while accompanying the condemned woman, he was promptly denounced by another gendarme and had to defend himself, as follows: "I did what I did to save her from falling. No one with any sense can suppose me to have had another reason; and if she had fallen down on the steps there would have been clamour about conspiracy and treason." The Queen's two defenders were likewise placed under arrest as soon as the trial was finished, for it was thought desirable to search them lest she should have conveyed to them some secret missive. The judges dreaded Marie Antoinette's inexhaustible energy though she was doomed to die that day.

But the poor, weary woman knew nothing of the troubles of those who had tried to help her. She had been taken back to prison. Her life was now numbered only by hours.

In her narrow cell two candles were burning on the table. As a special favour to the condemned, they were allowed to her on this night before she passed into the night eternal. Her jailer, who had hitherto been so strict, likewise showed indulgence when she asked for pen, ink, and paper. From this gloomy solitude she wished to send a farewell to those who were fond of her. So late was it now, that candles were scarcely needed. The first glimmer of dawn must have been showing in the sky when Marie Antoinette, summoning her last energies, began her last letter.

Concerning such "last words" of the dying, Goethe remarks: "At the close of life, thoughts hitherto unthinkable rise into the mind of one who meets his fate with resignation; they are like good spirits that diffuse their radiance upon the summits of the past." This mysterious farewell light shines from the Queen's last letter. Never had her thoughts been so composed and so clear as in the good-bye to Madame Elisabeth, her husband's sister, and (Marie Antoinette hoped) henceforward to be the guardian of her children. The handwriting of this letter, written on a prison table, is firmer, stronger, than that of all those penned upon the gilded writing-table in the Trianon. One might almost describe it as virile. The phraseology, too, is clearer, and

no undue restraint is imposed upon the feelings. It is as if, under
stress of imminent death, there had been scattered the clouds which
had so long and so disastrously prevented this woman from gaining a
glimpse into her own depths. Marie Antoinette wrote as follows:

"October 16th, at half past four in the morning.

"It is to you, Sister, that I am writing for the last time. I have just
been sentenced to death, but not to a shameful one, since this death
is shameful only to criminals, whereas I am going to rejoin your
brother. Innocent like him, I hope to show the firmness which he
showed during his last moments. I am calm, as one may well be
when one's conscience is clear, though deeply grieved at having to
forsake my poor children. You know that I existed only for them and
for you, my good and affectionate sister. You who, in the kindness
of your heart, had sacrificed everything in order to be with us—in
what a terrible position do I leave you! It was only during the trial
that I learned my daughter had been separated from you. Alas, poor
child, I do not dare write to her, for she would not receive my letter;
I do not even know if this one will reach you. However, through you
I send them both my blessing, in the hope that some day, when they
are older, they will be with you once more and will be able to enjoy
your tender care. If only they will both continue to think the thoughts
with which I have never ceased to inspire them, namely that sound
principles and the exact performance of duties are the prime foundation of life, and that mutual love and confidence will bring them happiness. I trust my daughter will feel that at the age she has now
reached she must always help her brother with the advice which her
greater experience and her affection will enable her to give him; and
that my son, in his turn, will give his sister all the care and will do
her all the services which affection can stimulate; that they will both
of them feel, whatever position they may find themselves in, they
cannot be truly happy unless united—that they will take example from
us. In our misfortunes, how much consolation we have derived from
our mutual affection! Again, in happy times, one's enjoyment is
doubled when one can share it with a friend—and where can one find
a more affectionate, a more intimate friend than in one's own family?
I hope my son will never forget his father's last words which I here
purposely repeat for him: Let him never try to avenge our death!

"I have to speak to you of one matter which is extremely painful. I know how much my little boy must have made you suffer. Forgive him, my dear sister; remember how young he is, and how easy it is to make a child say whatever one wants, to put words he does not understand into his mouth. I hope a day will come when he will grasp the full value of your kindnesses and of the affection you have shown both my children.

"It remains to entrust you with my last thoughts. I should have liked to write them before the trial opened; but, apart from the fact that I was not allowed to write, things have moved so swiftly that I really have not had time.

"I die in the Catholic, Apostolic, and Roman religion, in that of my fathers, that in which I was brought up, and which I have always professed. Having no hope of any spiritual consolation, not even knowing whether there are still priests of this religion in France, and feeling that should there be such I should expose them to great risks were they to visit me here, I sincerely ask God's forgiveness for all the faults I have committed since I was born. I trust that, in His goodness, He will hear my last prayers, as well as those which I have long been making that, in His pity and His goodness, He may receive my soul.

"I ask the forgiveness of all those whom I have known, and, especially of you, my sister, for the sorrow which, unwittingly, I may have caused them. I forgive my enemies the evil they have done me. I here bid farewell to my aunts and to my brothers and sisters. I had friends. The thought of being separated from them for ever and of their distresses is among my greatest regrets in dying. Let them know, at least, that down to the last they were in my mind.

"Adieu, my good and affectionate sister. I trust that this letter will reach you. Continue to think of me. I send you my most heartfelt love, and also to my poor, dear children. How heartbreaking it is to leave them for ever! Adieu, adieu. I must now devote myself entirely to my spiritual duties. Since all my actions are under restraint, it is possible that they will bring a priest to me. I declare, however, that I shall not say a word to him, and that I shall treat him as an absolute stranger."

The letter breaks off suddenly, without the customary greeting and without a signature. One may suppose that the writer was overcome by fatigue. Two candles were still burning on the table, and perhaps the Queen's life was extinguished before their flame.

This letter from the darkness, the messages it contained, reached hardly any of those to whom it was directed.

Shortly before the executioner came to take her to the scaffold, Marie Antoinette gave it to Bault, the governor of the prison, asking him to transmit it to her sister-in-law. Bault had been humane enough to supply her with writing materials, but he lacked courage to deliver the missive to Madame Elisabeth without authorization. Heads were falling fast now, and everyone was dubious about the safety of his own! He therefore, as his official duty demanded, handed the document to Fouquier-Tinville, who docketed it and filed it. When, two years later, the public prosecutor had to enter the tumbril which he had sent to the Conciergerie for so many other victims, the letter had vanished, the only person in the world who knew of its existence being a man of no account named Courtois. This insignificant and commonplace deputy was, after Robespierre's arrest, ordered by the Convention to arrange and edit the fallen dictator's papers, and Courtois, the sometime maker of sabots, became aware how much power is vested in the hands of one who has the disposal of secret State documents. Deputies who were compromised by the activities of the Reign of Terror now came hat in hand to him, whom previously they had not deigned to notice, promising him fantastic rewards if he would give them back their letters to Robespierre. Being a man with an eye to the main chance, he thought it would be well to impound as many of these documents as possible, and he therefore took advantage of the universal chaos to pilfer all the records of the Revolutionary Tribunal, in the hope of doing a good trade with them. But Marie Antoinette's letter, which also fell into his hands in these circumstances, the cunning fellow put aside. That might rise in value. Who could tell when there might not be a change in the wind? For twenty years he hoarded his plunder, and then the wind had indeed changed. There was once more a Bourbon monarch, Louis XVIII, on the throne of France, and the "regicides" of former days, those who had voted for the execution of his brother Louis XVI, felt their necks uneasy. To woo the new King's favour, Courtois wrote a hypocritical letter offering him as a gift the farewell epistle by Marie Antoinette which he had "saved from destruction." The trick did not serve his turn, for Courtois was proscribed like the others. But the letter had been recovered. One-and-twenty years after the Queen had penned it, this remarkable good-bye came to light. Too late, alas! Almost all those whom Marie Antoinette had wished to greet in her dying hours had followed her to the tomb. Madame Elisabeth was guillotined in May next year. The Dauphin either perished in the Temple, or else (the truth about the lad has never been cleared up) lived out his life elsewhere, his true identity unknown either to himself or to others. Fersen, too, had perished before the Restoration. Nor, indeed, was he mentioned therein, but to whom else can the words have applied: "I had friends. The thought of being separated from them for ever and of their distresses is among my greatest regrets in dying. Let them know, at least, that down to the last they were in my mind"? Regard for the proprieties made it impossible for Marie Antoinette to name openly, in her farewell letter, the man who was dearest to her. She hoped, however, that somehow, some day, the foregoing lines would come under his eyes; that, discreet though the phrasing was, her lover would recognize that down to the last she had been unalterably devoted to him. In the world of feeling, deep may call to deep, even from a vast distance. At any rate, as if he had been aware of her longing to be in touch with him in her final hours, he wrote in his diary on receipt of tidings of her death: "The most terrible pang of all is that she had to be alone during those last moments, lacking the consolation of having anyone to talk to."

CHAPTER LXIII

Drive to the Scaffold

At five in the morning, while Marie Antoinette was still writing her farewell letter, in the eight-and-forty sections of Paris the drums were beating. By seven the whole armed force of the capital was afoot; loaded cannons guarded the bridges; infantrymen with fixed bayonets lined the streets, and there were squadrons of cavalry to reinforce them—a vast display of soldiers against a lonely woman who herself wished for nothing but the end. Often enough the wielders of force are more afraid of their victim than is their victim of the wielders of force.

At seven the kitchen-maid of the prison governor stole into the Queen's cell. On the table the two wax candles were still burning; in the corner, a watchful shadow, sat the gendarme on duty. At first Rosalie did not see the prisoner, then, as she looked more closely, she perceived that Marie Antoinette, fully dressed and wearing her black widow's gown, was lying on the bed. Not asleep, only tired, and worn out by repeated hæmorrhages.

The country girl was full of passionate sympathy for this queen who was about to be put to death. "Madame," she said, coming close to the bed, "you had nothing to eat yesterday evening, and took almost nothing during the day. What can I bring you this morning?"

"Child, I want nothing more, since for me everything is finished," answered the Queen, without sitting up.

When the girl once more urged her to take some soup which had been specially prepared for her, she answered: "Very well, Rosalie, bring me the soup." She swallowed a few spoonfuls, and then the serving-maid began to help her undress. Marie Antoinette had been forbidden to go to the scaffold in the mourning she had worn when on trial before the Revolutionary Tribunal, since the authorities were afraid that this widow's dress might be regarded by the people as provocative. Well, what did a dress matter now? She made no objection, and decided to don a simple white gown.

But even for this last occasion, a last humiliation had been kept in store. For many days, now, she had been losing blood, and the shift she was wearing was soiled with it. Having a natural desire to go to her death clean, she wanted to put on fresh undergarments, and begged the gendarme to withdraw for a few minutes. But he, having been given strict orders not to let her out of his sight for a moment, said he had no choice but to refuse. The Queen, therefore, crouched in the narrow space between the bed and the wall, and, while she was changing her shift, the kitchen-maid stood between her and the gendarme, to hide her nakedness. But the blood-stained undergarment, what was to be done with that? She was ashamed at the thought of leaving her soiled linen for the prying eyes of those who, within a few hours, would enter her cell to scrutinize all that she had left there; so, rapidly rolling it up into a small bundle, she stuffed it into a crevice behind the stove.

Then she dressed herself with peculiar care. It was more than a year since she had set foot in the streets, more than a year since she had had a free outlook into the sky. This last progress should find her respectably and cleanly dressed. The desire that animated her was no longer feminine vanity, but a sense of dignity for a historical hour. She carefully smoothed her white gown, wrapped her neck in a muslin cloth, and put on her best shoes. Her white hair she covered with a two-winged cap.

At eight o'clock there came a knock at the door. No, it was not yet the executioner, but only a herald of the executioner, a priest, one of those who had taken the oath of fealty to the Republic. The Queen recognized no priest but the non-jurors, and she refused, courteously, to confess her sins and seek absolution from a man whom she regarded as an apostate. When he asked her whether he should accompany her upon her last journey, she answered indifferently: "As you please."

This seeming indifference was the wall of defence behind which Marie Antoinette was preparing her fortitude for the drive to the scaffold. When, at ten o'clock, Samson the executioner, a young man of great stature, entered to cut her hair, she made no protest and offered no resistance, nor yet when he tied her hands behind her back. Life, she knew, could no longer be saved, but only honour. Her honour demanded that there should be no sign of weakness. Steadfastness, that alone was needed, to show all who cared how a daughter of Maria Theresa could die.

At about eleven the gates of the Conciergerie were thrown open. Outside stood the tumbril—the name (misapplied) which has become traditional for the sort of knacker's cart or float in which, drawn by a heavily built horse, the victims of the Revolutionary Tribunal were driven to execution. Louis XVI, indeed, had made his royal progress to death in due state, seated in his closed court-chariot, protected by the glass wall from the worst indignities, from the vilest curiosity, from the crudest exhibitions of popular hatred. Since then, however, the Republic had made rapid advances. There must be equality even on the drive to the guillotine. No reason why an ex-queen should go to death more comfortably than other citizens, and a knacker's cart was good enough for Widow Capet! The seat was a bare board fixed to the uprights. Danton, Robespierre, Fouquier-Tinville, Hébert—all those who were now sending Marie Antoinette to her death—would take their last drive seated on the same hard piece of wood; and the condemned of today was only a few stages in front of her judges. Next month, Madame Roland, the month after, Madame Dubarry, were to travel the same road.

The first to emerge from the dark entry of the Conciergerie were some officers, who were followed by a company of soldiers with muskets at the ready. Then, composedly, and with a steady gait, came Marie Antoinette. Samson the executioner was holding her by a long cord, the end of the cord with which he had tied her hands behind her back; was holding her as if there were danger that his victim, though surrounded by hundreds of armed men, might still escape him. Some of the bystanders, despite themselves, were shocked at this unexpected and needless humiliation. None of the customary scornful cries were raised. Not a sound was uttered as the Queen walked to the tumbril. There Samson helped her to get in. Girard, the priest, who did not wear a cassock but was dressed in civilian attire, seated himself beside her. The executioner, with an unmoved countenance, remained standing throughout the drive, still with the cord in his hand. With no more concern than Charon ferrying the souls of the departed across the Styx did he daily convey his doomed freight to the other shore of life. On this occasion, however, during the journey he and his assistants held their three-cornered hats under their arms, as if, by this unwonted token of respect, they were asking pardon of the defenceless woman whom they were about to slay on the scaffold.

The tumbril rattled slowly over the stone pavement. Plenty of time had been allowed for the drive, since all who wished were to be given an opportunity of feasting their eyes on the unusual spectacle. On the hard seat the Queen was jolted by every movement of the roughly made cart, but, her pale face imperturbable, staring out into vacancy with her red-rimmed eyes, Marie Antoinette gave no sign of fear, no indication that she was aware of the inquisitive crowd that had gathered to see her going to her doom. In vain did the fiercest of her enemies try to detect a sign of weakness. Nothing could shake her equanimity; not even when, as she was passing the church of Saint-Roch, the women gathered there assailed her with cries of scorn; not even when Grammont the actor, wishing to enliven the gloomy scene, wearing his uniform of a National Guard rode a few paces beside the death-chariot swinging his sabre and shouting: "There she is, the infamous Antoinette! She's done for at last, my friends!" She seemed neither to hear nor to see. The savage noises of the street made no impression on her ears, the savage sights no impression on her eyes, for the bitterness of death was already past. Even Hébert had to admit next day in "Père Duchesne": "The whore, for the rest, was bold and impudent to the very end."

At the corner of the Rue Saint-Honoré, where the Café de la Régence now stands, a man stood waiting, an artist's block in one hand and a pencil in the other. It was Louis David, one of the greatest cowards but also one of the greatest painters of his day. Among the loudest of spouters while the Revolution was in full cry, he served the men of might so long as they were mighty, only to abandon them in the hour of danger. He painted Marat on the death-bed. When the Eighth Thermidor came, he emotionally gave his word to Robespierre "to drink the cup with him to the dregs"; but next day, that of the fateful sitting, the thirst for heroism had been quenched; he decided to stay at home, and thus saved himself from the guillotine. No one could more bitterly have denounced tyrants than did he during the Revolution, but he would be one of the first to attach himself to the rising fortunes of the new dictator; and in due time, when he made a picture of Napoleon's coronation and was for this service granted the title of baron, he showed how genuine had been his hatred of the aristocrats. A typical specimen of those who lick the boots of the powerful, always ready to flatter the successful but pitiless towards the vanquished, he was equally ready to limn the victor at the coronation and the vanquished on the way to the scaffold. From the same tumbril which was now bearing Marie Antoinette to her fate, Danton, who knew how contemptible was the man's spirit, hissed at him the exclamation: "You have the soul of a lackey!" But though he was a despicable creature, though he had the soul of a servant, he had an artist's eye and an artist's hand. In a trice he had sketched the Queen as she was passing, a cruelly magnificent drawing, made from the life with sinister skill; the picture of a woman prematurely old, no longer beautiful, to whom nothing but pride remains. Her mouth is arrogantly closed; her expression is one of profound indifference; with her hands tied behind her back she sits as challengingly upright on the wooden seat of the tumbril as if she were seated upon a throne. Every line of her stony countenance speaks disdain, and her pose is one of invincible resolution. Suffering transformed into defiance, pain metamorphosed into energy, give her tortured face a new and dreadful majesty. Not even hatred, which made this picture, can deny the awful dignity with which Marie Antoinette endured the shame of her drive to the place of execution.

The huge Place de la Révolution, now known as the Place de la Concorde, was thronged by a mighty crowd. Tens of thousands had been standing there since early morning, lest they should miss the unique spectacle of a Queen, as Hébert had coarsely phrased it, "being shaved by the national razor." They had been kept waiting there hours and hours. To while away the time, one talked to a pretty girl at one's side, one laughed and gossiped, one bought newspapers or caricatures from the hawkers, one fluttered the pages of the most topical pamphlets, such as *Les adieux de la Reine à ses mignons et mignonnes* and *Grandes fureurs de la ci-devant Reine.* In cautious whispers, one discussed with one's neighbour whose head was likely to fall tomorrow or next day. Between times, for refreshments, one bought lemonade, rolls, or nuts. The great scene was worth a little patience.

Towering above the heads of this inquisitive and lively throng were to be seen the only motionless objects in the great square, first of all the uprights of the guillotine, connected at the top by two cross-bars —a wooden bridge leading from this world to the next. Near the summit there gleamed in the chill October sunshine, like a sign-post on the way, the freshly sharpened knife. This gruesome instrument stood sharp and clear against the sky, and the birds, who knew naught of its sinister meaning, flew above it unheeding.

Near by, much taller than the gateway of death, towered the huge statue of liberty upon the pedestal which once had borne the monument of Louis XV. A seated figure, that of the unapproachable deity, her head crowned by the Phrygian cap, and the sword of justice in her hand; she sat there, petrified, the Goddess of Liberty, dreaming, dreaming. Her white eyes were staring across the restless crowd and across the "humane-killer" into distances invisible to human eyes. She did not see human beings at all, neither their life nor their death— this incomprehensible and eternally beloved goddess with the dreaming eyes of stone. She did not hear the voices of those who appealed to her; she did not notice the garlands that were laid upon her stony knees; she did not see the blood that drenched the earth beneath her feet. An everlasting ideal, an alien among human beings, she sat mutely staring into the distant void, contemplating her invisible goal. She neither asked nor knew what deeds were being done in her name.

There was a stir in the crowd, and a sudden silence. This silence was broken by savage shouts from the Rue Saint-Honoré. A squadron of cavalry rode into the Place, followed by the tumbril in which was seated the bound woman who had once been queen of France; behind her stood Samson the executioner. So still was it in the huge square that the stamping of the horses and the gride of the wheels was plainly audible. The thousands upon thousands of spectators regarded with a sort of consternation the pale victim, who seemed to ignore their presence. She was but awaiting the final test. In a few minutes death would come, to be followed by immortality.

The tumbril drew up beside the scaffold. Unaided, "with an air even more composed than when leaving the prison," the Queen mounted the wooden steps, tripping up them as lightly in her high-heeled black satin shoes as if they had been the marble staircase at Versailles. One last glance skywards over the heads of the onlookers! Did she, through the autumnal haze, discern the Tuileries, where she had dwelt nearly three years and had suffered so atrociously? Did she, during this last minute of her life, recall the day when a crowd similar to that now assembled, differing only in attitude of mind, had, in the gardens of the Tuileries, acclaimed her as successor to the throne? Who can tell? No one ever learns the last thoughts of the dying. The end had come. The executioner and his assistants seized her by the back, thrust her into position, kneeling, with her throat in the lower half of the round; the upper board was adjusted to the back of her neck; they pulled the string; a flash of the falling knife; a dull thud; and, by the hair, Samson picked up a bleeding head and lifted it on high for the multitude to gloat upon. Those who had been holding their breath for the last half minute now broke into a wild shout of "Long live the Republic!" Then the onlookers hastily scattered. "Parbleu, it is already a quarter past twelve, more than time for déjeuner; we must get home quickly." No need to loiter! Tomorrow, day after day for weeks and for months, those who like the sight and smell of blood will be able to foregather in the Place de la Révolution and watch the same tragedy reiterated a thousandfold.

The executioner has wheeled away the body in a little hand-cart, the head thrust betwixt the legs. A few gendarmes are left to guard the scaffold. No one troubles about the blood which is slowly soaking into the ground.

Except for the gendarmes the only spectator left in the Place de la Révolution is the Goddess of Liberty, motionless, petrified, looking out as before into the distance, towards her invisible goal. Of the happenings that morning in the square she has seen and heard nothing. Severe of aspect, disregarding the savageries and follies of mankind, she contemplates the eternal distance. She knows not, nor wishes to know, the deeds that are done in her name.

CHAPTER LXIV

The Keening

URING these months the pace of events was too lively in Paris for people to devote long thought to any particular individual among those who had passed by that bloody road to death. The quicker the progress of time, the shorter are people's memories. Within a few weeks, perhaps within a few days, there was scarcely anyone in Paris to remember that Marie Antoinette, sometime Queen of France, had been decapitated and that her remains had been buried in the cemetery of the Madeleine. On the day of the execution, Hébert uttered a howl of delight in "Père Duchesne": "I saw the head of the female Veto fall into the sack. If only, damn it all, I could convey to you the delight of the sansculottes when the arch-tigress was driven across Paris in the cart with the six-and-thirty uprights. . . . At length her accursed head was severed from her whorish neck, and the air resounded to cries of 'Vive la république!'" These mouthings received little attention, for in that epoch of the Red Terror people were chiefly concerned as to whether their own heads were firmly fixed upon their shoulders. A little while elapsed before the interment took place, since it was too expensive to dig a grave for one individual. The custom was to await reinforcements from the busy guillotine, and not until three score corpses were on hand was Marie Antoinette's coffin liberally besprinkled with quicklime and then lowered into a common grave with subsequent arrivals.

There was an end of the matter. In the Conciergerie the Queen's little dog ran restlessly hither and thither for a few days, sniffing about in one room and another, jumping on various beds in search of his mistress; then he, likewise, lost interest, and the prison governor compassionately took possession of him. An undertaker presented his account to the Commune as follows: "Widow Capet, for the coffin, 6 livres; for the grave and the gravediggers, 15 livres." An usher of the court collected the few poor remnants of clothing left by the Queen, made a list of them, and sent them to an infirmary, where pauper women wore them without knowing whose they had been. For a while there was no further thought of Marie Antoinette. When, a few years later, a German visited Paris and asked where the Queen had been buried, he could find no one in the whole town able to gratify his curiosity.

Nor did the execution of Marie Antoinette, which had for some time been expected, arouse much excitement across the frontier. The Duke of Coburg, who had been too faint-hearted to make a timely attempt for her rescue, breathed threatenings and slaughter in an order of the day. The Count of Provence, who, thanks to this execution, had made a long stride towards the fulfilment of his ambition to ascend the throne as Louis XVIII (since now only the poor little lad in the Temple remained to be hidden or thrust aside), showed a decorous sorrow by having Masses said for the soul of the departed. At Vienna, Emperor Francis, who had been too lazy to write so much as a letter which might have been helpful to his aunt, ordered the court to go into mourning. The ladies wore black; His Imperial Majesty refrained for a few weeks from visiting the theatre; the newspapers, according to instructions, expressed the utmost indignation at the behaviour of the wicked Jacobins in Paris. The authorities were so gracious as to take possession of the diamonds which Marie Antoinette had entrusted to Mercy, and subsequently to exchange the imprisoned commissaries for the late Queen's daughter; but when the question arose of repaying the sums of money advanced by various persons for the attempts at escape and of honouring the late Queen's drafts, the court of Vienna turned a deaf ear. At the Hofburg, speaking generally, no one had any wish to be reminded of the Queen's execution. Perhaps the imperial conscience was a trifle uneasy, yet not so much because a close relative had been sacrificed as because all the world was aware of the fact. A good many years later Napoleon remarked: "It was a fixed maxim in the House of Austria to maintain a profound silence concerning the Queen of France. At the name of Marie Antoinette they lowered their eyes and changed the conversation, wishing to evade a disagreeable and embarrassing topic. Such was the rule adopted by the entire family and recommended to Austrian envoys in foreign parts."

There was but one person stricken to the heart by the news: Fersen, the truest of the true. Day after day, in his deep distress, he awaited the horrible tidings: "For a long time I have been trying to prepare myself, and it seems to me that when the day comes I shall receive the news without too profound an emotion." But when the journals containing accounts of the Queen's execution reached Brussels, he felt utterly shattered, writing to his sister: "She for whom I lived, since I have never ceased to love her (how could I, even for a moment, cease to love her); she for whom I would have sacrificed everything . . . she whom I loved so dearly, and for whom I would have given my life a thousand times—is no more. God, why have you crushed me thus, and what have I done to deserve such a manifestation of your wrath? She is no more. My agony has reached its height, and I do not know how I go on living, I do not know how to support my suffering, which is intense and which nothing can ever efface. Always she will be present to my memory and I shall never cease to bewail her. . . . My dear, how I long to have died at her side, for her, for them, on the twentieth of June. This would have been much happier for me than to drag out a sad existence amid eternal regrets, amid regrets which will end only with my life, for her adored image will never be effaced from my memory." Only through his memory of her can he still live: "The sole object of my interest has ceased to exist; she alone meant everything to me; and now for the first time do I fully grasp how passionately I was devoted to her. I can think of nothing but her. Her image is continually with me, and will always be with me wherever I go. I care to speak of nothing but her, to recall the happy moments of my life. Alas, nothing is left of them but memories which, however, I shall preserve so long as my life lasts. I have arranged for agents in Paris to buy anything of hers which may be obtainable, for whatever I can get of this sort will be sacred to me. They are relics which will be the unceasing objects of my perpetual admiration." For him nothing can make good this loss. Months afterwards, he writes in his diary: "I feel so keenly day by day how much I have lost in losing her, and how perfect she was in every respect. There never has been and there never will be another such woman." The passing of the years did not seem to lessen the shock, and everything that happened served only to remind him of his loss. When, in 1796, he was in Vienna and saw Marie Antoinette's daughter at the imperial court, his eyes filled with tears. "My knees almost gave way beneath me as I was going downstairs after seeing her. I was profoundly moved by mingled feelings of joy and of sorrow."

Always when he saw this young woman, Maria Theresa Charlotte, afterwards Duchess of Angoulême, he found it hard to refrain from weeping, and the old passion for the mother was revived in a fatherly affection for the daughter. Not once, however, was she allowed to say or write a word to Fersen. We do not know whether this prohibition was the fruit of a secret court decree, of a decision that the victim was as far as possible to be forgotten; or whether, maybe, her confessor's influence was at work, since this priest may well have known of the "sinful" relations between Marie Antoinette and the Swedish nobleman. Anyhow, the Austrian court disliked Fersen's coming and was always ready to speed his departure. Never once did any surviving member of the House of Habsburg show gratitude to the man who had been the most faithful of the Queen's adherents.

After his beloved's death, Fersen became gloomy and harsh. The world seemed to him cold and unjust; life, devoid of meaning. His political and diplomatic ambitions were extinct. During the long years of warfare that ensued he wandered hither and thither through Europe as envoy, appearing now in Vienna, now in Karlsruhe, now in Rastatt, now in Italy, and returning from time to time to Sweden. He had intimacies with other women, but they were only superficial. Nothing could console him. Again and again we find in his diary entries that show him to have been little more than a living shadow. Many years later, on October 16th, the anniversary of the Queen's death, we find him writing: "For me this is a day of devotion, and I can never forget all that I have lost; my regrets will last as long as my life."

But there is another date to which Fersen always refers as fateful, the twentieth of June. He never found it possible to forgive himself for having obeyed Louis XVI's orders on this day of the flight to Varennes, and for having allowed Marie Antoinette to venture alone into the jaws of danger. Whenever June 20th came round, he was reminded of a personal offence, an undischarged sense of guilt was revived. Repeatedly he declared that it would have been better to allow himself to be torn to pieces by the populace than to survive his mistress, with no joy in his heart, and a perpetual victim of self-reproach. "Why, ah why, did I not die for her on the twentieth of June?" Again and again these words recur in his journal.

But fate loves the analogies of what we call chance, and is fond of playing in a mysterious way with figures. After many years his romantic desire was strangely fulfilled. On this very date, June 20th, Fersen perished, dying a violent death. This was in the year 1810. By degrees, though he never sought advancement, he had become a man of note in his homeland; he was a Swedish marshal and the most trusted among the king's counsellors; a man wielding much power, but harsh and severe; a masterful man. His spirit was that of the old regime. Since the days of the flight to Varennes and the frustrated escape, he had detested the people which had robbed him of his Queen. They were the mob; they were canaille; and his hatred was frankly reciprocated by the common folk. Being powerful and harsh, he had made enemies among his own order, and these had disseminated a rumour, which had found ready credence, that—in his desire to take vengeance on France—he wanted to make himself King of Sweden and drag the nation into war. When, therefore, in June 1810, Prince Christian of Holstein-Augustenberg died suddenly, the report ran in Stockholm that Marshal Fersen had poisoned the heir to the throne in order to smooth his own path. Now Fersen was in the same sort of danger as Marie Antoinette during the Revolution. During the days before the prince's burial, therefore, well-meaning friends, who had heard that sinister plans were afoot, warned the Marshal against attending the funeral. It would be wiser for him, they said, to stay at home. But the day fixed for the interment was June 20th, and he had an obscure urge to meet the fate of which he had dreamed. The result was, on this twentieth of June in Stockholm, what would have been the result twenty-one years earlier in Paris if the mob had discovered Fersen in the chariot as Marie Antoinette's companion. Hardly had his carriage left the palace when a raging crowd broke through the protecting cordon of troops, tore the grey-headed man down among them, and dispatched him, defenceless as he was, with sticks and stones. The visionary picture of June 20th had been fulfilled. The bleeding and mutilated corpse of "handsome Fersen," the last champion of the Queen of France, was left lying on the pavement in front of the Stockholm town hall, the life crushed out of it by the same savage untamable element—the indiscriminate wrath of the populace—which had brought Marie Antoinette to the scaffold. In life they had had to be sundered, but in death at least, symbolically united by the likeness of their destiny, they were not divided.

With Fersen the last had perished of those who retained loving memories of Marie Antoinette. Neither one who passes by the name of living nor one who has entered into the shadow of death is truly alive unless still sincerely loved by a fellow human being. Fersen's lament for his long-dead mistress was the last word of fidelity to her image. The rest was silence. Soon any others who had remained faithful to her had passed away; Trianon was falling into decay, its ornamental gardens ran wild; the pictures, the furniture which, in their harmony, had reflected her charm, had been sold by auction and scattered; thus it seemed that the last visible traces of her existence on earth had vanished. Time ran its course, bloodshed followed bloodshed, the Revolution was succeeded by the Consulate, Bonaparte had become Emperor Napoleon, and had sought, as second wife, another archduchess from the House of Habsburg. Yet Marie Louise, however incredible it may seem, never sought to inquire where this unhappy woman of her kin who had lived before her and suffered in the palace of the Tuileries was sleeping her last sleep. Never in so short a space of time had a queen been so coldly forgotten by her nearest relatives and successors.

Then there came a new turn of fortune's wheel, and memories were stirred by an uneasy conscience. Over the corpses of three millions, the Count of Provence had ascended the throne of France as Louis XVIII. Since those who had been barriers to his ambition—Louis XVI, Marie Antoinette, and their unhappy son Louis XVII—had long since been swept out of the way, and since the dead cannot arise and bring complaints against the living, would it not be well to provide them with a splendid tomb? Never before this had he who was now a monarch troubled to inquire where his brother might have been buried, but after his accession the search was duly instituted. It was by no means easy, when two-and-twenty years had elapsed, to find what was wanted in that notorious cemetery of the Madeleine, the old monastery garden which the chiefs of the Terror had manured with thousands of corpses. The grave-diggers had been hard-worked, with no time to distinguish one headless body from another. They had swiftly carted and swiftly interred, huddled indifferently together, the mortal remains which the insatiable guillotine vomited forth day after day. Neither cross nor crown marked the spot. All that was known was that the Convention had issued orders for the royal corpses to be buried with plenty of quicklime. The searchers, therefore, had an aim in their digging, and they went on indefatigably until their spades clashed upon a hard stratum which had been made by the slaking of the lime. Amid this, a mouldering garter enabled them to recognize that the handful of pale dust which was disinterred from the damp soil was the last trace of that long-dead woman who in her day had been the goddess of grace and of taste, and subsequently the queen of many sorrows.

FINIS

Chronological Table

1755.	November 2nd:	Birth of Marie Antoinette.
1769.	June 7th:	Written demand of Marie Antoinette's hand for his son made by Louis XV.
1770.	April 19th:	Marriage per procurationem in Vienna.
	May 16th:	Marriage at Versailles.
	December 24th:	Choiseul falls into disgrace.
1772.	January 11th:	Rohan arrives in Vienna.
	August 5th:	First Partition of Poland.
1773.	June 8th:	Entry of the Dauphiness into Paris.
1774.	May 10th:	Death of Louis XV.
		The necklace is offered to Marie Antoinette for the first time.—Fersen's first visit to Versailles.—Recall of Rohan from Vienna.—Beaumarchais sells his lampoon to Maria Theresa.
1777.	April–May:	Joseph II's visit to Versailles.
	August:	The marriage of Louis and Marie Antoinette at length consummated.
1778.	December 19th:	Birth of Maria Theresa Charlotte, "Madame Royale," in later days Duchess of Angoulême.
1779.		First pamphlet against Marie Antoinette.
1780.	August 1st:	First appearance at the Trianon Theatre.
	November 29th:	Death of Maria Theresa.
1781.	October 22nd:	Birth of the first Dauphin.
1783.	September 3rd:	Peace of Versailles.—Recognition of the United States by England.
1784.	April 27th:	First Night of *Le Mariage de Figaro* at the Théâtre Français.
	August 11th:	Concocted meeting with Rohan in the Grove of Venus.
1785.	January 29th:	Rohan buys the necklace.
	March 27th:	Birth of the second Dauphin.

	August 15th:	Arrest of Rohan at Versailles.
	August 19th:	Performance of *Le Barbier de Séville* at the Trianon, this being the last performance at the Trianon Theatre.
1786.	May 31st:	Judgment delivered upon the affair of the necklace.
	July 9th:	Birth of Princess Sophie Béatrix.
1788.		Early days of the intimacy with Fersen.
	August 8th:	Summoning of the States-General for May 1, 1789.
1789.		Necker again Minister of State.
	May 5th:	Opening of the States-General.
	June 3rd:	Death of the first Dauphin.
	June 17th:	The Third Estate declares itself to be the National Assembly.
	June 20th:	Oath of the Tennis Court.
	June 25th:	Freedom of the press.
	July 11th:	Necker expelled from France.
	July 13th:	Creation of the National Guard.
	July 14th:	Storming of the Bastille.
	July 16th:	Flight of the émigrés begins (Artois, Polignac).
	End of August:	Fersen at Versailles.
	October 1st:	Banquet to the Flemish regiment.
	October 5th:	March of the Parisian populace to Versailles.
	October 6th:	Drive of the royal family to Paris.—Founding of the Jacobin Club in Paris.
1790.	February 20th.	Death of Joseph II.
	June 4th:	Last Summer Stay at Saint-Cloud.
	July 3rd:	Meeting with Mirabeau.
1791.	April 2nd:	Death of Mirabeau.
	June 20th–25th:	Flight to Varennes.—Barnave and his friends in the Tuileries.
	September 14th:	The King swears to maintain the Constitution.
	October 1st:	Legislative Assembly.

1792.	February 13th–14th:	Fersen's final visit to the Tuileries.
	February 20th:	For the last time Marie Antoinette goes to the theatre.
	March 1st:	Death of Leopold II.
	March 24th:	Roland Ministry.
	March 29th:	Death of King Gustavus III of Sweden.
	April 20th:	France declares war on Austria.
	June 13th:	Dismissal of the Roland Ministry.
	June 19th:	The King exercises his constitutional right of veto.
	June 20th:	First storming of the Tuileries.
	August 10th:	Second storming of the Tuileries.—Danton becomes Minister for Justice.
	August 13th:	Suspension of the royal authority.—Transference of the royal family to the Temple.
	August 22nd:	First rising in Vendée.
	September 2nd:	Fall of Verdun.
	September 2nd–5th:	The September massacres.
	September 3rd:	Murder of the Princesse de Lamballe.
	September 20th:	French victory over the Prussians at Valmy.
	September 21st:	First meeting of the National Convention. —Abolition of the Monarchy, establishment of the Republic.
	November 6th:	French victory over the Austrians at Jemappes.
	December 11th:	Opening of the trial of Louis XVI.
1793.	January 4th:	Second Partition of Poland.
	January 21st:	Execution of Louis XVI.
	March 10th:	Establishment of the Revolutionary Tribunal.
	March 31st:	Evacuation of Belgium by the French.
	April 4th:	Dumouriez's desertion to the enemy.
	May 29th:	Rising in Lyons.
	July 3rd:	Separation of the Dauphin from Marie Antoinette.

	August 1st:	Marie Antoinette's removal to the Conciergerie.
	October 3rd:	Prosecution of the Girondists.
	October 9th:	Fall of Lyons.
	October 12th:	Preliminary hearing of Marie Antoinette.
	October 14th:	Opening of Marie Antoinette's trial.
	October 16th:	Execution of the Queen.
1795.	June 8th:	Alleged death of the Dauphin ("Louis XVII").
1814.		Louis XVIII, sometime Count of Provence, becomes King of France.
1824.		Charles X, sometime Count of Artois, becomes King of France.

Postface

IT IS usual at the end of a historical work to append a bibliography of the sources utilized, but in the case of Marie Antoinette it seems to me that it would be more appropriate to mention which sources have not been utilized and why. Even those documents which are as a rule most trustworthy, namely autograph letters, are here unreliable. As has been more than once pointed out in the foregoing pages, Marie Antoinette, being of an impatient disposition, was a careless letter-writer. Rarely did she on her own initiative and un-compelled sit down at that fine writing-table which can still be seen in the Trianon. It is not surprising, therefore, that ten, and even twenty years after her death hardly any letters in her handwriting were known to be extant, or anything in her handwriting at all beyond the countless bills at the foot of which she had scrawled the inevitable "Payez, Marie Antoinette." At that time the two chief series of letters, those written to her mother and the court of Vienna, and those more intimate missives sent to the Comte de Fersen, were still hidden away in the archives, where they remained until the nineteenth century was half-way through its course; and the originals of the few published letters to the Countess Polignac were likewise inaccessible. Great, therefore, was the surprise when, in the 'forties, the 'fifties, and the 'sixties of the nineteenth century there appeared for sale, at almost every Parisian auction of autograph documents, letters ostensibly in the Queen's handwriting, and, more remarkably still, all bearing her signature—whereas she seldom signed her name to a letter! Then, in rapid succession, came three extensive collections of letters, issued from the press: one by Count Hunolstein; a second (still the most abundant) edited by Baron Feuillet de Conches; and, for the third, that of Klinkowström, who published a bowdlerized version of the Queen's letters to Fersen. The delight of historians in this wealth of material was considerably chastened by the fact that, a few months after the publication of Hunolstein's and Feuillet de Conches's collections, doubts were cast upon the authenticity of much of the material. A tedious polemic followed, and ere long it became plain to every unprejudiced person that a forger who must be styled a genius at this particular sort of work had been boldly mixing false with true and reaping a rich harvest of ill-gotten gains.

Animated by an almost inexplicable delicacy, accomplished students of these matters have hitherto refrained from mentioning the name of this brilliant falsifier, one of the ablest that ever plied his trade. No doubt Flammermont and Rocheterie, the leading experts in the matter, made it obvious to those who read between the lines whither their suspicions were directed. Today there is no longer any reason for keeping silence, and thus depriving the history of forgery of the story of a case which presents unusual psychological interest. The over-zealous multiplier of the letters of Marie Antoinette was none other than the aforesaid editor, Baron Feuillet de Conches, a diplomat of high standing, exceptionally cultured, a remarkably amusing author, and extremely well informed upon all details of the history of French civilization. For ten or twenty years he had been hunting Marie Antoinette's letters in official archives and private collections, and had displayed remarkable skill in their discovery—an achievement which still commands our respect.

But this estimable and diligent student had one strong passion, and strong passions are always dangerous. He was an ardent collector of autographs, ranked as the scientific pope in this field, and penned an admirable essay on autograph collecting which will be found in his *Causeries d'un curieux*. His collection, or, as he proudly called it, his "cabinet," was the largest in France—but the born collector is insatiable. Probably because he was not sufficiently well off to fill his portfolios as tightly as he wanted, he forged a number of autograph letters by La Fontaine, Boileau, and Racine, many of which still come into the market from time to time, and which, as opportunity arose, he disposed of through Parisian and British dealers. Incontestably, however, his masterpieces were the forged letters of Marie Antoinette. He had an unrivalled knowledge of her story, her handwriting, and all the surrounding circumstances of her life. It was therefore easy enough for him, after discovering seven genuine letters from the Queen to the Duchesse de Polignac, to produce an equal number of excellent forgeries, and, growing bolder, to write a number of letters ostensibly penned by the Queen to those of her relatives with whom he knew her to have been in close touch. His exceptionally intimate knowledge both of the Queen's handwriting and of her literary style enabled him, unfortunately, to produce forgeries which (being free from historical blunders) almost defied detection. It must be frankly admitted that, with the best will in the world, in the case of many of these letters no expert can make up his mind whether they are genuine or false, whether they were thought and penned by Queen Marie Antoinette or invented and forged by Baron Feuillet de Conches. To give an example, I find it impossible to decide as to the genuineness of the letter to Baron Flachslanden, which is preserved in the Prussian State Library. The contents seem genuine enough, but suspicions of forgery are aroused by the fact that the handwriting is somewhat too composed and well rounded—and, above all, that the previous owner acquired it from Feuillet de Conches! Influenced by these considerations, my desire for historical accuracy has led me, in the present volume, inexorably to disregard documents whose only certificate is the extremely suspicious one of having been derived from the "cabinet" of the late Baron. Better less and genuine than more and of dubious authenticity, has been the fundamental psychological rule in the compilation of the present work.

As regards oral testimony concerning Marie Antoinette, we are little better off than in respect of the trustworthiness of letters. If as regards other epochs in history we have often to complain of an insufficiency of memoirs and the testimonies of eye-witnesses, as regards the French Revolution we have rather to complain of superabundance. In cyclonic decades, when without pause for reflection a whole generation is hurled from one political wave into the next, there is seldom time for thoughtful survey. Within five-and-twenty years the people of one brood experienced the most unexpected changes, passing with hurried strides through the last blossoming of the monarchy and then its death-agony, the first happy days of the Revolution, the ghastly period of the Terror, the Directorate, the rise of Napoleon, his Consulate, his dictatorship, the establishment of the empire, his aim at world dominion, numberless victories followed by his decisive defeat, the re-establishment of the monarchy, the Hundred Days when Napoleon was again in power. At length, after Waterloo, came the great pause, the tranquil pause of the Restoration when, after a quarter of a century, a world

wide storm of unparalleled violence had blown itself out. Men and
women recovered from their alarm and rubbed their eyes. They were
astonished, to begin with, to find themselves still alive; and then were
amazed at what a wealth of happenings they had lived through in
so short a space. (We ourselves shall feel just the same when the
inundation which has been sweeping us onwards since 1914 has finished its torrential flow.) Having got safe to shore, they wanted to
form quiet and consistent views of the confused happenings they had
witnessed and in which they had played their various parts. Everyone, in those days, wanted to read history in the form of memoirs of
eye-witnesses, that they might be helped thereby to reconstruct an
orderly picture of events—with the result that after 1815 there was a
luxuriant output of memoirs, just as, a century later, there was a
fungoid growth of war books after the World War. Professional
writers and publishers were quick to seize their chance. Before the
public interest ebbed, (this also we have ourselves seen), they wanted
to gratify the universal curiosity for memorials, memorials, memorials
of the great days. Everyone who had rubbed shoulders with some
individual of historic note was asked to recount his experiences. Since,
however, the small fry, who for the most part had been swept help-
lessly along by the current of events, could remember very few details, and did not know how to relate them interestingly, expert journalists, writing in their names, stuffed a fine thick piece of dough
with these few raisins, added a liberal allowance of sugar, and fla-
voured the whole with sentimentalist inventions in order to make a
book. Everyone who in those days had been inside the Tuileries, or,
for an hour or two, had been a grain of dust carried by one of the
cyclones of history through the prisons or the Revolutionary Tribunal,
posed as an author. The tailoress, the chambermaid, the first, second,
and third under-maids, the hairdresser, the prison warder in charge
of Marie Antoinette, the first and the second governesses of her children, every one of her friends, found it necessary to write a book. Last
not least, even the executioner, Monsieur Samson, thought fit to write
memoirs, or at least to make money by putting his name to a book
which others, more skilled than he with the pen, had hastily compiled.

It need hardly be said that these spurious reports contradict one another in almost every respect. As regards the decisive occurrences of

October 5 and 6, 1789, as regards the behaviour of the Queen during the storming of the Tuileries, and during her last hours, we have at our disposal seven, eight, ten, fifteen, twenty widely divergent accounts by persons who claim to have been eye-witnesses. Only in one respect are the writers unanimous, and that is as regards their political sentiments, for they are all unconditionally, touchingly, inviolably loyal—and this can readily be understood when we remember that their works were printed in the days of the Bourbon Restoration. A serving-man or a prison warder who during the Revolution had proclaimed himself the reddest of the Reds could not, under Louis XVIII, be profuse enough in his assurances that in secret he had always had the utmost veneration for the good, the noble, the pure, the virtuous Queen, could not exaggerate the extent of his devotion to this unfortunate lady. Had but a small fraction of those who in 1820 declared their inviolable loyalty really been, in 1792, as loyal as they maintained, Marie Antoinette would never have been sent to the Conciergerie and would never have mounted the steps of the scaffold.

Nine tenths of the memoirs published during that period are, therefore, either crude sensationalism, or else lickspittle productions of the most offensive kind; and he who is in search of historical truth will do well (deviating from the practice of previous writers) to brush aside as hopelessly untrustworthy the evidence of the vast majority of these chambermaids, hairdressers, gendarmes, and pages, on the ground that they have found it much too easy to "remember" whatever they wished to be believed.

That explains why, in the present biography of Marie Antoinette, I have thought it desirable to pay no heed to a large number of documents, letters, and reported conversations which my predecessors in this field have hesitatingly used. The reader will miss a good many anecdotes which may have charmed or amused him in the aforesaid biographies: beginning with that in which young Mozart is reported to have made a proposal of marriage to Marie Antoinette at Schönbrunn, and ending with that in which, on the scaffold, the Queen, accidentally treading on the executioner's foot, is said to have politely excused herself with a "Pardon, Monsieur" (an anecdote too good to be true!). The reader will also find no mention of numerous well-known letters, above all the touching one to the "cher cœur" (the Princesse de Lamballe)—for the very simple reason that they are certainly some of Baron Feuillet de Conches's forgeries, and were never written by Marie Antoinette; I have also omitted a number of witty or affecting remarks which belong to the "Marie Antoinette tradition"—have omitted them because they seem to be too witty or too affecting to be appropriate to the Queen's character, which was that of an average woman.

Though this may seem a loss to the sentimentalists, it will not be regarded as a loss in respect of historical genuineness; and the reader will find that there has been a gain of new and important material. Above all, a careful examination of the State archives in Vienna has shown that in the published correspondence between Maria Theresa and Marie Antoinette, though the letters as here reproduced purport to be complete, there has been a suppression of very important, and often the most important, passages, which were omitted because they were regarded as unduly intimate. Here I have used these repressed passages without reserve, for the reason that the conjugal relations between Louis XVI and Marie Antoinette are psychologically incomprehensible unless the reader has full knowledge of certain physiological matters which have long been veiled in mystery. Especially important, moreover, was the light thrown upon Fersen's literary remains by the researches of that distinguished investigator Alma Söderhjelm, who was able to discover numerous "retouchings" and excisions that had been effected on "moral" grounds. Thanks to her work, the pious fraud, the chaste legend, concerning Fersen's troubadour passion for the unapproachable Marie Antoinette—a legend based upon mutilations which, once discovered, make the documents all the more convincing—can no longer be sustained. Thus I have been able to show that the two were lovers in every sense of the word; and, further, to clear up a number of obscure or obscured details. Now that we hold freer views concerning the human and moral rights of a woman, even though she happens to be a queen, we can talk frankly, and are no longer afraid of facing spiritual truths; for we do not believe, as those of an earlier generation believed, that if we are to win admiration for a historical figure we must at any cost idealize a character, bedaub it with sentimentalism, or make it appear heroic, while leaving essential traits discreetly veiled and exaggerating others with the skill of the earlier writers of tragedy and romance. Not to idolize, not to deify, but to humanize, is the supreme task of creative psychological study; not to excuse with a wealth of far-fetched arguments, but to explain, is its true mission. That is what I have here attempted in the case of a woman of average character, who owes her long-lasting influence to an incomparable fate, and whose inward greatness was but the outcome of unprecedented misfortunes. My hope is that, in default of all exaggeration, this character will arouse the sympathy and enjoy the understanding of the present, precisely because she was of one flesh with ourselves.

Index